THE HELL OF GOOD INTENTIONS

THE HELL *of* GOOD INTENTIONS

AMERICA'S FOREIGN POLICY ELITE
AND THE DECLINE OF U.S. PRIMACY

Stephen M. Walt

FARRAR, STRAUS AND GIROUX *New York*

Farrar, Straus and Giroux
175 Varick Street, New York 10014

Portions of this book originally appeared, in slightly different form, in *Foreign Affairs* and *Chaos in the Liberal Order: The Trump Presidency and International Politics in the Twenty-First Century*. Grateful acknowledgment is made to the Council on Foreign Relations and Columbia University Press for permission to use these materials here.

Library of Congress Cataloging-in-Publication Data
Names: Walt, Stephen M., 1955– author.
Title: The Hell of good intentions : America's foreign policy elite and the decline of U.S. primacy / Stephen M. Walt.
Description: First edition. | New York : Farrar, Straus and Giroux, 2018. | Includes bibliographical references and index.
Identifiers: LCCN 2018007639 | ISBN 9780374280031 (hardcover)
Subjects: LCSH: United States—Foreign relations—1989– | Political consultants—United States.
Classification: LCC E895 .W35 2018 | DDC 327.73009/04—dc23
LC record available at https://lccn.loc.gov/2018007639

Designed by Richard Oriolo

Our books may be purchased in bulk for promotional, educational, or business use. Please contact your local bookseller or the Macmillan Corporate and Premium Sales Department at 1-800-221-7945, extension 5442, or by e-mail at MacmillanSpecialMarkets@macmillan.com.

www.fsgbooks.com
www.twitter.com/fsgbooks • www.facebook.com/fsgbooks

10 9 8 7 6 5 4 3 2 1

FOR MY FAMILY

CONTENTS

PREFACE

IN MARCH 2013, a member of the State Department's Policy Planning staff invited me to speak at the department and requested that I "be provocative." Happy to comply, I titled my talk "Why U.S. Foreign Policy Keeps Failing." A lively but friendly discussion followed, and it occurred to me afterward that my remarks might form the basis for a short book. I estimated it would take about a year to write.

Like the men and women responsible for U.S. foreign policy in recent years, I badly misjudged the difficulty of the task I had undertaken. Nonetheless, a full draft of the manuscript was complete in October 2016 and I anticipated the book would appear near the end of Hillary Clinton's first year as president. The timing would be ideal, I thought, as I expected Clinton to repeat many of her predecessors' mistakes, making a hard-hitting critique of U.S. grand strategy both timely and valuable.

Donald Trump's unexpected victory in November 2016 was an awkward surprise in more ways than one, but it was also an ideal opportunity to test my core argument about America's foreign policy elite. Candidate Trump had challenged many enduring orthodoxies about U.S. foreign policy, and he was openly dismissive of (and dismissed by) Democratic and Republican foreign policy experts alike. Once in power, however, Trump discovered that overcoming the foreign policy establishment was much harder than he had expected. Trump's presidential style is obviously different from his predecessors' and he has altered U.S. policy in some significant ways, but the foreign policy revolution that he promised back in 2016 remains unrealized. This book will help you understand why.

In some ways, this work is the logical continuation of a research program I began pursuing in graduate school. In *The Origins of Alliances* (1987), I argue that a proper understanding of the causes of international alliances could explain why the United States and its main allies were significantly stronger than the Soviet bloc, and could reduce concerns that key allies would realign with the Soviet Union if the United States did not constantly reassure them. *Revolution and War* (1996) explores the international effects of domestic revolutions and argues that efforts to overthrow revolutionary powers often contribute to spirals of hostility and thus make war with them more likely. *Taming American Power* (2005) explains why both friends and foes were concerned about America's dominant position after the Cold War, shows how other states were trying to counter U.S. power or exploit it for their own ends, and argues that the United States could have defused such efforts by adopting a more restrained foreign policy. And in *The Israel Lobby and U.S. Foreign Policy* (2007), John Mearsheimer and I show how a powerful domestic interest group can influence U.S. foreign policy in significant ways, to the detriment of broader U.S. national interests.

Each of these works cast a skeptical eye at important elements of U.S. foreign policy and tried to show how it could be improved. The present book develops that theme in detail, focusing on the enduring role that elite foreign policy institutions play in shaping U.S. strategy and managing America's relations with the wider world.

In particular, this book seeks to explain why the United States spent the past quarter century pursuing an ambitious, unrealistic, and mostly unsuccessful foreign policy. Having won the Cold War and achieved a position of primacy unseen since the Roman Empire, why did U.S. leaders decide to maintain a military establishment that dwarfed all others and expand an already far-flung network of allies, client states, military bases, and security commitments? Instead of greeting the defeat of its principal rival as an opportunity to reduce America's global burdens, why did both Democrats and Republicans embark on an ill-considered campaign to spread democracy, markets, and other liberal values around the world?

This strategy—sometimes termed "liberal hegemony"—has been a costly failure. Yet three successive administrations—under Clinton, Bush, and Obama—clung to it, even as the costs mounted and the quagmires multiplied. Why did Washington persist in the face of repeated setbacks, and how did the foreign policy establishment convince the American people to support policies that were neither necessary nor successful?

Part of the explanation is America's remarkable combination of wealth, power, and favorable geography. Because the United States is the world's most powerful nation, faces no threats in the Western Hemisphere, and is protected from the rest of the world by two enormous oceans, it can intervene in distant lands without placing its immediate survival in jeopardy. Yet this explanation is not the whole story, because those same favorable circumstances would also permit the United States to reduce many of its overseas commitments and focus more attention on problems at home.

Instead of pursuing a more restrained grand strategy, U.S. leaders opted for liberal hegemony because the foreign policy community believes spreading liberal values is both essential for U.S. security and easy to do. They convinced ordinary citizens to support this ambitious agenda by exaggerating international dangers, overstating the benefits that liberal hegemony would produce, and concealing the true costs. And because members of the foreign policy elite are rarely held to account, they were able to make the same mistakes again and again.

This book is highly critical of the foreign policy establishment, but the nature of my critique needs to be properly understood. America's foreign policy elite is not a conspiracy of privileged insiders who are consciously seeking to advance their own fortunes at the nation's expense. On the contrary, the institutions examined in this book are filled with dedicated public servants who genuinely believe that U.S. dominance is good for the United States and for the rest of the world. At the same time, however, the pursuit of liberal hegemony appeals to this elite's sense of self-worth, enhances their power and status, and gives them plenty to do. These individuals also operate in a system that rewards conformity, penalizes dissent, and encourages its members to remain within the prevailing consensus.

In short, most of the men and women examined in this book tried to advance the national interest as they saw it. Unfortunately, the strategy they pursued with such energy and dedication was fundamentally flawed, and their mistakes were sometimes egregious. With the best of intentions, America's foreign policy elite did great harm to others and considerable damage to the United States itself. And unless and until a new elite emerges with a different view of America's role and a greater willingness to pursue a strategy of restraint, the errors of the past twenty-five years are likely to be repeated.

A single book cannot produce a revolution in U.S. foreign policy. But it is my hope that this book will help hasten the day when the United States adopts a foreign policy that actually enhances its security and prosperity and makes America's core values more attractive to others. A foreign policy with those qualities would be closer to what the American people actually want, and easier to defend at home and abroad.

Stephen M. Walt
Brookline, Massachusetts

THE HELL OF GOOD INTENTIONS

Introduction

O N JANUARY 20, 2017, Donald J. Trump became the forty-fifth
president of the United States. It was the culmination of a political
odyssey that had defied the experts' predictions from the day he announced his candidacy. Hardly anyone expected him to do well in the
Republican primaries, and pundits repeatedly reassured the public that
his early successes could not be sustained. Yet he swept the Republican
field aside and won the GOP nomination despite strong opposition from a
number of top Republican leaders. He trailed Hillary Clinton throughout
most of the general election campaign, performed poorly in three televised
debates, and was endorsed by hardly any major U.S. newspapers. Days
before the election, pollsters generally saw his chances as bleak, judging
the probability of a Clinton victory to be 70 percent or higher.

Yet he won, and in singular fashion. He defeated a large field of Republican rivals, many of them with far more experience in politics and representing a range of familiar conservative views. He defied the established norms of U.S. political campaigning—refusing to release his tax returns, making vulgar comments about female journalists, openly mocking a handicapped reporter, and scorning the grieving family of a decorated U.S. soldier who had given his life for the country. He told supporters the entire election might be "rigged," threatened to arrest his opponent and "lock her up" if he won, and survived the exposure of well-documented accounts of past sexual predation and the release of an audiotape exposing deeply misogynistic attitudes.

Most remarkable of all, he won in the face of fervent opposition by established figures in both political parties. Prominent Democrats opposed Trump for obvious partisan reasons, but in 2016 a sizable number of Republican politicians declined to endorse his candidacy, and a handful—including former secretary of state Colin Powell—endorsed Clinton. Nor did he win the support of any living president, including George Bush *père et fils*.

As the campaign wore on, by far the most unified and fervent warnings about Trump came from the ranks of America's professional foreign policy elite. He was of course opposed by foreign policy experts in the Democratic Party, such as former secretary of state Madeleine Albright; and Hillary Clinton's supporters included literally dozens of familiar insiders with impressive foreign policy credentials, including Jake Sullivan, James Steinberg, Kurt Campbell, Anne-Marie Slaughter, and many, many more.[1] But opposition to Trump was, if anything, more vehement on the Republican side. In March 2016 the former State Department counselor and Johns Hopkins University professor Eliot A. Cohen organized an open letter signed by 122 former national security officials that denounced Trump's views on foreign policy, described him as "fundamentally dishonest," and judged him "utterly unfitted to the office." A few months later, fifty top Republican foreign policy experts—including former ambassador to India and NSC aide Robert Blackwill, former deputy secretary of state and World Bank president Robert Zoellick, former National Security Agency chief Michael Hayden, and former head of the Department of Homeland Security Michael Chertoff—released a public letter saying they would not vote for Trump and warning that he lacked "the temperament" to lead the country and would be "the most reckless president in American history."[2]

It was hardly surprising that Trump's ascendancy alarmed the foreign policy establishment. Not only had his conduct during the campaign raised doubts about his character and judgment, but he had repeatedly challenged some of the most enduring shibboleths of U.S. foreign policy. He had openly questioned the value of NATO and raised doubts about whether he would fulfill the treaty obligations the United States had undertaken toward its European allies. He had accused allies in Asia and Europe of "not paying their fair share" (which was not by itself a controversial claim) and said it might not be a bad thing if countries like South Korea or Japan built their own nuclear weapons. He had praised Russian president Vladimir Putin as a "strong leader" and refused to condemn Russia's seizure of Crimea, its aggressive use of cyberweapons, or its support for the Assad regime in Syria, which had killed several hundred thousand civilians in a long and bitter civil war. He called the multilateral agreement that had capped Iran's nuclear program "a terrible deal" and threatened to launch trade wars with China, Mexico, Canada, and South Korea. He also gave lengthy interviews on foreign policy that revealed a shallow, even ill-informed knowledge of international affairs.[3]

Among other things, Trump's startling victory revealed considerable public dissatisfaction with the foreign policy of the past three U.S. presidents. Far from rendering him unappealing or unfit for office, Trump's "America First" rhetoric took dead aim at the grand strategy that had guided the foreign policies of the Clinton, Bush, and Obama administrations. Instead of viewing the United States as the "indispensable nation" responsible for policing the globe, spreading democracy, and upholding a rules-based, liberal world order, Trump was calling—however incoherently—for a foreign policy he claimed would make Americans stronger and richer at home and less committed, constrained, and bogged down abroad.

To be sure, foreign policy was not the biggest issue in the 2016 campaign. Issues of race, class, and identity drove a substantial number of voters toward Trump, who was also aided by lingering hostility toward the nation's first black president and Hillary Clinton's own tarnished reputation and tiresome familiarity after more than two decades in the public eye. Media fascination with Trump fueled his rise as well, and he proved to be a far more effective marketer and user of social media than any of his rivals. It would be a mistake, therefore, to see foreign policy as the taproot of Trump's victory in 2016.

Yet foreign policy was far from irrelevant. For starters, a consistent theme of Trump's message was opposition to globalization in all its forms. He claimed that Washington had been negotiating "bad trade deals" with other states for decades, beginning with NAFTA in 1993, China's entry into the World Trade Organization in 2001, and especially the pending Trans-Pacific Partnership (TPP) in Asia and the Transatlantic Trade and Investment Partnership (TTIP) with Europe. According to Trump, this "false song of globalism" had cost millions of Americans good jobs and left the American economy far weaker. Globalization had also encouraged what he termed "senseless immigration policies" that threatened America's core identity and allowed dangerous criminals and violent extremists to enter the U.S. homeland.[4] If elected, he promised, he'd tear up those bad trade deals, "build a wall" with Mexico, keep "extremists" from coming to America, abandon the Paris Agreement on climate change (a phenomenon he claimed was a Chinese hoax designed to stifle U.S. businesses), bring the jobs lost to globalization back to the United States, and "make America great again."

Equally important, a long string of foreign policy failures under the previous three presidents reinforced Trump's antiestablishment message and cast doubt on Hillary Clinton's claim to be an experienced leader with the judgment and seasoning needed in the Oval Office.

Trump repeatedly criticized her performance as secretary of state, pointing out that as a senator, she had supported the 2003 invasion of Iraq, backed the ill-advised toppling of the Libyan leader Muammar Gaddafi in 2011, and called for deeper U.S. involvement in the Syrian civil war. Clinton may not have deserved all of Trump's gibes, but she could not counter his attack by citing a compelling list of undisputed foreign policy achievements, simply because there weren't any.

In fact, the track record of U.S. foreign policy since the end of the Cold War was difficult—maybe impossible—to defend, and certainly not in a way that American voters could relate to and understand. Instead of a series of clear and obvious successes, the years after the Cold War were filled with visible failures and devoid of major accomplishments. President Barack Obama had even suggested that modest achievements were all one could reasonably expect, telling an interviewer in 2014 that his approach to foreign policy "may not always be sexy . . . But it avoids errors. You hit singles, you hit doubles; every once in a while you may be able to hit a home run."[5] There were precious few home runs in the years since the Cold War ended, however, and plenty of pop-ups, strikeouts, and weak ground balls instead.

Some of these failures were missed opportunities, such as the bipartisan failure to capitalize on the Oslo Accords and achieve a lasting solution to the Israeli-Palestinian conflict. Other debacles—such as the Iraq and Afghan wars—were costly, self-inflicted wounds. In a few cases, what were advertised as farsighted and constructive U.S. initiatives—such as the decision to expand NATO or the policy of "dual containment" in the Persian Gulf—ended up sowing the seeds of future troubles. None of these decisions made Americans more secure or prosperous.

Nor was the United States successful at spreading its preferred political values. The collapse of the Soviet empire was a striking vindication for America's democratic ideals, and many observers expected these principles to take root and deepen around the world. These idealistic hopes went unfulfilled, however: existing dictatorships proved resilient, several new democracies eventually slid back toward authoritarian rule,

U.S.-led efforts at regime change produced failed states instead, and, over time, it was the United States that began to abandon its core principles. In the years after the September 11, 2001, terrorist attacks, top U.S. officials authorized torture, committed war crimes, conducted massive electronic surveillance of U.S. citizens, and continued to support a number of brutal authoritarian regimes in key regions. The 2008 financial crisis exposed deep corruption within key financial institutions and cast doubt on whether U.S.-style free-market capitalism was the best formula for sustained economic growth. Meanwhile, America's democratic order was increasingly paralyzed by ideological polarization and partisan gridlock, and new democracies increasingly modeled their constitutions on examples from other countries rather than on the United States.[6]

By the time the 2016 election ended, in fact, the United States no longer seemed to be a particularly attractive political or economic model for other societies. Instead of being a beacon for liberal ideals and a model of enlightened democratic rule, the country had become an inspiration for such leaders of xenophobic nationalist movements as Marine Le Pen in France or Geert Wilders in the Netherlands, who greeted Trump's election with enthusiasm and hoped to follow his example in their own countries.

From a broader perspective, both the overall condition of the world and America's status within it had declined steadily and significantly between 1993 and 2016. Despite a number of positive trends—including a sharp decline in the number of people living in extreme poverty—the optimistic visions of the early 1990s were not fulfilled. Great power competition had returned with a vengeance, weapons of mass destruction continued to spread, terrorists and other violent extremists were an active force in more places, the Middle East was in turmoil, and the euro crisis, Brexit decision, and illiberal trends in several member states left the European Union facing an uncertain future. U.S. foreign policy was not the primary cause of all of these developments, perhaps, but it played a significant role in many of them. When Trump told audiences that "our foreign policy is a complete and total disaster," he was telling it like it was.[7]

Most damning of all, Trump pointed an accusing finger at a foreign policy establishment that had failed to recognize its repeated errors, refused to hold those responsible for them accountable, and clung to discredited conventional wisdoms. Like the Wall Street bankers who caused the 2008 financial crisis, the architects of repeated foreign policy debacles never seemed to pay a price for their mistakes, or even to learn from them. A bipartisan coterie of senior officials circulated from government service to the private sector, from think tanks to corporate boards, from safe sinecures to new government appointments, even when their past service was undistinguished and the policies they had conceived, sold, and implemented hadn't worked. Pundits and policy wonks whose predictions and prescriptions had proved to be misguided were shielded from sanction as well, while those who challenged the bipartisan consensus were marginalized, ignored, or vilified even when they were right. And while members of the establishment routinely jockeyed for position and sparred over tactical issues, they remained united in the belief that the United States had the right and the responsibility to lead the world toward a broadly liberal future.

Foreign policy may have been a secondary issue in the 2016 campaign, therefore, but the combination of persistent failures abroad and an insular, unaccountable elite that refused to acknowledge them dovetailed perfectly with Trump's populist assault on existing institutions and his pledge to "shake the rust off of America's foreign policy."

What alternative did Trump offer? Although his foreign and national security policy positions lacked detail and clarity, several recurring themes emerged throughout the campaign. First and foremost, he emphasized that the central purpose of U.S. foreign policy should be to advance the American national interest, that the United States should engage with others in ways intended to benefit Americans. Although this might seem obvious, even a truism, Trump was telling his listeners what many of them wanted to hear: U.S. power and influence should be used not to help others or to advance a broader set of political values around the world, but rather to make Americans better off.

Consistent with this principle, Trump chastised U.S. allies in Europe and Asia for free-riding on American protection, and he made it clear that he expected them to contribute much more to collective defense if they expected to retain U.S. support. He said he would hold summits with U.S. allies in Asia and Europe that would "discuss a rebalancing of financial commitments" and "upgrade NATO's outdated mission and structure." In a Trump administration, in short, relations with America's most important and powerful allies would be fundamentally recast.

Trump also condemned U.S. efforts at "nation-building" in places like Iraq and Afghanistan. Complaining that "we're rebuilding other countries while weakening our own," he said that such efforts "began with a dangerous idea that we could make western democracies out of countries that had no experience or interests in becoming a western democracy." If elected, he promised the United States would be "getting out of the nation-building business."

Trump also took dead aim at globalization, especially the various institutions and agreements that had expanded global trade and investment dramatically over the past several decades. He called the North American Free Trade Agreement a "total disaster" and said that U.S. trade policy had led to "the theft of American jobs" and helped China "continue its economic assault on American jobs and wealth."

Paradoxically, he also suggested that he would try to improve relations with China and Russia, saying, "We should seek common ground based on shared interests," and stressing that "an easing of tensions, and improved relations with Russia . . . is possible, absolutely possible." Russia's interests in its "near abroad" would be respected, he implied, and he vowed to work with Moscow to counter the common threat from ISIS, even if this meant supporting the Assad regime in Syria.

Trump also sounded a defiant note against "radical Islam." He vowed to "work together with any nation in the [Middle East] that is threatened by the rise of radical Islam" and threatened to bar Muslims from entering the United States. He also said he had a "simple message" for ISIS: "Their days are numbered."

Finally, Trump sounded a consistent theme of American strength, resolve, and purpose. Declaring that the United States was now "a weak country," he promised to rebuild U.S. military power, saying that "our military dominance must be unquestioned . . . by anybody and everybody" and suggesting that the United States could get its way more often by being "more unpredictable."[8]

Trump's pronouncements may have lacked coherence, but the central message was clear: U.S. foreign policy was not delivering as promised. What the country needed, therefore, was a tough-minded emphasis on American national interests and a hard-nosed approach to allies and adversaries alike. In other words, America needed a radically different grand strategy.

Viewed as a whole, Trump's foreign policy program promised a radical departure from the internationalist agenda that had informed U.S. foreign policy since the end of the Second World War, and especially since the end of the Cold War. Instead of striving to expand and deepen a rules-based international order—one that actively sought to spread democracy, promote free trade, strengthen alliances and international institutions, and defend human rights—Trump was offering a self-centered, highly nationalist foreign policy that eschewed long-term efforts to spread American ideals and focused instead on securing short-term advantages.

Whether he understood it or not, Trump was also presenting a different take on the familiar notion of "American exceptionalism." The United States would still be different from other countries, but it would no longer be the "indispensable nation," the linchpin of a liberal world order, the first responder to major global challenges, or even a "reluctant sheriff." Instead, relations with other states would be conducted on a purely transactional basis, with an eye toward getting "the best deals" and forcing others to bear the greatest burdens. Given that this approach was a direct repudiation of the worldview that had guided U.S. foreign policy for more than sixty years, it is no wonder that foreign policy elites greeted his candidacy with a combination of horror and dismay.

And yet he won. Given the positions he had outlined in the campaign, Trump's victory raised two fundamental questions about the past, present, and future of U.S. foreign policy.

First, how could the U.S. have gone so badly off the rails that American voters would elect a completely inexperienced leader who had openly challenged well-established foreign policy wisdoms and who was opposed by senior foreign policy experts from both parties?

Second, could Trump pull off the revolution in foreign policy that he promised? Given the opposition he was bound to face from elites in both parties and a well-entrenched national security establishment, would he be able to steer the ship of state in a new direction? Would the foreign policy establishment manage to co-opt and corral him, or had he been bluffing all along? Whichever course he ultimately chose, what effects would his presidency have on U.S. security and prosperity, and on international politics more broadly?

The Argument

This book addresses each of these questions, focusing primarily on the political power of the foreign policy community here at home. I argue that Trump won in part because his claim that U.S. foreign policy was "a complete and total disaster" contained many elements of truth.[9] The American people understood that something had gone awry, which is why public opinion polls showed diminishing support for overseas adventures and why voters kept gravitating toward candidates who promised to do less abroad and more at home.

It is worth remembering, for example, that in 1992, voters ignored George H. W. Bush's impressive foreign policy achievements and opted instead for Bill Clinton, whose campaign mantra was "it's the economy, stupid." In 2000, George W. Bush won support by criticizing Clinton's overemphasis on "nation-building" and by promising voters a foreign policy that would be "strong but humble." After Bush failed to deliver as promised, however, in 2008 Americans picked Barack Obama because he had opposed the war in Iraq and promised to repair relations with the rest of the world. Though personally popular, Obama did not end the cycle of foreign policy failure either, and by 2016 many voters clearly preferred Trump's "America First" to Hillary Clinton's commitment to continue the same policies that had repeatedly backfired.

What had gone wrong? U.S. foreign policy did not fail because the United States faced a legion of powerful, crafty, and ruthless adversaries whose brilliant stratagems repeatedly thwarted Washington's noble intentions and well-crafted designs. Nor did it fail because the United States experienced an improbable run of bad luck.

On the contrary, U.S. foreign policy failed because its leaders pursued a series of unwise and unrealistic objectives and refused to learn from their mistakes. In particular, the deeper cause of America's recurring foreign policy failures was the combination of overwhelming U.S. primacy, a misguided grand strategy, and an increasingly dysfunctional foreign policy community.

With respect to the former, victory in the Cold War had left the United States, as President George H. W. Bush and National Security Advisor Brent Scowcroft later recalled, "with the rarest opportunity to shape the world."[10] This position of primacy was the permissive condition that allowed Washington to pursue a highly ambitious foreign policy—to "shape the world"—without having to worry very much about the consequences. Yet because the United States was already wealthy, powerful, and secure, there was little need to "go abroad in search of monsters to destroy" and little to gain even if these efforts succeeded. The result was a paradox: U.S. primacy made an ambitious grand strategy *possible*, but it also made it less *necessary*.

Ignoring these realities, which implied that the United States could have reduced its overseas commitments somewhat and focused more attention on domestic priorities, each post–Cold War administration embraced an ambitious grand strategy of "liberal hegemony" instead. This strategy is *liberal*, not in the sense of being left-leaning (as in the familiar dichotomy between "liberal" and "conservative"), but because it seeks to use American power to defend and spread the traditional liberal principles of individual freedom, democratic governance, and a market-based economy.[11] The strategy is one of *hegemony* because it identifies America as the "indispensable nation" that is uniquely qualified to spread these political principles to other countries and to bring other states into a web of alliances and institutions designed and led by the United States. Not only do its proponents see the preservation of U.S. primacy and the expansion of a predominantly liberal world order as essential for U.S. security and prosperity; in their eyes, this objective is good for the rest of the world as well.

But as the past twenty-five years have shown, the strategy of liberal hegemony is fundamentally flawed. Instead of building an ever-expanding zone of peace united by a shared commitment to liberal ideals, America's pursuit of liberal hegemony poisoned relations with Russia, led to costly quagmires in Afghanistan, Iraq, and several other countries, squandered trillions of dollars and thousands of lives, and encouraged both states and non-state actors to resist U.S. efforts or to exploit them for their own benefit. Instead of welcoming U.S. leadership, allies took advantage by free-riding, adversaries repeatedly blocked U.S. initiatives, and hostile extremists found different ways to attack, divert, and distract. America's superior economic and military assets could not rescue an approach to the world that was misguided at its core.

So why did the United States adopt a grand strategy that performed so poorly, and why did three very different presidents continue this approach even after its limitations became apparent? I argue that liberal hegemony remained the default setting for U.S. foreign policy because the foreign policy establishment was deeply committed to it and in an ideal position to promote and defend it. As the nearly unified opposition to Trump has shown, the consensus behind this approach transcended party lines and survived repeated disappointments.

Leading members of the foreign policy establishment undoubtedly believed that liberal hegemony was the right strategy for America, but they also understood that it was very good for them. Open-ended efforts to remake the world in America's image gave the foreign policy establishment plenty to do, appealed to its members' self-regard, and maximized their status and political power. It bolstered the case for maintaining military capabilities that dwarfed those of the other major powers, and it allowed special interest groups with narrow foreign policy objectives to lobby for their preferred policies and logroll with others, thereby making it more likely that the government would give each some of what it wanted. Liberal hegemony, in short, was a full-employment policy for the foreign policy elite and the path of least resistance for groups seeking to convince the U.S. government to do something somewhere far away on behalf of somebody else.

By 2016, however, the track record of the past twenty-five years and the costs it had imposed on the nation could not be fully concealed. Awareness of repeated failures opened the door to Trump's populist assault on what many of his supporters saw as an aloof, insular, and unaccountable elite. Dissatisfaction with the status quo helped propel Trump to the White House, but would he be able to overcome opposition from the establishment and pull off the revolution in foreign policy that he promised?[12]

PLAN OF THE BOOK

The remainder of this book is organized as follows.

In chapter 1, I evaluate the foreign policy performance of the three post–Cold War presidents: William Clinton, George W. Bush, and Barack Obama. I describe America's position in the world at the end of the Cold War, its expectations for the future, and the policies it pursued. The tale is not a happy one. In 1993 the United States was the unipolar power, on good terms with the other major powers, and an inspiring model for millions around the world. Democracy was expected to spread far and wide, and great power rivalry was supposedly a thing of the past. Today, by contrast, we live in a multipolar world, relations with Russia and China have deteriorated sharply, and liberal values are under siege. U.S. efforts to halt proliferation, pacify the Middle East, and reduce the danger from terrorism have repeatedly failed. It is, in short, a dismal record.

But why did U.S. foreign policy perform so badly? In chapter 2, I argue that it failed because the strategy of liberal hegemony rested on an inaccurate and unrealistic understanding of world politics, paid insufficient attention to political conditions in other countries, overstated America's ability to shape complex societies, and encouraged other states and non-state actors to resist or exploit U.S. efforts. America was very powerful, and its intentions may even have been (mostly) benevolent, but the strategy it adopted after 1993 was doomed to fail.

But if liberal hegemony contained obvious flaws and led to repeated disappointments, why did the United States adopt it and why didn't U.S. leaders learn from their mistakes? Chapter 3 addresses this question through a detailed portrait of the American foreign policy establishment, one that highlights the bipartisan consensus uniting most of the individuals and organizations that make up this community. Instead of being a disciplined meritocracy that rewards innovative thinking and performance, the foreign policy community is in fact a highly conformist, inbred professional caste whose beliefs and policy preferences have evolved little over the past twenty-five years, even as the follies and fiascoes kept piling up. The establishment's deep commitment to liberal hegemony is also sharply at odds with the preferences of most Americans.

If that is the case, then how did Washington sell the public a foreign policy that most of them did not want, and how did the foreign policy elite sustain public support for policies that kept failing? One reason, already mentioned, is the favorable geopolitical position the United States still enjoys. Because the country is so strong and so secure compared with other nations, it can pursue misguided and unsuccessful policies for a long time without putting its survival at risk.

The second reason is the ability of the foreign policy establishment to dominate public discourse on these issues, making it less likely that Americans will question the wisdom of liberal hegemony. Chapter 4 shows how politicians, officials, pundits, and other influential members of the establishment sold the strategy of liberal hegemony by manipulating the "marketplace of ideas": (1) inflating threats, (2) exaggerating the benefits of global leadership, and (3) concealing the costs of an expansive global role in order to convince the population that garrisoning the world and trying to spread liberal ideals was both essential to their security and destined to succeed (eventually).

Chapter 5 considers why liberal hegemony remained the default strategy despite its obvious shortcomings. A key reason, I suggest, is the foreign policy establishment's ability to avoid full accountability. Key ideas are rarely questioned, lessons learned are soon forgotten, and members of the foreign policy elite are rarely, if ever, penalized for their mistakes. Instead, it is the dissidents and critics who end up marginalized or penalized, even when they are proved right. When the same people keep getting reappointed and the same tired rationales are rarely challenged, there is no reason to expect the guiding principles of U.S. foreign policy to change or the results to improve.

Until Trump. His election in 2016 showed that although the American people would tolerate a long series of foreign policy failures, these shortcomings could not be concealed forever. The final question, therefore, is whether Trump would manage to steer the ship of state in a new direction, and whether his efforts to do so would leave the country better off. Sadly, the evidence to date suggests that this will not be the case. Instead, chapter 6 argues that Trump's handling of the presidency provides a textbook illustration of how *not* to fix U.S. foreign policy. In particular, it shows how the foreign policy community forced Trump back toward the same familiar paths—aided in no small part by Trump's ignorance, deficiencies of character, and poor policy choices. Instead of implementing a systematic and well-thought-out readjustment to liberal hegemony and playing different groups in Washington off against one

another, Trump soon united key elements of the foreign policy community against him and lost political support. He also turned out to be a
chaotic manager whose White House was a snake pit where top aides
came and went with alarming frequency and whose inexperienced staff
made repeated and sometimes embarrassing mistakes. Add to that toxic
mix Trump's own errors of judgment, rash statements, and decidedly
unpresidential behavior, and you have a recipe for disaster.

Thus, the battle between the Donald and the foreign policy
"Blob"—to use former deputy national security advisor Ben Rhodes's
dismissive term for the Beltway establishment—was a protracted one
and continues today. But the United States has already paid a substantial
price, with the costs still mounting. Trump's stewardship of U.S. foreign
policy has had serious negative consequences and has squandered the
hard-won positions of influence the United States had established since
the Second World War. The United States is still fighting wars in distant
lands and bearing a disproportionate share of global security burdens,
but it is now led by an impulsive and frequently angry narcissist whose
erratic behavior has alarmed U.S. allies but done little to contain or co-
opt America's adversaries. Instead of bringing America's commitments
and capabilities into better balance, Trump has undermined the latter
without decreasing the former, and has given other states ample reason
to question Washington's judgment and competence.

Chapter 7 explains how this situation might be corrected. After
briefly considering possible objections to my argument, I lay out an alternative grand strategy based on the geopolitical concept of "offshore
balancing." This approach eschews trying to remake the world in America's image and would focus U.S. foreign policy on upholding the balance of power in three key regions: Europe, East Asia, and the Persian
Gulf. Offshore balancing rejects isolationism and calls for the United
States to remain diplomatically and economically engaged with other
nations, but it would rely primarily on regional actors to uphold local
balances of power and commit the United States to intervene with its
own forces only when one or more of these balances was in danger of
breaking down.

Absent a crushing international setback, however, the foreign policy establishment will not embrace a strategy that would diminish its own power, status, and sense of self-worth. If outsiders such as Obama or Trump could not pull off a more fundamental change, who could? I argue that meaningful and positive change will occur only if a well-organized and politically potent reform movement emerges, one that can puncture the elite consensus behind liberal hegemony and generate a more open and sustained debate on these issues. A single leader cannot do it alone, especially someone as unqualified and unfit as the current president. It is the foreign policy establishment that has to change for a new strategy to emerge, and that means building new institutions and sources of political power inside the "Blob." If such a movement does not arise or proves too weak to generate meaningful change, U.S. foreign policy will not improve. The United States will undoubtedly survive, but its citizens will live less secure and bountiful lives.

It did not have to be this way. The United States is an exceptionally lucky country, one that is wealthy and vastly powerful, and it has no serious enemies nearby. That remarkable good fortune gives its leaders enormous latitude in the handling of foreign affairs. But as I show in the next two chapters, the men and women responsible for U.S. foreign policy over the past twenty-five years have repeatedly made bad choices and squandered many of these enduring advantages. They may have acted with the best of intentions, but their recurring failures are part of the reason Donald Trump became president.

1. A DISMAL RECORD

WHEN THE SOVIET UNION collapsed, in 1991, Americans could have taken a well-earned victory lap and reconsidered the expansive grand strategy they had pursued for the previous four decades. They could have asked themselves whether the level of global engagement mandated by the Cold War strategy of containment still made sense in these radically new circumstances. In the absence of a peer competitor or a strong ideological rival, was it still necessary or wise for the United States to maintain an extensive array of global security commitments and to work overtime to shape events around the world? The sudden disappearance of America's only serious rival might have encouraged U.S. leaders to question the wisdom of trying to guide political, economic, and military relations on every continent, and led them to retrench slightly and focus more attention on domestic needs.

Yet this possibility did not get much of a hearing in the early 1990s.[1] A handful of academics and policy analysts called for a significant reduction in America's global commitments, but their views attracted scant attention in official circles and had zero impact on U.S. foreign and defense policy.[2] Allies in Europe and Asia worried that the United States might cash in its "peace dividend" and reduce its global presence substantially, but the foreign policy establishment never considered this possibility for more than a moment. The world had changed, but a serious reassessment of U.S. grand strategy never took place.

Even before the U.S.S.R. imploded, top officials in the Bush administration believed that the United States should preserve or expand its existing commitments and maintain overwhelming military superiority in order to deter the emergence of new "peer competitors."[3] But their ambitions did not stop there. As President George H. W. Bush and National Security Advisor Brent Scowcroft later recalled, they found themselves "standing alone at the height of power" with "the rarest opportunity to shape the world and the deepest responsibility to do so wisely for the benefit of not just the United States but all nations."[4]

As Richard Haass, former director of the State Department's Policy Planning Staff and later the president of the Council on Foreign Relations, described it, the central objective of U.S. foreign policy became one of integrating other countries "into arrangements that will sustain a world consistent with U.S. interests and values, and thereby promote peace, prosperity, and justice."[5] The process of "integration" was not passive: on the contrary, the United States actively pressured other states to adopt more representative political systems, open themselves to trade and investment, and accept a set of global institutions that were to a large extent made-in-America. States that welcomed U.S. primacy were supported and defended; those that resisted it were isolated, contained, coerced, or overthrown. Terrorist and insurgent groups that opposed U.S. dominance would be tracked, targeted, and, if possible, destroyed. Presidents Bill Clinton, George W. Bush, and Barack Obama all shared these broad objectives and actively pursued them, albeit in somewhat different ways.

The United States, in short, was not a "status quo" power. Having won the Cold War, helped liberate Eastern Europe, and freed Kuwait from Saddam Hussein's clutches, U.S. leaders now set out to create a liberal world order through the active use of U.S. power. Instead of defending its own shores, maximizing prosperity and well-being at home, and promoting its ideals by force of example, Washington sought to remake other countries in its own image and incorporate them into institutions and arrangements of its own design.

Victorious nations often succumb to hubris, and the heady sense of possibility that followed America's Cold War triumph was to be expected. Nor did these hopes appear unwarranted. The smashing U.S. victory in the 1991 Gulf War had exorcized the ghosts of Vietnam and the 1979 Iranian hostage debacle, and U.S. military supremacy was now apparent to all. The U.S. economy grew impressively for most of the 1990s, new democracies were springing up in Latin America and the former Soviet empire, and there were even hopes for lasting peace in the broader Middle East.

Small wonder, then, that prominent intellectuals believed that the era of great power competition and grand ideological rivalries was finally behind us and humankind could concentrate on amassing wealth in a benevolent "new world order." American power would be marshaled for (nearly) everyone's benefit, and other states were expected to welcome Washington's leadership, accept its well-intentioned guidance, imitate the American model of democratic capitalism, and be grateful for the benefits U.S. primacy would provide.

Unfortunately, the results of this ambitious attempt to remake the world have been dismal. Pursuing liberal hegemony did not make the United States safer, stronger, more prosperous, or more popular. Nor did it make the rest of the world more tranquil and secure. On the contrary, America's ambitious attempt to reorder world politics undermined its own position, sowed chaos in several regions, and caused considerable misery in a number of other countries.

To see this clearly, we need only compare the world the United States faced in the early 1990s with the world it confronts today. It is not a pretty picture.

The Unipolar Moment and the End of History

A BENEVOLENT STRATEGIC ENVIRONMENT

When the Cold War ended, the United States found itself in a position of global primacy unseen since the Roman Empire. It had the world's largest and most advanced economy—with a gross domestic product roughly 60 percent larger than its nearest competitor—and in 1992 it produced roughly 25 percent of the world's goods and services.[6] It continued to set the pace in scientific research and technological innovation, its universities and research labs were the best in the world, and the U.S. dollar remained the world's reserve currency, a luxury that allowed Washington to run larger trade deficits and to offset costs onto other countries in other ways.

The United States was also the only country in the world with a global military presence. Not only did it have "command of the commons" (the oceans and much of the world's airspace), it had the capacity to take decisive military action almost anywhere.[7] In the 1990s, in fact, U.S. military spending exceeded the defense expenditures of the next twenty or thirty largest countries *combined*. Many of these states were close U.S. allies, so America's practical lead over its remaining rivals was in fact even larger. Its armed forces also enjoyed impressive qualitative advantages, with U.S. spending on military R & D alone exceeding the entire defense budgets of Germany, Great Britain, France, Russia, Japan, or China.[8] Even the deaths of nineteen U.S. Rangers in a bungled raid in Somalia in 1993 did not undermine the widespread sense of U.S. military omnipotence.

Moreover, the United States was on good terms with all the other major powers. The major European states were bound to the United States through NATO, and Washington also had formal alliances with Japan, South Korea, Australia, New Zealand, and the Philippines as well as close strategic partnerships with Egypt, Israel, Saudi Arabia, and Jordan (among others). Relations with Russia were surprisingly cordial as the unipolar era began, as Moscow wanted Western help to transition to a market economy and was eager to forge cooperative security arrangements as well. China's rising power was of some concern to U.S. leaders, but Beijing was still committed to Deng Xiaoping's policy of "peaceful rise." Accordingly, the United States opted to integrate China into existing institutions such as the new World Trade Organization in the hope that extending a friendly hand would convince Beijing to be a partner rather than a rival.

Given America's abundant advantages, many experts believed that the "unipolar moment" might last for years—and possibly decades. Writing in *Foreign Affairs* in 1990, the columnist Charles Krauthammer of *The Washington Post* suggested that preserving U.S. dominance was readily affordable and that the only thing that might topple the United States from its lofty perch was a prolonged economic downturn caused by wasteful entitlement spending at home.[9] The political scientists William Wohlforth and Stephen Brooks of Dartmouth College agreed, arguing that U.S. primacy might last even longer than the forty-plus years of bipolarity that preceded it.[10] These and other apostles of U.S. dominance repeatedly emphasized that the costs of U.S. primacy were modest and would be easy for the world's largest economy to bear.[11]

The strategic situation was not entirely rosy, of course, but the dangers that troubled U.S. leaders after the Cold War were far less ominous than the threats the United States had faced in the recent past. Instead of competing with a continent-size superpower driven by a revolutionary ideology that had won millions of sympathizers around the world, America's main adversaries were now an array of weak "rogue states" such as Iraq, Iran, Cuba, North Korea, Libya, Syria, Afghanistan (under the Taliban), and Serbia. These regimes were all unsavory dictatorships, some of them sought to acquire weapons of mass destruction, and each was a troublesome influence within its own region. But they were all third- to fifth-rate powers when compared with the mighty United States, and none of them posed an existential threat to the United States or to any of its vital interests.[12] As General Colin Powell, chairman of the Joint Chiefs of Staff, wryly noted in 1991, "I'm running out of demons. I'm running out of enemies. I'm down to Castro and Kim Il Sung."[13]

Moreover, the first Gulf War and the subsequent containment of Iraq suggested that the United States and its allies could take care of any of these states rather easily if it became absolutely necessary. From a broad historical perspective, the United States could hardly have asked for a more benign security environment.

A FAVORABLE POLITICAL AND ECONOMIC TIDE?

In 1993 the tides of history appeared to be flowing America's way. Victory in the Cold War seemed to be a striking vindication of America's core ideals of individual liberty, free elections, and open markets. The so-called velvet revolutions in Eastern Europe and a "third wave" of democratic transitions in Latin America and elsewhere convinced many observers that liberal democracy was the only logical end point for modern or even postmodern societies. The expansion and deepening of the European Union (EU) in 1992—culminating in its decision to adopt a common currency, the euro—fit this upbeat narrative as well. Indeed, as a self-proclaimed "civilian power," the EU seemed to offer further evidence that democracy, the rule of law, and the progressive expansion of international institutions could create durable "zones of peace" among countries that had fought repeatedly in the past.

The spread of liberal norms and institutions—democracy, free speech, rule of law, market economies, etc.—was closely linked to hopes for significant progress in human rights. With Soviet-style authoritarianism discredited and more states becoming democratic, it seemed inevitable that government abuses would decline and humans would live increasingly free and secure lives. America's dominant position put it in an ideal place to press other states to protect basic human rights and to help states making the transition to democracy build the requisite legal institutions and other supporting elements of civil society.

The political scientist Francis Fukuyama captured the zeitgeist perfectly in a famous 1989 essay (and subsequent 1993 book), arguing that the grand ideological struggles of the past were now behind us and that mankind had reached "the end of history."[14] In the future, he suggested, there would be "no struggle or conflict over 'large' issues and consequently no need for generals or statesmen; what remains is primarily economic activity." The chief danger we faced, warned Fukuyama, might be boredom. Another well-known scholar, John Mueller, offered the rosy view that great power war had become unfashionable and obsolescent, and the Harvard professor Stanley Hoffmann told *The New York Times* that foreign policy realism—which emphasizes the perennial and often tragic struggle for power between states—was "utter nonsense today."[15] These (and other) optimistic views reflected the widespread sense that the world had left great power politics behind and was moving steadily toward a peaceful liberal order.

Reinforcing the sense of optimism about democracy and human rights was the belief that economic globalization was opening the door to a new era of peace and prosperity. The Communist world had embraced the market; new technologies of transportation, communication, and digitalization were shrinking distance and lowering transaction costs; ambitious new global agreements were removing political barriers to trade and investment; and global manufacturing now depended on complex but highly efficient supply chains that made goods cheaper and war even less feasible. International institutions such as the new World Trade Organization (WTO) would manage these new arrangements and enable all states to benefit from increased economic cooperation, assuming that they met the relevant requirements for membership and agreed to abide by the rules that these various organizations had laid down.[16]

Needless to say, these same pundits saw the United States as the linchpin of this benevolent new economic order. In *The Lexus and the Olive Tree*, Thomas L. Friedman's bestselling anthem to globalization, the *New York Times* columnist argued that countries hoping to succeed in a globalized world had to don the "Golden Straitjacket"—open markets, democratic institutions, the rule of law, etc.—and described the United States as the state that had gone furthest toward perfecting what he called "DOSCapital 6.0." And Friedman seemed to be onto something, because the U.S. economy performed well during the 1990s. *Time* magazine dubbed the U.S. Treasury secretaries Robert Rubin and Larry Summers and the Federal Reserve chief Alan Greenspan "the Committee to Save the World," and the idea that U.S. officials and Wall Street financial institutions were better at running a modern economy than anyone else reinforced the so-called Washington Consensus. If poorer states wanted to succeed in an increasingly integrated and competitive world economy, they would have to become more like the United States.

Taken together, these trends heralded a bright future for the United States but also for much of the world. Liberal values were on the march, and powerful secular trends seemed to be pulling much of the world inexorably in the direction that U.S. leaders wanted it to go. A few recalcitrant "rogue states" might hold out for a while, but over time, more and more countries would become democratic, respect human rights, and enter an ever-expanding global economy. U.S.-led international institutions would facilitate cooperation and enhance transparency, reinforcing liberal norms and uniform legal standards even more. American power was the foundation on which globalization supposedly rested— or, as Friedman quipped, "Without America on duty, there will be no America Online."[17]

SOLVING GLOBAL PROBLEMS

Primacy also seemed to put Washington in an ideal position to address an array of vexing global issues. Given the vast power at America's disposal and the lack of serious rivals, the United States would be free to use its influence, wealth, prestige, and, if necessary, its superior military forces to address problems that had defied solution for decades.

1. The Arab-Israeli Conflict

In the aftermath of the first Gulf War, the 1991 Madrid Peace Conference had made a promising start toward resolving the long and bitter Arab-Israeli conflict. Then, in 1993, the Oslo Accords brought new hope that the elusive final status agreement between Israel and the Palestinians might finally become a reality. The Palestinian Liberation Organization had accepted Israel's existence, Israeli prime minister Yitzhak Rabin was genuinely interested in a permanent peace, and the Clinton administration seemed to be in an ideal position to broker the deal. For the first time since Israel's founding in 1948, a lasting peace in the Middle East appeared within reach.

2. Proliferation

Addressing the danger posed by nuclear weapons seemed increasingly feasible as well. The United States had long sought to discourage the spread of nuclear weapons (and other weapons of mass destruction) and had labored to create the 1968 Nuclear Non-Proliferation Treaty and to persuade close U.S. allies to abandon their own nuclear ambitions. Although the problem had not disappeared in the early 1990s, the United States seemed to be in an excellent position to keep the lid on it. Iraq was now under strict UN sanctions, and inspectors from the United Nations Special Commission (UNSCOM) were dismantling its nuclear programs. Its neighbor, Iran, had sought nuclear weapons during the reign of Shah Reza Pahlavi, but the Islamic Republic had zero nuclear centrifuges operating when the Clinton administration took office in 1993 and still had none when George Bush became president eight years later. The United States joined with Russia and several European states to convince Ukraine, Kazakhstan, and Belarus to give up the nuclear weapons they had inherited when the U.S.S.R. broke up; Washington and Moscow subsequently negotiated new reductions in their own nuclear forces; and the Nunn-Lugar Cooperative Threat Reduction program was gradually placing Russia's vast stockpile of nuclear materials under more reliable custody and reducing the danger of "loose nukes."[18] Washington was keeping a watchful eye on North Korea, and the Clinton administration eventually decided against preventive war and instead negotiated the so-called Agreed Framework in 1994, which sought to persuade Pyongyang to forgo a nuclear weapons capability in exchange for civilian nuclear power plants and other material benefits.[19] Proliferation and other related issues remained a concern, but they appeared to be problems the United States could manage.

3. International Terrorism

International terrorism seemed to be a manageable problem as well. U.S. officials were aware that Al Qaeda and other terrorist groups were hostile and dangerous, and attacks on the World Trade Center (1993), the Khobar Towers dormitory in Saudi Arabia (1996), the U.S. embassies in Tanzania and Kenya (1998), and the USS *Cole* in Yemen (2000) underscored the challenge. But top U.S. officials also believed that the threat could be contained and that significant adjustments in U.S. strategy—such as distancing itself from its various Middle East clients or reducing its military presence there—were not required. Instead, they believed that the long-term solution was the further spread of U.S. ideals: as two former Clinton administration counterterrorism officials later wrote, "Democratization, however hazardous and unpredictable the process may be, is the key to eliminating sacred terror over the long term."[20]

As the post–Cold War era began, in short, the United States was in the catbird seat. Not only was it richer and stronger than any of the other major powers, it was allied with most of them and on good terms with the others, and it faced no peer competitors, regional rivals, or existential dangers. Key geopolitical trends seemed to be breaking America's way, and the liberal prescription for perennial peace and expanding prosperity appeared to be fulfilling its promise. It was time to abandon ancient hatreds and local quarrels and get busy getting rich in a rapidly globalizing world, one whose defining features were made in America and underpinned by American power.

But even if the winds of progress were at America's back, U.S. leaders still believed it would take an active effort to lead the world to this bright new future. As Secretary of State Warren Christopher told the Senate Foreign Relations Committee in 1993, the United States was standing "on the brink of . . . a new world of extraordinary hope and possibility." But, he also cautioned, "the new world we seek will not emerge on its own. We must shape the transformation that is under-way."[21]

Shaping that transformation is precisely what Presidents Clinton, Bush, and Obama all tried to do. Although their diplomatic styles differed and their specific policies and priorities varied in certain respects, liberal hegemony remained the default strategy for all three administrations. All three assumed that U.S. leadership was essential to global progress, and each sought to use American power to spread democracy, expand U.S. influence and security commitments, and reinforce a rules-based, liberal world order. How well did their efforts go?

Getting Used to Disappointment

By almost any measure, and in nearly every key area of foreign policy, the United States is in worse shape today than it was in 1992. The "unipolar moment" turned out to be surprisingly brief, the United States suffered repeated setbacks in several important areas, and the strategic environment has deteriorated sharply. Liberal democracy is in retreat in many places, and America's image as a vanguard of stable and competent governance was eroding long before Donald Trump appeared on the scene. U.S. efforts to address important regional problems have repeatedly failed, existing global institutions are visibly fraying, and terrorism and nuclear weapons have spread despite extensive U.S. efforts to contain them. Some regions—most notably the Middle East—are now mired in conflicts that may take decades to resolve. Although there have been isolated foreign policy achievements over the past twenty-five years, the failures are far more numerous and consequential than the successes.

A DETERIORATING STRATEGIC ENVIRONMENT

1. Great Power Relations

When the "unipolar era" began, the United States was the sole great power. Russia and China were both relatively weak, U.S. relations with both countries were reasonably good, and Washington's attention was focused primarily on a set of even weaker "rogue states," on terrorism, and on WMD proliferation. Today, Russia and China are significantly stronger than they were, both are at odds with Washington, and Moscow and Beijing are collaborating more closely than at any time since the 1950s. Several of the rogue states that Washington targeted in the 1990s remain defiant, and the rest are now "failed states" that may pose even greater risks. America's image of military dominance has been tarnished, the danger from terrorism has increased, and efforts to halt proliferation have been disappointing.

Relations with Russia deteriorated largely because the United States repeatedly ignored Russian warnings and threatened Moscow's vital interests. The most important step was the decision to expand NATO eastward, beginning with the admission of Poland, Hungary, and the Czech Republic in 1999; the subsequent entry of Bulgaria, Estonia, Latvia, Lithuania, Romania, Slovakia, and Slovenia in 2004; and the U.S. proposal to invite Ukraine and Georgia to prepare "action plans" for NATO membership in 2008.

As Russia experts like the late George Kennan warned, expanding NATO to the east was a "tragic mistake" that made a future conflict with Russia far more likely.[22] It also violated the assurances that Western officials (notably Secretary of State James Baker) had given to Soviet leaders prior to German reunification, including a pledge that NATO's jurisdiction and military forces would not move "one inch to the east."[23] U.S. leaders felt they could act with near impunity, however, because the Russian economy was in free fall and there was little Moscow could do, even in areas adjacent to its territory. A similar disregard for Russian concerns led President George W. Bush to withdraw from the U.S.-Soviet Anti-Ballistic Missile Treaty in 2002 and announce plans to deploy ballistic missile defenses in Eastern Europe, triggering Russian fears of a possible U.S. first-strike capability.

By 2000, Russia's official *National Security Concept* was warning of "attempts to create an international relations structure based on domination by developed Western countries . . . under U.S. leadership," and some of these fears were well-founded.[24] The United States bombed Serbia during the 1999 Kosovo War (without prior authorization by the UN Security Council), toppled Saddam Hussein in 2003, backed the "Orange Revolution" in Ukraine in 2004, and ousted the Libyan leader Muammar Gaddafi in 2011. This last step was especially significant because Moscow had gone along with UN Security Council Resolution 1973—which authorized military action "to protect civilian life" but not to topple the Libyan government—only to see the United States and its allies use the resolution as an opportunity to remove a leader they had long despised.[25] As former secretary of defense Robert Gates later acknowledged, "the Russians felt they had been played for suckers on Libya," which helps explain why Russia later backed the Syrian leader Bashar al-Assad so firmly and blocked UN action against him.[26]

Similarly, Obama's early insistence that "Assad must go" in Syria threatened Moscow's only remaining Middle East ally, and then, in 2013, U.S. officials openly sided with the pro-Western demonstrators who ousted Viktor Yanukovych, the democratically elected, pro-Russian leader of Ukraine. Moscow responded by seizing Crimea and backing breakaway militias in eastern Ukraine, thereby halting Ukraine's drift into the Western orbit.[27] The United States and its NATO allies responded with economic sanctions and the deployment of additional air and ground units in Eastern Europe, plunging relations with Moscow to the lowest level since the Cold War.

Russia is still significantly weaker than the United States but no longer a basket case. Although its economy remains dependent on energy exports and vulnerable to falling energy prices, its military power has been partly restored, and Moscow now has some capacity to defend its vital interests, especially in areas close to home. The seizure of Crimea, along with Moscow's successful military intervention in support of the Assad regime in Syria, underscored Russia's return to great power status and the waning of America's unipolar moment.

U.S. relations with China have become increasingly fraught as well.

In the 1990s, U.S. officials had hoped to integrate China into existing international institutions and make it a "responsible stakeholder" that would not challenge U.S. dominance. As late as 2002, in fact, the Bush administration's *National Security Strategy* counseled China to forgo advanced military capabilities and focus on greater social and political freedom instead.[28]

China ignored this self-serving advice, however, and by 2016 had emerged as an increasingly confident and ambitious rival. It was using some of its rapidly growing wealth to modernize its military forces, with an eye toward contesting the dominant position in Asia that the United States had enjoyed since the end of World War II. As China grew stronger, its leaders abandoned Deng Xiaoping's doctrine of a "peaceful rise" and began active efforts to shift the regional status quo in its favor. In a triumphal speech to the 19th Party Congress in October 2017, Chinese president Xi Jinping described global power trends as increasingly favorable, said that the Chinese nation "now stands tall and firm in the East," and declared that China would be "a global leader in terms of comprehensive national power and international influence" by mid-century.[29]

Within Asia itself, China has begun to challenge U.S. military pre-eminence in the maritime areas close to China and to advance its own territorial claims in the South China and East China seas. This policy has led to repeated incidents with Vietnam, the Philippines, and Japan, largely over disputed territorial claims in the adjacent waters. Beijing also began a sustained effort to build up and garrison a number of partially submerged reefs and shoals in the South China Sea, rejecting a ruling by the Permanent Court of Arbitration in The Hague that challenged its territorial claims there. A further sign of Beijing's more confrontational posture was its seizure of an unmanned U.S. undersea drone in December 2016, even though the drone was operating outside the waters Beijing had previously claimed. And with the United States bogged down in the Middle East and elsewhere, in 2013 Beijing announced an ambitious "One Belt, One Road Initiative," a multibillion-dollar infrastructure project to develop transportation networks in Central Asia and the Indian Ocean.[30]

The Bush administration sought to balance a rising China by forming a "strategic partnership" with India, and the Obama administration took the next step by announcing a "pivot" (or "rebalancing") toward Asia in 2011. In addition to moving additional U.S. military forces to the region, the Obama team negotiated the Trans-Pacific Partnership (TPP), a controversial twelve-nation multilateral trade agreement that excluded China and was intended to reinforce U.S. economic and political influence in Asia.

Yet in a move clearly designed to provide an alternative to the U.S.-led liberal order, Beijing began to develop its own set of international institutions. Chief among them was a new Asian Infrastructure Investment Bank, which had attracted fifty-seven "founding members" by 2016. The Obama administration refused to participate and tried to persuade other countries to follow its lead, but Washington could not even convince such close U.S. allies as Israel, Germany, or Great Britain to stay out of the new organization. And when President-elect Donald Trump announced that he would abandon the TPP as soon as he took office, Beijing immediately offered to organize regional trade under the auspices of a "Regional Comprehensive Economic Partnership" that excluded the United States.[31]

By 2016, it was increasingly clear that the world's two most powerful countries were headed for an intense security competition, one that was likely to shape great power politics for many decades to come.[32] Not surprisingly, the deteriorating U.S. relationship with both Russia and China gave the two Asian giants ample incentive to cooperate with each other. In 1992 the two states announced that they were forming a "constructive partnership"; in 2001 they signed a formal treaty of friendship and cooperation. And when Chinese president Xi Jinping visited Moscow in 2015, Russian president Vladimir Putin spoke openly of a "special relationship" between the two states. Although they share a long border, have fought in the past, and are in many respects not natural allies, a shared desire to rein in American power has led Beijing and Moscow to share intelligence and military technology, conduct joint military exercises, sign a number of long-term oil and gas development deals, and coordinate diplomatic positions within the UN Security Council.

Instead of being on reasonably good terms with all the major powers and being decisively stronger than all of them, by 2016 the United States had an increasingly contentious relationship with two of the world's great powers and U.S. policies had pushed them closer together.

2. From Rogue States to Failed States

American efforts to address the supposed threat from "rogue states" fared no better. The United States remains on bad terms with the rogue states that are still in power—North Korea, Iran, and the Assad regime in Syria—and all three governments continue to defy U.S. pressure. Syria has been wrecked by a brutal civil war, but Assad seems likely to remain in power, and Iran and North Korea are in stronger positions than they were twenty-five years ago.

With the partial (and minor) exception of Serbia, the rogue states the United States has successfully overthrown—Ba'athist Iraq, the Afghan Taliban, and Muammar Gaddafi's regime in Libya—ended up as failed states in the aftermath of U.S. intervention. Instead of becoming stable, pro-Western democracies, or even more moderate authoritarian regimes with a high degree of internal order, each became an active war zone, a breeding ground for violent extremism, and a further source of regional instability. Toppling Saddam Hussein in Iraq also removed a key counterbalance to Iranian influence and greatly enhanced Iran's position in the Persian Gulf region.

3. A Tarnished Military Reputation

By 2016 a series of internal scandals; the long, costly, and unsuccessful campaigns in Iraq and Afghanistan; and the ability of a number of weaker foes to defy sustained U.S. pressure had eroded the armed forces' reputation for competence and military supremacy. The United States still possessed the world's most capable military forces, but they no longer seemed unstoppable.

In Afghanistan, the toppling of the Taliban in 2001 seemed like a miraculous demonstration of U.S. military prowess, belying preinvasion fears that the United States would end up in the same sort of quagmire that had ultimately defeated the Soviet Union. Some seventeen years later, however, it is clear that those fears were well-founded. None of the long line of U.S. commanders managed to find the magic formula to defeat the Taliban and achieve victory, and the Afghan government remained corrupt, internally divided, and incapable of securing its own territory without extensive U.S. military backing and lavish economic support. The much-publicized 2009 "surge" of additional U.S. troops failed to turn the tide, and by 2016 the United States seemed trapped in a war it could neither win nor leave.[33]

The Bush administration's ill-fated decision to invade Iraq in 2003 offers a similarly tragic lesson. The invading force had little difficulty defeating Iraq's third-rate army, but U.S. civilian and military leaders had failed to plan for the occupation and were repeatedly surprised by the challenges it posed. A potent insurgency soon emerged, sectarian violence exploded, and the occupying troops responded in ways that made these problems worse. The subsequent "surge" in 2007 was a tactical success but a strategic failure, as it did not produce the necessary political reconciliation between Iraq's Shia, Sunni, and Kurdish populations. Iraq's new Shia-dominated government eventually insisted that the United States leave, and the Bush administration negotiated a schedule for withdrawal in 2008. Barack Obama eventually implemented this agreement (albeit more slowly than intended), only to be surprised when the new insurgent group ISIS emerged in 2014, inflicted a series of defeats on the Iraqi government forces that the United States had spent billions of dollars training and equipping, and proceeded to seize control of a significant slice of Iraqi and Syrian territory and proclaim the formation of a new "caliphate." Viewed as a whole, the Iraq War was an eloquent reminder of the limits of military power: having broken Iraq and ignited a bitter sectarian struggle, Washington had no idea how to fix it.[34]

U.S. military interventions elsewhere were no more successful. Relying primarily on covert action teams, Special Forces, and armed drones, the United States had interfered in Somalia and Yemen on several occasions from the early 1990s onward, and in each case the political situation got worse and anti-American extremists grew stronger.[35] Even the twin interventions in the Balkans—the 1996 Dayton Agreement and the 1999 Kosovo War—produced at best mixed results, as the new states that emerged from these conflicts remain fragile and the ethnic tensions that produced these conflicts continue to fester. As Admiral Mike Mullen, former chairman of the Joint Chiefs of Staff, admitted when asked about U.S. efforts at regime change in 2016, "We're 0 for a lot."[36]

By 2016, what had once appeared to be an irresistible tool of American influence had been humbled, and the mismatch between U.S. commitments and aspirations and its military capabilities was increasingly apparent. The 2008 financial crisis, ballooning federal deficit, and subsequent budget sequester eventually forced across-the-board cuts in defense spending, yet the United States was still fighting in Afghanistan, still waging war against ISIS in Iraq, still reinforcing vulnerable NATO allies in Eastern Europe, still attempting to "rebalance" toward Asia, and still conducting an unknown number of counterterrorist operations in dozens of other countries.

When Donald Trump took the oath of office, the United States was committed to defending more countries than at any time in its history. It had formal defense commitments with at least sixty-six countries, including the twenty-eight other members of NATO, the twenty signatories of the Rio Treaty in the Western Hemisphere, and such Asian allies as Japan, South Korea, Australia, and the Philippines. Afghanistan, Argentina, Bahrain, Egypt, Israel, Jordan, Kuwait, Morocco, New Zealand, and Pakistan had all been designated "major non-NATO allies," and the United States was tied to dozens of other countries through a bewilder-

ing array of security arrangements and defense cooperation agreements.[37] In 2014 a RAND Corporation study of U.S. security partnerships
noted that "the most striking observation is the sharp increase in 1992,
after the end of the Cold War, in both bilateral and multilateral agreements."[38] The available resources had shrunk, the number of opponents
had grown, and still America's global agenda kept expanding.

By almost any measure, the strategic environment the United
States faces today is worse than it was in 1993, and America's overall
position within that environment has eroded. In 2014, the chairman of
the Joint Chiefs of Staff, General Martin Dempsey, judged the world to
be "more dangerous than it ever has been." In 2016, Richard Haass
gloomily noted that "the question is not whether the world will continue to unravel, but how fast and how far." Or as Henry Kissinger observed darkly, "The United States has not faced a more diverse and
complex array of crises since the end of the Second World War."[39] Even
if one allows for the hyperbole that pervades much contemporary commentary on U.S. foreign policy, this is hardly the world that U.S. foreign-
policy makers anticipated when the Cold War ended. To the contrary,
the broad downward trend is a telling indictment of America's post–
Cold War grand strategy.

LIBERALISM IN RETREAT

When the Cold War ended, U.S. leaders expected that a rising liberal
tide would accelerate the spread of democracy, human rights, and open
markets and would usher in an unprecedented era of peace and global
prosperity, all under Uncle Sam's benevolent but watchful eye. By 2016
these confident expectations of an ever-rising liberal tide had dissipated,
and liberalism was in retreat both at home and abroad.

1. Democracy Demotion

The Clinton, Bush, and Obama administrations all made democracy
promotion a central goal of U.S. foreign policy and were confident that
U.S. power could reinforce a powerful secular trend. The Clinton

administration's national security strategy of "engagement and enlargement" put this objective at the heart of U.S. foreign policy, and George W.
Bush said that his own national security strategy was based on a "great
and guiding goal: to turn this time of American influence into generations of democratic peace."[40] Barack Obama was less outspoken on the
topic than his predecessors, perhaps, but many of his senior aides were
deeply committed to promoting liberal values, and Obama himself repeatedly called for foreign governments to be more open, transparent,
and accountable.[41] As he told the UN General Assembly in 2010, "There
is no right more fundamental than the ability to choose your leaders and
determine your destiny."[42] Or, as the State Department's *Quadrennial
Diplomacy and Development Review* declared in 2015, "Democracy, accountable government, and respect for human rights are essential for a
secure, prosperous and just world."[43] This commitment to promoting
certain human rights extended to religious freedom, which successive
U.S. officials declared to be a cherished constitutional value, a strategic
interest, and a foreign policy priority.[44]

Nor were such statements merely empty rhetoric. In addition to using military power to topple such dictators as Saddam Hussein or
Muammar Gaddafi, the United States used an array of softer policy instruments to promote or solidify democratic change in other countries.
The U.S. Agency for International Development allocates more than
$1 billion annually to strengthening political parties and democratic in-
stitutions, with the U.S. State Department spending roughly half that
much on similar programs. The federal government also subsidizes the
nonprofit National Democratic Institute and the International Republican Institute, organizations run by the two main U.S. political parties
whose mission is aiding their counterparts overseas. The U.S. taxpayer
also supports the National Endowment for Democracy, a bipartisan,
nongovernmental organization created by Congress that is "dedicated
to fostering the growth of a wide range of democratic institutions
abroad."[45] According to former assistant secretary of state Victoria Nuland, a leading proponent of U.S.-sponsored regime change, the U.S. gov-

ernment invested more than $5 billion to strengthen democracy in Ukraine alone.[46]

Yet despite the rhetorical priority given to this goal and the repeated use of U.S. wealth and power to advance it, efforts to promote democracy and human rights have gone into reverse. In 2012 the Economist Intelligence Unit's annual *Democracy Index* reported that "between 2006 and 2008 there was stagnation of democracy; between 2008 and 2010 there was regression across the world." The 2015 edition was even gloomier, noting "a decline in some aspects of governance, political participation and media freedoms, and a clear deterioration in attitudes associated with, or that are conducive to, democracy."[47] More shocking still, in 2016, declining trust in government led the *Democracy Index* to downgrade the United States from a "full" to a "flawed" democracy.[48]

Similarly, the 2018 edition of Freedom House's annual report on *Freedom in the World* warned that democracy "faced its most serious crisis in decades" and found that "Seventy-one countries suffered net declines in political rights and civil liberties, with only 35 registering gains. This marked the 12th consecutive year of decline in global freedom." Over that twelve-year period, in fact, "113 countries have seen a net decline, and only 62 have experienced a net improvement."[49]

These trends are apparent nearly everywhere: liberal institutions are eroding in Poland and Hungary, Turkey's ruling AKP Party has sharply curtailed press freedoms and imprisoned thousands of suspected opponents, and right-wing populist parties are increasingly active across Europe. The Obama administration persuaded the Egyptian military dictator Hosni Mubarak to step down in February 2011, but a military coup crushed Egypt's brief experiment with electoral democracy two years later. Elections in Afghanistan are rife with fraud, and the government in Kabul remains divided, corrupt, and ineffective to this day. U.S.-backed reform efforts in Myanmar convinced the military to give up power and hold free elections, but the new, mostly civilian-led government subsequently launched a brutal campaign of violence against the Rohingya, a Muslim minority group. After a period of decline, mass killings peaked again in 2013, with massacres or civil wars occurring in Egypt, the Central African Republic, Nigeria, and several other countries.[50] By 2016, what began as a peaceful protest movement for modest reforms in Syria had become a brutal civil war between the Assad regime and its equally despicable and dangerous opponents. Meanwhile, the youngest beneficiary of U.S. efforts at democracy promotion—the fledgling Republic of South Sudan—had fallen back into civil war before its third anniversary.[51]

"Between 2000 and 2015," observed democracy expert Larry Diamond of the Hoover Institution in 2016, "democracy broke down in 27 countries . . . Meanwhile, many existing authoritarian regimes have become even less open, transparent, and responsive to their citizens . . . [And] democracy itself seems to have lost its appeal. Many emerging democracies have failed to meet their citizens' hopes for freedom . . . just as the world's established democracies, including the United States, have grown increasingly dysfunctional."[52]

As Diamond suggests, part of the problem was the various ills afflicting Western-style liberal democracy itself, including the paralysis that repeatedly hobbled the U.S. political system, the pervasive and corrupting role that money plays in U.S. elections, and the regulatory failures exposed by the 2008 financial crisis. The inability of European leaders to devise prompt and effective responses to the eurozone crisis sapped popular confidence as well, and public opinion polls across the Western world revealed declining support for democracy itself. For example, a 2014 study based on *Eurobarometer* surveys found that "satisfaction with democracy [in the EU] receded by seven percentage points between autumn 2007 and 2011, while trust in national parliaments decreased by eight percentage points."[53] As Thomas Carothers of the Carnegie Endowment rightly noted, "Democracy's travails in both the United States and Europe have greatly damaged the standing of democracy in the eyes of many people around the world."[54]

Compounding these problems was the failure of countries like the United States to uphold the ideals they eagerly preached to others. The

discovery that U.S. officials had authorized torture, extraordinary rendition, and targeted assassinations, and the revelations about prisoner
abuse in Iraq, Afghanistan, and the U.S. prison at Guantanamo made
U.S. complaints about other states' human rights conduct seem gratu-
itous at best and hypocritical at worst.[55] Similarly, revelations that the
National Security Agency was illegally compiling a vast trove of electronic data on U.S. and foreign citizens—and that top officials had lied
about these activities—cast doubt on America's professed commitment
to civil liberties and the rule of law, straining relations with key allies.
U.S. support for authoritarian governments such as Saudi Arabia, Uzbekistan, Pakistan, and Singapore; its ready acceptance of the coup that toppled
the democratically elected government of Mohamed Morsi in Egypt;
and its refusal to sanction the questionable human rights behavior of such
allies as Israel and Turkey helped tarnish America's democratic brand
as well.[56]

At the same time, authoritarian regimes proved to be more resilient
than U.S. leaders had anticipated. China's one-party state weathered the
2008 financial crisis well and continued to enjoy impressive levels of
economic growth, Russia regained its status as a great power and began
defending its interests more successfully, and quasi-democratic leaders
such as Recep Erdogan in Turkey and Viktor Orbán in Hungary remained popular despite their increasingly authoritarian conduct.

The antidemocratic backlash also hit the philanthropic foundations
and nongovernmental organizations that were working to strengthen
democracy and promote human rights around the world. Between 2012
and 2015, for example, "more than 60 countries have passed or drafted
laws that curtail the activity of non-governmental and civil society organizations. Ninety-six countries have taken steps to inhibit NGOs from
operating at full capacity, in what the Carnegie Endowment calls a
'viral-like spread of new laws'" designed to limit what these organizations can do or in some cases shut them down altogether.[57]

To sum up: both Democratic and Republican administrations
wanted to make the world more democratic, foster greater freedom,

and improve human rights, and they believed that powerful secular forces around the world would make this goal easy to achieve and lead to a more peaceful and prosperous world. Not only were their hopes not borne out, U.S. actions at home and abroad have undermined these idealistic objectives and helped ignite the populist backlash that ushered Donald Trump into the White House.

2. Globalization and Its Discontents

The backlash against liberal democracy gained additional momentum when globalization failed to deliver as promised. Lowering political barriers to global trade and investment did boost world trade, helped countries like China and India lift millions of people out of deep poverty, reduced the costs of goods for U.S. consumers, and increased overall living standards in many places. But in the developed world—and especially the United States—the benefits of rapid globalization went mostly to the wealthy and well-educated: Wall Street won big, but Main Street did not. As Branko Milanovic has shown, incomes of the Asian middle class and the "global 1%" increased by roughly 60 percent between 1988 and 2008, while income gains for the lower and middle classes in the West over the same period were less than 10 percent.[58] According to Martin Wolf of the *Financial Times*, between 1980 and 2016 the top 1 percent in North America received as much of the aggregate increase in real incomes as the bottom 88 percent did.[59] Over time, the combination of rapid technological change and increasingly mobile global capital disrupted formerly dominant industries and eliminated thousands of middle- and lower-class jobs.[60] The benefits for the country as a whole might be undeniable, but globalization had harmed key sectors and regions, and government institutions failed to create adequate compensatory or adjustment mechanisms. By 2016, a growing sense of vulnerability in the face of powerful but anonymous market forces had produced a strong domestic backlash in the United States, Great Britain, and a number of other countries, paving the way for such populist politicians as Donald Trump and Bernie Sanders and helping inspire the "Brexit" campaign in the United Kingdom.[61]

Globalization also made the international economic order more vulnerable to financial crises, beginning with the 1997 Asian financial panic and later the 2008 Wall Street crisis and subsequent global recession. The follies and corruption within key financial institutions were eventually exposed, and Wall Street no longer seemed populated by brilliant and farsighted "Masters of the Universe." The financial crisis raised serious doubt about the competence of the U.S. economic leadership and accelerated the search for new institutional models. The subsequent problems of the eurozone—a direct result of the Wall Street collapse—put the European Union under unprecedented strains as well and dampened earlier expectations of an "ever-deeper Union."

Proponents of globalization also believed that an array of existing international institutions would facilitate cooperation between states, dampen conflicts between them, and help overcome familiar dilemmas of collective action. Instead of growing more capable and legitimate, however, the U.S-led institutions that seemed invincible in the early 1990s—NATO, the World Bank, the International Monetary Fund, and the World Trade Organization—"are now in rapid and unmistakable decline."[62] Even more charitable appraisals acknowledge that existing institutions are not working well and are badly in need of reform, yet the measures needed to update and improve them have been almost impossible to implement.[63]

A final consequence was the growing backlash against immigration. Globalization facilitated the movement of large numbers of people, including economic migrants seeking better employment and refugees fleeing conflict zones in the Balkans, Afghanistan, sub-Saharan Africa, or the Middle East. Although immigrants and refugee populations comprised relatively small minorities in their host countries, the inevitable cultural frictions, fears of job displacement, and concerns about crime and/or terrorism fueled opposition to immigration and aided the rise of right-wing nationalist movements across the industrialized world. Nationalism turned out to be alive and well, and when tensions arose between the desire for national sovereignty and an increasingly globalized world economy, it was the latter that lost out.[64]

The bottom line: the liberal vision of an increasingly democratic and economically open world—a world that many U.S. elites believed was in the offing when the Cold War ended—did not emerge as expected. History did not end; if anything, it galloped off in the opposite direction. Nor were these setbacks the result of a series of unfortunate accidents or a run of bad luck; they were mostly due to inflated expectations, hubris, and bad policy choices.

By the time Donald Trump took the oath of office, visions of a robust and globalized world economy—guided by Washington and underpinned by American power—had largely evaporated. As the political economist Jonathan Kirshner noted in 2014, "actors throughout the world are disenchanted with the American model and with the U.S. orchestration of global economic governance. Many are now searching for alternative conceptions, and, feeling empowered, for greater voice in determining the rules of global governance and recognition of their own, often distinct, interests."[65] Here, as in many other areas, the strategy of liberal hegemony came up short.

MAKING GLOBAL PROBLEMS WORSE

When the unipolar era began, U.S. leaders believed that America's privileged position would allow them to address and eventually solve a wide array of global problems. Although the United States made some progress on a number of challenges and was able to manage or resolve crises in several places, the overall record of the past three presidents was unimpressive.

Perhaps most obviously, repeated U.S. efforts to resolve the Israeli-Palestinian conflict all ended in abject failure. Bill Clinton oversaw the Oslo peace process in the 1990s, George W. Bush negotiated the Middle East "Road Map" and convened a summit meeting in Annapolis, and Barack Obama spent eight years trying to halt the continued expansion of Israeli settlements and coax the two sides toward a final status agreement.

Yet by 2016 the two-state solution that all three presidents had favored was further away than ever. The settler population in the territories Israel conquered in 1967 had grown from roughly 281,000 in 1993 to more than 600,000, and a network of Israeli roads, checkpoints, military bases, and settlements crisscrossed the West Bank, making a viable Palestinian state effectively impossible.[66] Given the potential leverage that all three presidents had at their disposal, their inability to make meaningful progress toward a solution they believed to be, as Obama put it, "in Israel's interest, the Palestinians' interest, America's interest, and the world's interest" was a humiliating display of U.S. impotence and diplomatic incompetence.[67]

Efforts to limit the danger from weapons of mass destruction—especially nuclear weapons—achieved only slightly better results. On the positive side, the Clinton administration successfully persuaded Ukraine, Belarus, and Kazakhstan to give up the nuclear arsenals they had inherited from the former Soviet Union, and the 1994 Agreed Framework with North Korea delayed its development of nuclear weapons for a few years. The so-called Nunn-Lugar programs helped place Russia's vast and poorly secured stockpile of nuclear materials under more reliable control; and sustained pressure from the United States and its European allies eventually persuaded the Libyan leader Muammar Gaddafi to abandon his own WMD programs in exchange for a pledge that the United States would not overthrow him.[68] The Obama administration also convened several well-attended Nuclear Security Summits that highlighted the need for further work on this problem.

But on the negative side, the Agreed Framework with North Korea broke down after 2000, and Pyongyang eventually withdrew from the Non-Proliferation Treaty in 2003, tested a nuclear weapon in 2006, and had amassed a stockpile of at least a dozen bombs by 2016. India and Pakistan resumed nuclear tests in 1998 despite strenuous U.S. objections and continued to expand their nuclear arsenals in later years. UN inspectors dismantled Iraq's nascent nuclear research program after the 1991 Gulf War, but neighboring Iran eventually mastered the full nuclear fuel cycle and produced a stockpile of enriched uranium that brought it within striking distance of a weapons capability. The Joint Comprehensive Plan of Action (JCPOA) completed in 2015 rolled back Iran's enrichment capacity and uranium stockpile and increased the time it would take for Tehran to "break out" and build a weapon, but Iran was now a latent nuclear weapons state with the ability to get a bomb if it ever wanted to.

With hindsight, it is not surprising that U.S. efforts to halt the spread of nuclear weapons achieved relatively little after 1993. Washington kept demanding that other states refrain from developing WMD, at the same time making it clear that it intended to keep a vast nuclear arsenal of its own.[69] If the mighty United States believed its security depended on having a powerful nuclear deterrent, then surely a few weaker and more vulnerable states might come to a similar conclusion. Moreover, the U.S. decision to ignore its earlier pledge and topple Muammar Gaddafi in 2011 showed the world that Washington could not be trusted and that states with no deterrent were vulnerable to attack. That lesson was not lost on countries such as North Korea or Iran, which had every reason to fear U.S.-led regime change and thus ample incentive to preserve a nuclear option.[70]

Last but by no means least, the U.S. response to international terrorism has been costly and counterproductive despite some modest successes. The Clinton administration recognized that groups like Al Qaeda posed a growing challenge in the 1990s, but it never developed an effective response to them.[71] On the contrary, Clinton's most significant attempts to deter, preempt, or retaliate for attacks on U.S. facilities or personnel were embarrassing debacles: a cruise missile strike on an Al Qaeda camp in Afghanistan in August 1998 missed Osama bin Laden, and a subsequent strike on an alleged chemical weapons facility in Sudan was in all likelihood an error based on faulty intelligence.[72] Nor did Clinton or his aides ever reevaluate the policies that had helped to inspire movements like Al Qaeda in the first place, such as the strategy of "dual containment" in the Persian Gulf and unconditional U.S. support for Israel.[73]

The most obvious failure of U.S. counterterrorism policy, of course, was September 11.[74] The Bush administration responded to the attacks by launching a "global war on terror," with the president vowing "to rid the world of evil."[75] Unfortunately, this mind-set led directly to the fateful decision to invade Iraq, which Bush and his aides believed would "send a message" to America's enemies and spark a democratic transformation of the region, which they assumed would make it harder for extremists to recruit new followers.

They could not have been more wrong. The occupation of Iraq fueled anti-Americanism across the Arab and Islamic world, and Iraq quickly became a magnet for extremists eager to take up arms against Uncle Sam. According to Peter Bergen and Paul Cruickshank, the Iraq conflict "greatly increased the spread of the Al Qaeda ideological virus, as shown by a rising number of terrorist attacks . . . from London to Kabul, and from Madrid to the Red Sea."[76] There were also incidents of blowback in the United States itself, such as the fatal shooting of thirteen U.S. Army soldiers at Fort Hood in 2009 by a U.S. Army psychiatrist who had become convinced that the United States was at war with Islam itself.[77]

As the "virus" spread, the war on terror kept expanding and the number of enemies kept growing. Greater reliance on drone strikes and "targeted killings" by U.S. Special Forces kept the costs of the war low, but these measures could not eliminate the problem and frequently made things worse. As terrorism experts Bruce Hoffman and Fernando Reinares noted in 2014, "despite its systematic attrition as a result of the U.S. drone campaign . . . al-Qaeda has nonetheless been expanding and consolidating its presence in new and far-flung locales."[78]

Al Qaeda was barely present in Somalia in 2001, for example, but a series of bungled U.S. interventions galvanized an Islamic resurgence and eventually spawned al-Shabaab, a radical Islamist group that conducted a lethal attack on a Nairobi shopping mall in 2013 and remains a dangerous force today.[79] U.S. counterterror operations and political interference had similar effects in Yemen, which gradually descended into a brutal civil war and remains a haven for Al Qaeda and other radical extremists.[80]

Perhaps the clearest sign that the "war on terror" had not gone as planned was the emergence of ISIS. An even more extreme offshoot of Al Qaeda, the group seized power in portions of western Iraq and Syria in 2014, proclaimed a new "caliphate," and used social media and online propaganda to attract thousands of recruits from around the world. ISIS agents and sympathizers conducted attacks in a number of countries—including France, Libya, Turkey, and the United States itself—and refugees from its tyrannical rule began fleeing to other countries.

Bin Laden was dead, but "bin Ladenism" was clearly alive and well. In December 2013, the heads of the House and Senate Intelligence Committees, Senator Dianne Feinstein (D-CA) and Representative Mike Rogers (R-MI), told CNN that "terror was up worldwide . . . there were more groups than ever and there was huge malevolence out there," and both agreed that Americans were not safer than they had been a year or two previously. Two years later, the CIA director, John Brennan, one of the leading architects of the war on terror, was admitting to a congressional committee, "our efforts have not reduced [ISIS's] terrorism capability and global reach."[81]

The problem, as some U.S. officials had recognized from the start, was that there was no shortage of new extremists to replace those whom the United States had killed or captured. As the head of the U.S. Africa Command, General Thomas D. Waldhauser, admitted in 2017, "We could knock off all the ISIL and Boko Haram this afternoon . . . But by the end [of the] week, so to speak, those ranks would be filled."[82] Further evidence that the war on terror had become an endless, ever-expanding effort were the revelations that 17 percent of U.S. commando troops were now deployed in Africa (up from a mere 1 percent in 2006) and engaged in more than one hundred separate missions, and that the United States was building a $100 million drone base in Niger to facilitate further attacks on extremist groups in West Africa and Libya.[83]

Nor was it obvious that all this effort and expense was necessary or cost-effective. Over time, it became increasingly clear that most terrorists were not brilliant criminal masterminds but incompetent bunglers.

The 9/11 attacks were not a harbinger of horrific mass attacks to come; they are more properly seen as a tragic incident when Al Qaeda got extremely lucky. And as John Mueller and Mark G. Stewart have shown, even if the losses suffered on 9/11 are included, international terrorism still poses an exceedingly small threat to American lives.[84] In 2001, the year the 9/11 attacks occurred, more Americans died from peptic ulcers than from all acts of terrorism.[85] Thus, the enormous political, economic, and human costs of the war on terror—including the instability it has sown in many countries—was based on a panicked and faulty estimate of the true danger America faced.

To be sure, the war on terror can claim some tangible achievements: a team of Navy SEALS eventually found and killed bin Laden, the drone war eliminated most of Al Qaeda's original leaders, and U.S. airpower helped a coalition of Iraqis, Kurds, and Iranian militias retake the territory ISIS had seized and forced the organization back underground. Along with improving homeland security efforts, these policies made large-scale attacks on the United States even less likely than they already were.

Viewed as a whole, however, the U.S. response to terrorism is no more impressive than the rest of its recent foreign policy. U.S. leaders understood that terrorism was a problem back in 1993; the problem is more widespread today. Violent extremists are active in more places than ever before and with more far-reaching political consequences, often as a direct result of misguided U.S. responses. Like other key aspects of U.S. foreign policy, the "war on terror" has been a costly failure.

CONCLUSION

No country as wealthy, powerful, and energetic as the United States fails every time, and U.S. foreign policy has produced a number of important successes in recent years. American diplomats brokered the peace treaty between Israel and Jordan in 1994 and the agreements that ended the Bosnian War in 1996. A combination of U.S. pressure and the

Nunn-Lugar Cooperative Threat Reduction program improved nuclear security in Russia and the former Soviet republics, and the Bush administration's Proliferation Security Initiative probably discouraged the export of dangerous weapons technologies. Bill Clinton successfully mediated the 1999 Kargil crisis between India and Pakistan, the PEPFAR program helped reduce the incidence of AIDS in Africa, and U.S. officials handled several potentially serious incidents with China (including a midair collision between a Chinese fighter and a U.S. reconnaissance plane) with skill and sensitivity.

Some observers might include in this list of successes the restoration of diplomatic relations with Cuba and the multilateral agreement that capped Iran's nuclear program and lengthened the time it would take for Tehran to acquire the bomb. There were also a number of dogs that didn't bark—such as an all-out war on the Korean Peninsula, a military clash over Taiwan, or an actual nuclear exchange—and the United States can plausibly claim some credit for these "nonevents." To say that U.S. foreign policy has been mostly a failure is not to say that it fails at everything.

Nor is U.S. foreign policy solely responsible for the negative developments described above. Some of these adverse trends—such as China's rapid rise and growing military potential—would probably have occurred no matter what the United States government did. The euro crisis may have begun when the U.S. housing bubble burst and U.S. financial markets crashed, but Washington is not responsible for the design flaws and other errors that made the euro vulnerable.

But considering where the United States and the world were in 1993 and where both are today, and looking back at the major initiatives the United States undertook and the most fateful decisions U.S. leaders made, America's outsize responsibility for today's problems is hard to deny. U.S. leaders may have had the best of intentions and the fondest of hopes, but their ambitious effort to "shape the world . . . for the benefit of all nations" fell woefully short. The next chapter explains why.

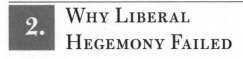

2. WHY LIBERAL HEGEMONY FAILED

T HE PREVIOUS CHAPTER described how the optimistic hopes with which the post–Cold War era began had come crashing to earth by 2016. Longtime adversaries were stronger and more assertive; traditional U.S. allies were weaker and more divided; and America's ambitious attempt to shape regional politics, spread liberal values, promote peace, and strengthen global institutions had mostly come to naught despite repeated and often costly efforts.

The taproot of these failures was the U.S. commitment to a grand strategy of "liberal hegemony": an ambitious effort to use American power to reshape the world according to U.S. preferences and political values. Despite important differences in style and emphasis, the Clinton, Bush, and Obama administrations were all deeply committed to this basic approach.

Yet liberal hegemony proved an elusive goal. At its most basic level, the strategy failed because it rested on mistaken views of how international politics actually works. It exaggerated America's ability to reshape other societies and underestimated the ability of weaker actors to thwart U.S. aims. The United States had enormous power and in some cases good intentions, but these virtues could not overcome the strategy's inherent flaws.

What Is "Liberal Hegemony"?

The grand strategy of liberal hegemony seeks to expand and deepen a liberal world order under the benevolent leadership of the United States.[1] At the domestic level, a liberal order is one where most states are governed according to liberal political principles: democracy, the rule of law, religious and social tolerance, and respect for basic human rights. At the international level, a liberal order is characterized by economic openness (i.e., low barriers to trade and investment) where relations between states are regulated by law and by institutions such as the World Trade Organization and the Non-Proliferation Treaty or multilateral alliances such as NATO.

Proponents of liberal hegemony do not believe that liberal orders arise spontaneously or sustain themselves automatically. On the contrary, they believe that such orders require active leadership by powerful countries that are deeply committed to liberal ideals. Not surprisingly, supporters of this strategy believe the United States is uniquely qualified to play that role. In practice, therefore, liberal hegemony rests on two core beliefs: (1) the United States must remain much more powerful than any other country, and (2) it should use its position of primacy to defend, spread, and deepen liberal values around the world.

To a large extent, the pursuit of liberal hegemony has been an effort to expand the partially liberal order that the United States created and led during the Cold War. From the start of that conflict, U.S. leaders drew a sharp distinction between the democratic "free world" and the un-free world of Soviet-style communism.[2] They pushed hard to dissolve the systems of imperial preference that such countries as Great Britain employed, along with other forms of protectionism, in favor of a more open international economic order that would encourage trade and growth and create opportunities for U.S. businesses. And they recognized that any system of states needed norms or rules (i.e., "institutions") to facilitate mutually beneficial cooperation—at the same time taking care to ensure that these rules were consistent with U.S. interests.

To be sure, the international order that emerged after World War II was only partly liberal. The Communist world was largely excluded, of course, and some key U.S. allies were not democracies, let alone liberal democracies. There was also considerable *disorder* within this system at various times and places, and the United States did not hesitate to break the rules (or rewrite them unilaterally) as the need arose. Nonetheless, the Cold War liberal order worked well for the United States and its allies, and their triumph over the Soviet bloc made that order look especially attractive to the countries that built it. With the United States in an overwhelming position of primacy after the Cold War, the time seemed ripe to make that order truly global in scope.

THEORIES AND ASSUMPTIONS

Liberal hegemony rests on a number of core premises or assumptions about the nature of world politics and the U.S. role in the current international system.[3] Together, these beliefs make the strategy appear to be necessary, affordable, and achievable, as well as consistent with core American values.

The intellectual foundation on which liberal hegemony rests is a family of interrelated theories of international relations: (1) democratic peace theory, (2) economic liberalism, and (3) liberal institutionalism. Democratic peace theory claims that well-established liberal democracies do not fight wars with each other and are strongly inclined to cooperate on key issues.[4] Economic liberalism argues that open international orders with high levels of trade and foreign investment maximize efficiency and overall economic growth. As states become increasingly interdependent, so the argument runs, the costs of conflict increase and the likelihood of war declines because states will not want to jeopardize the economic ties on which their prosperity depends.[5] Liberal institutionalism posits that strong international regimes—i.e., rules, norms, and formal organizations such as the WTO or the United Nations—can facilitate cooperation among states, discourage overly competitive behavior, and make it less likely that violent disputes will occur or escalate.[6] Taken together, these theories implied that the United States could foster a more prosperous and peaceful world by spreading democracy, promoting economic globalization, and creating, expanding, or strengthening international institutions.

As previously described, this hopeful vision was especially appealing in the early to mid-1990s, when history seemed to be moving America's way and spreading these principles was thought to be easy to do. Confident that market-oriented democracy offered the surest and swiftest path to prosperity and peace, U.S. leaders believed that a universal desire for freedom, wealth, and comfort would supplant old-fashioned concerns about status, power, and identity.

Pundits and policymakers also imagined that great power rivalries would fade or disappear and that traditional realpolitik would no longer be a useful guide to statecraft in this brave new postmodern world. Bill Clinton captured the prevailing optimism perfectly during the 1992 presidential campaign, declaring "the cynical calculus of power politics simply does not compute. It is ill-suited to a new era."[7] In the heady days of the 1990s, in short, the liberal prescription for perennial peace and expanding prosperity seemed to be within America's grasp. As discussed in chapter 1, its proponents believed it was time to abandon ancient hatreds, atavistic ethnic loyalties, and pesky local quarrels and get busy getting rich in a globalized world, one whose defining features were made-in-America and underpinned by American power.

AMERICA'S EXCEPTIONAL ROLE

Liberal hegemony's proponents also believed that the United States had a unique role to play in creating, expanding, and managing this emerging liberal order. The Clinton administration's official *National Security Strategy* described the United States as a "beacon of hope to peoples around the world" and "indispensable to the forging of stable political relations."[8] The late Samuel P. Huntington of Harvard, a prominent public intellectual and former government official, saw U.S. primacy as "central to the future of freedom, democracy, open economics and international order."[9] To explain why the United States was entitled to lead the world, Secretary of State Madeleine Albright famously described America as "the indispensable nation . . . that sees farther than others do."[10] Prominent neoconservatives agreed wholeheartedly, with Charles Krauthammer of *The Washington Post* praising U.S. power as "the land mine that protects civilization from barbarism."[11] A cottage industry of think tank reports and strategy documents recycled this mantra, warning of the dangers of diminished U.S. "leadership" and offering advice on how to expand, strengthen, revitalize, justify, or guarantee it for the long haul.[12]

Although he became president in the wake of the Iraq War and the 2008 financial crisis, Barack Obama never questioned the probity of America's uniquely ambitious world role. At his Nobel Peace Prize acceptance speech in 2009, for example, he told his audience that "the United States of America has helped underwrite global security for more than six decades with the blood of our citizens and the strength of our arms," and he made it clear that this role would not change on his watch. He made the same point in his 2012 State of the Union speech, declaring that "America remains the one indispensable nation in world affairs—and as long as I'm president, I intend to keep it that way." His administration's 2015 *National Security Strategy* referred to U.S. "leadership" more than thirty-five times, implying that the world might descend into chaos were Washington not firmly in charge.[13]

This belief in the necessity for American leadership flows in part from the recognition that powerful states sometimes need to cajole others into cooperating in order to achieve common goals. If the world's most powerful country disengaged completely and did not encourage other states to address global problems, selfish national interests might loom larger and achievable solutions to challenges such as climate change might never be reached.

Yet the importance attached to U.S. leadership also reflected the conviction that the United States was uniquely positioned to spread democracy and other liberal ideals to the rest of the world, and that doing so would be to everyone's benefit. Advocates of liberal hegemony believed that its blessings would be apparent to nearly everyone and that America's noble aims would not be doubted. These deep convictions about America's unselfish role help us understand why U.S. policymakers believed that active U.S. leadership was both essential and feasible. As President George W. Bush declared in his second inaugural address, "It is the policy of the United States to seek and support the growth of democratic movements and institutions . . . with the ultimate goal of ending tyranny in our world . . . America's influence is not unlimited, but fortunately for the oppressed, America's influence is considerable, and we will use it confidently in freedom's cause."[14]

THE POWER OF AMERICAN POWER

Confidence was indeed a key ingredient in liberal hegemony, because it also assumed that American power—and especially its unmatched military supremacy—would provide the means to advance this revisionist agenda. For starters, a healthy margin of superiority would deter the emergence of new peer competitors and dampen future security competition in Europe, Asia, and the Middle East. Convinced that no state would willingly face the "focused enmity" of the mighty United States, proponents of liberal hegemony saw deep U.S. engagement as the key to preventing the renationalization of great power politics and renewed great power rivalry in Europe or Asia.[15] Proponents also believed that the United States should stand ready to stop mass killings or other human rights abuses, if necessary by force, which in turn required U.S. engagement anywhere where such tragic events might occur.[16]

Most important, advocates of liberal hegemony assumed that U.S. primacy gave Washington ample leverage over others and a reliable capacity to shape events around the world. As a task force of experienced foreign policy insiders put it in 2000, "Relative to any potential competitor, the US is more powerful, more wealthy, and more influential than any nation since the Roman empire. With these extraordinary advantages, America today is uniquely positioned to shape the international system to promote international peace and prosperity for decades or even generations to come."[17] During the heyday of American primacy, U.S. foreign policy mavens did not think small.

If other states balked, U.S. policymakers were convinced that the United States had the tools to force them to comply. It could impose economic sanctions, give aid to a hostile regime's foreign or domestic opponents, undermine rivals through covert action, and use military force to compel them to capitulate. If necessary, the United States could invade and depose hostile regimes at little cost or risk to itself. Once these obstreperous tyrants were gone, the United States and the rest of the liberal international community could step in and help liberated and grateful populations create new and legitimate democracies, thereby expanding the liberal, pro-American order even more. Convinced that world politics were already going their way, U.S. officials were confident that they could accelerate the process reliably, safely, and cheaply.

A SHRINKING PLANET

Proponents of liberal hegemony also saw the world as a "global village" increasingly connected by trade, travel, and technology. They envisioned a world where borders were increasingly permeable (if not irrelevant), where information flowed at the speed of light and faraway events could reverberate with surprising rapidity. Distance no longer divided the world and the vast Atlantic and Pacific Oceans could not protect the United States from new nuclear arsenals, unexpected financial crises, transnational terrorists, global pandemics, cyberattacks, and a host of other dangers. As Secretary of State Albright remarked in 1998, "the idea of an ocean as protection is as obsolete as a castle moat."[18] According to the State Department's 2010 *Quadrennial Diplomacy and Development Review* (*QDDR*), "People, money, and ideas can move around the world so quickly that conflict, even in distant countries, has become a far greater threat to the United States."[19] In a complicated and tightly interdependent world, a weak failed state might be a greater danger than a hostile and heavily armed great power. Dangerous ideologies or destabilizing cyber-weapons could spread with the click of a mouse, and the hazards of disease, criminal activity, and violent extremism might fester and grow if they were not checked and eventually eliminated.

Yet that same shrinking globe also made it easier for the United States to shape the world and address these various dangers. The absence of a peer competitor eliminated the risk of dangerous escalation, and an array of new technologies—including precision-guided munitions, enhanced surveillance and data management tools, sophisticated cyber-weapons, and improved communications capabilities—would enable the United States to project power with greater ease than ever before, without having to worry about local resistance or hostile retaliation. After warning about new threats such as violent extremism, WMD proliferation, or climate change, the State Department's *QDDR* suggested that "the forces that fuel these challenges—economic interdependence and the speedy movement of information, capital, goods, and people—are also creating unprecedented opportunities."[20]

The idea that serious dangers might emerge from almost anywhere made liberal hegemony seem *necessary*, while the perceived ability to project power and influence at low cost and risk made global activism seem *feasible*. Threats might emerge from any quarter, but the United States could keep them at bay with a sophisticated combination of force, diplomacy, and economic and political engagement.

Thus, as the unipolar era took shape, officials and commentators across the political spectrum believed that the United States had the right, the responsibility, and the ability to expand and consolidate a liberal world order and that doing so would keep the United States safe and prosperous.

They were also confident that most states would recognize America's be-nevolence, welcome U.S. leadership, and gratefully embrace Washing-ton's blueprint for a liberal order. Only "rogue states" led by illegitimate dictators and other international troublemakers would be inclined to re-sist the exercise of U.S. power, and most of these states were compara-tively weak and politically isolated. In any case, they were assumed to be headed for the dustbin of history, with a helping hand from Uncle Sam.

THE UNIVERSALIST TEMPTATION

Lastly, liberal hegemony is attractive because it appeals to Americans' self-regard and taps into powerful elements in America's political DNA. As Louis Hartz and others have shown, the United States is the quintessen-tial liberal society, in the sense that its founding principles and governing institutions privilege individual rights over group identities.[21] Once committed to the "self-evident" truth that all humans possess the right to "life, liberty, and the pursuit of happiness," Americans cannot deny these rights to others without betraying their own beliefs. And as John Mearsheimer emphasizes, because Americans regard these principles as the ideal blueprint on which to found a just society and promote world peace, it is almost inevitable that they will seek to share these wonder-ful ideals with those who presently lack them.[22] John Quincy Adams may have recognized that the early republic was too weak to "go out in search for monsters to destroy," but the temptation to spread liberal ide-als became more alluring as the United States grew stronger. Once the country stood at the pinnacle of power, it was impossible to resist.

LIBERAL HEGEMONY IN PRACTICE

In practice, the pursuit of liberal hegemony involved (1) preserving U.S. primacy, especially in the military sphere; (2) expanding the U.S. sphere of influence; and (3) promoting liberal norms of democracy and human rights. Although the three post–Cold War administrations pursued these goals in somewhat different ways, each was strongly committed to all three objectives.

PRESERVING U.S. PRIMACY

The first element in the strategy of liberal hegemony was maintaining—
if not extending—the position of primacy the United States had acquired
over the previous four decades, especially after the collapse of the Soviet
Union. George H. W. Bush's national security team signaled this inten-
tion clearly in 1992, recommending in a draft version of the Department
of Defense's official *Strategic Guidance* that the United States maintain a
margin of superiority sufficient to discourage other states from even attempting to compete with American power.[23] None of Bush's successors
ever questioned the need to maintain a significant power advantage over
allies and adversaries alike. As former deputy secretary of state Strobe
Talbott observed in 2003, "a recurring and animating premise of US foreign policy has always been the righteous *im*balance of power; that is, an
imbalance in favour of the US, its friends, its allies, its protégés and, cru-
cially, its fellow democracies."[24]

U.S. defense spending did decline by about a third in the early
1990s—as the country enjoyed a brief post–Cold War "peace dividend"—
but the United States still accounted for more than 35 percent of global
military expenditures and spent more than twice as much as the number
two power (China). Defense spending began to rise in Bill Clinton's
second term, however, with the Pentagon seeking sufficient strength to
wage two "major regional conflicts" simultaneously. Significantly, none
of the "regional conflicts" it envisioned were close to the United States,
or even in the Western Hemisphere.

National security spending increased sharply after the 9/11 attacks, and by 2007 it was higher in real terms than it had been at the
peak of the Reagan administration. The 2008 financial crisis and the
subsequent drawdowns from Iraq and Afghanistan slowed but did
not reverse the upward trend, and defense spending did not decline
until a congressionally mandated "budget sequester" went into effect
in 2013.

Although Barack Obama took office after the 2008 financial crisis and sometimes emphasized the need to rebuild U.S. economic strength, he reaffirmed the goal of continued military dominance. Obama repeatedly affirmed the need for active U.S. leadership, and his 2010 *National Security Strategy* called for the U.S. military to "maintain its conventional superiority and . . . nuclear deterrent capability, while continuing to enhance its capacity to defeat asymmetric threats, preserve access to the global commons, and strengthen partners."[25] The United States still spent more on national security in 2016 than the next dozen or so countries combined, and it sometimes devoted a higher percentage of its much larger GDP to defense than most of its allies or even such potential adversaries as Russia and China.[26] In addition to maintaining powerful fleets in all the world's oceans and thousands of nuclear weapons, the United States still had nearly 175,000 army, navy, or air force personnel deployed at hundreds of bases or other facilities in more than 130 countries as Obama's second term neared its end.[27] In a revealing sign of Washington's global ambitions, every inch of the planet was now assigned to one of six "unified combatant commands."[28]

Most important, U.S. leaders did not seek primacy in order to protect the American homeland from invasion or attack. Rather, they sought it in order to promote a liberal order abroad. "To effectively promote liberty over the long haul," wrote Michael McFaul, the future U.S. ambassador to Russia, in 2002, "the United States must maintain its overwhelming military advantage over the rest of the world."[29] Or, as the neoconservative pundits William Kristol and Lawrence Kaplan wrote in 2003, "What is wrong with dominance, in the service of sound principles and high ideals?"[30] America's military forces were extremely busy after 1993, but they weren't fighting to repel invaders from American soil or even to protect key allies. Rather, they were sent in harm's way to shape political conditions or address security concerns in such faraway places as Afghanistan, Bosnia, Iraq, Kosovo, Libya, Somalia, and Yemen.[31]

In short, apart from the obvious deterrent role played by the U.S. nuclear arsenal, U.S. primacy was for the most part not used to keep dangerous adversaries from attacking the United States or vital U.S. interests. Instead, it was used to shape the international environment according to U.S. preferences, to topple authoritarian leaders at odds with Washington, or to advance other broadly liberal objectives. Bill Clinton and Barack Obama used military force more cautiously and discreetly than George W. Bush did, but all three post–Cold War presidents saw U.S. military power as an invaluable tool for advancing an ambitious global agenda. In Nobel Peace Prize recipient Barack Obama's last year in office, for instance, the American military dropped more than 26,000 bombs in seven different countries.[32]

EXPANDING AMERICA'S SPHERE OF INFLUENCE

After the Cold War ended, U.S. officials might have concluded that there were no longer any serious threats to contain and that extensive overseas commitments and a global military presence were no longer needed. Or they might have sought to preserve a few key alliances as a hedge against future troubles while shifting most of the burden onto local powers that had more at stake in key regions. But consistent with a strategy of liberal hegemony, U.S. leaders instead chose to expand U.S. security commitments in Europe, Asia, and the Middle East and to take on demanding new missions in Africa and Latin America. They did so in part to spread liberal ideals, but also because they believed that doing so would make conflict less likely and enhance U.S. security even more.

In Europe, the United States drove the process of expansion that grew NATO from sixteen to twenty-eight members by 2009.[33] This policy sought to consolidate democratic rule in Europe, safeguard these states against a resurgent Russia, and forestall a new division of Europe. But because many new NATO members were small, weak, and close to Russia, expansion in effect committed the United States to protect a group of vulnerable and hard-to-defend states that had little military capability of their own to contribute. Washington was at best ambivalent about European efforts to develop military capabilities outside the NATO framework during this period, for fear such steps would reduce

U.S. influence over its European partners and create a counterweight to U.S. power over the longer term.[34]

Concerns about China drove a steady increase in U.S. security commitments in Asia, and the focus on balancing China intensified as Beijing grew stronger and more assertive. The United States reinforced its bilateral alliance with Japan in the mid-1990s and moved closer to Singapore, Indonesia, and Vietnam, and the Bush administration eventually negotiated a new "strategic partnership" with India. This process continued during the Obama administration, which emphasized Asia's growing economic and strategic importance and began a well-publicized "rebalancing" of U.S. forces to Asia.

U.S. involvement in the Middle East expanded even more dramatically, and at much greater cost. Despite the strategic importance of Middle East oil and the country's long-standing commitment to several local powers, the United States had previously relied on local allies to uphold the balance of power and had kept its own ground and air forces out of the region. That approach changed in 1993, when the Clinton administration announced a new policy of "dual containment." Instead of preserving a balance of power in the Persian Gulf by playing Iran and Iraq off against each other, the United States would keep significant ground and air forces in Saudi Arabia, Bahrain, and Kuwait, in order to contain both.[35]

The United States plunged even more deeply—and fatefully—into the Middle East after the September 11 terrorist attacks, when the Bush administration first invaded Afghanistan to remove the Taliban and disrupt Al Qaeda, and then, in 2003, invaded Iraq and ousted Saddam Hussein. Regime change in Iraq was intended to demonstrate U.S. power, send a message to other rogue states, and begin to transform the Middle East from a source of anti-American terrorism to a sea of pro-American democracies.[36] But instead of producing a stable democracy and enhanced U.S. influence, the invasion and occupation triggered a violent insurgency that left Iraq deeply divided, enhanced Iran's regional position, and eventually allowed an even more radical extremist group— ISIS—to establish itself in parts of Iraq and Syria in 2014.

Barack Obama won election in 2008 by pledging to end the long wars in Afghanistan and Iraq, but his effort to do so was only partly successful. He eventually withdrew the bulk of U.S. ground forces from both countries and relied instead on airpower, drones, special operations units, and targeted killings of suspected terrorists. But U.S. troops were still fighting in Iraq and Afghanistan when his term ended, and the United States was still actively involved in counterterrorism operations in Yemen, Somalia, Libya, Syria, and many other countries.

The growing list of U.S. burdens did not end there. In 1998 the United States had begun providing military training and several billion dollars' worth of economic assistance to the Colombia government to help it defeat the FARC insurgency and to limit illegal narcotics flowing to the United States. The war on terror also led to a dramatic increase in the U.S. security role in Africa, including repeated interventions in Somalia, expanded drone operations, and a host of military training and advising efforts. By 2016, in fact, nearly two thousand U.S. Special Operations forces were "active in twenty [African] nations in support of seven major named operations."[37]

Under liberal hegemony, in short, the United States kept taking on new security commitments without reducing any of its other obligations. As noted in the previous chapter, by 2016 the United States was committed to defending more countries than at any time in its history, while simultaneously trying to pacify several distant war-torn societies and conducting violent counterterrorism operations in many other places.[38] America's "sphere of influence" had never been greater, though how much influence the United States actually exercised in these places was far from clear.

PROMOTING LIBERAL VALUES

Expanding U.S. security commitments was closely linked to the larger goal of spreading liberal values and institutions. Strengthening democracy in Europe was a key justification for NATO expansion, for example, and a major motive behind the U.S. effort to broker peace in Bosnia in 1996 and the decision to wage war over Kosovo in 1999. The United States also backed the pro-democracy "color revolutions" in Georgia in 2003 and Ukraine in 2004, and subsequently supported a popular uprising against Ukrainian president Viktor Yanukovych in 2013.[39] This almost-reflexive instinct to spread liberal values—including religious tolerance and women's rights—also helps explain why Washington spent billions of dollars and thousands of lives trying to create workable democracies in Afghanistan and Iraq.

This enduring commitment to building a liberal world order also accounts for the Obama administration's haphazard and ultimately unsuccessful response to the "Arab Spring." After a brief period of vacillation, Obama declared, "It will be the policy of the United States to promote reform across the region, and to support transitions to democracy," and Washington subsequently backed Tunisia's fledgling democracy, the removal of the Egyptian dictator Hosni Mubarak in 2011, and the toppling of Muammar Gaddafi in Libya later that same year.[40] And when antigovernment protests began in Syria, the Obama administration quickly concluded "Assad must go" and eventually gave millions of dollars in covert aid to groups seeking to oust the regime.[41] Washington also midwifed the creation of a short-lived democracy in South Sudan, attempted to bolster democracy in Yemen by orchestrating the removal of the strongman Ali Abdullah Saleh in 2012, and successfully pressed for a partial end to military rule in Burma.[42]

Washington's approach to economic globalization sought similar objectives in less obvious ways. By definition, globalization involves reducing barriers to international trade and investment and allowing market forces to operate more widely, a goal that U.S. leaders believed would increase global wealth, strengthen emerging democracies, and reduce the likelihood of war. Moreover, economic institutions such as the World Trade Organization and multilateral trade pacts like the TPP or the Transatlantic Trade and Investment Partnership (TTIP) increasingly included provisions on transparency, shared labor and environmental standards, and compatible legal and regulatory frameworks. In actual practice, therefore, globalization required participating states to conform their domestic politics to a broad set of international norms, most of them heavily influenced by U.S. preferences and values.[43]

To be sure, the commitment to spreading liberal principles did not prevent Washington from supporting authoritarian governments in such countries as Saudi Arabia, Uzbekistan, Pakistan, or Singapore or keep it from turning a blind eye to human rights abuses practiced by close allies like Israel, Egypt, or Turkey. Nor did Washington seem overly concerned about the human costs its policies inflicted on others. These inconsistencies led to predictable (and valid) charges of hypocrisy, which undermined America's image as a consistent defender of liberal principles. These lapses notwithstanding, U.S. leaders were genuinely committed to expanding a liberal world order, even if some of their actions fell well short of that ideal.

Indeed, as described at length in chapter 1, the energetic pursuit of liberal hegemony was mostly a failure. The United States was still very powerful, but its strategic position declined sharply between 1993 and 2016. Extending U.S. security commitments far and wide did not make Europe, Asia, or the Middle East more peaceful and in some cases caused wars that would not have occurred otherwise. And as we have seen, the broad effort to spread liberal values did not succeed. By 2017, in fact, democracy was in retreat in many places and under considerable strain in the United States itself.

WHY DID LIBERAL HEGEMONY FAIL?

At its core, liberal hegemony sought to remake world politics in America's image and for America's benefit. Despite its overweening ambition, it is not surprising that the strategy attracted wide support in the wake of America's Cold War triumph. By portraying U.S. values as the ideal model for others and assigning Washington primary responsibility for peace, prosperity, and progress, the strategy appealed to Americans' sense of virtue and self-regard. It also gave the foreign policy commu-

nity in Washington a new and lofty purpose, while making those idealistic goals seem easy to achieve.

Moreover, the strategy's promised benefits were undeniably appealing: Who wouldn't prefer to live in a world where war is rare; where
goods, investment, and people can move freely; where evildoers are
contained or, better yet, punished; and where human rights are increasingly respected—especially if all these wonderful things could be
achieved at little cost or risk? Given how most U.S. foreign policy experts saw the post–Cold War world, it might have been more surprising
if the United States had *not* succumbed to these idealistic visions.

Yet as we have seen, the bipartisan pursuit of liberal hegemony led
to repeated and costly failures, and its shortcomings became increasingly apparent over time. What were its main deficiencies and negative
consequences? What exactly had gone wrong?

FRAGILE FOUNDATIONS

For starters, liberal hegemony rested on a distorted understanding of
international politics, which led its proponents to exaggerate its
expected benefits and underestimate the resistance the United States
would generate while pursuing it. The liberal internationalists who ran
foreign policy in the Clinton and Obama administrations believed that
the spread of democracy and rising economic interdependence would
attenuate existing conflicts and create an increasingly harmonious
world, with robust international institutions taking care of any minor
conflicts that remained. The neoconservatives who shaped the Bush administration's foreign policy were less enamored of global institutions
(which they saw as constraints on America's freedom of action), but they
believed that forceful demonstrations of American power and resolve
would intimidate potential opponents and encourage most states to
jump on America's bandwagon. Despite minor differences, both liberal
and neoconservative proponents of liberal hegemony assumed that the
United States could pursue this ambitious global strategy without triggering serious opposition.

Unfortunately, the theories that underpinned these optimistic expectations are flawed. Although it is true that liberal democracies have fought few wars with each other, there is still no satisfactory explanation for why this is the case. The absence of a compelling theory means that some other factor besides regime type may account for this phenomenon, and we simply do not know if a world with a significantly greater number of democracies would in fact be more peaceful or make the United States more secure.

Even if it did, however, history also warns that newly democratized states are especially prone to internal and external conflicts. Even if the long-term effects proved to be salutary, efforts to spread democracy make trouble more likely in the short-to-medium term.[44] Democratic peace theory also says little about how liberal states should deal with authoritarian regimes, except to suggest that overthrowing them is the path to perpetual peace. As a guide for policy, therefore, democratic peace theory promises more than it can deliver, and it is a potent recipe for trouble between liberal and non-liberal countries.

Liberal theories of economic interdependence are also of limited value. To be sure, lowering barriers to trade and investment is good for global economic growth, and high levels of economic interdependence may reduce the likelihood of war in some cases. But as the two world wars and many civil wars remind us, high levels of economic interdependence do not make war impossible and thus do not free states from having to worry about what powerful rivals might do to upset the balance of power.[45] Even extensive economic globalization will not eliminate the possibility of rivalry, suspicion, and war, and may in some cases exacerbate these problems. The most recent wave of globalization also led to recurring financial crises—most notably in 2008—and has had wrenching social and political effects in many countries. Contemporary globalization is no panacea, in short, and certainly does not herald an end to traditional geopolitics.

Finally, liberal hegemony overstates the ability of international institutions to regulate relations among states and to resolve deep conflicts of interest. There is no question that even a world of sovereign states needs rules to manage interactions among them. To take an obvious example, modern international aviation would be impossible without detailed arrangements for governing and regulating access to airspace and managing daily flight operations. As multilateral organizations such as NATO, the World Bank, or the World Trade Organization have shown repeatedly, international institutions can facilitate cooperation when states have clear and obvious incentives to work together, but they cannot stop powerful states from acting as they wish and thus cannot remove the danger of conflict and war. International institutions are simply a tool that states use to advance their interests, and they inevitably reflect the interests of the most powerful states.[46] Most present-day institutions have long conformed to U.S. preferences because the United States was by far their most powerful member; it is equally unsurprising that China now seeks a greater role in existing forums and in some cases is seeking to create parallel institutions of its own.[47]

U.S. leaders have also recognized that masking the exercise of power within a multilateral institution can make U.S. dominance more tolerable to others and help overcome some of the obstacles to effective international cooperation. Yet even the most powerful institutions could not bring peace to the Middle East; eliminate terrorism; create stable states in Afghanistan, Iraq, Syria, or Sudan; prevent the 2008 financial crisis; reverse the centrifugal forces in the European Union; resolve maritime disputes in Asia; or produce a timely and effective response to the long-term problem of climate change.

BALANCING, BUCK-PASSING, AND BLOWBACK

At the same time, liberal hegemony ignores an even more important principle of international relations: imbalances of power make other states nervous, especially when the strongest state uses its power with little regard for others' interests. It was entirely predictable that the so-called rogue states would look for ways to keep American power in check, for example, because the United States had made spreading democracy a centerpiece of its grand strategy and taken dead aim at a number of these countries. It was equally unsurprising that China, Russia, and a number of other states were alarmed by U.S. efforts to spread liberal values, because such efforts, if successful, threatened existing political arrangements in all non-liberal states and the privileged positions of their ruling elites.[48]

Yet America's dominant position also alarmed some of America's closest allies, including some fellow democracies. The French foreign minister Hubert Vedrine repeatedly complained about American "hyperpower" during the 1990s, and he once said that "the entire foreign policy of France . . . is aimed at making the world of tomorrow composed of several poles, not just one." The German chancellor Gerhard Schröder echoed this concern, warning that the danger of U.S. unilateralism was "undeniable."[49] Not surprisingly, both states actively opposed bold U.S. initiatives—such as the invasion of Iraq— on more than one occasion.

Their concerns were well-founded—not because the United States deliberately used its power to harm friendly countries like France, but because America's vast capabilities made it easy to hurt them by accident. The invasion of Iraq is a perfect illustration: it eventually led to the emergence of ISIS, whose online recruiting and brutal conduct inspired terrorist attacks in a number of European countries and contributed to the refugee crisis that engulfed Europe in 2015. European officials were correct to oppose the war back in 2003; they understood that destabilizing the Middle East might harm them in ways they could anticipate, if not entirely foresee. Removing Saddam Hussein also eliminated Iran's principal regional rival and enhanced its position in the Persian Gulf, thereby threatening close U.S. partners such as Saudi Arabia. Washington obviously did not intend to harm its allies when it decided to invade Iraq, but that is precisely what it did. As the Oxford historian Timothy Garton Ash noted in April 2002, "the problem with American power is not that it is American. The problem is simply the power. It would be dangerous even for an archangel to wield so much power."[50]

Even as they were alarmed by U.S. dominance, key U.S. allies also took advantage of it by free-riding, thereby forcing Washington to bear greater burdens in places like Afghanistan. Such behavior was only to be expected: Why should other states take on difficult and costly burdens when Uncle Sam wanted to do most of the work? Letting Washington do the heavy lifting allowed these states to spend their money on other things, and it had the added virtue of placing additional constraints on the overeager American Gulliver. And then, when Washington tried to get its allies to do more on matters where their own interests were more engaged—such as the Balkan Wars of the 1990s or the Libyan intervention of 2011—it discovered that its allies could not do the job without considerable U.S. help.

Opponents balanced U.S. power in other ways. Some adversaries sought to deter U.S. pressure by pursuing weapons of mass destruction, while others moved closer to each other in order to thwart U.S. aims. Cooperation increased between Russia and China as NATO moved east and Washington pivoted toward Asia; and Russia eventually fought a short war with Georgia, seized Crimea from Ukraine, and used cyberattacks and "hybrid warfare" to stop NATO from moving farther east and to undermine the liberal order in Europe. Similarly, Syria and Iran worked together to defeat U.S. efforts in Iraq and ensure that the United States was not free to go after either of them. None of these efforts sufficed to alter the global balance of power, but they made it more difficult for the United States to achieve its ambitious aims and insulated these states from U.S. pressure.

Finally, the United States also faced growing opposition from various Islamic extremists whose hostility was driven by U.S. support for Israel, Egypt, Jordan, and Saudi Arabia and by the expanded U.S. military presence throughout the Muslim world. Over time, U.S. efforts to counter Al Qaeda, the Taliban, Hezbollah, Hamas, ISIS, Boko Haram, and other extremist groups produced an ever-expanding, open-ended set of conflicts in Yemen, Somalia, Iraq, Syria, Pakistan, Afghanistan, and several other countries.

Moreover, the growing perception that the United States was fundamentally hostile to Islam began to inspire terrorist attacks in a number of countries, including the United States itself. In November 2009, for example, Major Nidal Hasan, an army psychiatrist, murdered thirteen people and injured more than thirty others at the Fort Hood army base in an attack motivated by his belief that the United States had declared war on Islam.[51] And in 2012 a report by the FBI's counterterrorism unit found that "anger over U.S. military operations abroad was the most commonly cited motivation for individuals involved in cases of 'home-grown' terrorism." In response to the report, the terrorism expert Marc Sageman predicted that "continued US military action will inevitably drive terrorist activities in this country, because some local people here will identify themselves with the victims of those actions abroad."[52]

Instead of a peaceful world order and near-universal acceptance of benevolent U.S. leadership, therefore, the post–Cold War world continued to operate according to the more traditional dictates of realpolitik. Other states remained acutely sensitive to the balance of power, declined to cooperate with Washington unless doing so was in their interest, and played hardball when necessary to safeguard key strategic priorities. Opponents of U.S.-led liberal hegemony sometimes resorted to violence— as Russia did when it seized Crimea or as Islamic extremists have done through the use of terror—even at considerable cost and risk to themselves. Such behavior was only to be expected; what was surprising was America's failure to anticipate it.

EXAGGERATING THE UTILITY OF FORCE

Liberal hegemony also failed because U.S. leaders exaggerated what American power—especially its military power—could accomplish. America's potent military arsenal freed Americans from the fear of being conquered or coerced, but it did not allow Washington to dictate to others or give U.S. leaders reliable control over domestic political developments in other countries.

In part, superior power did not translate into reliable control because the targets of U.S. pressure cared more about the issues at stake and were willing to pay a high price to defend their independence or other vital interests. States such as Serbia, Libya, Iran, Iraq, Syria, and North Korea were vastly weaker than the United States, but none of them capitulated at the first hint of U.S. pressure. Indeed, most U.S. opponents were willing to absorb considerable punishment without saying "uncle," thus limiting Washington's ability to impose its will upon them.

It is true, for example, that President Slobodan Milosevic of Serbia eventually cut a deal on Bosnia in 1996 and was forced to give up control of Kosovo in 1999. Serbia was a very weak state, however, and it still took a seventy-eight-day air campaign to force Milosevic to concede. Moreover, neither Bashar al-Assad, Saddam Hussein, Kim Jong Il and Kim Jong-un, Muammar Gaddafi, nor any of Iran's leaders ever capitulated outright to U.S. demands; indeed, some U.S. foes remained defiant right up to the moment they were overthrown.[53] The Afghan Taliban are still fighting after more than seventeen years of war, and the lengthy U.S. occupation of Iraq never gave Washington the ability to tell the country's post-Saddam leaders what to do.

And remember: each of these states was far weaker than the United States. If Washington could not intimidate, browbeat, or compel these minor powers to do its bidding, what did that reveal about the actual leverage the "unipolar power" enjoyed and its ability to use military force and other forms of pressure to expand a liberal order?

Proponents of liberal hegemony—whether in the more restrained Democratic version or the more muscular GOP approach—also forgot that military power is a crude instrument. It is useful for certain purposes, but not for others, and it always produces unintended consequences. Vast wealth, sophisticated weaponry, and innovative doctrines made it possible for the United States to project power to distant regions and defeat any number of weaker military opponents on the battlefield, which is why the United States could topple the Taliban, remove Saddam Hussein, and defeat Muammar Gaddafi rapidly and with little loss of American life. But the ability to destroy third-rate armies and oust foreign leaders did not enable the United States to create new and effective political institutions to replace defeated regimes. Fighting and governing are very different activities, and being able to blow things up with great precision does not confer a similar capacity to administer conquered territory effectively. As the deputy national secretary advisor Ben Rhodes admitted at the end of Obama's presidency, "the [U.S.] military can do enormous things. It can win wars and stabilize conflicts. But a military can't create a political culture or build a society."[54]

Nor is military power a particularly flexible instrument, the growing reliance on more precise tools (such as remotely piloted drones or elite special operations units) notwithstanding. Using military force is ultimately a political act with its own logic and momentum, and it cannot be turned on and off like a light switch or simply dialed up or down as circumstances require. Committing forces to battle engages U.S. prestige, and allies and enemies will soon weigh in, soldiers will be killed and wounded, and the public will expect benefits commensurate with the costs. If success is not immediately forthcoming, neither civilian officials nor senior military commanders are likely to admit that they miscalculated. Nor will they be inclined to stop before victory is achieved. Setbacks will create pressures to escalate, and wars begun in response to false fears or false hopes can easily turn into open-ended campaigns.

Proponents of liberal hegemony were convinced that they could use military power selectively and cheaply in the service of an ambitious global agenda; they found themselves trapped in unwinnable quagmires instead. The Iraq War is the most obvious example of this problem, but every major case of U.S. military intervention after 1992—in Afghanistan, Bosnia, Iraq, Kosovo, Libya, Somalia, and Yemen—took significantly longer and cost substantially more than U.S. leaders expected, while achieving much less than they promised. *Every single one.*

DIPLOMATIC RIGIDITY

Excessive faith in U.S. power also encouraged U.S. officials to eschew genuine diplomacy—that is, the adjustment of competing interests for mutual benefit—and to rely excessively on ultimatums and coercive pressure. As Chas W. Freeman, a former assistant secretary of defense and longtime U.S. diplomat, has noted, "for most in our political elite, the overwhelming military and economic leverage of the United States justifies abandoning the effort to persuade rather than muscle recalcitrant foreigners into line."[55]

Compounding this problem was the widespread tendency to see world politics as a Manichaean struggle between virtuous liberal states and malevolent, rights-abusing tyrants. Instead of attributing conflicts between states to differing perceptions, competing historical narratives, or straightforward clashes of national interest, U.S. officials and influential pundits routinely portrayed them as confrontations between good and evil. Whether in the form of the "rogue states" targeted by the Clinton administration or the dictators lumped into the Bush administration's "Axis of Evil," U.S. adversaries were routinely demonized as immoral and illegitimate governments whose very existence violated America's deepest political convictions.[56] Barack Obama was less inclined to use such moralistic language than his predecessors, but he reminded the audience at his Nobel Prize acceptance speech, "Make no mistake: evil does exist in the world."

Because they saw opponents as evil and believed they held the high cards, U.S. officials tended to view concessions made to secure a deal as a form of surrender, even if the resulting agreement gave them most of what they wanted. In short, instead of genuine bargaining, Washington tended to simply tell others what it wanted them to do. If they refused to comply, U.S. leaders tightened the screws or reached for the sword.

In the negotiations preceding the 1999 Kosovo War, for example, U.S. officials blamed Serbia for the entire conflict, made little effort to construct an agreement that would preserve Belgrade's minimum interests, and assumed that Serbian president Slobodan Milosevic would capitulate as soon as NATO showed it was willing to use force. Instead, it took a lengthy air campaign to get the Serbs to concede—an effort that accelerated Serbian ethnic cleansing, caused hundreds of civilian casualties, and destroyed billions of dollars' worth of property—and Belgrade did so only after securing a deal that was more favorable than the original U.S. ultimatum. Had the United States been more empathetic and flexible from the start, the entire war might have been avoided.[57]

The same uncompromising approach allowed Iran to go from zero nuclear centrifuges in 2000 to more than nineteen thousand by early 2015. More interested in regime change than in halting Iran's progress toward a latent nuclear capability, for years the United States demanded that Iran halt all nuclear enrichment, refusing to consider any arrangement that might leave Tehran with control over the full nuclear fuel cycle. U.S. officials refused to meet directly with their Iranian counterparts and rejected or derailed several Iranian proposals that would have frozen its enrichment capacity at much lower levels.[58] Even after serious talks began in 2009, the Obama administration walked away from a "confidence-building" agreement that would have substantially reduced Iran's stockpile of low-enriched uranium.[59] Instead of negotiating in earnest Washington kept imposing stiffer economic sanctions and issuing veiled threats to use force ("all options are on the table") if Iran did not comply. This pressure probably played a role in Tehran's eventual willingness to cut a deal, but the 2015 nuclear agreement also required flexibility on America's part, including dropping the demand that Iran give up its entire enrichment capability. More than a decade of U.S. intransigence left Iran considerably closer to a nuclear bomb than it would have been had Washington engaged in genuine diplomacy sooner.

A similar rigidity hamstrung the U.S. response to the crises in Syria and Ukraine. In the former case, U.S. insistence that "Assad must go," combined with its initial refusal to allow Iran to participate in peace discussions, crippled early efforts to stop the fighting, facilitated the growth of radical Islamic groups, and helped prolong an admittedly challenging conflict.[60] In Ukraine, the United States called for Moscow to cease all of its activities in Ukraine, withdraw from Crimea, and let Ukraine join the EU and/or NATO if it eventually met the membership criteria for these organizations. Instead of pursuing a compromise that would satisfy each side's core objectives, the United States was in effect demanding that Moscow abandon all of its interests in Ukraine, full stop. Such an outcome might be highly desirable in the abstract or from a purely American perspective, but it blithely ignored Russia's history, its proximity to Ukraine, and its own security concerns. It is hard to imagine any Russian leader capitulating to these demands absent a long and costly struggle that would have done enormous damage to Ukraine itself.

Finally, diplomacy based on threats, ultimatums, and a refusal to compromise rarely produces durable outcomes. Weaker parties usually retain some bargaining power—especially where their core interests are concerned—making it difficult for even the most powerful states to get absolutely everything they might want from the other side. Equally important, if the weaker side is forced to capitulate under duress and in ways it regards as unfair, it will resent the result and seek to reopen the issue when conditions are more favorable. For diplomacy to work, both parties have to get some of what they want, or those making the largest concessions will have little incentive to abide by the deal over the longer term.

By exaggerating their ability to bend other states to America's will, U.S. leaders undermined their own diplomatic efforts and missed important opportunities to resolve conflicts without having to use force.

THE LIMITS OF SOCIAL ENGINEERING

By definition, liberal hegemony committed the United States to remaking other societies. A liberal world order requires other states to embrace liberal principles, and the United States tried to give them a healthy shove in that direction. This effort failed, however, because it exaggerated America's ability to conduct large-scale social engineering in societies whose history, internal characteristics, and social institutions were radically different from the U.S. experience. America's accomplishments fooled both Democrats and Republicans into thinking that liberal democracy was the magic formula for economic growth and political tranquillity and convinced them that a universal desire for wealth and liberty would trump "old-fashioned" national, ethnic, or religious identities and obviate concerns about the relative power of competing groups in other countries. If history was moving in a progressive direction and other societies couldn't wait to become like us, they would be quick to abandon old ways of thinking, embrace democracy, resolve internal conflicts peacefully, and eagerly join the liberal world order that Uncle Sam was creating. If this rosy vision were accurate, hardly anyone would even think of resisting America's well-intentioned effort to usher other countries into the twenty-first century.

Alas, this view was at best naïve and at worst wildly off-base. The "velvet revolutions" in Eastern Europe and a "democratic wave" in Latin America were encouraging signs as the 1990s began, but secular trends in favor of liberal democracy were far from universal and authoritarian regimes proved surprisingly resilient in Russia, China, the Middle East, and parts of Asia. It had taken centuries for fairly stable democratic institutions to emerge in Western Europe and North America, and that lengthy process had been contentious and often violent. To believe that the United States could create liberal orders in the Balkans, Afghanistan, Iraq, or elsewhere in the Middle East in a few years was fanciful if not downright delusional. By 2017, in fact, it was not even clear if liberal democracy would survive in parts of Europe.

Trying to spread democracy via regime change was doomed to fail for another reason. Changing an entire system of government inevitably creates winners and losers, and the latter will often take up arms to oppose the new order. At the same time, regime change creates power vacuums that facilitate these acts of resistance. Local sources of identity, allegiance, and obligation—whether national, ethnic, tribal, sectarian, or whatever—do not suddenly disappear when a tyrant is toppled, and some of the people the United States was trying to help resented America's heavy-handed interference and were willing to fight and die to resist it. As a research team led by the former senior advisor on Afghanistan and Pakistan in the Office of the Secretary of Defense wrote in 2016, "civilian harm by U.S., international, and Afghan forces contributed significantly to the growth of the Taliban . . . and undermined the war effort by straining U.S.-Afghan relations and weakening the legitimacy of the U.S. mission and the Afghan government." The same team observed similar effects in Yemen, Iraq, Syria, and Pakistan.[61] The more the United States tried to spread its liberal principles, the more opposition it created.

Furthermore, U.S. officials in Afghanistan, Iraq, Yemen, and Libya lacked the detailed local knowledge necessary to guide successful state-building. As an infamous PowerPoint slide from the Afghan War made clear, state-building in the context of a counterinsurgency campaign was an absurdly complex process that could barely be comprehended, let alone implemented successfully (see Figure 1).[62] Personal accounts from participants in these efforts make it abundantly clear that the people responsible for these efforts did not know which local leaders to trust or support, did not understand the complex and subtle networks of allegiance and authority in which they were trying to work, and inevitably trampled on local customs and sensitivities.[63]

Over time, some U.S. commanders and diplomats eventually acquired some of the knowledge that might have helped them be more successful. But then their tour of duty would end, and their replacements would have to learn the same lessons over again. As one former U.S. Army commander ruefully recalled, "we haven't fought the wars overseas for the past fifteen years. We've fought them one year at a time for the past fifteen years."[64] This problem explains why, in 2016, a U.S. Army commander had to apologize for distributing anti-Taliban leaflets that juxtaposed Koranic verses with images of dogs, a combination deeply offensive to Afghan Muslims.[65] The United States had been fighting in

FIGURE 1: Afghanistan Stability/COIN Dynamics

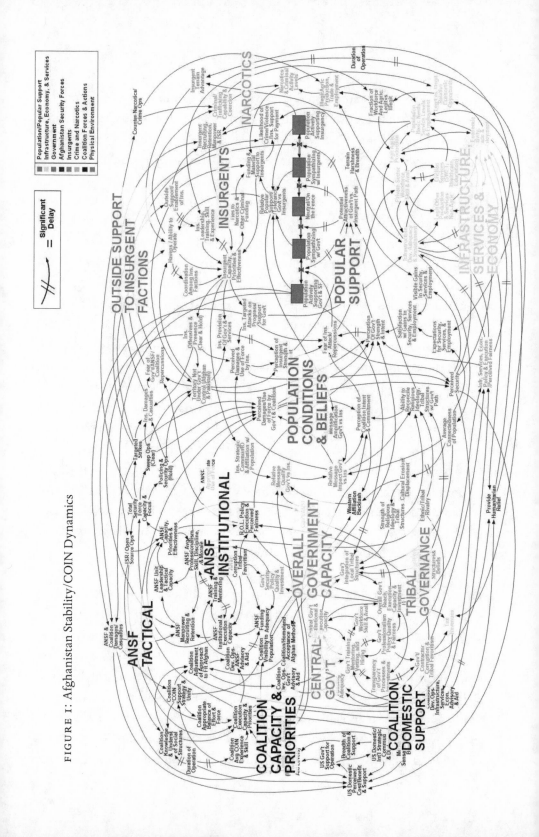

Afghanistan for a decade and a half, yet top commanders still did not understand key elements of the culture in which they were operating.

Moreover, even well-intentioned efforts to aid local populations repeatedly foundered in a sea of corruption and administrative incompetence.[66] Pouring development and reconstruction aid into societies in the absence of effective institutions guaranteed that much of the aid would be squandered or, even worse, would end up in the hands of America's enemies. In Afghanistan, for example, "the U.S. military was paying vast sums to Afghan security firms to guard supply convoys while much of the money was being passed on to the Taliban to guarantee safe passage."[67] Even worse, the central government in Kabul had little incentive to implement the reforms that might help the United States defeat the Taliban, as the billions of dollars of U.S. economic aid on which leaders in Kabul depended (and routinely diverted for their own gains) would evaporate if the war were ever won.[68] And because U.S. officials kept insisting that defeat or withdrawal was not an option, they could not pressure America's local clients to undertake meaningful reforms by threatening to leave them to their fates.

Of course, it didn't help that many of these interventions were taking place in the Middle East, a region where the United States was especially unpopular. The use of military force and economic pressure to topple regimes or spread democracy inevitably reinforced well-established opposition to Western interference in the Arab/Muslim world and thereby discredited the new elites the United States sought to support. Comments made by the Syria expert Joshua Landis about America's failed effort to support moderate groups in the Syrian civil war apply with equal force elsewhere: "America failed not because it didn't try, but because its moderates were incompetent and unpopular. As soon as they began taking money and orders from America, they were tarred by radicals as CIA agents who were corrupt and traitors to the revolution. *America was toxic, and everything it touched turned to sand in its hands.*"[69]

These recurring failures are neither surprising nor atypical; on the contrary, rigorous scholarly studies of earlier efforts at "foreign-imposed regime change" by the United States, Great Britain, and other democracies have shown that toppling a foreign government rarely produces a successful democracy, enhances the rule of law, or leads to significant progress on human rights.[70] What is surprising is how long it took for these lessons to sink in.

THE IMPACT OF DISTANCE

A final justification for liberal hegemony was the idea that the world was shrinking, that grave dangers could emerge from virtually anywhere, and that it was therefore necessary for the United States to try to monitor and guide events almost everywhere. If we were all citizens in a shrinking "global village," then keeping order all over the world was essential to protecting Americans back home.

But as Patrick Porter argues convincingly, the popular image of a "global village" was mostly a myth.[71] Advances in military technology did not give hostile states a usable capacity to threaten the U.S. homeland in strategically consequential ways, because hostile foreign powers could be reliably deterred by America's vastly greater retaliatory capabilities. Globalization might increase the risks from terrorism, cyberwarfare, and infectious diseases somewhat, but these dangers remained modest when compared with other threats. In any case, projecting U.S. power into more places was not an effective way to deal with them.

Nor did these various technological developments make it easier for the United States to govern distant lands. Satellite reconnaissance, sophisticated targeting systems, long-range aircraft, and unmanned drones allowed Washington to bring force to bear in many places, but establishing political control still required "boots on the ground," with all the attendant costs and risks. Supporting expeditionary forces far from home was still expensive—especially in a remote and landlocked country like Afghanistan—and poorly armed local insurgents turned out to be surprisingly effective when fighting on their home turf. Trying to make America safer by intervening in many different places just made the problem of violent extremism worse, and public support for costly overseas crusades soon waned.

NEGLECTING THE HOME FRONT

Liberal hegemony had one final shortcoming, although it did not become fully evident until the 2016 election. Trying to reshape politics all over the world and carrying the other burdens of global leadership was costly and time-consuming, and it took time, attention, and resources away from pressing domestic concerns. Every hour a president spent fretting about Iraq or Afghanistan or Somalia or Colombia was an hour he could not devote to domestic concerns, and every dollar spent on foreign military bases and overseas interventions was a dollar that could not be devoted to improving the lives of Americans at home or left in taxpayers' pockets. As we shall see in chapter 3, the American people were never all that enthusiastic about liberal hegemony, and with good reason.

These opportunity costs were especially important because the combination of globalization and rapid technological change was having a profound impact on the American workforce. Globalization may have been good for highly educated elites and especially Wall Street, but middle-class incomes were stagnating, blue-collar manufacturing jobs were disappearing, and the reeducation and retraining programs that Washington was providing were far from adequate. The country's crumbling infrastructure was badly in need of repair—a 2017 report by the World Bank found that the United States had an infrastructure investment gap of almost $4 trillion, the largest of any country in the world—but infrastructure spending had to compete with existing entitlement programs and costly overseas interventions.[72] Not only had liberal hegemony failed to achieve its explicit international goals, it contributed to the domestic discontent that fueled Donald Trump's surprising electoral triumph.

SUCCESS STORIES

Liberal hegemony's shortcomings become even clearer when one examines those rare episodes when U.S. foreign policy worked well. As discussed in chapter 1, U.S. diplomacy helped end the Bosnian War and helped broker the peace treaty between Israel and Jordan, and the Nunn-Lugar Cooperative Threat Reduction program improved nuclear security in Russia and other former Soviet territories until it fell victim to the crisis over Ukraine. The creation of the World Trade Organization, the PEPFAR program in Africa, the Proliferation Security Initiative, the 2015 nuclear deal with Iran, the 2015 Paris Agreement, and the restoration of diplomatic relations with Cuba were all legitimate achievements, as was the successful multilateral effort that convinced Libya to dismantle its WMD programs.

What do these success stories have in common? In each case the United States did not try to impose solutions on others solely by issuing ultimatums and ratcheting up more and more pressure, or by trying to topple hostile governments with which it disagreed. On the contrary, in these cases it recognized that there were limits to U.S. leverage, and it adjusted its goals to win greater international support and to reach a mutually acceptable agreement with the other parties. When Washington sought cooperation from others and took others' interests into account, its efforts were generally successful.

As previously discussed, the poster child in this category is the 2015 Joint Comprehensive Plan of Action, which blocked Iran's ability to acquire nuclear weapons. As long as the United States insisted that Iran give up its entire enrichment capacity, it made no headway whatsoever, and the Islamic Republic just kept expanding its centrifuge capacity and stockpiling more and more enriched uranium. Once Washington began negotiating in earnest, however, it was able to assemble a broad international coalition and impose more effective economic sanctions. Equally important, U.S. negotiators abandoned the futile hope that pressure alone would convince Tehran to give up its entire enrichment capacity. That concession to reality opened the door to a compromise that avoided war, blocked Iran's path to a bomb, and allowed Tehran to save face. The election of the moderate Iranian president Hassan Rouhani in 2013 surely facilitated the agreement, but it took flexibility on America's part to seize the opportunity.

The disarming of Libya in 2003 offers a similar lesson. There is no doubt that coercive pressure—including tough multilateral economic sanctions—helped persuade Muammar Gaddafi to give up his relatively primitive WMD programs in exchange for restored economic and diplomatic ties. Fear of regime change in the wake of the U.S. invasion of Iraq may also have played some role in his decision, but the other key ingredients were Gaddafi's own fears of Al Qaeda and the Bush administration's pledge to leave him in power if he allowed U.S. officials to cart away his WMD equipment. The Obama administration's decision to renege on this pledge in 2011 does not negate the broader lesson: diplomacy worked in 2003 because the United States offered carrots as well as sticks.[73]

Furthermore, in many of these cases, the United States was willing to negotiate in earnest with regimes whose values and governing principles were very different from its own. Washington didn't demand that other states become democratic before joining the Proliferation Security Initiative or receiving Nunn-Lugar Threat Reduction funds, for example, and it did not insist that Vietnam and Brunei become democracies before joining the Trans-Pacific Partnership negotiations.

These same features can also be seen in the U.S. approach to China. U.S. leaders understood that China was too big to push around, so they generally refrained from issuing ultimatums or relying solely on threats or sanctions. They were sometimes critical of China's authoritarian system and human rights record, but Clinton, Bush, and Obama quickly learned that hectoring Beijing on these issues accomplished little. U.S. leaders recognized that Sino-American relations were likely to be increasingly conflictive, and they took a number of steps designed to constrain Chinese influence, but they also understood that cooperation was still necessary on climate change, global health, North Korea, and international economic issues. In short, when dealing with Beijing, U.S. officials forgot about regime change and the other revisionist elements of liberal hegemony, concentrated on managing relations with the world's number two power, and did about as well as could be expected.

The lesson is clear: when the United States abandoned liberal hegemony and adopted a more realistic and flexible approach, its ability to achieve specific foreign policy goals increased significantly.

CONCLUSION

After more than two decades, the failures of liberal hegemony were impossible to hide. Yet until the inauguration of Donald Trump, its central principles remained hardwired into American foreign policy discourse and went mostly unchallenged in the corridors of power. Barack Obama may have been elected in good part to correct his predecessors' excesses, but even he sought to expand the sphere of democratic rule and oust a few dictators, and he was willing to take on new security obligations, just as Bill Clinton and George Bush had done. Obama tried to use more limited means and to get others to bear a bit more of the burden, but the foreign policy establishment remained committed to maintaining U.S. dominance, spreading liberal values, and expanding U.S. commitments. Liberal hegemony remained the guiding star of U.S. strategy even though Washington still had no idea how to make it work.

The election of Donald Trump exposed a final flaw in the strategy of liberal hegemony: it had created a world order that was overly reliant on the United States and thus potentially vulnerable to the vagaries of U.S. domestic politics. By viewing their country as the "indispensable power" and making it the linchpin of security arrangements around the world, U.S. officials had unwittingly created a security architecture that depended on America's being engaged, powerful, resolute, and effective nearly everywhere. Instead of encouraging regional powers to resolve their differences and develop security arrangements that didn't require a lot of active American guidance, U.S. leaders had created a world order that would disintegrate rapidly if the United States stopped bearing the global burdens it had once eagerly embraced. No wonder U.S. foreign policy elites viewed Trump's arrival with alarm; the liberal world order to which they were deeply committed was more delicate than it appeared, and they knew it.[74]

With the benefit of hindsight, the decision to embrace a grand strategy of liberal hegemony and to pursue it despite repeated failures seems baffling. It was the height of hubris for Americans—who are, after all, only 5 percent of the world's population—to believe they had discovered the only workable model for a modern society and the only possible blueprint for a durable and peaceful world order. It was naïve for them to think they could create stable and successful democracies in deeply divided societies that had never been democratic before. It was positively delusional to assume that this objective could be achieved rapidly and at low cost. It was unrealistic to believe that other states would not be alarmed by America's efforts to reshape world politics and to assume further that opponents would not devise effective ways to thwart U.S. designs. And it was stubborn to the point of insanity to keep chasing the same elusive objective after so many repeated setbacks.

So why did liberal hegemony remain the default condition of U.S. grand strategy? Part of the answer—but only part—is the vast power the United States possessed and the favorable geopolitical position it enjoyed after the Soviet Union collapsed. To borrow Bill Clinton's explanation for his embarrassing affair with a White House intern, the United States opted for liberal hegemony and kept trying to make it work "because it could."

The end of the Cold War had left the United States in a position of preponderance unseen since the Roman Empire. This good fortune could not protect the country from every conceivable danger, but it was still the most secure great power in modern history.[75] The combination of vast power—along with what the historian C. Vann Woodward called the "free security" resulting from America's providential location—was the permissive condition that allowed the United States to intervene with near impunity all over the world without having to worry too much about the short-term consequences back home.[76]

Because the United States was so rich, powerful, and secure, it could afford to follow a misguided grand strategy for a long time without bankrupting itself completely or leaving itself vulnerable to foreign invasion. Had it faced a serious peer competitor after 1993 or some number of powerful and hostile neighbors, it would have been forced to devote more attention to protecting the U.S. homeland and it would have been less willing to take on costly new commitments or to try to shape political conditions in distant lands. Since World War II, however, and especially since 1993, the United States has had the luxury of being able to intervene wherever it chooses and then withdraw if things go badly—as it did in Vietnam, Iraq, Somalia, and Libya—leaving the local populations to their fates.

At the same time, these advantages also left the country with relatively little to gain from its ambitious campaign to remake the world. The benefits of an ambitious and successful foreign policy are not zero, of course, but in 1993 the United States was already rich and secure, already led stable alliances with a number of other powerful states, was on fairly good terms with many other countries, and was positioned to do well in a globalizing world economy. Even if liberal hegemony had worked much better than it did—for example, by successfully turning Iraq and Afghanistan into thriving democracies—it would not have improved America's overall position all that much.

Indeed, because the United States was already wealthy, strong, and secure, it could have just as easily chosen to draw down its overseas commitments somewhat, passed the burdens for regional security in some areas onto other states, and devoted more time, money, and attention to improving the lives of citizens back home. This approach might even have enhanced U.S. leverage over its remaining allies, who might have worked harder to preserve U.S. backing and been more sensitive to Washington's wishes.[77]

We are left with a puzzling paradox. Primacy made pursuing liberal hegemony *possible*, but it also made it less *necessary*. Understanding why that fateful choice was made, and why three very different presidents clung to it despite its failings, requires a closer look at the institutions and organizations that shape how Americans think about these decisions and how elected officials ultimately choose to act. That task begins in chapter 3.

3. DEFINING THE "BLOB": WHAT IS THE "FOREIGN POLICY COMMUNITY"?

D URING THE 2016 PRESIDENTIAL CAMPAIGN, Donald Trump showed scant regard for the individuals who had been in charge of U.S. foreign policy. Saying "we have to look for new people," Trump stated that he wasn't going to be "surrounding myself with those who have perfect resumes but very little to brag about except responsibility for a long history of failed policies." When prominent Republican foreign policy VIPs published an open letter questioning his qualifications and character, Trump retorted, "The names on this letter are the ones the American people should look to for answers on why the world is a mess, and we thank them for coming forward so everyone in the country knows who deserves the blame for making the world such a dangerous place."[1]

Were Trump's criticisms justified? The answer—unfortunately—is yes, because most of the problems afflicting U.S. foreign policy are the result of conscious choices rather than unpredictable acts of fate. Primacy and "free security" made it possible for the United States to meddle in distant regions, and it insulated Americans from some of the consequences, but the specific commitments and initiatives that U.S. leaders undertake are still matters of political choice. As Thomas Oatley notes, "the United States has never been forced by foreign invasion to fight a war at home. Instead, American policymakers have been able to choose when, where, and if to participate in wars . . . in every instance . . . [they] could have chosen not to use force without placing the territorial integrity or national sovereignty of the United States at risk."[2] Yet in recent years the threat or use of force has often been the default option despite its disappointing results.

Let us therefore look more closely at the people and institutions that make or influence these decisions, and explore what is guiding their choices.

FOREIGN POLICY AND DEMOCRATIC POLITICS

In a democracy, foreign policy is not simply the product of a president's vision. It is also shaped by competing forces in civil society and by what might be termed the "foreign policy community." The impact of civil society will be especially large in a liberal democracy such as the United States, with its tradition of divided government, constitutional guarantees of free speech and association, and ambivalent attitude toward centralized power. These forces will be even more powerful when there is no compelling danger to focus the national mind and when policymakers are freer to act as they see fit or as domestic pressures dictate.

In theory, these features ought to make American democracy more effective at conducting foreign policy than most, if not all, authoritarian regimes. Indeed, a large scholarly literature makes precisely this argument, declaring that democracies typically outperform dictatorships in many areas of public policy.[3] As the careers of Mao Zedong and Saddam

Hussein illustrate, incompetent despots can cling to power for decades, even when their policies are profoundly harmful, provided they retain reliable control over the army, the police, and other tools of repression. Democratic leaders, by contrast, are accountable to the public, and the constant fear of electoral sanction disciplines the exercise of power, encourages them to appoint effective subordinates, and is said to discourage frivolous or risky initiatives.

Furthermore, the formal separation of powers and other institutional "checks and balances" supposedly makes it difficult for democratic leaders to wield power arbitrarily. The president may be the chief executive and commander in chief, but Congress controls the purse strings and in theory can limit what the president is able to do at home or abroad. An independent judiciary provides a further check on executive power and can be a potent source of accountability—again, in theory—because officials who break the law are subject to indictment, prosecution, and punishment.

Third, because democracies also encourage free speech, open discourse, and an independent media, they are said to benefit from a "marketplace of ideas."[4] Citizens in a democracy should have better access to information, and vigorous debate will supposedly winnow out bad ideas and allow better alternatives to emerge. When mistakes are made, citizens and officials in a democracy can figure out that something is amiss and correct the error more rapidly than a typical authoritarian regime would.[5]

In addition to these structural advantages, one might expect U.S. foreign policymaking to benefit from the dramatic expansion of state capacity and the specialized training that those charged with handling U.S. foreign relations typically receive. During the nineteenth century, notes the historian Ernest May, only a small group of U.S. leaders and private citizens showed "any deep interest in foreign affairs."[6] Even America's rise to world power did not immediately produce a large community of foreign policy experts in and outside government. As President Woodrow Wilson prepared for the Paris Peace Conference in 1919, the dearth of official foreign policy expertise led Wilson's closest advisor,

Colonel Edward House, to create an ad hoc group known as "The Inquiry" to advise the president on U.S. interests and objectives.[7]

Organizations and individuals engaged primarily in international affairs grew in number throughout the interwar period, though participation in the highest reaches of government was still dominated by an "Eastern Establishment," as embodied by elite associations such as the Council on Foreign Relations (CFR), the Foreign Policy Association, and the Carnegie Endowment for International Peace. Philanthropies such as the Ford Foundation and the Rockefeller Brothers Fund became active after World War II, funding a variety of international affairs programs at universities and civic associations.[8] And as the *Washington Post* columnist Joseph Kraft later observed, "the main function [of the establishment] . . . was to drive isolationism from the field, to make internationalism not only respectable but beyond serious question."[9]

By the 1960s, however, as America's global role grew, education expanded, and foreign policymaking required more specialized expertise, "a revolution was taking place in the structure of America's foreign policy leadership. Power passed almost imperceptibly from the old Eastern Establishment to a new Professional Elite, from bankers and lawyers who would take time off to help manage the affairs of government to full-time foreign policy experts."[10]

At first glance, this expansion of professional expertise would appear to be a significant improvement over the "old guard" establishment, and it should have produced more intelligent and successful policy decisions. Instead of relying on a self-selected group of elites drawn primarily from the corporate world, U.S. foreign policy would be handled by a more diverse group of experts who had specialized training in economics, military affairs, history, diplomacy, or regional studies. In theory, the clash of competing views among these well-informed professionals would generate a livelier debate, thereby ensuring that alternative policy choices were vetted in advance and making major blunders less likely. When mistakes did occur—as they inevitably would—this same well-trained policy community would quickly identify the misstep(s) and alter course.

In the next three chapters I argue that this optimistic vision is an illusion, especially in an era when U.S. dominance allowed it to pursue ambitious foreign policy goals at seemingly low cost and with little risk of significant escalation.[11] America's democratic institutions did not perform nearly as well as this upbeat scenario envisioned, and the contemporary foreign policy community has been characterized less by competence and accountability and more by a set of pathologies that have undermined its ability to set realistic goals and pursue them effectively.

To put it in the bluntest terms, instead of being a disciplined body of professionals constrained by a well-informed public and forced by necessity to set priorities and hold themselves accountable, today's foreign policy elite is a dysfunctional caste of privileged insiders who are frequently disdainful of alternative perspectives and insulated both professionally and personally from the consequences of the policies they promote. It was impolitic for the deputy national security advisor Ben Rhodes to dismiss this community as "the Blob," but the label nonetheless contains important elements of truth.[12]

The foreign policy community in contemporary America has been strongly committed to the strategy of liberal hegemony. Within that world, organizations and individuals committed to America's global leadership role and to an ambitious foreign policy agenda are far more numerous and much better funded than groups arguing for greater U.S. restraint. Despite occasional differences over tactics and the setbacks of the past two decades, today's foreign policy community still exhibits a striking consensus in favor of trying to run the world.

DEFINING THE FOREIGN POLICY COMMUNITY

By the "foreign policy community," I mean those *individuals and organizations that actively engage on a regular basis with issues of international affairs.* This definition incorporates both formal government organizations and the many groups and individuals that deal with foreign policy as part of their normal activities, seeking either to shape public perceptions of international issues or to influence government policy directly.[13] For an individual to be considered part of this community, working on some aspect of foreign policy must be either their principal professional vocation or a major private commitment occupying a substantial part of daily life.

To illustrate: members of the "foreign policy community" would include Foreign Service officers, intelligence analysts at the CIA, a senior fellow at a foreign policy think tank, a professor of international relations at a college or university, a staff member serving the Senate Foreign Relations Committee, or a journalist whose beat deals with some aspect of U.S. foreign relations. It would also include an active member of a local World Affairs Council chapter, a defense analyst at the Congressional Budget Office or the RAND Corporation, a lobbyist working for Human Rights Watch, or a program officer at a philanthropic foundation whose agenda includes international affairs.

There will always be borderline cases, of course, but this definition would exclude an employee at a think tank who works on health care or a congressional staffer assigned to the Judiciary Committee, unless they are actively involved in foreign policy issues in some other capacity. It would also exclude private citizens whose foreign policy–related activity is limited to voting in elections or writing the occasional letter to the editor of their local paper, but who do not engage global issues on a regular basis.[14]

FORMAL INSTITUTIONS OF GOVERNMENT

The foreign policy community begins with the individuals and agencies of government charged with handling different aspects of U.S. foreign relations. The list here is enormous, and it includes the president, the vice president, the National Security Council, the relevant personnel in the Departments of State, Defense, Energy, and Treasury, the various intelligence services, the relevant congressional committees, research organizations such as the Congressional Budget Office or the Los Alamos National Laboratory, and the vast array of smaller agencies performing specialized foreign policy tasks.

This world has expanded dramatically over the past half century. For example, the president's own foreign policy staff—embodied in the National Security Council—has grown from fewer than twenty people in 1961 to roughly two hundred under President George W. Bush and more than four hundred under President Obama.[15]

The U.S. military is down from its Cold War peak, but there are still nearly 1.4 million men and women on active duty and roughly one million in the National Guard and military reserves. The Department of Defense employs more than 700,000 civilians, and the Department of State consists of roughly 25,000 Foreign Service and civil service personnel (plus 45,000 locally employed civilians worldwide), while the intelligence community comprises seventeen separate agencies with an annual budget well in excess of $50 billion and employing some 100,000 people. More than four million Americans now hold some sort of security clearance, and close to one million are cleared to read top secret material.[16]

Obviously, most members of this sprawling bureaucratic agglomeration do not exercise substantial authority over major foreign policy decisions. But as Michael Glennon notes, the ability of presidents, cabinet secretaries, and other political appointees to chart a different course in foreign policy is inevitably constrained by the size, inertia, and the de facto autonomy of what he calls the "Trumanite Network" (a reference to the 1947 National Security Act), whose permanent members endure across successive administrations.[17]

The sheer size of the foreign policy and national security bureaucracy impedes effective policymaking in two ways. First, coordinating action across multiple agencies and constituencies is time-consuming, especially when a new policy has to be created and coordinated through the interagency process.[18] Second, the presence of a vast foreign affairs bureaucracy dilutes accountability: when so many fingerprints are on any major policy decision, it becomes harder to determine responsibility for success or failure and thus harder to reward good judgment and penalize incompetence.

MEMBERSHIP ORGANIZATIONS

Outside government, elite and mass attitudes about foreign policy are also influenced by various "membership organizations" that are made up of self-selected individuals with a particular interest in America's relations with the rest of the world. Examples include the World Affairs Councils, the Foreign Policy Association, the Council on Foreign Relations, or the Veterans of Foreign Wars, and each of these groups engages in activities intended to strengthen public awareness of critical international issues and to help members deepen their own understanding of such topics. Within this category one also finds more specialized membership organizations such as Greenpeace and Oxfam, whose work focuses primarily on other issues but sometimes has an important foreign policy dimension as well.

THINK TANKS

According to James McGann, there are more than eighteen hundred public policy "think tanks" in the United States today, approximately one-quarter of them located in the nation's capital.[19] Their ranks include broad, general-purpose research organizations such as the Brookings Institution, the American Enterprise Institute (AEI), the Heritage Foundation, the Cato Institute, the Center for Strategic and International Studies, the Bipartisan Policy Center, and the Carnegie Endowment for International Peace, along with dozens of smaller, more specialized organizations such as the Center for Strategic and Budgetary Assessments, the Center for a New American Security (CNAS), the Aspen Institute, the Hudson Institute, the Center for International Policy, the Washington Institute for Near East Policy, Resources for the Future, the Center for the National Interest, and the Peterson Institute for International Economics. The venerable Council on Foreign Relations is a membership organization—albeit a selective one—as well as a think tank, with a staff of more than eighty foreign policy professionals and offices in New York and Washington.

Think tanks perform several functions within the foreign policy community. Staff members conduct independent research, testify to Congress and other government agencies, and appear frequently as media commentators. Most think tanks engage in extensive outreach efforts via their own websites, blogs, publications, seminars, legislative breakfasts, and other events, all intended to enhance their visibility inside Washington, facilitate fundraising, and increase their influence over policy. Think tanks can also play a critical role in many stages of a foreign policy professional's career: they provide entry-level opportunities for young policy wonks seeking to make their way into government positions, and they provide sinecures for former government officials, including those seeking to return to public service at a later date. In this sense, the D.C.-based think tank community provides an arena where foreign policy ideas can be discussed, debated, criticized, and defended, and some parts of it operate almost as a "shadow government" preparing people and policies for future administrations.[20]

Although certain think tanks and research organizations are explicitly nonpartisan and aspire to high standards of scholarship, the line between research and policy advocacy is increasingly blurred.[21] As Steven Clemons, an experienced veteran of several think tanks, acknowledged some years ago, such organizations "are less and less committed to genuine inquiry designed to stimulate enlightened policy decisions and more and more oriented to deepening the well-worn grooves of paralyzed debate."[22]

Indeed, the overall academic quality of D.C.-based think tanks has declined noticeably over the past thirty years. In the 1980s, for example, the Foreign Policy Studies group at Brookings contained a number of scholars who published regularly in top academic journals and university presses, and several senior fellows were subsequently appointed to tenured positions at elite universities.[23] Although full-time Brookings fellows sometimes teach as adjunct faculty members at local universities today, they rarely publish in academic venues and would be unlikely to be considered eligible for senior positions in a top academic department.

In many cases, in fact, think tanks are advocacy organizations masquerading as independent research bodies. Organizations such as the Progressive Policy Institute or the Center for American Progress serve these functions for Democrats, while the American Enterprise Institute and the Heritage Foundation work mostly on behalf of the GOP. These organizations exist to provide intellectual ammunition for partisan political warfare and are understandably sensitive to the interests of major donors and the political leaders whose agendas they seek to promote. In this way, many prominent think tanks are important adjuncts to the next category.

INTEREST GROUPS AND LOBBIES

Interest groups are a central element of American democracy. Because the U.S. Constitution guarantees freedom of speech and association, groups of citizens can coalesce around any issue that unites them and try to convince politicians to adopt policies they favor. They can do so by lobbying legislators or government officials directly, helping draft congressional resolutions or formal legislation, steering campaign contributions to politicians who support their views, and engaging in activities designed to convince the public to embrace their policy preferences.[24]

Despite the cliché that "politics stops at the water's edge," foreign policy is hardly immune to interest group influence. On the contrary, there is a plethora of interest groups and lobbies on nearly every significant foreign policy issue, each trying to shape mass and elite opinion and persuade government officials to follow its preferred course of action. Here one finds advocacy groups such as Amnesty International, Human Rights Watch, or the Arms Control Association; ethnic lobbies like the American-Israel Public Affairs Committee, the Armenian Assembly of America, or the United States India Political Action Committee; lobbyists and think tanks funded by corporations favoring increased defense spending; pro-peace groups such as the American Friends Service Committee; business associations like the U.S. Chamber of Commerce; and many, many more.

This category also includes so-called letterhead organizations, such as the Committee on the Present Danger, United Against Nuclear Iran, the Project for the New American Century (or its successor, the Foreign Policy Initiative), or the Coalition for a Realistic Foreign Policy. "Letterhead organizations" are ad hoc groups that bring together eminent figures to issue open letters and statements intended to shape public debate and influence the policy agenda.

THE MEDIA

My definition of the foreign policy community would also include those parts of the media that cover foreign affairs, for they play a key role in shaping what elites and publics know and believe about the world at large and about U.S. foreign policy itself. Prominent components include major news organizations (Reuters, the Associated Press, etc.); elite newspapers and magazines such as *The New York Times*, *The Wall Street Journal*, or *The Washington Post*; and influential broadcast venues such as National Public Radio, Fox News, MSNBC, C-Span, or the *PBS NewsHour*. Specialized journals such as *Foreign Policy*, *Foreign Affairs*, and *The National Interest* belong here as well, along with general interest publications that frequently cover international issues, such as *The New Republic*, *The New Yorker*, and *The Atlantic*. Of course, individual journalists such as Thomas Friedman, Dana Priest, Helene Cooper, or David Ignatius and celebrity hosts like Fareed Zakaria, Rachel Maddow, Wolf Blitzer, and Sean Hannity must be considered part of the broad foreign policy community, along with the vast number of bloggers and websites that focus heavily on foreign affairs.

ACADEMIA

Although some university-based scholars have little interest in policy issues or other real-world concerns, many political scientists, lawyers, historians, economists, and other scholars write books and articles about foreign policy and contribute in other ways to public discourse on these topics. University-based scholars also educate and train many of the people who end up working in government, media, and the think tank world, and some of them serve in government themselves, including at very senior levels. As one would expect, the faculty ranks at most schools of public policy or international affairs are filled with people who have combined scholarly careers with periods of public service, and many of these individuals remain engaged in a variety of policy-related activities after leaving office.[25]

SOURCES OF SUPPORT

Nor can we exclude the private groups and individuals who provide financial support for many of these activities. Relevant actors here include philanthropies that support research or advocacy in international affairs, such as the Ford, MacArthur, Smith Richardson, Stanton, Scaife, Rockefeller, Koch, and Hewlett foundations, and the many similar but smaller philanthropies that help support groups working on foreign policy issues. Private individuals with an interest in foreign policy can donate to political action committees, universities, think tanks, or lobbies, sometimes in impressive amounts, in order to advance their particular foreign policy objectives. The financier George Soros helped fund the New America Foundation and the Center for American Progress, and the Israeli-American businessman Haim Saban has given millions of dollars to the Democratic Party and provided the initial funding for the Saban Center for Middle East Policy at Brookings. The Foundation for Defense of Democracies and other neoconservative organizations have received generous funding from the gambling mogul Sheldon Adelson and the hedge fund billionaire Paul Singer. The Carnegie Endowment for International Peace began with a bequest from the industrialist Andrew Carnegie, and the Council on Foreign Relations has received generous support from many private individuals throughout its long history.

Corporations with a clear interest in foreign and national security policy are active here as well, and think tanks such as AEI, the Center for Strategic and Budgetary Assessments, and the Center for a New American Security all rely heavily on contributions from defense contractors and other major corporations. More worrisome still, in recent years a number of prominent think tanks have become partly dependent on donations from foreign governments, raising serious questions about their objectivity.[26]

Universities are equally reliant on donor support, of course, some of it clearly motivated by a donor's interest in foreign policy. In 2006, for example, the neoconservative financier Roger Hertog funded grand strategy programs at several prominent U.S. universities; these were patterned after an existing program at Yale and intended to promote a more hawkish perspective on college campuses.[27] Similarly, the Charles Koch Institute has recently begun funding research and training programs on international security at MIT, Tufts, Harvard, Texas A&M, and Notre Dame.[28] And in 2016 the Pearson Family Foundation pledged a whopping $100 million to endow a center for the study of global conflict at the University of Chicago (a gift it subsequently regretted and has sued to reverse).[29]

What does this broad picture of the foreign policy community reveal? To paraphrase Karl Marx, top government officials make foreign policy, but they do not make it entirely as they please. They draw upon expertise from the think tank world and from academia, and they are often constrained by bureaucratic opposition, public skepticism, media scrutiny, and the interplay of interest groups within society. Even presidents do not operate with complete freedom, as the decisions they make are constrained by the broad consensus within the foreign policy community and by the choices presented to them by their subordinates. As Michael Glennon notes, "true top-down decisions that order fundamental policy shifts are rare . . . When it comes to national security, the President is less decider than presider."[30] To understand the recurring tendencies of U.S. foreign policy, therefore, we need to consider the characteristics of this broad community in greater depth.

LIFE IN THE "BLOB"

A SENSE OF COMMUNITY

Partisan differences notwithstanding, a key feature of the "foreign policy community" is that it *is* a community, especially at the highest levels.

Many of its leading members know one another and participate in overlapping activities and organizations. The boundaries between many of these organizations are permeable, and prominent figures within this community often work for several different organizations over the course of a career, sometimes simultaneously.

For example, a typical foreign policy career path might begin on Wall Street or in academia, proceed to a period of government service, and then move to a think tank or even into journalism.[31] An equally plausible trajectory might start with government service, then migrate to academia, a think tank, or the private sector before returning to government at some later stage.[32] Alternatively, a different individual might rise to prominence in the private sector, academia, or journalism and then parlay that reputation into a government career or use the wealth acquired through business activity to fund a research or lobbying organization that advanced his or her political views. Some individuals wear several hats at once: teaching at a university, serving as a nonresident fellow at an inside-the-Beltway think tank, and doing private consulting for government agencies, individual officials, or for-profit corporations.[33]

The foreign policy community is also highly networked, with leading members connected by personal associations and by their participation in overlapping groups and activities. Senior figures often know one another personally and know other prominent figures by reputation, and many inhabit overlapping professional and social groups. There are also prominent "power couples," such as the journalists Peter Baker (*The New York Times*) and Susan Glasser (*Foreign Policy, Politico,* and *The New Yorker*); the CNAS cofounder and former assistant secretary of state Kurt Campbell and former undersecretary of the treasury Lael Brainerd; or former assistant secretary of state Victoria Nuland and neoconservative pundit Robert Kagan.

As a classic example of an elite foreign policy network, consider the Aspen Strategy Group (ASG). Its stated mission is "to provide a bipartisan forum to explore the preeminent foreign policy challenges the

United States faces." One of its flagship events is a four-day summer workshop, but it also organizes task forces and other meetings and publishes occasional briefings and reports on issues of interest. Participants are a "who's who" of foreign policy luminaries, including such former government officials as Madeleine Albright, Brent Scowcroft, Nicholas Burns, Thomas Donilon, Anne-Marie Slaughter, and Robert Zoellick; journalists like CNN's Fareed Zakaria or *The Wall Street Journal*'s Carla Robbins; think tank presidents like Richard Haass of the Council on Foreign Relations, former Carnegie Endowment president Jessica Mathews, former Brookings head Strobe Talbott; and academics (who may also be former officials) such as Eliot Cohen of Johns Hopkins, Mitchell Reiss (formerly of the College of William and Mary), and Philip Zelikow of the University of Virginia. ASG members serve in many other capacities as well: Talbott, Scowcroft, and the Clinton-era national security advisor Sandy Berger all served on the Global Board of Advisors of the Council on Foreign Relations, while Albright and Zakaria have served on CFR's board of directors. Cohen is a member of the American Enterprise Institute's Council of Academic Advisors, and Slaughter is the former dean of Princeton's Woodrow Wilson School of International and Public Affairs and current president of the New America Foundation.

The neoconservative movement provides another example of a mutually supportive network of well-connected insiders. Over the past three decades, neoconservatives such as Richard Perle, Robert Kagan, Max Boot, Danielle Pletka, Eric Edelman, Elliott Abrams, William Kristol, and James Woolsey (among many others) have populated a dizzying collection of centers, think tanks, lobbies, consulting groups, and letterhead organizations such as the American Enterprise Institute, the Center for Security Policy, the Project for the New American Century (PNAC), the Hudson Institute, the Jewish Institute for National Security of America (JINSA), United Against Nuclear Iran, the Middle East Forum, the Foundation for Defense of Democracies (FDD), and several others while working or writing for publications like *The Weekly Standard* and, in some cases, for mainstream foreign policy organizations like the Council on Foreign Relations or the Center for Strategic and Budgetary Assessments.[34]

Connections of this kind are invaluable for individuals seeking to rise (or remain) within the foreign policy community, for there is no single, clear, and established route to power inside the U.S. political system. Unlike the professions of law, medicine, or accounting, there are no required courses of study that must be completed before one can practice foreign policy and there is no procedure for professional certification. Prominent members of this community may have advanced degrees in political science, history, international affairs, or public policy, but such training is not a prerequisite for entry or advancement. Sandy Berger was a U.S. national security advisor to Bill Clinton, and Thomas Donilon held the same post under Barack Obama: both were lawyers with little or no formal training in international affairs, yet each eventually took on major responsibilities in this area.[35] Similarly, Barack Obama's chief foreign policy speechwriter, Deputy National Security Advisor Ben Rhodes, was an aspiring novelist with B.A. degrees in English and political science from Rice and an M.A. in Creative Writing from NYU, but he had no advanced training in foreign policy, national security, diplomacy, or international economics. Donald Trump's first choice as secretary of state, Rex Tillerson, has a bachelor's degree in civil engineering, spent his entire professional career at Exxon, and had never served in government before his appointment in 2017.

The point is not that these (or other) officials were unqualified; it is that the path to a prominent position in the foreign policy community is highly contingent and has no formal prerequisites. Doctors, lawyers, accountants, and other professionals must devote years to formal study and pass a rigorous certifying exam, but aspiring foreign policy gurus need only establish a close relationship with a successful politician or acquire a solid reputation among established figures within some part of the existing community.[36] For instance, former national security advisor Donilon worked for several Democratic Party stalwarts and at the same law firm as Secretary of State Warren Christopher (whom he served as chief of staff), and his counterpart Sandy Berger had been a personal friend of Bill Clinton's since the 1972 McGovern campaign.

Given the recurring need to bring new blood into the establishment, a number of foreign policy institutions have created fellowships and internships designed to identify, recruit, socialize, and advance the careers of young people eager for a career in this world. The Council on Foreign Relations reserves five-year "term memberships" for candidates under thirty-five, and its International Affairs Fellowships place academics and other professionals in government positions for a year at no cost to the U.S. taxpayer. Similarly, the Center for a New American Security has its "Next Generation National Security Fellowship," whose recipients participate in a leadership development program, a monthly dinner series, and private discussions where they can "engage with those who have led before them, developing a deeper understanding of U.S. national security interests and policies."[37] Another variant is the annual fellowships awarded by the Truman National Security Project, which is self-described as "a highly competitive leadership development program for exceptional individuals who show promise to become our country's future global affairs leaders."[38]

In this sense, today's foreign policy community operates much as the old "Eastern Establishment" did, insofar as new entrants are recruited, groomed, and promoted based on judgments made by established figures. But there is an important difference. Until sometime in the 1950s, top foreign policy leaders usually had successful careers outside government and did not depend on working on foreign policy for their livelihoods. Men such as Paul Nitze, McGeorge Bundy, James Forrestal, John McCloy, Averell Harriman, Dean Acheson, Robert Lovett, John Foster Dulles, and the like were successful lawyers, bankers, academics, or businessmen whose work in the private sector or in academia had made them financially secure before they entered public service. "Old boy" networks and organizations such as the Council on Foreign Relations helped recruit and prepare them for positions of leadership in foreign policy, even if they had not established a visible public presence beforehand.

By contrast, the modern foreign policy professional has to survive inside the foreign policy community itself. Although a few individuals may alternate between foreign policy work and wholly separate activities (such as working for a law firm or an investment bank on matters unrelated to foreign affairs), today's foreign policy experts tend to move between different sectors without changing professions: they do "foreign policy" no matter where they happen to be working. Thus, former U.S. ambassador to the United Nations Samantha Power first rose to prominence as a journalist focusing on human rights issues, taught courses on that subject for a number of years at Harvard, then joined Barack Obama's Senate staff and presidential campaign, was subsequently appointed a White House aide in 2009, and became ambassador in 2013 before returning to Harvard in 2017. Her roles changed, but she was "doing foreign policy" the entire time. When officials leave government, they rarely leave the field; thus, when former Brookings Institution fellow Ivo Daalder stepped down as U.S. ambassador to the European Union, he was soon chosen to be the new president of the Chicago Council on Global Affairs. Similarly, former undersecretary of defense Douglas Feith left the Bush administration in 2005 and became a senior fellow at the Hudson Institute, where he continues to work on foreign policy issues today.

The nature of the foreign policy job market encourages entrepreneurship and assiduous self-promotion, as acquiring a reputation for being smart, creative, and knowledgeable about some key aspect of foreign policy is the path to professional advancement. As Janine Wedel suggests, professional success in this world "depends not just on quick study, but on connecting and forging networks, on conferences and cross-pollination among politics, business, and media."[39] Ambitious foreign policy professionals rise by writing articles, op-eds, policy briefs, task force reports, and books that attract favorable attention, by cultivating connections to influential insiders, by impressing superiors with their dedication and effectiveness, and by convincing politicians that they are reliable and, above all, loyal.

Moreover, the days when a public servant such as George Marshall would decline opportunities to profit from public service are long gone. Today, a successful career in Washington—and sometimes even a badly tarnished one—can pave the way to a lucrative career in the private sector, provided one does not stray outside the "respectable" consensus. It has become a common practice for top officials to form or join consulting groups or lobbying organizations (e.g., Kissinger Associates, the Chertoff Group, the Scowcroft Group, the Albright Stonebridge Group, the Cohen Group, Barbour Griffith & Rogers, etc.) in order to profit from contacts made and knowledge acquired while in public service. As the journalist Mark Leibovich observes in his acerbic but entertaining portrait of Washington, *This Town*, "everyone is now, in effect, a special interest, a free agent, performing any number of services, in any number of settings."[40]

The career of the former U.S. ambassador to India, Robert Blackwill, offers a revealing but hardly unique example of the ways that members of the foreign policy community can shape perceptions and policy no matter where they are operating. A former Foreign Service officer and protégé of Henry Kissinger's, Blackwill taught for a number of years at the Harvard Kennedy School and was one of the "Vulcans" who advised George W. Bush during the 2000 presidential campaign.[41] As Bush's ambassador to India, Blackwill helped orchestrate an expanding U.S.-Indian security partnership and backed the controversial U.S.-India Civil Nuclear Agreement completed in 2008. He later served on Bush's National Security Council, where he worked on Iraq and tried to secure Ayad Allawi's appointment as interim prime minister. After leaving government, Blackwill became president of the lobbying firm Barbour, Griffith & Rogers, where he continued to press for the policies he had backed while in government (including closer ties with India and Allawi's candidacy in Iraq).[42] He was subsequently appointed Henry A. Kissinger Senior Fellow at the Council on Foreign Relations, and he continues to write, speak, and advise prominent politicians on different aspects of foreign affairs. A lifelong Republican and staunch internationalist, Blackwill was also an early and vocal opponent of Donald Trump, helping to organize the open letters by former GOP officials that judged Trump unfit for office during the 2016 campaign.

Blackwill's example illustrates how prominent members of the foreign policy community can exercise influence regardless of where they are employed, in good part because they are experienced, well-connected, and respected by people in power. But as discussed at greater length in chapter 4, this environment also creates powerful incentives for conformity. Because professional success depends first and foremost on one's reputation, those who wish to rise to power and wield continued influence must take pains to remain within the acceptable range of opinion. As the *Financial Times'* Washington correspondent Edward Luce observes, "Today's climate makes it hard for a contrarian to advance in government. It is better to be wrong in good company than right and alone."[43] This pressure to conform also helps explain why Washington think tanks with ostensibly different political orientations sometimes sponsor joint events: the goal is to attract as large an audience as possible, and the range of disagreement is often less than one might suppose.[44]

Ironically, moving higher in this world does not give most people greater latitude to take unpopular positions or to say what they really think. If anything, pressure to conform increases the closer one gets to the corridors of power. University-based scholars (and especially those with tenure) and anyone not desperate to land a job in government are freer to challenge the prevailing consensus and sometimes rewarded for doing so. By contrast, people who aspire to rise within the inside-the-Beltway establishment will be more inclined to shift with the prevailing winds. It should be no surprise, therefore, that there was little opposition to the 2003 Iraq War in the corridors of power or in the major think tanks that dominate discourse inside the Beltway. A majority of Democratic senators (including Hillary Clinton and Joe Biden) voted for the war in 2003, and prominent Democratic foreign policy experts like

Richard Holbrooke and James Steinberg were open supporters as well. Experts at the American Enterprise Institute, the Brookings Institution, and the Council on Foreign Relations were among the loudest and most persistent voices backing the war, and even some moderates who opposed a full invasion, such as former Carnegie Endowment president Jessica Mathews, still favored "the selective use of military force" to enable "coercive inspections."[45] As one might expect, the most consistent voices opposing the invasion were outside Washington and had little or no effect on the decision.

There is an important personal dimension here as well. To be a respected and well-connected member of the broader foreign policy community opens doors, confers status, creates lucrative opportunities, and feeds one's ego and sense of self-worth. It's *cool* to have a White House pass or a top secret security clearance, and it's gratifying to be nominated for membership in an elite organization like the Council on Foreign Relations or invited to testify on the Hill. It's a heady experience to feel that one is "in the know," to participate in conferences attended by other foreign policy VIPs, to be asked to advise a regional commander or consult for the National Intelligence Council—all the more so when one is young, ambitious, somewhat insecure, and eager to get ahead. But the higher one rises, the greater the benefits and the more exclusive the company becomes, so the incentive to avoid any steps that might lead to being cast off the heights of Olympus grows ever greater. Given how hard they have worked to make it up the mountain, it's easy to understand why most members of the foreign policy establishment go to great lengths to stay there. And that means keeping their reputations intact and keeping their thoughts and recommendations "within the lines" (at least in public).

To be sure, the sense of community and the pressures to conform do not prevent personal animosities, tactical disagreements, and a lot of sharp-elbowed infighting from taking place inside the foreign policy world, even among those who agree on many policy issues. Individuals inside the establishment are often competing to climb the next rung up the ladder of government service, and they inevitably want their particular issues or concerns to garner more attention and resources. Because top jobs are scarce and resources are finite, there is no shortage of backstabbing, character assassination, self-promotion, and contention even among those who are all equally committed to liberal hegemony.

There will also be cases—such as the Iran nuclear deal or the merits of intervention in the Syrian civil war—where there are deep and genuine disagreements within the elite over what U.S. policy should be. But such disagreements take place within a broader climate of opinion that sees U.S. primacy and active global leadership as good for America and good for the world.

To be clear: most foreign policy professionals are genuine patriots who seek to make the world a better place, at least as they would define it. But they also have an obvious personal interest in the United States pursuing an ambitious global agenda. The busier the U.S. government is abroad, the more jobs there will be for foreign policy experts, the greater the share of national wealth that will be devoted to addressing global problems, and the greater their potential influence will be. A more restrained foreign policy would give the entire foreign policy community less to do, reduce its status and prominence, decrease the importance of teaching foreign policy in graduate schools, and might even lead some prominent philanthropies to devote less money to these topics. In this sense, liberal hegemony and unceasing global activism constitute a full-employment strategy for the entire foreign policy community.

"DON'T JUST STAND THERE, DO SOMETHING!": THE ACTIVIST BIAS OF U.S. FOREIGN POLICY INSTITUTIONS

The above features help us understand why the United States routinely errs on the side of doing too much rather than too little. Just as there is an imbalance of power between the United States and the rest of the world, there is also an imbalance of power inside America's foreign policy community. Groups and organizations that support extensive U.S. involvement in world affairs and vigorous U.S. leadership are far more numerous, well-funded, and influential in Washington than groups or organizations that favor greater restraint, less intervention, more burden-sharing with key allies, and, overall, a more realistic foreign policy. Indeed, the latter are almost, though not quite, nonexistent. Although the various groups and individuals that make up most of the foreign policy community do not agree on every policy issue, there is a strong consensus supporting the active exercise of American power.

Within the U.S. government, agencies concerned with foreign policy must compete with other demands on national resources. For predictable budgetary reasons, therefore, the agencies of government that deal with global issues tend to favor greater U.S. activity rather than less. Senior military commanders tend to be warier of military intervention than their civilian counterparts are, but the Pentagon, the intelligence community, and the uniformed military still depict a world filled with dangers, where American power—especially military force—is the answer to a wide range of global problems.[46] Just look at the U.S. Navy, which marketed itself until recently as "A Global Force for Good." Indeed, it would be remarkable if any branches of government charged with some aspect of U.S. foreign relations did not aspire to do more, if only to maintain their present share of the budget.

Similarly, membership organizations such as the World Affairs Councils of America (WACA) and the Foreign Policy Association (FPA) were created to inform the public about world affairs and encourage greater interest in an active foreign policy. As WACA's website notes, the founders of these closely related organizations "were concerned that at the end of World War I, Americans would choose an isolationist foreign policy over one of engagement, so they worked to nurture grassroots citizen involvement in international affairs."[47] Although formally nonpartisan, both of the above organizations remain strongly committed to an active U.S. role in world affairs.

At WACA's 2012 National Conference, for example, the keynote speakers included then-CIA director David Petraeus, former undersecretary of state Marc Grossman, former ambassador Paula Dobriansky (who chairs WACA's board of directors), the *New York Times* reporter

David Sanger, former national security advisor Stephen Hadley, the longtime Middle East advisor Dennis Ross, and a flock of mainstream academics, journalists, and former officials. A similar lineup of well-credentialed insiders appeared in 2014, including the army general David Perkins, Vali Nasr of the Johns Hopkins School of Advanced International Studies, Susan Glasser of *Politico*, and Moisés Naím of the Carnegie Endowment. The 2015 and 2016 programs were no different, including numerous speakers from such mainstream think tanks as Brookings or the Carnegie Endowment, establishment journalists such as Evan Thomas or Michael Duffy; well-connected consultants such as former State Department officials Evans Revere (now with the Albright Stonebridge Group) or Anja Manuel of RiceHadleyGates LLC; or other former officials such as Robert Zoellick, Jeffrey Garten, and R. James Woolsey.[48]

These (and other) speakers are all dedicated internationalists, which is why they were invited. Experts with a more critical view of U.S. foreign policy—such as Andrew Bacevich, Peter Van Buren, Medea Benjamin, Glenn Greenwald, Jeremy Scahill, Patrick Buchanan, John Mueller, Jesselyn Radack, or anyone remotely like them—were notably absent. And who provides the funding for these gatherings? Not surprisingly, financial support comes from, among others, NATO, Raytheon, Northrup Grumman, Goldman Sachs, and the German Marshall Fund, all organizations strongly committed to preserving U.S. global leadership.

Educating American citizens about world affairs is a worthy activity, and WACA, its local affiliates in major metropolitan areas, and the FPA do not take formal positions on specific foreign policy issues. Nonetheless, in both design and in practice, these organizations exist to encourage a more active U.S. role in international affairs and to combat any tendency to reduce the level of U.S. engagement or alter the basic outlines of U.S. policy.

The bias in favor of liberal hegemony is even more pronounced in the largest mainstream think tanks and research organizations such as the Brookings Institution, the Carnegie Endowment for International Peace, the American Enterprise Institute, and the Heritage Foundation. These organizations do not have a strict "party line" on many issues, and the people who work at them do not always agree on specific policy problems or foreign policy priorities. Nonetheless, several of these organizations were originally created to convince Americans to play a more active role in world affairs, and all of them lean strongly in the direction of greater U.S. engagement.

Since its founding in 1922, for example, the Council on Foreign Relations—which is both a membership organization with nearly five thousand full-time members and an independent think tank with a staff of roughly eighty full-time professionals—has been committed to promoting an activist foreign policy. As former CFR president Leslie Gelb proudly wrote in 1995, "If the Council as a body has stood for anything these 75 years, it has been for American internationalism based on American interests." Its flagship journal, Foreign Affairs, routinely publishes articles prescribing what the United States should do to address contemporary international problems, and it only occasionally offers works challenging the orthodox view of America's global role. Its annual meeting in New York features speeches and presentations by council fellows and a bevy of mainstream foreign policy figures, with nary a dissenting voice in the mix.

Similarly, the Carnegie Endowment for International Peace long ago abandoned its original mission of promoting global peace and now describes its role as "advancing cooperation between nations and promoting active international engagement by the United States."[49] The more hawkish American Enterprise Institute goes even further, consistently defending larger defense budgets and issuing reports explicitly aimed at countering alleged isolationist tendencies.[50]

One sees much the same pattern at the Atlantic Council, the Center for a New American Security (CNAS), the Center for Strategic and Budgetary Assessments (CSBA), the Center for Strategic and International Studies (CSIS), the Center for American Progress (CAP), and the New

America Foundation. The Atlantic Council's mission statement says that it "promotes constructive leadership and engagement in international affairs based on the Atlantic Community's central role in meeting global challenges," and its leadership and staff are drawn from a bipartisan array of experienced foreign policy insiders. Concerned that the United States might be turning inward, in 2015 the council launched a new "Strategy Initiative" intended to "reinvigorate U.S. and trans-Atlantic leadership in the world." In short, like most inside-the-Beltway think tanks, the Atlantic Council remains firmly committed to liberal hegemony and U.S. global leadership.

The same is true of CNAS. Its cofounders—former assistant secretary of state Kurt Campbell and former deputy secretary of defense Michèle Flournoy—created the organization to give the Democratic Party a more muscular, pro-military voice on foreign and defense policy and to counter perceptions that Democrats were "soft" on national security. Partly funded by defense contractors such as Lockheed Martin and led by once-and-future DOD officials and former military officers, CNAS is strongly committed to promoting U.S. engagement abroad. In 2014, for example, Flournoy and CNAS president Richard Fontaine publicly criticized what they called "the siren song of disengagement," warning "if the United States is seen as abandoning its role as the primary supporter of international order, other powers—or the forces of chaos—will fill the gap."[51] And as we shall see, in 2016 CNAS became even more outspoken in opposing any significant adjustment in America's global role.

The other predominantly Democratic think tank, the Center for American Progress, generally takes a more moderate line than CNAS does, but its positions on most foreign policy questions nonetheless reflect the same commitment to liberal hegemony.[52] In 2014, for example, the CAP senior fellow Brian Katulis published a full-throated defense of U.S. global engagement that accused progressives of "muddled thinking" and opposed any meaningful reduction in U.S. military power or America's global role.[53]

Yet another Democratic Party institution, the Progressive Policy Institute, purveys an even more hawkish line on most foreign policy issues. Its president, Will Marshall, was an outspoken advocate for war in Iraq and Libya, openly advocates what he calls "muscular liberalism" and U.S. military dominance, and has written that "advancing democracy—in practice, not just in rhetoric—is fundamentally the Democrats' legacy, the Democrats' cause, and the Democrats' responsibility."[54] Marshall redoubled his efforts in 2017, launching a new think tank and political action committee (New Democracy) intended to counter left-wing tendencies in the Democratic Party and warning of the need to "close the security confidence gap" and affirm "the animating principle of liberal internationalism."[55]

The evolution of the New America Foundation (NAF) is in some ways the most revealing tale of all. Founded in 1999, NAF was originally intended to be an incubator for unconventional ideas on foreign, domestic, and economic policy. Consistent with that mission, it hosted a realist-oriented American Strategy Program headed by Steve Clemons. That program included an innovative project on Middle East policy run by a former Israeli peace negotiator, Daniel Levy, and its ranks eventually included South Asia and Middle East expert Anatol Lieven and the husband-and-wife team of Flynt and Hillary Leverett, two former government officials with decidedly independent views on U.S. Middle East policy. NAF was also home to iconoclastic public intellectuals such as Michael Lind, a prominent Reagan-era conservative who had become increasingly skeptical of U.S. interventionism. In its initial incarnation, therefore, NAF was a notable outlier in the Washington think tank world.

Over time, however, NAF moved steadily toward the inside-the-Beltway mainstream. Its second president, the journalist Steve Coll, was a consistent advocate for U.S. global engagement and a vocal proponent of nation-building efforts in Afghanistan and Iraq. Coll's successor, Anne-Marie Slaughter (former dean of Princeton's Woodrow Wilson School and former director of policy planning at the State Department),

is a staunch liberal internationalist who openly supported U.S. interventions in Iraq, Libya, and, most recently, Syria. By 2015, what had
begun life as an outside-the-box research and advocacy organization—
in particular, one that openly questioned Washington's interventionist
proclivities—had joined the chorus of mainstream foreign policy think
tanks.

Apart from a handful of left-wing or antiwar organizations—such
as the Institute for Policy Studies, the Center for International Policy, and
the American Friends Service Committee—the only major inside-the-
Beltway think tank that consistently challenges the dogma of liberal
hegemony is the Cato Institute, whose libertarian, small-government philosophy inclines it to a skeptical attitude toward America's overactive
foreign policy agenda. But the ranks of once-and-future officials and ambitious policy wonks clamoring to sell assorted internationalist missions
are larger, much more generously funded, and significantly louder than
this modest set of dissenting voices, and they can usually drown out the
latter without much difficulty.

The result, notes Vox.com's Zack Beauchamp, "is that Washington's foreign policy debate tends to be mostly conducted between the
center and the right. The issue is typically how much force America
should use rather than whether it should use it at all, or how to tweak a
free-trade agreement rather than whether it should be accepted at all.
Debates over pressing policy issues . . . lack a left-wing voice of any
prominence."[56]

Many of the special interest groups and lobbies active on foreign
policy issues help reinforce America's expansive global role because
their chief purpose is to persuade the public and the U.S. government to
take action to support their particular pet projects. Human rights advocates want the United States to do more to protect the victims of abuse
by foreign governments, which explains why some prominent "liberal
hawks" supported military action against Saddam Hussein in 2003,
Muammar Gaddafi in 2011, and Bashar al-Assad in 2014.[57] Ethnic lobbies
want Washington to do more to support Israel, India, Armenia, Poland,

or whomever; and exiles from countries like Cuba or Iran want Washington to do more to weaken the foreign regimes from which they fled.[58] Arms control organizations want U.S. officials to use the power at their disposal to prevent the spread of WMD or to make existing nuclear arsenals more secure. Corporations want government officials to help them gain greater access to foreign markets, and defense contractors want the Defense Department (and U.S. allies) to buy more weapons.[59] Some of these objectives might be desirable, at least some of the time, but if each of these different groups gets even a fraction of what it wants, the United States will be very busy indeed.

The activist bias is equally evident in the most influential parts of the establishment press. Although editorial boards and columnists of elite newspapers such as *The New York Times*, *The Wall Street Journal*, and *The Washington Post* are sometimes critical of specific foreign policy initiatives, liberal hegemony remains the default setting, and they rarely present their readers with alternative perspectives. The days where a noninterventionist like Robert McCormick, the late publisher of the once-isolationist *Chicago Tribune*, could occupy a prominent place in media circles are long gone. A more typical view today is *The New York Times'* Thomas L. Friedman, who was a prominent supporter of the invasion of Iraq and remains a consistent cheerleader for U.S. global activism.[60] But even Friedman was outdone by *Politico*'s Michael Hirsh, who once wrote that "for all its fumbling, the role played by the United States is the greatest gift the world has received in many, many centuries, possibly all of recorded history."[61]

Yet Hirsh is not really an outlier. In addition to Friedman, for example, *The New York Times'* lineup of foreign affairs columnists also includes David Brooks, Bret Stephens, Nicholas Kristof, and (less frequently) Roger Cohen. Each of these commentators would use U.S. power for somewhat different purposes, but all are dedicated internationalists who believe the United States should pursue a wide array of goals in distant lands. Brooks is a neoconservative who wrote for the *National Review*, *The Wall Street Journal*, and *The Weekly Standard* before coming to the *Times*; he was also an ardent proponent of the invasion of Iraq, and he continues to favor a muscular approach to U.S. foreign policy. In 2014, for example, he complained that President Barack Obama's handling of foreign affairs suffered from a "manhood" problem, and he warned of a "spiritual recession" that might discourage Americans from pursuing idealistic missions abroad. "If America isn't a champion of universal democracy," he fretted, "what is the country for?" Stephens has a similar profile to Brooks; he is an unapologetic neoconservative, a former columnist for *The Wall Street Journal*, and the author of *America in Retreat*, a polemical attack that accused the Obama administration of "isolationism."[62] Cohen and Kristof focus more on human rights issues and are less inclined to favor military solutions than Friedman, Brooks, or Stephens, yet each is a strong proponent of using American power to right wrongs in faraway places, even when U.S. vital interests are not engaged.[63]

The editorial stances of *The Washington Post* and *The Wall Street Journal* are even more consistently interventionist than that of the *Times*. Since the end of the Cold War, for instance, the *Post*'s op-ed page has been given over to regular columnists such as Charles Krauthammer, Robert Kagan, Richard Cohen, David Ignatius, former Bush administration speechwriter Michael Gerson, George Will, Jim Hoagland, the late Michael Kelly, Max Boot, and William Kristol (longtime editor of the right-wing *Weekly Standard* and briefly a columnist for *The New York Times* as well). Each of these pundits supported an interventionist foreign policy, though Will became increasingly skeptical of military intervention as the failures continued to mount.[64] Guest commentators skeptical of liberal hegemony or in favor of a more restrained U.S. role appear occasionally in the *Post*, but they have never been part of its regular stable of writers. Needless to say, the editorial page editor Fred Hiatt is an enthusiastic proponent of liberal hegemony as well.

Such views deserve a place in America's elite press; the problem is that alternative views are largely absent. In particular, none of these newspapers features any regular columnist representing a libertarian view of America's global role, or even one that might be characterized as consistently "realist" in orientation. The latter omission is especially striking insofar as realism is a venerable tradition in the academic study of foreign policy, and realists such as Henry Kissinger, George Kennan, Brent Scowcroft, Richard Nixon, and Colin Powell were prominent and influential figures in the past. Yet one would be hard-pressed to find someone regularly espousing a similar worldview in any major media outlet today.

In fact, rather than broaden the range of views they present on foreign policy, the *Times*, the *Post*, and the *Journal* have been doubling down on mainstream hawkish pundits instead. The *Times* hired the hardliner Bret Stephens away from the *Journal* in 2017, and in 2018, the *Post* added the neoconservative writer Max Boot and the *Journal* selected the right-wing historian Walter Russell Mead. All three men are ardent defenders of liberal hegemony (and each was an enthusiastic proponent of the Iraq War); more to the point, their hiring merely duplicated perspectives that were already well represented at all three publications.

What about right-wing media outlets such as Fox News, Breitbart, and the Drudge Report? Although these outlets were consistently critical of Clinton's and Obama's handling of foreign policy, they did not call for significant reductions in America's global role. Moreover, these outlets feed viewers an alarming diet of stories about the growing threat from Islam, terrorism, a rising China, immigrants, etc., along with any number of other global dangers. Far-right media outlets are skeptical of the global institutions favored by liberal internationalists (if not actively hostile to them), but they are strongly supportive of U.S. military primacy and do not believe the United States should decrease its global role significantly.

America's media landscape is not a monolith, of course, and mainstream media figures such as Dana Priest, Rajiv Chandrasekaran, Jane Mayer, Matt Lee, and James Risen have produced important critical accounts of key aspects of U.S. foreign policy. Outside the mainstream, people such as the late *Rolling Stone* reporter Michael Hastings, Glenn

Greenwald of *The Intercept*, Tom Engelhardt of Truthdig, and the left-wing broadcaster Amy Goodman of *Democracy Now* have offered well-informed critiques of America's imperial tendencies. The Public Broadcasting Service documentary series *Frontline* has produced a number of hard-hitting programs questioning key elements of recent U.S. foreign policy, and satirists such as Jon Stewart, Trevor Noah, John Oliver, Samantha Bee, and Stephen Colbert have been sharp-eyed and witty critics of some of America's foreign policy follies. The work of these individuals reminds us that media coverage of foreign affairs is not one-dimensional and that alternative views are available if one knows where to look. But on the whole, the commanding heights of U.S. media are still dominated by individuals who favor an active U.S. foreign policy—however much they disagree over specific priorities or programs—and that view shapes what they tell readers, viewers, and listeners about world politics in general and U.S. foreign policy in particular.

Last but not least, the academic institutions most relevant to issues of foreign policy exhibit many of the same traits as the rest of the foreign policy community. This tendency is especially evident at schools of public policy and international affairs, whose raison d'être emphasizes identifying global problems and proposing solutions for them. And despite academia's reputation as a bastion of dovish, left-wing thought, most of these institutions do not question the strategy of liberal hegemony.

This situation is to be expected. The leadership and faculty at most of these institutions tend to be leading figures in the foreign policy community, and they are inclined to favor maintaining U.S. leadership. Past deans of Harvard's John F. Kennedy School of Government include Joseph S. Nye, Albert Carnesale, and Graham T. Allison, who all held senior foreign policy positions in the U.S. government or important advisory posts. The current dean of the Fletcher School of Law and Diplomacy at Tufts University is former NATO supreme allied commander James Stavridis, and his predecessor was Ambassador Stephen Bosworth, a career diplomat who served as Obama's special envoy to North

Korea. Former deputy secretary of state James Steinberg was dean of the Lyndon Baines Johnson School of Public Affairs at the University of Texas and now heads the Maxwell School of Citizenship and Public Affairs at Syracuse. The arms control expert and former State Department official Michael Nacht ran the School of Public Policy at the University of Maryland and the Goldman School of Public Policy at UC-Berkeley, and Anne-Marie Slaughter was dean of Princeton's Woodrow Wilson School prior to her appointment as director of policy planning and her subsequent hiring by the New America Foundation. The list goes on: the career State Department official Robert Gallucci was dean of Georgetown's School of Foreign Service before assuming the presidency of the MacArthur Foundation, and former Clinton-era NSC staffer James Goldgeier was until recently dean of American University's School of International Service.

There is nothing conspiratorial about the tendency of these institutions to favor liberal hegemony and active U.S. leadership. After all, students enroll in schools of public policy and international affairs because they care about the real world and want to make it better. Faculty members at these institutions write books and articles and serve in government for similar reasons: they want to make the United States more secure or more prosperous or to benefit humankind more broadly. It would be odd, therefore, if most scholars working on international topics—especially those working in professional schools—opposed an active U.S. role on the world stage or were consistently skeptical about the wisdom of using American power to advance supposedly worthy ends.

This commitment to improving the world is admirable, but self-interest and ambition play important roles as well. The more foreign policy problems that the United States tries to solve, the greater the demand for trained experts to work on them and the greater the need for schools in which they can receive this training. Identifying new and urgent problems facilitates fundraising from foundations and alumni and creates more opportunities for ambitious faculty members to go to Washington to address their pet issue. Support for liberal hegemony also minimizes cognitive dissonance: if you've invested years of your life defending the necessity for U.S. global leadership, thinking about its shortcomings, costs, or failures might be uncomfortable if not actively painful. To a large extent, therefore, the most important academic institutions concerned with the real world of foreign policymaking will be strongly inclined to support the strategy of liberal hegemony.

The existence of an "activist bias" within the broad foreign policy community does not mean that this approach is necessarily wrong or imply that the policies that this community develops, promotes, and implements are always misguided. Similarly, to point out that people within the broad foreign policy community have an interest in lots of U.S. involvement overseas is not to suggest that they embrace liberal hegemony solely for selfish, greedy, or vainglorious reasons.

Rather, it is simply to observe that there is a broad and strong consensus uniting most people who work on a regular basis on issues of international affairs and foreign policy. Until the Trump experiment, this consensus was shared by the two main political parties, most government officials, and the bulk of the policy analysts, journalists, editors, and academics who work on these issues. Despite repeated failures over the past two decades, liberal hegemony was largely unchallenged within the foreign policy community.

LIBERAL HEGEMONY UNDAUNTED: A TALE OF THREE TASK FORCES

To see this phenomenon more clearly, let us examine three prominent efforts to identify what U.S. grand strategy should be in the twenty-first century. The first attempt was conducted in the aftermath of September 11 but before the 2008 financial crisis; the second was written after the crisis hit, and when it was also clear that the Iraq and Afghan wars were going badly; and the third emerged near the end of the Obama administration and after the Ukraine crisis and the emergence of ISIS. All three reports were bipartisan efforts, and each offered remarkably ambitious and strikingly similar blueprints for America's role in the world.

THE PRINCETON PROJECT ON NATIONAL SECURITY:
FORGING A WORLD OF LIBERTY UNDER LAW (2006)

Between 2003 and 2006 the Woodrow Wilson School of Public and International Affairs at Princeton University sponsored an ambitious bipartisan initiative, known as the Princeton Project on National Security, with the goal of developing "a sustainable and effective national security strategy for the United States." The project was directed by Anne-Marie Slaughter and G. John Ikenberry, and the honorary cochairs were former secretary of state George Shultz and former national security advisor Anthony Lake. Funded by grants from the Ford Foundation and the philanthropist David Rubenstein of the Carlyle Group, the project brought nearly four hundred participants from the foreign policy community together in an extended series of conferences, workshops, round tables, and working groups. Its stated purpose was "to write a collective 'X article,' to do together what no one person in our highly specialized and rapidly changing world could hope to do alone."[65]

Completed in 2006, the result was a dense, sixty-page report entitled *Forging a World of Liberty Under Law: U.S. National Security in the 21st Century* (hereafter *FWLL*). It is a textbook expression of the strategy of liberal hegemony that has united neoconservatives and liberals since the end of the Cold War.

FWLL's first sentence begins with a stern warning: "On the fifth anniversary of September 11, the world seems a more menacing place than ever." The United States "feels increasingly alone," and faces "many present dangers." A far-reaching and ambitious response is needed: U.S. national security strategy "must address all the dangers we face—diffuse, shifting and uncertain as they are—and seize all the opportunities open to us to make ourselves and the world more secure." In short, like most national security documents, the report begins by portraying a world brimming with numerous threats, all of them requiring a U.S. response.

The report then prescribes a breathtaking set of national security imperatives based on the overarching belief that "America must stand for, seek and secure a world of liberty under law." In short, the ultimate aim of U.S. foreign policy is not to protect the well-being of the American people, but rather to ensure that every citizen on the entire planet lives in a stable and well-governed liberal democracy. To do this, the United States cannot simply be a status quo power; it "must develop a more sophisticated strategy of recognizing and promoting the deeper preconditions for successful liberal democracy." In particular, U.S. power must be used to create "Popular, Accountable, and Rights-regarding (PAR) governments" around the world, a process it describes (without irony) as "bringing the world up to PAR."

But that's not all. Washington must also "make UN reform a top priority, as part of a broader effort to rebuild a liberal international order." The report recommends creating a "Concert of Democracies," calls for "reviving the NATO alliance," and says that Washington must lead "efforts to reform the main international financial and trade institutions." High levels of defense spending are necessary to preserve "a balance of power in favor of liberal democracies," and the United States must simultaneously maintain a strong U.S. nuclear deterrent while working to "revitalize the Non-Proliferation regime." The latter goal will require "a range of counter-proliferation measures," including (as a last resort) "preventive military action." America's "primary task" regarding a rising China is to convince Beijing that it can "achieve its legitimate ambitions within the current international order," though it is left to Washington to decide whether Beijing's ambitions are "legitimate" or not.

Wait, there's more! The United States must also "make critical investments in our public health system," "establish an East Asia security institution that brings together the major powers," "invest more in public education," and "do everything possible to achieve a peace settlement" between Israel and the Palestinians. Nor can Americans shy away from interfering in other countries' political systems: on the contrary, "U.S. strategy must include the creation of institutions and mechanisms whereby the international community can . . . encourage sound practices within states without using force or illegitimate modes of coercion."

This list is but a sample of the report's recommendations; and admonitions to "rectify our irresponsible fiscal policies" and reallocate "enough public resources to provide sufficient economic security for American workers" are thrown in for good measure. By the time one is finished reading, it is hard to think of any international issue the authors do not regard as a vital concern for the United States, even though no president could attempt—let alone achieve—more than a handful of these initiatives.

The Princeton Project's overweening ambition was partly the result of its inclusive design: if you ask four hundred experts to devise a grand strategy, everyone's pet project will have to be mentioned and a lot of logrolling is inevitable. Yet *FWLL* is hardly an outlier insofar as it mirrors other important statements of post–Cold War grand strategy, including the Clinton administration's *National Security Strategy of Engagement and Enlargement* (1995) and the Bush administration's post-9/11 *National Security Strategy* (2002). Like these earlier documents, *FWLL* depicts a hostile world where diverse dangers lurk, sees U.S. power as a consistent force for good, and believes the United States must remake the world in its image without compromising the very principles it is trying to promote. The report ends with Henry Kissinger observing that the "ultimate test of U.S. foreign policy" lies in protecting "the extraordinary opportunity that has come about to recast the international system." If that lofty goal is indeed the "ultimate test" of U.S. foreign policy, then the United States has an awful lot to do.

"THE PROJECT FOR A UNITED AND STRONG AMERICA" (2013)

Roughly ten years after the Princeton Project began its deliberations, a second bipartisan task force presented a new set of recommendations for U.S. grand strategy. Cochaired by James Goldgeier of American University's School of International Service, a Democrat, and Kurt Volker of Arizona State University's McCain Institute, a Republican, the bipartisan Project for a United and Strong America had a similar objective: to examine the role "the United States should play in the world."

Plus ça change, plus c'est la même chose. Though written in the wake of the 2008 financial crisis and after the Bush Doctrine had crashed and burned in Iraq and Afghanistan, the project's final report is every bit as ambitious as the earlier Princeton version. Indeed, its central message is that setbacks abroad and financial pressures at home are no reason to scale back U.S. global involvement. Convinced that "any short-term savings would come at significant long-term cost," the report calls for the United States to "remain true to the principles of advancing democratic values and exercising strong American global leadership."

The authors make their case through the usual rhetorical devices and arguments. The United States is portrayed as an exceptional nation with "the unique ability to lead but an imperative to do so—for the protection of its own national interests and values." The United States "remains in an extraordinarily strong position globally" (which makes an ambitious foreign policy possible), yet "the challenges confronting U.S. interests and values remain substantial and complex." These challenges range "from a full spectrum of security threats" to economic, environmental, ideological, political, and humanitarian challenges. Moreover, the Internet and globalization have "ushered in an unprecedented empowerment of individuals and small actors" and created "unprecedented risk." The United States may be a global superpower with no peer competitors, but it still faces a troubled and dangerous world.

The solution, as always, is American "leadership," with the ultimate aim of spreading democracy. The United States "must play an active, day-to-day role in shaping events" and "work to advance a liberal, democratic world order" through "tangible and sustained actions" (including the use of military force).

To be sure, the report acknowledges that fiscal pressures may require the United States to "absorb some reductions in defense spending." But not to any significant degree, for it also calls for the United States to maintain "the capacity to deter any potential military rival and defeat any potential adversary." In addition, the United States must protect the global commons, curb nuclear proliferation, conduct counterterrorism operations around the globe, and "anchor regional stability" in several distant areas. Washington should act with allies when it can but still preserve "the capacity to conduct successful operations on its own, anywhere in the world."

Why? Simple: because vital interests are everywhere. "Europe remains crucial to our common efforts to manage global challenges," the report opines, and "the United States must also . . . give priority to alliance relationships in the Asia-Pacific region" while "[s]imilar efforts are needed with our security partnerships in the Middle East." But that's not all: the United States should upgrade its partnerships with Brazil, Indonesia, and Turkey, keep Iran from achieving a nuclear capability, prevent reversals in Afghan stability, rebuild cooperative ties with Pakistan, counter Al Qaeda (everywhere), and end the civil war in Syria (among other things). By the time one finishes reading, there isn't a square inch on the planet left to itself.

Mindful of economic constraints, the report also recommends prompt action to reduce the national debt, strengthen economic competitiveness, and maintain a level playing field in global markets. Revealingly, the justification for these actions is not the well-being or comfort of the American people; instead, the report places "a priority on strength at home *in order to underpin a strong U.S. role in the world*" (my emphasis). A strong economy is desirable not because it would allow Americans to lead more bountiful or fulfilling lives; it is necessary so that the United States can swing a big stick around the world.

EXTENDING AMERICAN POWER: STRATEGIES TO
EXPAND U.S. ENGAGEMENT IN A COMPETITIVE
WORLD ORDER (2016)

A final example of a blue-ribbon defense of liberal hegemony is the Center for New American Security's *Extending American Power*, released in

May 2016. Like the reports already discussed, it views the United States as the "indispensable" linchpin of the present world order, warns that any alteration of America's role in the world would have catastrophic consequences, and offers up a lengthy to-do list of projects Washington must undertake around the globe.

Given the composition of the task force, these conclusions are precisely what one would expect. The cochairs were former Clinton-era State Department official James Rubin and the ubiquitous neoconservative pundit Robert Kagan. Participants included experienced foreign policy VIPs: Michèle Flournoy, Robert Zoellick, Kurt Campbell, Stephen Hadley, James Steinberg, and Eric Edelman, and the witnesses invited to testify at the group's working sessions were equally familiar faces, including Stephen Sestanovich, Elliott Abrams, Dennis Ross, Victoria Nuland, and Martin Indyk. The only mildly contrarian witnesses were Ian Bremmer of the Eurasia Group and Vali Nasr of the School of Advanced International Studies at Johns Hopkins, but neither occupies a position outside the foreign policy mainstream.

The result—surprise!—is another well-worn defense of liberal hegemony. The report begins by lauding the "immense benefits" the current world order has produced and declares that "to preserve and strengthen this order will require a renewal of American leadership in the international system." Yet it never tells the reader exactly what that "order" is or acknowledges that recent U.S. efforts to "extend" it have produced costly quagmires and deteriorating relations with other major powers instead. Nor does it ask if there are elements in the existing order that should be rethought. Instead, the report simply posits that a liberal world order exists and that it cannot survive without the widespread application of American power.

To maintain America's "leadership role," the report calls for significant increases in national security spending and recommends that the United States expand its military activities in three major areas: Europe, the Middle East, and Asia. It leaves open the possibility that the United States might have to do more in other places too, so its real agenda may be even more ambitious.

In Europe, Washington must "stabilize Ukraine and anchor it in Europe," "establish a more robust US presence in Central and Eastern European countries," and "restore capacity for European strategic leadership." The latter goal is not something the United States can do alone, however, and the contradiction here is hard to miss. Why should one expect Europe to develop a renewed capacity for "strategic leadership" if the United States reserves that role for itself and Europe's leaders can still count on Uncle Sam to ride to the rescue?

In Asia, the United States should continue the Obama administration's "pivot" and implement the Trans-Pacific Partnership, and it may have to "impose regional costs" on China for its actions in the South China Sea and inflict "commensurate economic penalties to slow Chinese dominance." At the same time, Washington should "facilitate China's continued integration so as to blunt its historical fears of 'containment.'" In other words, the United States should make a sustained effort to contain China—and maybe even work to retard its rise—but Beijing won't mind if Washington does so politely.

In the Middle East, the task force wants to "scale up" the effort against ISIS, with the United States taking the leading role. It also calls for a no-fly zone in Syria and says that Washington "must adopt as a matter of policy, the goal of defeating Iran's determined effort to dominate the Middle East." The report does not explain how Persian Iran will manage to "dominate" the Arab Middle East with a defense budget that is less than 5 percent of America's and in the face of potential opposition from more heavily armed states such as Israel, Egypt, Saudi Arabia, Turkey, and several others.[66]

In short, the CNAS report recommends that the United States maintain every one of its current international commitments, double down on policies that have repeatedly failed, and take on expensive, risky, and uncertain projects in several regions at once. Although some of its individual recommendations may make sense, the overall package is the same boundless vision of U.S. "leadership" that has guided U.S. foreign policy since the Soviet Union broke apart.

And like the two earlier reports discussed above, *Extending American*

Power is silent regarding America's geographic position, resource endowments, demographic characteristics, underlying economic interests, or core strategic requirements. It does not try to rank vital interests, assess potential threats to those interests, or consider different ways these dangers might be reduced. Like its predecessors, the CNAS report simply declares that the U.S. has vital interests everywhere, says that a liberal world order will preserve them, and maintains that preserving this order requires deploying and using American power in every corner of the world.

My point is not that these three studies (and others like them) provided specific blueprints for action that had a direct and immediate impact on the foreign policy of particular administrations. Rather, such reports are simply a revealing window into the mind-set of the U.S. foreign policy community. Indeed, they tell us more about the way this community thinks than they do about the actual strategic challenges the United States faces.[67] Such documents define the range of "acceptable" opinion within the community and thereby serve to set limits on the policy options that can be proposed without jeopardizing one's professional reputation. By ruling out alternatives from the beginning, such exercises help keep U.S. grand strategy within the same narrow and familiar contours.

What is perhaps most striking about these three exercises in mainstream grand strategizing is how insensitive they are to the actual state of the world. It doesn't matter where the United States is located, what its internal condition is, where principal dangers might lie, how the balance of power in regions might be changing, or whether the main challenge the United States faces is a large and well-armed peer competitor like the former Soviet Union, a rising revisionist power like China, a complex multipolar world of contending regional powers, or a shadowy terrorist network like Al Qaeda. No matter what the question is, the answer is always the same: the United States must take the lead in solving every global issue, and it must keep interfering in other countries in order to keep the liberal world order alive.

MIND THE GAP: ELITES VERSUS THE PUBLIC

The American people, however, have a different view. Members of the foreign policy community may share similar policy preferences, but in the words of the political scientists Lawrence R. Jacobs and Benjamin I. Page, "the general public stands somewhat to the side."[68] The foreign policy community has been firmly wedded to liberal hegemony, but the American people have a more sensible and realistic view of what is desirable and feasible.

According to Page and another coauthor, Jason Barabas, "the most conspicuous gap between citizens and leaders is a familiar and long-standing one: more leaders than citizens tend to be 'internationalists,' at least in the simple sense that they say they favor the United States taking an 'active part' in world affairs."[69] More recently, Page and Marshall Bouton of the Chicago Council on Global Affairs have documented a persistent "disconnect" between elite and mass attitudes on foreign affairs, one they believe presents "serious problems for democratic values." In their words, "official U.S. foreign policy often differs markedly from the policies most Americans want" (i.e., a less costly, ambitious, and burdensome foreign policy).[70]

Needless to say, this is precisely the sentiment Donald Trump tapped into in 2016. On the one hand, most Americans reject out-and-out isolationism, with more than 60 percent saying that the United States should "take an active part in world affairs" (as opposed to "staying out"). On the other hand, most do not believe that the United States should be the only "global leader," and they remain wary of unilateral U.S. action. This percentage, it is worth noting, has been more or less constant since the late 1970s.[71] In 2016, for example, fewer than 10 percent thought the United States should be the "preeminent world leader in solving international problems," and only 37 percent thought it "should be the most active of leading nations."[72]

U.S. citizens also believe that the United States is bearing too large a share of global burdens, and they are far more skeptical about an "activist" foreign policy than most members of the foreign policy community appear to be. In 2002, for example, immediately following the 9/11 attacks, public support for U.S. military action and general interest in world affairs rose significantly. Yet even then, 62 percent of Americans believed that the United States did not have the responsibility to play the role of "world policeman," and 65 percent felt that Washington was playing that role "more than it should."[73] In 2006, 57 percent of Americans said that the United States was "doing more than its share" to help others in the world.[74] By 2013, more than 52 percent of Americans surveyed agreed with the statement "the US should mind its own business internationally and let other countries get along the best they can on their own"—the highest percentage ever recorded since the question was first asked in the 1960s. In 1964, 54 percent of Americans believed that "we should not think so much in international terms but concentrate on our own national problems and building up strength here at home"; by 2013, the number endorsing that sentiment had risen to 80 percent.[75] And in 2016, 64 percent felt that "the United States is playing the role of world policeman more than it should be."[76]

The gap between elites and the public is equally evident when specific scenarios are invoked. In 2009, for example, 50 percent of Council on Foreign Relations members supported Obama's Afghan "surge" and said that U.S. troop levels in Afghanistan should be increased, but only 32 percent of the general public agreed. Eighty-seven percent of CFR members thought the initial U.S. decision to use force there was correct, but only 56 percent of the public shared that view. (Ironically, CFR members also had a gloomier view of the U.S. military effort, with 90 percent believing the war was not going well, as compared with 57 percent of the general public.)[77] A similar gap between elites and the public was apparent in 2013: 51 percent of the public believed the United States "did too much" in world affairs, and 17 percent thought it did "too little," but only 21 percent of CFR members thought the country was doing too much and 41 percent maintained that it was doing "too little."[78]

This same pattern recurred as the Obama administration debated military action in response to the Assad regime's use of chemical weapons in the Syrian civil war. According to a *New York Times* poll, although 75 percent of Americans believed the Assad regime had used chemical weapons and 52 percent saw this act as a potential threat to the United States, majorities in excess of 80 percent said they were either "very" or "somewhat" concerned that U.S. intervention would cause civilian casualties, be long and costly, and "lead to a more widespread war." And contrary to the foreign policy community's reflexive commitment to spreading U.S. values, when ordinary citizens are asked whether the United States "should try to change a dictatorship to a democracy where it can" or "stay out of other countries' affairs," 72 percent choose "stay out" and only 15 percent say "change where it can."[79] A CNN poll yielded similar results, with 69 percent of respondents saying it was not in the U.S. national interest to get involved in the Syrian conflict.[80]

Public support for global activism continued to decline in subsequent years. A *Wall Street Journal*/NBC News poll in April 2014 found that only 19 percent of those asked wanted the United States to be "more active" in world affairs (down from 37 percent in 2001), while the percentage favoring a "less active" role increased from 14 in 2001 to 47.[81] As the 2016 election campaign intensified in the spring of 2016, the Pew Research Center reported that 57 percent of Americans believed that the United States should "deal with its own problems and let other countries deal with theirs the best they can," while only 37 percent felt that the United States "should help other countries deal with their problems." Forty-one percent now felt that the country was doing "too much" in world affairs; only 27 percent thought it was doing "too little."[82] In 2007, public opinion was evenly split (39 percent to 40 percent) over whether the president should focus more on domestic or foreign policy; by 2013, 83 percent said the former and only 6 percent (!) chose the latter.[83]

Public opinion can be fickle, and it often responds to vivid events or to the cues provided by elites. For example, support for military action against ISIS soared after the extremist group beheaded two American journalists in the summer of 2014, only to fall to earth again a few months later.[84] Furthermore, when elites are strongly united behind some foreign policy action, public opinion tends to follow along.[85] As the next chapter will show, Americans have tolerated an overly ambitious foreign policy in part because the foreign policy establishment keeps telling them it is necessary, feasible, and affordable.

Nonetheless, there is a persistent and significant gap between the foreign policy community's enthusiasm for liberal hegemony—with the costs and risks it entails—and the views of the American people at large. The latter do not want to retreat to Fortress America, shut down the Department of State, or sever all foreign alliances, but the broader public is far less supportive of the ambitious crusades that the foreign policy establishment has conducted since the end of the Cold War and far more concerned with conditions back home.

The obvious question, therefore, is how has the foreign policy elite overcome the public's reluctance to take on costly overseas commitments—a reluctance borne of the remarkable security that the United States already enjoys? I tackle that question directly in the next chapter.

4. SELLING A FAILING FOREIGN POLICY

WHEN A STATE is as secure as the United States, convincing its citizens to seize the mantle of global leadership will not be easy. Indeed, a long tradition of American thinking about foreign affairs emphasizes the need to preserve the nation's exceptional qualities—such as its deep commitment to liberty—by remaining aloof from the intrigues, rivalries, and cruelties associated with power politics. In his Farewell Address in 1796, for example, George Washington warned his fellow citizens not to become entangled in the affairs of other nations, arguing that America's "detached and distant situation invites and enables us to pursue a different course."[1] Or as Charles Ames, a prominent anti-imperialist figure, warned in 1898, "Once we enter the field of international conflict as a great military and naval power, we shall be one more bully among bullies."[2] Aware of this tradition, Bill Clinton told the White House press secretary George Stephanopoulos early in his presidency, "Americans are basically isolationist."[3] Given the country's providential geopolitical position and fortunate history, convincing Americans to pursue liberal hegemony should be a tough sell.

To make that sale, its advocates have to convince the public that liberal hegemony is necessary, affordable, and morally desirable. Proponents need not convince everyone to embrace these policies, however; a core of elite support is sufficient provided the rest of the population goes along. If the costs are not too great and advocates can point to some degree of success, the forces favoring liberal hegemony will face little opposition.

But "the more demanding the policy is, in terms of its call on American resources or lives," warns the historian John A. Thompson, "the broader and deeper such support must be."[4] Accordingly, the foreign policy community uses a number of arguments to convince the public to support (or at least tolerate) its efforts to shape world politics in accordance with U.S. designs.

First, advocates of activism *inflate threats* to convince Americans that the world is a dangerous place and that their security depends on active U.S. engagement. Second, supporters *exaggerate the benefits* of liberal hegemony, arguing that it is the best way to defuse potential dangers, enhance prosperity, and spread cherished political values. Lastly, government officials try to *conceal the costs* of their ambitious foreign policy in order to persuade Americans that it is a bargain even when successes are few and far between.

RIGGING THE MARKETPLACE OF IDEAS

In fact, selling liberal hegemony is easier than one might think, as debates on foreign and national security policy are not a fair fight among the competing alternatives.

As discussed in chapter 3, access to information and open debate (i.e., the "marketplace of ideas") are supposed to help democracies avoid major policy blunders and minimize the consequences when they do occur.[5] When the subject is foreign policy, however, these mechanisms often break down. Vested interests within the government and the broader foreign policy establishment have significant advantages in shaping what the public knows about international politics and foreign policy, and these advantages tilt the competition among policy alternatives in their favor. In other words, the marketplace of ideas is rigged.

MANIPULATING INFORMATION

For starters, citizens lack direct access to reliable information about most foreign policy issues. If the economy is in free fall and millions of people are losing their jobs, if roads and bridges are crumbling, or if government agencies bungle a disaster relief effort, ordinary citizens can see this for themselves. But few Americans have independent information about Al Qaeda's inner workings, the details of U.S. trade agreements, the history of Iran's nuclear research program, the scope and impact of U.S. drone operations, or whether Russia did in fact hack the Democratic National Committee's computers in 2016. For these and countless other international topics, citizens have to rely on what the government officials or well-connected experts tell them, and the media that reports on these issues depends on these same sources for information as well. As a result, people inside the foreign policy community have considerable latitude to shape what the public thinks about key issues.

Governments can also influence what the public knows by classifying information, so as to keep citizens in the dark about the actions top government officials undertake.[6] To take an obvious example, an extensive and costly Senate investigation into the Central Intelligence Agency's use of torture has yet to be released to the public—even in a highly redacted form—although U.S. taxpayers funded the crimes the committee was investigating and paid millions of dollars for the report.[7]

Top officials can also leak classified information in order to make the case for the policies they prefer. To persuade Americans to back the invasion of Iraq, for example, the Bush administration used a well-orchestrated campaign of leaks and false statements to convince Americans that Saddam Hussein was stockpiling biological and chemical weapons, actively seeking a nuclear bomb, and in cahoots with Osama bin Laden.[8] Vice President Dick Cheney told CNN in March 2002 that Saddam was "actively pursuing nuclear weapons," and in August he announced, "There is no doubt that Saddam Hussein now has weapons of mass destruction." In September 2002 President Bush told reporters, "You can't distinguish between Al Qaeda and Saddam when you talk about the war on terror," and Secretary of Defense Donald Rumsfeld told an interviewer that the alleged links between Saddam Hussein and Al Qaeda were "accurate and not debatable." National Security Advisor Condoleezza Rice told a CNN interviewer, "We don't want the smoking gun to be a mushroom cloud," implying that Iraq might already have nuclear weapons, and President Bush repeated the same warning in October.[9] As John Schuessler observes, "The democratic process may act as a constraint on leaders' ability to go to war, but deception provides a way around that constraint."[10]

Officials with access to classified information can also tie a president's hands by leaking it. As the newly elected president Barack Obama pondered military requests to increase troop levels in Afghanistan during the spring and summer of 2009, military leaders leaked a report by the U.S. commander Stanley McChrystal warning that the war "would likely result in failure" if the request were not approved. This transparent gambit to box in the new president worked, and Obama ordered a "surge" of additional troops later that year.[11]

The desire to control what the public knows also encourages government officials to go after independent whistle-blowers and journalists who publish leaked information. Indeed, government efforts to prosecute leaks increased sharply after 2008, President Obama's pledge to conduct the most "open" government in American history notwithstanding.[12]

The combination of leaking and selective prosecution empowers those with control over information and makes it harder for critics to evaluate the merits of the government's case.[13] According to Benjamin Page and Marshall Bouton, this asymmetry helps explain why government officials are often able to ignore public opinion about foreign policy. In their words, "The executive branch can use its information control to conceal or misrepresent what it is doing abroad. This diminishes the ability of voters to hold officials accountable."[14]

FOCUSED INTERESTS VERSUS THE NATIONAL INTEREST

The marketplace of ideas is distorted further because the focused interests that benefit from liberal hegemony have more influence over public debate than the public does. This phenomenon is well known to students of democracy: if there are key groups with a focused interest in a particular policy while the majority of citizens are either indifferent or distracted, the more focused groups will exert a disproportionate impact on policy, even if they do not get their way every time.[15]

The think tanks and lobbies described in chapter 3 are a perfect illustration of this tendency. These groups work overtime to publicize their work and get their experts onto talk shows, op-ed pages, or other visible venues, and they take up a disproportionate share of the bandwidth in debates on foreign policy. Because the vast majority of foreign policy think tanks and lobbying organizations support liberal hegemony and U.S. "global leadership" (even if they sometimes disagree about the best way to advance that goal), what the public hears about these issues is biased toward an interventionist approach.

To be sure, when competing interest groups are equally powerful, their respective efforts to sway elite and mass opinion can produce the rich and lively debate the "marketplace of ideas" metaphor depicts. The vigorous debate over the 2015 nuclear agreement with Iran is an apt example: both supporters and opponents were well-organized and had similar opportunities to make their respective cases.[16] But balanced debate does not occur in many areas of U.S. foreign policy—especially not over the wisdom of liberal hegemony itself.

Proponents of liberal hegemony also benefit from the enduring power of nationalism, including the reverence accorded the military as the embodiment of patriotic service. In a country where sports events typically begin with the national anthem and feature color guards, tributes to veterans, or awe-inducing flybys by B-2 bombers, advocates of military dominance and global leadership enjoy powerful rhetorical advantages while advocates of restraint risk being seen as favoring a weaker America. No wonder the Defense Department paid at least fifty professional sports teams a total of $10 million to conduct patriotic ceremonies at games as part of a broader campaign to reinforce public support and enhance recruiting. In effect, U.S. taxpayers were paying for a public relations program designed in part to convince them to pay even more.[17]

The implication is clear: debates over foreign policy and grand strategy are not a fair fight, let alone a genuine "marketplace" where the best ideas invariably win out.

TABOOS, DOGMAS, AND THE "CONVENTIONAL WISDOM"

The benefits of open debate diminish further when topics become taboo and questioning them can be harmful to one's career. To say a particular topic is taboo is not to say that no one ever raises the issue or challenges the reigning orthodoxy, only that it is understood to be politically risky for anyone seeking a prominent role in government or the foreign policy establishment. What John Kenneth Galbraith dubbed the "conventional wisdom" goes unchallenged, and errors are more likely to be repeated than corrected. Or as Walter Lippmann once warned, "Where all think alike, no one thinks very much."[18]

As the task forces described in the previous chapter illustrate, the elite consensus in favor of liberal hegemony is wholly bipartisan. It is also deeply ingrained in the foreign policy establishment. Ambitious foreign policy wannabes rarely question the desirability of U.S. primacy, the need for nuclear superiority, the necessity of NATO, the desirability of the "special relationship" with Israel, the need to protect access to

Middle East oil and defend an array of Asian allies, and the inevitability of conflict with "rogue states" such as North Korea and Iran.[19] The origins of these unquestioned dogmas vary, but each one adds to the global tasks the United States is supposed to perform. Until very recently, anyone who questioned these basic principles or proposed a more restrained foreign policy risked being labeled an "isolationist," a loaded term that seeks to marginalize alternative views by tying them to the now-discredited individuals who opposed U.S. entry into World War II.[20]

A similar bias distorts discussions about the use of military force. Foreign policy mavens do debate the pros and cons of specific military actions—such as the merits of intervention in Syria's civil war—but not the basic right of the United States to use force wherever and whenever it wishes. A corollary to this principle is the reluctance of Washington insiders to endorse peace as a central goal of U.S. foreign policy—even though it is very much in the U.S. interest—for fear of being seen as "soft."[21] As Leslie H. Gelb, president emeritus of the Council on Foreign Relations and a quintessential foreign policy insider, admitted in 2009, his initial support for the Iraq War "was symptomatic of unfortunate tendencies within the foreign policy community, namely the disposition and incentives to support wars to retain political and professional credibility."[22]

At worst, taboos such as these force politicians and their advisors to refrain from expressing their true beliefs so that they can stay within the boundaries of "acceptable" opinion. Such informal prohibitions also discourage members of the foreign policy community from asking tough questions about well-established policies even when those policies are visibly failing. Questionable but politically safe ideas pollute the public sphere, few will say the emperor has no clothes, and those who do so openly will not be taken seriously.

CONSTRAINTS ON THE MEDIA

Nor can the media be relied upon to challenge the dominant narratives that underpin liberal hegemony, at least not on a consistent basis. To take an obvious example, the most popular Sunday TV talk shows rarely present views from outside the Beltway mainstream and instead show a marked bias for hawkish positions. This is partly a question of design, as the main purpose of such programs as NBC's *Meet the Press* and ABC's *This Week* is to spotlight senior officials or other prominent politicians rather than to deepen public awareness or foster wide-ranging debate. Proponents of aggressive U.S. policies appear on these programs far more often than advocates of restraint, with three hard-line members of Congress—John McCain (R-AZ), Lindsay Graham (R-SC), and Mike Rogers (R-MI)—being especially prominent in recent years.[23] Even if one omits consistently hawkish outlets like Fox News, the deck is stacked.

Furthermore, as we saw in chapter 3, many prominent media figures genuinely believe that the United States should be committed all over the world and are therefore quick to defend the expansive role that liberal hegemony prescribes.[24] During the 1990s, for example, mainstream media coverage in *The Washington Post*, the *Los Angeles Times*, and *The New York Times* was strongly biased in favor of increased defense spending, with hawks and Defense Department officials quoted three times more frequently than advocates of spending cuts.[25] As Michael Glennon points out, many of the reporters and columnists working on foreign policy and national security are part of the same inside-the-Beltway culture and subject to the usual pressures to conform. Moving outside the consensus behind liberal hegemony could also jeopardize access to top officials—the lifeblood for any ambitious journalist—and put existing friendships and future professional opportunities at risk.[26]

Of course, government officials understand that favorable media coverage is essential to sustaining public support for an ambitious foreign policy, so they work hard to obtain it. In 2008, for example, the *New*

York Times reporter David Barstow revealed that the Pentagon had recruited a network of retired military officers who were given VIP briefings and access to classified information. Media outlets looking for expert "military analysts" to appear on air were then given these names. As an internal Pentagon memorandum put it, the retired officers would be "message force multipliers" and "surrogates" who would appear as authoritative, independent voices supporting the Bush administration's policies. Participants were told not to reveal their relationship with the Pentagon and were expected to stay "on message." If you weren't on board, one participant told Barstow, "you'll lose all access," and another former officer was dismissed from the program after telling Fox News that the United States was "not on a good glide path" in Iraq.[27]

Subsequent investigations by the Pentagon's inspector general and the General Accounting Office found that this program did not violate any federal laws, but the real issue is that the American people were being fed biased but seemingly "authoritative" accounts of how the military campaign was proceeding. This covert public relations campaign didn't help the United States win in Iraq or Afghanistan, but it did help mislead the American people about how well these wars were going.

The modern practice of "embedding" reporters with combat units may have similar effects. Allowing reporters to accompany combat units can make for vivid coverage and in theory should produce more informed stories, but it also makes journalists even more dependent on the Pentagon for access to stories "from the front" and encourages them to portray the soldiers that are protecting them in favorable terms.[28]

Finally, media scrutiny of key foreign and national security policy issues is also affected by the media's willingness to respect government secrecy. Especially after 9/11, media managers have been understandably reluctant to publish stories that might aid America's enemies, and government officials have been quick to use this concern to influence how controversial topics are covered.

In 2004, for example, *The New York Times* bowed to government pressure—including a direct request from President Bush himself—and delayed for nearly a year the publication of a story exposing the National Security Agency's domestic eavesdropping program. The reason? Administration officials told the *Times* that the story "could jeopardize continuing investigations and alert would-be terrorists that they might be under scrutiny."[29]

As discussed in the previous chapter, a number of journalists, academics, and media figures do important critical work on key elements of recent U.S. foreign policy and provide a useful counterpoint to conventional narratives about America's global activities.[30] The diversity of discourse on foreign policy in the United States is higher than in authoritarian countries, where censorship and official government media make it much harder for alternative voices to be heard. Indeed, the election of Barack Obama in 2008 and Donald Trump in 2016 could be seen as confirmation that many Americans understood that U.S. foreign policy had veered off-course. It would be wrong, therefore, to conclude that the "marketplace of ideas" does not operate at all, or to view media coverage of foreign affairs as nothing but "fake news" designed to keep U.S. citizens in the dark.

Nonetheless, the clash of ideas and policy proposals is not a fair fight on a level field. Individuals and groups with money and status enjoy powerful advantages, and special interests with strong preferences on particular issues normally wield disproportionate influence over what gets written, printed, or broadcast. As shown in the previous chapter, most of these groups strongly favor some version of liberal hegemony. In the competition for the public mind, therefore, it remains easier for advocates of liberal hegemony to make their case, even in the wake of repeated policy failures.

But exactly how does this work? What are the main arguments the foreign policy establishment employs to justify global engagement in general and the goal of liberal hegemony in particular?

STEP 1: THREAT INFLATION

A time-honored method for selling an ambitious foreign policy is to exaggerate foreign dangers. If the public believes that the country faces imminent threats from abroad, it is more likely to support energetic efforts to contain, compel, isolate, degrade, or eliminate them.

Threat inflation has a long history in U.S. foreign policy, especially since the United States took on the mantle of global leadership after World War II.[31] At the beginning of the Cold War, for example, the chair of the Senate Foreign Relations Committee, Arthur Vandenberg, advised President Harry Truman that the best way to win passage of a controversial aid program for Greece and Turkey was to give a speech that would "scare the hell out of the American people." Truman did just that, and Americans were soon convinced that they faced a vast and looming threat from "monolithic Communism." Hard-line advocacy groups such as the Committee on the Present Danger hyped these fears, as did official documents such as NSC-68 (1950), a National Security Council policy paper that offered an alarming portrait of Soviet capabilities and intentions and argued that Moscow's recent acquisition of atomic weapons threatened the entire free world and necessitated a major U.S. defense buildup.[32]

By the early 1950s Americans believed that international Communism was on the march, and many accepted Senator Joseph McCarthy's claims that numerous Communist agents had penetrated the Department of State and other key U.S. institutions. Over the next two decades, U.S. leaders fretted about bomber gaps, missile gaps, and "windows of vulnerability," even though the United States had clear nuclear superiority until the late 1960s. During the Indochina War, U.S. leaders repeatedly argued that defeat or withdrawal would cause other dominoes to fall and U.S. allies to lose confidence, thereby undermining America's entire global posture and turning the country into a "pitiful, helpless giant."[33] Yet fourteen years after Saigon fell, it was the Soviet Union that ended up on the ash heap of history.

In short, U.S. policy throughout the Cold War was frequently driven by worst-case assumptions about the dangers facing the United States. Nonetheless, the Soviet Union was a great power with an industrialized economy, and its large conventional forces and nuclear weapons arsenal did threaten U.S. allies in Europe and Asia. Soviet leaders never formally abandoned Bolshevism's revolutionary aims, and millions of sympathizers around the world genuinely embraced the ideology of Marxism-Leninism. U.S. leaders may have exaggerated these and other dangers, but the threat was hardly a phantom.

Indeed, threat inflation may be a more significant problem today because the foreign dangers the United States faces are less daunting than in earlier eras. It is one thing to build in a margin for error when dealing with a serious threat, but quite another to convince the country that a minor problem is really a grave and imminent danger. If Americans become convinced that minor problems are really existential hazards, they will squander vast sums chasing monsters of their own imagining. Even worse, policymakers may take preventive actions that are in fact counterproductive, thereby turning minor problems into larger ones. What are the main rhetorical ploys that threat inflators use to justify greater exertion abroad?

"DELAY MEANS DEFEAT; ACTING NOW WILL GUARANTEE VICTORY"

Threat inflators see a world chock-full of dangers, where failing to respond quickly will have ominous consequences. Yet they also portray these same threats as easily overcome if their recommendations are undertaken promptly. In other words, threat inflators typically portray a world that is highly elastic: our entire way of life is in peril if we do not act quickly, but a vigorous and immediate response will rout our adversaries and usher in decades of durable peace.

Such claims often rest on peculiar beliefs about the basic nature of world politics. Threat inflators typically reject balance-of-power logic—which argues that powerful or aggressive states usually face ever-increasing resistance—and instead maintain that states are more likely to "bandwagon" with threatening states. If the United States does not maintain decisive military superiority or fails to respond in some far-flung corner of the earth, so the argument runs, its allies will lose confidence and quickly realign with America's enemies. As Paul Nitze, the author of NSC-68, put it in that famous document, "In the absence of affirmative action on our part [i.e., a major military buildup] . . . our friends will become more than a liability to us, they will become a positive increment to Soviet power."[34] If this tendency were widespread, even minor shifts in the balance of power could have ominous consequences.

Relatedly, threat inflators believe that U.S. credibility is extremely important and inherently fragile. As Max Fisher notes, this idea "is pervasive, almost to the point of consensus, in much of Washington's foreign policy community."[35] Any time the United States chooses not to respond to some external event, threat inflators warn that this decision will destroy U.S. credibility, undermine allies' resolve, and embolden America's opponents. Thus, hawks claimed that the U.S. failure to attack the Assad regime after it used chemical weapons in 2013 (thereby crossing a "red line" President Obama had implicitly drawn) had a "catastrophic" effect on U.S. credibility.[36] When the United States does respond, however, the effects are fleeting, and Washington has to demonstrate its will and prowess again the next time a potential challenge arises.

Repeated scholarly studies on reputation and credibility show that the world does not work this way: states judge how others will respond primarily based on the interests at stake and not on how the country acted in a radically different context.[37] To take an obvious illustration, how the United States responds to a crisis in a minor power far away says little or nothing about how it would respond to a direct attack on the U.S. homeland or against an important U.S. ally. Yet threat inflators argue the opposite, implying that the United States must respond in places that don't matter in order to convince adversaries it will act in places that do.

Finally, given that the United States is wealthy, militarily capable, and has no powerful enemies near its own territory, threat inflators have to construct elaborate and improbable sequences of events in order to convince Americans that faraway events might eventually cause them significant harm.[38] For example, the claim that any failed state could become a safe haven for anti-American terrorists transforms weak and strategically insignificant areas such as Afghanistan or Yemen into vital battlegrounds, thereby justifying open-ended counterterrorism and state-building efforts. Yet this argument requires all of the following statements to be true: (1) distant terrorist cells set a high priority on attacking the United States, (2) they can evade all the post-9/11 measures taken to enhance the security of the U.S. homeland, (3) an attack, if it does occur, will inflict enormous costs, and (4) the area in which they are currently operating is vital to their success, and alternative "safe havens" do not exist. Apart from the exceedingly remote possibility of a terrorist attack with a powerful weapon of mass destruction, no conceivable foreign-based terror attack could ever cause that much damage. Moreover, trying to eradicate all the groups that might aspire to attack the United States, while simultaneously eliminating every conceivable safe haven, would cost far more than the harm such groups might inflict.

OVERSTATING ENEMY CAPABILITIES

During the Cold War, threat inflators routinely portrayed the Soviet Union as a military colossus, even though the United States and its allies routinely outspent the Warsaw Pact on defense by as much as 25 percent each year.[39] But Soviet power was not a chimera, even if it was often overstated. Once the U.S.S.R. collapsed, however, the tendency to exaggerate enemy capabilities became more pervasive and consequential.

Beginning in the early 1990s, for example, U.S. officials and establishment pundits have treated such third-rate military powers as Iraq and Iran as if they were major conventional threats, even though neither had any ability to attack the United States directly and scant ability to threaten other U.S. interests. The United States and its allies had defeated Iraq's overmatched armed forces easily in the 1991 Gulf War, and a decade of punishing sanctions meant that Saddam Hussein's forces were even weaker in 2003. Yet both the Clinton and Bush administrations continued to portray Iraq as a powerful and dangerous adversary.

Exaggerating Iraq's capabilities was also a key ingredient in the Bush administration's recipe for preventive war. U.S. officials accused Iraq of seeking nuclear weapons and claimed that it had a large and sophisticated arsenal of chemical and biological weapons. For example, Secretary of State Colin Powell's infamous briefing to the UN Security Council painted an alarming portrait of Iraq's alleged WMD programs, claims that turned out to be completely false.

Similarly, hard-liners have long depicted Iran as a major military power that is about to dominate the Persian Gulf, even though Iran has little conventional power projection capabilities and its defense budget in 2016 was a mere $12.3 billion (compared with $63.7 billion for Saudi Arabia, $17.8 billion for Israel, and more than $600 billion for the United States).[40] To make the case for economic sanctions and possibly a future preventive strike, hard-line anti-Iranian groups repeatedly accused Tehran of actively seeking nuclear weapons (just as they once accused Saddam Hussein) even though National Intelligence Estimates have repeatedly concluded that Iran has no active nuclear weapons program. Moreover, Iran's nuclear potential was capped by the Joint Comprehensive Plan of Action (JCPOA) in 2015.[41] Or they insist that Iran's local proxies (e.g., Hezbollah in Lebanon, the Assad regime in Syria, and the Houthis in Yemen) make up the sinews of an emerging "Persian Empire," a view that overstates the influence of these various groups and Iran's ability to direct them.[42]

Threat inflation has consistently shaped the American response to international terrorism. The danger is not zero, of course, but the actual threat that Al Qaeda, ISIS, or other terrorist organizations pose does not merit the obsessive attention it has received. Even if the toll from the 9/11 attacks were included, the risk that an American will be killed or injured in a terrorist incident is vanishingly small—perhaps 1 chance in

4 million each year—yet U.S. officials continue to describe foreign terrorists in ominous terms.[43] In 2014, for example, Secretary of Defense Chuck Hagel described the Islamic State (or ISIS) as a threat "beyond anything we've ever seen," and in 2015 FBI director James Comey said it was "the danger we're worrying about in the homeland most of all."[44] Testifying about ISIS in June 2016, then–CIA director John Brennan told the Senate Select Committee on Intelligence, "I have never seen a time when our country faced such a variety of threats to our national security."[45] Organizations such as ISIS posed a considerable danger to the people they ruled and caused some degree of harm elsewhere, but they remain weak and under-resourced actors and are nowhere close to being an existential threat.[46]

According to the U.S. National Counterterrorism Center, for example, there were forty-seven Islamic terrorist attacks in Western countries between 2012 and 2016. These attacks killed 269 people, more than half of them in a single attack in a Paris nightclub in November 2015.[47] By comparison, roughly fifteen thousand Americans are murdered each year by guns, yet the federal government does little to address the problem, even in the wake of such mass shootings as the Sandy Hook massacre in December 2012 or the slaughter of fifty-eight concertgoers in Las Vegas in October 2017. Lightning strikes and bathroom accidents take more American lives than terrorism, yet no politician is declaring a War on Thunderstorms or announcing a National Campaign against Slippery Tile.

To say that government officials, think tank experts, and assorted interest groups inflate threats is not to say that the United States faces no dangers or to imply that hostile powers cannot affect U.S. interests. However, overstating the dangers they pose is still costly when it distracts U.S. leaders from other problems or leads them to act in ways that make the problem worse.

"OUR ENEMIES ARE HOSTILE, IRRATIONAL, AND IMPOSSIBLE TO DETER"

In addition to exaggerating enemy capabilities, threat inflators typically describe potential enemies as irrevocably hostile, irrational, and impossible to deter, which in turn implies that they must be removed. In the run-up to the Iraq War, for example, the Brookings Institution senior fellow Kenneth Pollack's influential book *The Threatening Storm* portrayed Saddam Hussein as an inveterate risk-taker who could not be contained—an alarmist portrait that helped convince skeptical liberals that it would be too dangerous to leave Saddam in place.[48]

In much the same way, those who called for tougher sanctions and/or preventive war against Iran routinely portrayed its leaders as fanatical religious extremists who would welcome martyrdom and would therefore be quick to use nuclear weapons. Former CIA director R. James Woolsey described Iran's leaders as "theocratic, totalitarian, and genocidal maniacs"; the columnist Bret Stephens (formerly of *The Wall Street Journal* and now at *The New York Times*) justified preventive war by describing Iran as a "martyrdom-obsessed, non-Western culture with global ambitions"; and Michael Rubin of the American Enterprise Institute suggested that "it is plausible [Iran's leaders] might believe Islamic interests make Iran's weathering a retaliatory nuclear strike worthwhile."[49] Such portraits occasionally reached absurd lengths, as when the neoconservative historian Bernard Lewis warned in a 2006 *Wall Street Journal* op-ed that Iran might be planning a nuclear attack on Israel and went so far as to identify the date: August 22.[50] That particular date was significant, Lewis argued, because it "is the night when many Muslims commemorate the night flight of the prophet Muhammad on the winged horse Buraq, first to 'the farthest mosque,' usually identified with Jerusalem, and then to heaven and back (c.f., Koran XVII.1). This might well be deemed an appropriate date for the apocalyptic ending of Israel and if necessary of the world." In Lewis's portrayal, Iran's leaders were suicidal religious fanatics awaiting a symbolic date on which to launch a mass slaughter in which they would also perish. August 22 came and went with no attack, of course, and Iran has no active nuclear weapons program today. Remarkably, this bizarre and baseless alarm appeared not on some obscure far-right website, but on the op-ed page of one of the country's most influential newspapers.

A variation on this same theme is to claim that animosity toward the United States does not arise from straightforward conflicts of interest or opposition to specific U.S. policies, but rather from a deep-seated antipathy to what America stands for. As George W. Bush famously explained after the September 11 attacks, the terrorists "hate our freedoms." Or as he subsequently told a prime-time news conference, he was "amazed that people would hate us . . . because I know how good we are." In fact, numerous independent surveys have shown that anti-Americanism around the world is largely a response to U.S. *policy*—not a rejection of "American values."[51]

Nonetheless, threat inflators still depict foreign opposition as the result of deep antipathy to America itself. This argument reinforces a key article of faith for proponents of liberal hegemony—the idea that the United States is an exceptional country that is always a force for good in the world—and implies that only misguided or evil people could possibly oppose whatever the United States does around the world. As such, insisting that opponents "hate our freedoms" conveniently absolves Washington of any responsibility for foreign hostility and implies that nothing can be done to reduce it. If America's enemies are implacably hostile no matter what we do, the only option is to eliminate them. Or as Vice President Dick Cheney put it in 2003, "We don't negotiate with evil; we defeat it."[52]

"AXES OF EVIL"

Another obvious way to magnify threats is to assume that adversaries form a unified coalition seeking to inflict maximum damage on U.S. interests. During the Cold War, for example, hawks repeatedly warned of a "Communist monolith" and were slow to recognize the deep schisms that divided the international Communist movement. Even after the Sino-Soviet split was apparent, top officials still saw left-wing governments as reliable Soviet allies, despite the abundant evidence that Moscow had difficult relations with most of its Third World client states.

Yet U.S. officials and foreign policy analysts continue to invoke similar arguments today, repeatedly lumping states and groups together though they have little in common. During the 1990s, for example, top U.S. officials and foreign policy professionals repeatedly warned of the threat from a motley collection of "rogue states" whose ranks included Iraq, Cuba, Iran, North Korea, Serbia, Libya, and Syria.[53] None of these recalcitrant regimes was especially powerful, and there was little cooperation among them; indeed, some of them—such as Iran and Iraq—were bitter enemies.

Yet in 1992 the U.S. House of Representatives Task Force on Terrorism released a staff report entitled "Tehran, Baghdad & Damascus: The New Axis Pact," which warned of a "Tehran-controlled strategic axis stretching from the Mediterranean to Iran . . . an integral part of a much larger 'Islamic Bloc' that is being consolidated by Tehran and that also includes Sudan and the Muslim countries of central and south Asia." At about the same time, Clinton's first national security advisor, Anthony Lake, warned of a growing threat from what he termed "backlash states" and called for vigorous U.S. action to contain them.[54] The states on Lake's list—Cuba, Iraq, Libya, Iran, and North Korea—were all at odds with the United States for different reasons, but none posed a grave threat to U.S. security and there was hardly any coordination between them. Taken together (with Serbia and the Taliban regime in Afghanistan thrown in), these states had a combined GDP of $165 billion in 1998. That amount was about one-third smaller than America's defense budget in the same year and equal to a mere 2 percent of the U.S. economy. Yet lumping these diverse and largely isolated states under the general heading of "rogue state" made them sound like a unified gang of dangerous international troublemakers.

George W. Bush did the same thing in his 2002 State of the Union speech, famously placing Iran, Iraq, and North Korea into the "Axis of Evil." According to former White House speechwriter David Frum, this misleading phrase was chosen deliberately to hype the threat and help justify military action against Iraq.[55] The Bush administration also went to great lengths to link Saddam Hussein with Osama bin Laden and Al Qaeda in order to make Iraq seem hostile, dangerous, and deserving of a U.S. attack. The disinformation campaign worked so well that a majority of Americans erroneously believed that Iraq had been directly involved in the 9/11 attacks.

As the post-9/11 "war on terror" proceeded, other hawks began to refer to a growing threat from "Islamofascism," thereby suggesting that a diverse set of Islamic terrorists had a common agenda and a unified strategy. Like the term "Axis," such phrases imply a high degree of coordination among these diverse groups and connect them rhetorically to Nazi Germany—as clear a case of evil as one could imagine—thereby suggesting that Islamic radicals and/or rogue states are equal to the dangers the world faced back in the 1930s. Such terms also subtly invoke the triumphal U.S. narrative of World War II—the "Good War," where virtuous Americans came together to save the world from a set of aggressive dictatorships. Small wonder that hard-liners quickly labeled the war on terror "World War IV," thereby implying that the United States was confronted by the same sort of threat it had faced in 1941 and needed to make an equivalent effort to defeat it.[56]

Unfortunately, sloppy historical analogies such as these make it harder to devise effective strategies for isolating, dividing, and ultimately defeating these various foes. Treating every group that employs terrorist methods as part of a common movement also gives some of them greater incentive to join forces, which is the last thing the United States wants.

"OUR ALLIES ARE WEAK AND UNRELIABLE
(YET WE MUST STILL PROTECT THEM)"

The flip side to exaggerating one's opponents' unity is overstating the fragility or fecklessness of America's many allies. Compared with potential adversaries such as ISIS, China, or Iran, the United States is blessed with a number of wealthy and capable partners. Of the ten countries with the largest defense budgets, for example, six are formal allies of the United States. China and Russia are the only countries in the top ten who are at odds with the United States, and neither of these states has other allies with substantial global influence.

Indeed, when one takes contemporary alliances into account, America's strategic situation is in some ways better than it was at the height of the Cold War. In the 1980s the United States and its allies together outspent all potential threatening states (e.g., the Soviet Union, the Warsaw Pact, Cuba, Iran, Iraq, Libya, North Korea, Syria, and Vietnam) by a margin of more than two to one. That margin increased to more than five to one when the Soviet Union collapsed, even though U.S. defense spending also declined during this period.[57]

Given these favorable realities, what is a dedicated threat inflator to do? One response is to assume that U.S. allies are unreliable and to warn that they will abandon the United States and bandwagon with America's rivals if the United States does not protect them against every conceivable danger. Accordingly, hawks warn that U.S. allies in the Persian Gulf would quickly abandon the United States and appease Iran were it to acquire nuclear weapons.[58]

A second response is to denigrate allied capabilities and suggest that having lots of allies makes it harder—not easier—to protect key U.S. interests.[59] There is some truth in this assertion, insofar as some of the states the United States has promised to protect—such as Estonia, Latvia, or Montenegro—have little military potential, and other U.S. allies—such as Germany—have become overly reliant on American protection and let their own military capabilities atrophy. Indeed, some of America's current alliances are better seen as one-sided "protectorates" that add to U.S. defense burdens but do not contribute new capabilities with which to meet them.[60]

But if some allies increase U.S. defense burdens without enhancing U.S. security, the proper response is to be more selective when extending guarantees and to insist that these allies bear a greater share of collective burdens. Such sensible steps won't happen, however, if U.S. leaders continue to believe it is a major strategic achievement whenever they take on costly security obligations for others.

EXPLOITING UNCERTAINTY

Threat inflation thrives when dangers are difficult to measure. Tanks, planes, ships, and defense budgets are easy to count and compare, but gauging other dangers can be more difficult. Anyone with a decent imagination can dream up an infinite number of frightening scenarios, and it is sometimes hard to prove that some hypothetical danger is overblown.

One sees this problem today in the tendency to hype threats from terrorism and, to a somewhat lesser extent, from cyberwarfare. Because terrorist organizations plot in secret (at the same time issuing lurid threats), we can never be 100 percent certain that a devastating attack is not in the works. Even if most of the post-9/11 plots against the United States were either FBI "sting" operations or involved incompetent bunglers, and even if the actual danger America faced from Al Qaeda or its various offshoots—including the "Islamic State"—was vastly overstated, there is no way to be completely sure that the next terrorist plot will fail.[61]

Similarly, because cyber threats are always evolving, and because one needs sophisticated technical knowledge to assess the danger accurately, it is easy for threat inflators (or Hollywood scriptwriters) to concoct alarming scenarios in which hackers, terrorists, foreign governments, or clever teenagers blind our armed forces, crash the air traffic control system, shut down power grids, crater the world economy, or launch whatever other nightmare scenario they can imagine.[62] The ability to dream up new dangers is nicely illustrated by Benjamin Wittes of Brookings and Gabriella Blum of Harvard Law School, who write, "In our new world, you can pose a threat to the security of every state and person on the planet—and each can also threaten you . . . Today, each person needs to fear an exponentially higher number of people and entities than only a decade ago. The threats to your personal security now include not merely governments and corporations but also other individuals around the world: stalkers, identity thieves, scammers, spammers, frauds, competitors, and rivals—everyone and everything from the government of China to the NSA . . . You can be attacked from anywhere—and by nearly everyone."[63] Shorter version: be afraid. Be very afraid.

This is not to say that such dangers are imaginary. Indeed, Russia's efforts to influence the 2016 presidential election and the use of damaging viruses, ransomware, and denial-of-service attacks by Iran, North Korea, Russia, the United States, and some private entities demonstrates that the threat is far from ephemeral.[64] The broader point, however, is that the uncertainties surrounding this pervasive and rapidly evolving technology make it more likely that we will overstate or misjudge the actual danger we face.

It is revealing, for example, that the chorus of experts warning about sophisticated forms of cyberwar, cyber espionage, cybercrime, and cyberterrorism failed to anticipate what is arguably the most politically significant use of digital technology to date. I refer, of course, to Russia's efforts to influence the 2016 U.S. election by flooding Facebook, Twitter, Instagram, and other social media platforms with counterfeit accounts disseminating phony stories and messages intended to deepen divisions within the United States and weaken the Democratic presidential candidate Hillary Clinton. Russia didn't hack voting machines or bring down the power grid on Election Day, but its low-tech effort to plant false stories reportedly reached some 126 million Americans through Facebook alone.[65] A number of prescient Internet scholars had previously warned that social media platforms might have powerful but largely unseen effects on election outcomes, but no one seems to have anticipated that a foreign power might use these same platforms to advance its own political agenda here in the United States.[66]

What this incident also revealed was the fragile and polarized condition of American democracy, which gave Russia's interference more impact than it deserved. As Paul Pillar put it in January 2017, "Sure, what the Russians did is worthy of condemnation, but Americans ought to be most disturbed by the fact that there already were enough reasons to shake such faith [in the existing democratic order] that the Russians would have known they had a vulnerable target."[67] In any case, the central point remains valid: when threats are inherently hard to measure, threat inflation is more likely to thrive.

If an imagined attack of any kind would be extremely damaging, taking extreme measures to prevent it may well be justified. This is the reasoning behind Vice President Dick Cheney's infamous "one percent doctrine": if there was only a 1 percent chance of something terrible happening (such as a Pakistani plot to give Al Qaeda a nuclear weapon), Cheney told aides to act as if it were a certainty.[68] Because dreaming up scary scenarios is child's play (especially when compared with the effort needed to make a rigorous threat assessment), the "one percent" doctrine guarantees that threats will be exaggerated. Nor does this approach tell us which of the infinite number of Very Bad Things That One Cannot Completely Rule Out deserve the most attention or the greatest claim on government resources. It does make liberal hegemony look more attractive, however: if there's a 1 percent chance that something really bad might emerge from almost anywhere, then the United States had better do more to root out potential dangers wherever they might arise.

WHY DOES THREAT INFLATION WORK SO WELL?

External dangers do exist, and the United States does not always exaggerate them. Threat inflation is still a serious problem, however, because it diverts resources from other priorities and can lead to policies that make existing dangers worse. Scaring the hell out of the American people may win popular support for an ambitious foreign policy, but it can also lead to costly missteps. Unfortunately, both politicians and pundits have learned all too well that a poorly informed public is quick to lap up such phrases as "a new Munich" or "another Hitler" and all too willing to succumb to worst-case fears about terrorist masterminds, wily dictators, and vast conspiracies.

Part of the problem lies in the incentives political leaders face when dealing with uncertain dangers. As Jack Goldsmith has argued, U.S. leaders overreact to terrorism because they receive daily reports about possible attacks and they fear the political consequences of appearing insufficiently vigilant. In his words, "It is hard to overstate the impact that the incessant waves of threat reports have on the judgment of people inside the executive branch who are responsible for protecting American lives."[69] Excessive vigilance is wasteful, but it shields officials from accusations of not having done enough to protect the nation.

Threat inflation also prevails because individuals and groups with an interest in exaggerating threats are more numerous and better funded than those who seek to debunk them, and they often enjoy greater political prestige. The entire military-industrial complex has obvious incentives to overstate foreign dangers in order to persuade the body politic to give it additional resources. Hawkish think tanks get generous support from defense contractors and individuals; by comparison, groups offering less frightening appraisals are generally less well-funded and less influential.

The unusual case of Micah Zenko, formerly the Douglas Dillon Senior Fellow at the Council on Foreign Relations, is instructive in this regard. Zenko has done important work on a variety of national security topics, but what made him noteworthy was his willingness to challenge the alarmist views that predominate in the national security establishment. Even more remarkably, he did so from a position at the Council on Foreign Relations, the beating heart of the mainstream foreign policy world. Zenko's iconoclasm was sufficiently unusual to earn him a featured profile in *The American Conservative* under the headline

"The Anti-Warrior." The article described Zenko's work as "a constant effort to take the threat landscape out of the funhouse mirror and restore some perspective: the gentle blasphemy of threat deflation."[70] Zenko is not the only threat-deflating voice in contemporary policy debates, but he was one of the few with a prominent position at a mainstream foreign policy think tank.

Foreign governments that depend on U.S. protection will also do what they can to keep the American people scared, thus ensuring that the United States will continue to protect them. When the Obama administration decided not to intervene in the Syrian civil war, for example, Arab officials—such as former Saudi Arabian intelligence chief Prince Turki al-Faisal—bemoaned the loss of U.S. "credibility" and warned that U.S. passivity would embolden Iran.[71] The crisis in Ukraine elicited a chorus of similar complaints from NATO's East European members, further underscoring their dependence on U.S. protection. Not to be outdone, U.S. allies in Asia routinely question U.S. credibility in the face of a rising China while refusing to increase their own defense spending significantly.[72]

Hawks back home are quick to trumpet these warnings, of course, which they cite as "independent" evidence to support their own alarmist views. Thus former vice president Cheney, whose recommendations after 9/11 did so much to destabilize the Middle East, warned in 2013, "our friends no longer count on us, no longer trust us, and our adversaries don't fear us."[73] Needless to say, this symbiotic relationship between liberal hegemony's proponents in the United States and the foreign powers that benefit from U.S. protection reinforces the perceived need to respond to even minor events in every corner of the world.

To repeat: my argument is not that the United States faces no foreign dangers or that its vital interests are reliably secure against any and all challenges. Nor am I suggesting that threat inflation leads directly and unavoidably to a strategy of liberal hegemony. When U.S. leaders are sufficiently alarmed, in fact, liberal values will get short shrift, and leaders will readily join forces with friendly dictators, provided the latter are useful for dealing with the problem at hand.

On balance, however, threat inflation encourages ambitious, revisionist strategies like liberal hegemony. After all, if the world is indeed filled with dangers and Americans do not want them to grow, Washington must use its power to shape events in many different places.

STEP 2: EXAGGERATE THE BENEFITS

Having labored to convince Americans that the world is overflowing with dangers, step two in the defense of liberal hegemony is to persuade the public that U.S. dominance and "global leadership" offer the best strategy for dealing with these risks. In particular, defenders maintain that liberal hegemony—including, when necessary, regime change in other countries—will enhance U.S. security, increase American prosperity, and spread basic liberal values. As discussed in chapter 1, these claims formed the central justification for the U.S. grand strategy throughout the Cold War, and they underpin America's expansive global role today.

SECURITY

With regard to the first goal—security—proponents of liberal hegemony claim that any reduction in America's global military position will invite chaos around the world and eventually place Americans at risk. Absent U.S. dominance and "deep engagement," great power competition will reemerge in Europe, the Middle East, and Asia, and states that now enjoy U.S. protection will rearm and possibly acquire nuclear weapons. Thus, the Council on Foreign Relations president Richard Haass claims that "for the past 75 years, the visible hand of the U.S., more than any other factor, has created and maintained conditions of stability." He goes on to warn, darkly, that "the consequences of a lasting American retreat from the world would be dire."[74] U.S. military power and intelligence assets are also said to be essential for addressing threats from terrorism, drug lords, refugees, and other nontraditional security threats.[75] In short, liberal hegemony supposedly makes Americans safer by keeping a diverse set of dangers at bay.

Unfortunately, these familiar rationales overstate the security benefits that liberal hegemony supposedly provides. Many of America's numerous global commitments and far-flung activities are not intended to keep the United States from being conquered or coerced; at most, the United States engages in distant areas in order to ward off future developments that might—repeat, might—one day impinge on U.S. security in some unspecified fashion. The alleged benefits are a hedge against uncertain dangers that might never come to pass, no matter what Washington does.

Second, it is not obvious that U.S. military forces must be committed all over the world in order to keep regional competition from reemerging, or that these commitments will work as promised. In claiming that the United States has long "created and maintained U.S. stability," for example, Haass ignores the many places (Indochina, the Middle East, Central America, etc.) where U.S. intervention did exactly the opposite. Deep U.S. engagement did help dampen security competition in Europe during the Cold War, for example, but a return to pre-1945 levels of rivalry today is unlikely no matter what the United States does in the foreseeable future. Alarmists now worry about a resurgent Russia, but the EU has more than three times Russia's population and each year spends four times more on defense than Russia does. Far from being an ascending, would-be hegemon, Russia is in fact a kleptocracy in decline, a state whose population is aging and shrinking and whose economy rests on energy exports whose value is likely to decline over time. Russian president Vladimir Putin has played a weak hand well—aided in no small part by American blunders—but Russia is too weak to challenge the United States directly or to threaten other major powers in Europe or Asia.

Third, although U.S. security guarantees have discouraged some states from seeking nuclear weapons, they are not the only reason potential nuclear states decide to forgo them. Britain, France, and Israel all developed nuclear weapons despite close security ties with the United States, and India is expanding its arsenal even as its ties to the United States grow. Thus U.S. primacy and its nuclear umbrella are neither necessary nor sufficient to keep some states from pursuing nuclear weapons. Moreover, a perceived threat *from* the United States is the main reason why North Korea, Iraq, Syria, Libya, and Iran were interested in acquiring a nuclear deterrent, though only North Korea succeeded. In terms of discouraging proliferation, therefore, the benefits of liberal hegemony are exaggerated.

Nor is liberal hegemony the best response to terrorism. U.S. intelligence agencies and military forces have been on the front lines of the counterterror campaign for at least two decades, yet the number of violent extremists and the number of places where they are active is greater now than they were when Al Qaeda first emerged in the early 1990s. This disappointing result should not surprise us, as opposition to America's expansive global role—especially its repeated interference in the Middle East—has been a key motivating element for Al Qaeda, ISIS, and other violent extremists for a long time now.

Instead of making Americans safer, liberal hegemony has been making them less secure than they would otherwise be. At best, the security benefits of military dominance and global activism are smaller than is usually claimed.

PROSPERITY

Liberal hegemony's defenders also exaggerate the economic benefits that military dominance and "deep engagement" allegedly provide. In theory, primacy could enhance U.S. prosperity by (1) making the United States a more attractive destination for foreign investment and helping solidify the dollar's role as a reserve currency, (2) allowing Washington to extract rents and other payments from states that depend on U.S. protection, or (3) helping sustain a globalized world economy from which Americans (and others) gain. But as Daniel Drezner convincingly argues, in each case "the economic benefits from military predominance alone seem, at a minimum, to have been exaggerated in policy and scholarly circles."[76] To take but two examples, U.S. primacy after the Cold War did not discourage key allies from rapidly expanding their economic ties with China and did not enable Washington to strike more favorable trade deals than other large and advanced economies (as such the EU) did.[77]

In fact, defenders of liberal hegemony rarely invoke the first or second arguments.[78] Instead, they see U.S. primacy and its global military role as central to the preservation of an open world economy. In this view, extensive global economic cooperation requires geopolitical stability, freedom of navigation, strong institutions such as the World Bank or WTO, and a host of other public goods.[79] The United States has been the most important provider of such goods since 1945, and simple self-interest dictates that it continue to perform this role. Were America's military role to diminish, they suggest, freedom of navigation would be imperiled, access to energy and other vital resources might be curtailed, protectionism would reemerge, and the benefits of globalization would be lost, leaving many Americans worse off.

There may be some truth to this argument, insofar as all economic orders rest to some degree on an underlying structure of political and military power.[80] Moreover, the global institutions favored by many proponents of liberal hegemony do help facilitate cooperation on economic issues. And were the United States to revert to full-blown protectionism and ignite a global trade war—as the Trump administration may now be doing—the results for America and the world could be disastrous.

But on the whole, the purely economic benefits of liberal hegemony and global military dominance are less than their proponents claim. U.S. citizens benefit from global trade and investment, but U.S. military dominance is not necessary for maintaining an open trading order or the multilateral institutions that make it possible.[81] Given that almost all states benefit to varying degrees from today's globalized economy, it is not clear why any of them would retreat from it were America's global military role to decline. If the United States withdrew most of its forces from the Middle East and reduced its military role in Europe, for example, why would Japan, China, the EU, or any other members of the G20 decide to raise new protectionist barriers, dismantle the WTO, or take other steps that would only make them poorer?

Furthermore, the scary economic scenarios used to justify liberal hegemony may not be anywhere near as bad as fearmongers suggest. Preserving access to Persian Gulf energy supplies has long been seen as a vital U.S. interest, as a significant reduction in Persian Gulf oil production would drive energy prices up, reducing global economic growth and hurting U.S. consumers directly. For this reason, the United States is committed to keeping oil and gas flowing from the Gulf to world markets, and it maintains a costly rapid deployment force for precisely this purpose.

Fortunately, the risk that oil and gas will be cut off is low. Oil prices have fluctuated significantly over the past four decades, and spikes have sometimes caused economic problems, but the world economy never came close to collapsing. The 1973 Arab oil boycott did have significant negative effects on many countries (including the United States), but neither the Iranian revolution of 1979 nor the long Iran-Iraq War had major effects on the world or the American economy. More recent events—including the 2003 Iraq War or the various conflicts arising from the "Arab Spring"—had even less impact.[82] If serious conflicts in the oil-rich Persian Gulf have only minor effects on global prosperity, then the benefits of protecting it militarily are small.[83]

This is not to say that there is no connection between U.S. security commitments and U.S. prosperity. Were the United States to disengage from all its overseas commitments, and were this decision to lead eventually to major conflicts in Europe, the Middle East, or Asia, and thus to a precipitous drop in world trade, the U.S. economy would clearly suffer. But if relations between other states became only slightly more contentious, the United States could continue to trade with all of them. Once again, proponents of liberal hegemony have exaggerated its benefits, including its contribution to American prosperity.

PROMOTING AMERICAN VALUES

Finally, most members of the foreign policy establishment believe that U.S. leadership and global dominance help preserve and advance America's most cherished political values. Woodrow Wilson promised that World War I would make the world "safe for democracy"; Franklin Roosevelt invoked "Four Freedoms" to prepare Americans for World War II; and Harry Truman justified U.S. aid to Greece and Turkey by saying it was necessary to defend a "way of life . . . distinguished by free institutions, representative government, free elections, and guarantees of individual liberty." Such declarations help rally public support for ambitious and difficult international challenges and may help deflect criticism when conditions at home fall short of professed U.S. ideals or when the United States finds itself bombing civilians, torturing captives, or violating international law. While obviously at odds with professed U.S. values, such acts can be defended as necessary evils in the struggle to end tyranny and (eventually) create a more benign world.[84]

As described in previous chapters, the absence of a peer competitor after the demise of the Soviet Union allowed this evangelical impulse to burst forth with new vigor. A commitment to spreading liberal values was the foundation of Bill Clinton's strategy of "engagement and enlargement," George W. Bush's "Freedom Agenda," and Barack Obama's vocal embrace of the Arab Spring. It is also the moral principle behind NATO expansion and the main reason so-called liberal hawks backed the war in Iraq.

The claim that liberal hegemony promotes the moral values for which America stands is thus a recurring thread in the complex tapestry of recent U.S. foreign policy and a reflexive justification for much of what the United States does on the world stage. Although this impulse has been present from the founding of the Republic, it has become increasingly pronounced as U.S. power has grown.

But as we have seen, efforts to spread U.S. values have not been nearly as effective as its proponents maintain. If anything, overzealous efforts to export America's ideals have unwittingly subverted them at home and abroad, and the exuberant faith in the superiority of American political institutions that prevailed at the end of the Cold War had given way to dark doubts about these same institutions by 2016.[85]

STEP 3: CONCEAL THE COSTS

Threat inflation makes liberal hegemony seem necessary; overstating its benefits makes it seem desirable. For its advocates, the last line of defense is to claim that the strategy is cheap. In a ringing defense of "deep engagement," for example, Stephen Brooks, John Ikenberry, and William Wohlforth point out that U.S. defense spending consumes a significantly lower percentage of GNP than it did during the 1950s or 1960s and assert that modestly higher defense spending does not hinder economic growth. In their view, pursuing liberal hegemony is just not that expensive. Or as the journalist Steve Coll (former president of the New America Foundation and now head of Columbia School of Journalism) put it, "As an investment in shared prosperity (or, if you prefer, global hegemony), the running cost of American military power may be one of history's better bargains."[86]

It would be nice if this were true, but there are good reasons to doubt it. The U.S. may spend a smaller percentage of GNP on national security than it once did, but the proper question to ask is whether it is spending more than it should. Modestly higher levels of defense spending may not affect overall economic growth very much, but every dollar spent on the military is still a dollar that cannot be left in the hands of American taxpayers or spent on other public goods, including long-term investments in future prosperity.

Moreover, the economic impact of America's global role may be more deleterious than defenders of liberal hegemony maintain. At moments of perceived emergency such as the Korea and Vietnam Wars or the 9/11 terror attacks, national security spending surges. The United States typically finances these expenditures not by raising taxes—which would make the cost of the war obvious and immediate—but by borrowing the money abroad. As Sarah Kreps has shown, this approach helps sustain popular support by hiding the immediate cost of these wars and shifting the burden onto future generations (who will end up paying off the loans).[87] Unfortunately, relying on borrowed money also creates asset bubbles at home and makes financial crises like the 2008 Wall Street crash more likely.[88] In this way, the global role mandated by liberal hegemony and the desire to conceal costs from the U.S. taxpayer foster greater financial instability.

Convincing Americans that liberal hegemony is affordable is easier to do if the costs really *are* low, which is why both Bill Clinton and Barack Obama were leery of sending large numbers of U.S. ground troops into harm's way. Clinton authorized "no-fly zones" over Iraq for eight years and ordered occasional air strikes against that unhappy country, but he rejected calls to topple Saddam Hussein with military force. Clinton also stayed out of Rwanda, sent peacekeeping forces into Bosnia reluctantly in 1996, and chose to wage the 1999 Kosovo War solely from the air, resisting military requests to send ground troops as well. Fareed Zakaria aptly dubbed Clinton's gingerly approach to global leadership "hollow hegemony," one that reflected Clinton's awareness that the American appetite for costly overseas engagements was limited.[89]

Barack Obama did much the same for similar reasons. Although he agreed to send additional ground troops into Afghanistan early in his presidency, he set a time limit for the deployment and tried hard to stick to it. He withdrew most U.S. ground forces from Iraq and sent small contingents of Special Forces and intelligence personnel to the conflict zones in Yemen, Libya, Somalia, Syria, and Nigeria. He was equally wary of openly sending arms or advisors to Syria for fear that doing so would fuel the conflict and place the United States on a slippery slope to deeper involvement. Obama understood that the stakes in these conflicts did not justify large and expensive deployments, and the American

people agreed with that assessment. Accordingly, his administration relied on drone strikes, training missions, and cyberattacks, which kept
the costs of continued U.S. global leadership relatively low for the United
States. Even so, such exercises in restraint—especially Obama's decision
not to intervene in Syria—typically faced strong criticism from the foreign policy establishment, whose "playbook" favors what Obama later
called "militarized responses."[90]

Yet Obama's more discreet approach was neither a repudiation of
liberal hegemony nor an embrace of a less ambitious grand strategy.
Obama did not reduce any of America's security commitments; in
fact, they increased on his watch. He did not end any of the wars he inherited, did not resist the temptation to back regime change on more
than one occasion, and did not reduce the use of drones, targeted killings, or special operations forces (indeed, they also increased during his
presidency). Obama sought to keep the costs of the strategy low, but he
never questioned the strategy itself.

George Bush's post-9/11 decision to transform the Middle East, beginning with the invasion of Iraq, is only a partial exception to this pattern. It was an enormous roll of the dice, but administration officials
convinced themselves that the war would be swift and cheap. When
one of Bush's top economic advisors, Larry Lindsey, estimated that the
war might cost $200 billion, Secretary of Defense Donald Rumsfeld
dismissed his estimate as "baloney" and Lindsey lost his job a few months
later. Similarly, Deputy Secretary of Defense Paul Wolfowitz told a congressional committee that Army Chief of Staff Eric Shinseki's estimate
that the occupation would require several hundred thousand troops
was "wildly off the mark" and said that Iraqi oil revenues would pay
the costs of the postwar occupation. His goal, of course, was to convince skeptics that the war would cost very little—and maybe even turn
a profit.[91]

Once Iraq and Afghanistan became quagmires, the Bush administration did its best to conceal the true cost of each one. Instead of funding them through the normal Defense Department budget, it asked

Congress to approve "supplemental" budget authority for each campaign. But as the Nobel Prize–winning economist Joseph Stiglitz and Linda Bilmes have documented, these supplemental budgets—totaling some $800 billion—covered only a fraction of the $4 to $6 *trillion* the two wars will eventually cost the American taxpayer.[92]

Defenders of liberal hegemony also tend to ignore its opportunity costs. More than a half century ago President Dwight D. Eisenhower tried to focus the nation's attention on the sacrifices excessive military spending imposed, telling a group of newspaper editors, "Every gun that is made, every warship launched, every rocket fired signifies, in the final sense, a theft from those who hunger and are not fed, those who are cold and are not clothed."[93] As a five-star general and victorious World War II commander, Eisenhower hardly needed to be convinced about the importance of national security. But he was reminding his fellow citizens that they would face a bleaker future if they ignored the opportunity costs that overly ambitious foreign policy goals entailed.

Eisenhower's prudence now seems quaint, even radical. To be sure, the three task forces discussed in the previous chapter—the Princeton Project on National Security, the Project for a United and Strong America, and the CNAS report *Extending American Power*—as well as such books as Richard Haass's *Foreign Policy Begins at Home* all acknowledge the need for fiscal responsibility. But they favor fiscal prudence not so that Americans can enjoy more prosperous lives, but to ensure that the U.S. government has the resources it needs to remain "indispensable" in world affairs. "For the United States to continue to act successfully abroad," writes Haass, "it must restore the domestic foundations of its power." Improving the lives of ordinary Americans is of secondary importance; what matters to the foreign policy elite is preserving America's capacity to shape events around the globe.[94]

CONTAINING CASUALTIES: THE ALL-VOLUNTEER FORCE

Originally implemented near the end of the Vietnam War, the all-volunteer force (AVF) disguises the costs of an expansive grand strategy in two ways. First, although recruits have to be paid higher wages than draftees, the overall cost to society declines because productive workers are not diverted into military jobs. From a purely economic point of view, forcing a talented software designer, biochemist, or engineer to train for and perform purely military tasks is not the most efficient allocation of their talents.[95]

Second, because members of the armed services have joined voluntarily, they cannot easily complain about being sent in harm's way and are less likely to question the merits of using U.S. power abroad. Surveys of recent military personnel bear this out, as most veterans remain highly patriotic, proud of their service, and more supportive of recent U.S. military operations than the general public.[96]

The AVF also insulates the political establishment from the direct consequences of relentless global activism. Because only a small proportion of American society is directly affected when these wars go badly, and because the men and women paying the blood price tend to be less well-educated or politically mobilized than the rest of the citizenry, politicians need not fear a sharp political backlash. Recent academic studies suggest that conscription decreases public support for war in general, which suggests that resuming a draft would make politicians far more cautious about sending U.S. forces into combat.[97] Imagine how U.S. college students might have reacted if the wars in Iraq, Afghanistan, and elsewhere had been waged by young people forced to serve solely because they received a low lottery number.

A desire to keep the visible costs of liberal hegemony down may also explain the enormous effort now devoted to protecting U.S. personnel from harm—a practice critics deride as "force protection fetishism."[98] To some degree, this concern stems from the belief that public support for overseas military operations would decline rapidly if U.S.

casualties were high, especially when vital interests are not at stake. Similar concerns also explain why the Pentagon barred photographers from filming returning U.S. war dead from 1991 to 2009: it is easier for the American people to overlook the human costs of U.S. interventions if they see fewer pictures of flag-draped coffins.[99]

The American people may not be as sensitive to casualties as current doctrine implies.[100] What matters, however, is that U.S. political and military leaders apparently believe they are. According to the *U.S. Army Field Manual 100-5*: "The American people expect decisive victory and abhor unnecessary casualties. They prefer quick resolution to conflicts and reserve the right to reconsider their support should any of these conditions not be met."[101]

Protecting men and women in combat is a laudable goal, but it can be counterproductive if carried too far. Body armor, medical and evacuation teams, and other protective measures all cost money, and key military objectives may be jeopardized if commanders are overly reluctant to put troops at risk.[102] The desire to protect U.S. troops also encourages overreliance on airpower, leading to greater civilian casualties and undermining efforts to "win hearts and minds." The result is another paradox: the Pentagon has to keep U.S. casualties low in order to preserve public support back home, but doing so makes it harder to win these wars, and public support for them eventually evaporates anyway.

These points do not mandate a return to conscription or imply that the United States should not try to protect its soldiers. Rather, they reveal the elite's recognition that the American people would reject liberal hegemony if the number of U.S. lives lost was too high. This constraint arises not because Americans are unusually sensitive to casualties (though there is surely nothing wrong with caring about the lives of soldiers, sailors, and aircrews), but because the public understands that most of the combat missions undertaken over the past two decades have not been necessary and thus not worth a lot of blood or treasure.

BLOWBACK

Supporters of liberal hegemony also obscure its geopolitical costs, usually by denying that U.S. policy sometimes can provoke greater resistance by others. One technique is to deny that foreign hostility has anything to do with U.S. policy and interpret it simply as an expression of envy, resentment, or deep-seated rejection of U.S. values. This reaction was especially widespread after 9/11, when assorted foreign policy experts flocked to the airwaves and op-ed pages to deny that Al Qaeda's attack had anything to do with U.S. support for Israel, its close ties and military presence in Saudi Arabia, or any other tangible element of U.S. Middle East policy.[103] Even the blue-ribbon *9/11 Commission Report* tiptoed around this issue, confining most of its discussion of the role of U.S. policy in motivating the 9/11 plot to appendices that few people read.[104]

Yet there is overwhelming evidence that anti-American terrorism is often inspired by what the United States has done around the world. That fact does not justify terrorism, of course, or imply that U.S. policy was necessarily wrong, but it does mean that a heightened risk from terrorism should be counted among the costs of what the United States is doing. Moreover, a 2012 study by the FBI's counterterrorism division found that "anger over U.S. military operations abroad was the most commonly cited motivation for individuals involved in cases of 'homegrown' terrorism."[105] If that is indeed the case, then the costs of liberal hegemony are larger than we often think.

Second, Americans will underestimate the costs of U.S. foreign policy when they are unaware of what the government is doing. If Americans do not know the full extent of U.S. drone strikes and Special Forces operations, for example, they will not understand why some victims of these attacks are angry and eager to retaliate. The late Chalmers Johnson called this phenomenon "blowback," which he defined as "the unintended consequences of policies that were kept secret from the American people."[106] Some members of the public may be aware of dubious things the government has done—such as drone strikes or waterboarding—but they may miss the connection between actions taken at one time and place and the negative reactions occurring years later or in some other region. In this way, the full costs of liberal hegemony are further obscured.

The emergence of the so-called Islamic State (or ISIS) illustrates this dynamic perfectly. ISIS arose from the insurgent group Al Qaeda in Iraq and the Levant, which formed in response to the U.S. occupation of Iraq in 2003. Its leader, Abu Bakr al-Baghdadi, was a cleric who was imprisoned by the U.S. occupation forces and radicalized further by the experience.[107] When Barack Obama sent U.S. troops back to Iraq to "degrade and destroy" ISIS in 2014, he was trying to solve a problem America had created.

Most societies have trouble recognizing that their own actions might be the cause of some other group's hostility. The United States is hardly the worst offender in this regard, and it has sometimes shown an admirable willingness to confront past wrongs. But given its power, its ambitions, and its global reach, concealing the role U.S. policy plays in provoking foreign opposition encourages Americans to understate the full cost of liberal hegemony.

IGNORING THE DEATHS OF OTHERS

Defenders of liberal hegemony insist that other states benefit from America's expansive global role. This claim is undoubtedly true for many states that enjoy U.S. protection, which makes them more secure and allows them to devote more resources to other national goals. It is clearly not true in many other cases, yet Americans are to a large extent unaware of that fact. Like most people, Americans care less about the deaths of the citizens of other states than they do about losses suffered by their own countrymen and -women. Even so, greater awareness of the harm done to others would undoubtedly lead more people to question Washington's actions.[108] In 2016, for example, reliable reports about civilian casualties from Saudi air strikes in Yemen generated widespread media and congressional criticism and eventually led the United States to restrict the sale of some military items to the kingdom and to revise its training procedures for Saudi forces.[109]

To limit public opposition to its own military operations, therefore, the U.S. government provides as little information as possible about the victims of U.S. foreign policy, military and civilian alike. "We don't do body counts," said commanding general Tommy Franks during the initial invasion of Afghanistan, a view echoed by former secretary of defense Donald Rumsfeld.[110] Nonetheless, Bush administration officials repeatedly claimed that independent estimates of Iraqi and Afghan casualties after the U.S. invasion were too high, and President Bush told reporters that estimates of several hundred thousand Iraqi "excess deaths" following the U.S. invasion were "just not credible."[111] Yet classified reports released by *WikiLeaks* show that the U.S. government's own estimate of Iraqi casualties were on a par with the figures of the Iraq Body Count and other independent groups.[112] Other estimates, including a careful survey of excess deaths that was published in the British medical journal *The Lancet*, were significantly higher.[113]

The U.S. government has also done its best to conceal the full extent of its use of armed drones and targeted killings, making it difficult to determine the number of civilians who died as a result of these activities. Independent research groups have estimated that U.S. drone strikes and targeted assassinations killed roughly 3,700 people (and roughly 500 civilians) between 2002 and 2014, but the U.S. government did not provide its own tally until 2016, and the low totals it eventually reported were widely disputed.

This same pattern continued into 2017. According to a spokesman for U.S. Central Command, the U.S. air campaign against ISIS was "one of the most precise air campaigns in military history." The Pentagon reported that 466 Iraqi civilians had died as a result of coalition air strikes and said that only one out of roughly 1,500 U.S. air strikes led to any civilian deaths. Yet a detailed and rigorous investigation by *The New York Times*—based on hundreds of on-the-ground interviews—

concluded that roughly one of every five U.S. air strikes produced at least one civilian death, a percentage thirty-one times higher than the Pentagon's estimates.[114]

Taken together, the desire to keep the costs to the United States low and the willingness to ignore the costs to others makes it easier to keep today's wars going and makes tomorrow's wars more likely. As Rob Malley and Stephen Pomper of the International Crisis Group observed in response to the *New York Times* report just cited, "It's a treacherous trifecta: the promise of greater precision and certainty of fewer U.S. casualties; which leads to more frequent use of military force in more diverse theatres without a substantial U.S. ground presence; which entails diminished ability both to gather information about who is being targeted before a strike and assess what happened afterward. With the human costs of wars substantially shifted to the other side, it has become easier to initiate, perpetuate, and forget them."[115]

As discussed at greater length in the next chapter, the U.S. government is equally reluctant to acknowledge excesses or atrocities by U.S. personnel. The Bush administration tried to minimize opposition to the most controversial aspects of the war on terror—the use of torture, extraordinary rendition, and aggressive surveillance—by keeping these programs secret. When U.S. Marines massacred twenty-four Iraqi civilians in Haditha in 2005, for example, the Pentagon at first blamed the deaths on an insurgent bomb attack and did not acknowledge U.S. responsibility until journalists at the scene presented compelling evidence refuting the official account.[116] And when the U.S. Air Force bombed a hospital run by the international aid group Médecins sans Frontières in 2015, U.S. officials initially claimed that the hospital was "collateral damage" and only subsequently admitted that U.S. forces had failed to observe proper rules of engagement and had mistakenly targeted the facility itself.[117] The Defense Department's internal investigation concluded that the attack was "unintentional," and sixteen U.S. personnel were disciplined, but no criminal charges were filed.[118]

In a democracy with a free press and norms guaranteeing free speech it is impossible to run a costly and unsuccessful foreign policy without people eventually becoming aware of it. As the evidence and anecdotes recounted above reveal, eventually the truth will out and a degree of public reckoning can begin. But the longer proponents of liberal hegemony can hide what is going on and delay the moment of revelation, the easier it will be to conduct business as usual. By the time the evidence is in and failure is apparent, the United States will have moved on to some new problem and repeated the same failed formula.

CONCLUSION

The arguments used to sell liberal hegemony form a seamless web. If Americans are convinced that they face a diverse array of powerful enemies who can be neither accommodated nor deterred, they will support active efforts to eliminate them and will not worry that using force might make the problem worse. If they believe that deep engagement will enhance U.S. prosperity and promote key U.S. values, they will be more likely to support an expanded U.S. role around the world. If the costs to the United States seem low and Americans are unaware of the costs borne by others, they will be even less likely to question what the government is doing.

The arguments used to sell liberal hegemony may be mutually reinforcing, but the campaign to sell it to the American people is not an elaborate conspiracy orchestrated by an unscrupulous, shadowy elite meeting in secret at Aspen, Davos, Bilderberg, or under the auspices of the Trilateral Commission. On the contrary, the foreign policy community in the United States conducts most of its work in full view: writing books, articles, blogs, and task force reports; posting media events on the Internet; appearing on TV and radio; testifying on Capitol Hill; consulting with government agencies; and serving in government themselves. There is no secret cabal running U.S. foreign policy; it is hiding in plain sight.

Yet most of the groups and individuals who favor an activist foreign policy also stand to benefit from it in large and small ways. The main government agencies responsible for conducting U.S. foreign policy have an obvious interest in an ambitious global agenda because it justifies their claim to a sizable share of the federal budget. Arms manufacturers, civil servants, ethnic lobbies, human rights activists, and other special interests have obvious reasons to favor liberal hegemony, especially if they can convince the public to back the particular projects that they favor. The more U.S. foreign policy tries to accomplish, the greater the need for foreign policy expertise and the more opportunities for ambitious foreign policy mandarins to rise to prominence. Whatever their private beliefs may be, most members of today's foreign policy community know that challenging the central premises of liberal hegemony is not a smart career move.

It is easy to understand, therefore, why the foreign policy establishment clings to this strategy, and why most of its members were and remain hostile to Donald Trump. Liberal hegemony enhances the foreign policy community's power and status and makes U.S. global leadership seem necessary, feasible, and morally desirable. But given the considerable costs and dubious benefits it has produced in recent years, how are we to explain its persistence? Why did the rest of the country tolerate failure for so long instead of demanding something better? It is time to consider this question in detail.

5. IS ANYONE ACCOUNTABLE?

WHEN A BIPARTISAN CHORUS of foreign policy professionals denounced Donald Trump's candidacy during the 2016 campaign, Trump fired back promptly, calling them "nothing more than the
failed Washington elite looking to hold onto their power, and it's time
they were held accountable for their actions."[1] Their concerns about
Trump may have been valid, but so was his depiction of an out-of-touch
community of foreign policy VIPs whose unthinking pursuit of liberal
hegemony had produced few successes and many costly failures.

In a perfect world, the institutions responsible for conducting or
shaping U.S. foreign policy would learn from experience and improve
over time. Policies that worked poorly would be abandoned or revised,
and approaches that proved successful would be continued. Individuals

whose ideas had helped the United States become stronger, safer, or more prosperous would be recognized and rewarded, while officials whose actions had repeatedly backfired would not be given new opportunities to fail. Advisors whose counsel proved sound would rise to greater prominence; those whose recommendations were lacking—or, worse yet, disastrous—would be marginalized and ignored.

This notion may sound idealistic, but it is hardly far-fetched. Any organization striving to succeed must hold its members—especially its leaders—accountable for results. No corporation seeking to stay in business would stick with a management team that never met a quarterly target, and no baseball team would keep the same manager and lineup after finishing dead last five years running. In a competitive world, holding people accountable is just common sense.

But it doesn't work this way in American politics, and especially not in foreign policy. Instead, failed policies often persist and discredited ideas frequently get revived, while error-prone experts "fail upward" and become more influential over time. U.S. leaders sometimes turn to the same people over and over, even when they have repeatedly failed to accomplish the tasks they were previously given. The reverse is sometimes true as well: people who do get things right can go unrecognized and unrewarded, and they may even pay a considerable price for bringing unpleasant truths to light.

In short, when it comes to foreign policy, F. Scott Fitzgerald had it exactly backward. Far from having "no second chances in American life," foreign policy practitioners appear to possess an inexhaustible supply of them. This worrisome tendency applies to both ideas and policies and to the people who conceive and implement them.

WHY BAD IDEAS SURVIVE

We would like to think that the government was getting wiser and that past blunders would not be repeated. And in some areas—such as public health, environmental protection, or transportation safety—there has been considerable progress. But the foreign policy learning curve is shallow, and bad ideas are remarkably resilient. Like crabgrass or kudzu, misguided notions are hard to eradicate, no matter how much trouble they cause or how much evidence is arrayed against them.

Consider, for example, the infamous "domino theory," which has been kicking around since Dwight D. Eisenhower was president. During the Vietnam War, U.S. officials and influential pundits repeatedly claimed that withdrawal would undermine American credibility and produce a wave of realignments that would enhance Soviet power and, in the worst case, leave the United States isolated and under siege. The metaphor was evocative—assuming that states actually did behave like dominoes—and it played on fears that other states would flock to whichever superpower seemed most likely to triumph.[2] Yet no significant dominoes fell after the United States withdrew from Vietnam in 1975; instead, it was the Soviet Union that collapsed some fourteen years later. Scholarly investigations of the concept found little evidence for its central claims, and the above two events should have dealt this idea a fatal blow.[3] Yet it reemerged, phoenixlike, in recent debates over Afghanistan, Syria, and the nuclear agreement with Iran. Americans were once again told that withdrawing from Afghanistan would call U.S. credibility into question, embolden U.S. opponents, and dishearten key U.S. allies.[4] In the same way, President Obama's reluctance to intervene in Syria and his decision to pursue a nuclear deal with Iran is supposedly what led Russian president Vladimir Putin to act more aggressively in Ukraine.[5] Despite a dearth of supporting evidence, it seems nearly impossible to quash the fear of falling dominoes.

Similarly, the French and American experience in Vietnam might have taught us that occupying powers cannot do effective "nation-building" in poor and/or deeply divided societies, and that lesson might have made future presidents wary of attempting regime change in the developing world. The Soviet defeat in Afghanistan in the 1980s and the turmoil the United States confronted in Somalia after 1992 should have driven the lesson home even more powerfully. Yet the United

States has now spent more than a decade and a half trying unsuccessfully to do regime change and nation-building in Iraq, Afghanistan, Libya, Yemen, and several other places—at considerable cost but with scant success. The futility of this task could not have been more obvious when Barack Obama took office in 2009, but he still chose to escalate the war in Afghanistan, acquiesced in the ill-advised campaign to topple Muammar Gaddafi in Libya, and continued to interfere throughout the Arab and Islamic world despite abundant evidence that such actions strengthened anti-American extremism.

Why is it so hard for states to learn from mistakes? And on the rare occasions when they do learn, why are the key lessons so easily forgotten?

THE LIMITS OF KNOWLEDGE

Foreign policy is a complicated business, and observers invariably offer competing explanations for policy failures and draw different lessons from them. Did the United States lose in Vietnam because it employed the wrong military strategy, because its South Vietnamese clients were irredeemably corrupt and incompetent, or because media coverage undermined support back home? Did violence in Iraq decline in 2007 because "the surge worked," because Al Qaeda overplayed its hand, or because prior ethnic cleansing had separated Sunnis from Shia and thus made it harder for either to target the other? Because policy implications depend on how the past is interpreted and explained, consensus on the proper "lessons" of a given policy initiative is often elusive.

"THIS TIME IS DIFFERENT"

The lessons drawn from past experience may also be discarded when policymakers believe that new knowledge, a new technology, or a clever new strategy will allow them to succeed where their predecessors failed. As Ken Rogoff and Carmine Reinhart showed in their prizewinning book *This Time Is Different: Eight Centuries of Financial Folly*, economists and financial professionals have repeatedly (and wrongly) concluded that they had devised new and foolproof ways to prevent financial panics, only to be surprised when the next one occurred.[6]

In much the same way, Vietnam taught a generation of U.S. leaders to be wary of counterinsurgency campaigns, but the lesson was forgotten as time passed and new technologies and doctrines made their way into the armed forces. The Vietnam experience had inspired the so-called Powell Doctrine, which prescribed that the United States intervene only when vital interests were at stake, rely on overwhelming force, and identify a clear exit strategy in advance.[7] Yet after routing the Taliban in 2001, top U.S. officials convinced themselves that a combination of special operations troops, precision-guided munitions, and high-tech information management would enable the United States to overthrow enemy governments quickly and cheaply, avoiding lengthy occupations. The caution that informed the Powell Doctrine was cast aside, leading to new quagmires in Iraq and Afghanistan.

Those unhappy experiences guided Barack Obama's more cautious approach to military intervention and his decision to rely on airpower and drones rather than ground troops in most instances. Yet the lesson of these earlier debacles was beginning to fade by 2014, as proponents of a more muscular foreign policy began insisting that the real problem was not the original decision to invade, but rather the decision to withdraw before total victory had been achieved.[8] Senator Marco Rubio (R-FL) told an interviewer, "It was not a mistake to go into Iraq," and Senator Lindsay Graham (R-SC) declared, "At the end of the day, I blame President Obama for the mess in Iraq and Syria, not President Bush." In addition to masking culpability for the earlier blunder, such comments are intended to convince elites and the public to support more operations of this kind, and, if necessary, for longer.[9] To the extent that these efforts to rewrite history succeed, earlier lessons will be forgotten and the same mistakes will be repeated.

IF YOU'RE STRONG, YOU DON'T HAVE TO BE SMART

A wealthy country like the United States has an array of well-funded universities, think tanks, and intelligence agencies to analyze global issues and figure out how to deal with them. These same assets should also help the country learn from experience and correct policies that aren't working. But because the United States is already powerful and secure, mistakes are rarely fatal and the need to learn is not as great as it would be if America's position were more precarious.

The tendency to cling to questionable ideas or failed practices will be particularly strong when some set of policy initiatives is inextricably linked to America's core values and identity. Consider the stubbornness with which U.S. leaders pursue democracy promotion, despite its discouraging track record. History shows that building stable and secure democracies is a long, contentious process, and foreign military intervention is usually the wrong way to do it.[10] As discussed in chapters 1 and 2, U.S. efforts to export democracy, or do nation-building more generally, have failed far more often than they have succeeded. Nonetheless, a deep attachment to the ideals of liberty and democracy make it hard for U.S. leaders to accept that other societies cannot be remade in America's image.

When a large-scale upheaval like the Arab Spring occurs, therefore, U.S. leaders are quick to see it as a new opportunity to spread America's creed. "Our national religion is democracy," noted the Syria expert Joshua Landis in 2017, "when in doubt we revert to our democracy talking points . . . It is a matter of faith."[11] Even when U.S. leaders recognize that they cannot create "some sort of Central Asian Valhalla," as former secretary of defense Robert Gates put it in 2009, they find it nearly impossible to stop trying.

CUI BONO?: BAD IDEAS DO NOT INVENT THEMSELVES

Lastly, bad ideas persist when powerful interests have an incentive to keep them alive. Although open debate is supposed to weed out dubious notions and allow facts and logic to guide the policy process, self-interested actors who are deeply committed to a particular agenda can interrupt this evaluative process. As Upton Sinclair once quipped, "It is difficult to get a man to understand something when his salary depends on his not understanding it."

The ability of self-interested individuals and groups to interfere in the policy process appears to be getting worse, in good part because of the growing number of think tanks and "research" organizations linked to special interests. Their raison d'être is not the pursuit of truth or the accumulation of new knowledge, but rather the marketing of policies favored by their sponsors. And as discussed at greater length below, these institutions can also make it harder to hold public officials fully accountable for major policy blunders.

For example, the disastrous war in Iraq should have discredited and sidelined the neoconservatives who conceived and sold it, as the war showed that most, if not all, of their assumptions about politics were deeply flawed. Once out of office, however, most of them returned to well-funded Washington sinecures and continued to promote the same highly militarized version of liberal hegemony they had implemented while in government. When key members of the foreign policy elite are insulated from their own errors and hardly anyone is held accountable for mistakes, learning from past failures becomes nearly impossible.

In some cases, in fact, influential groups or individuals can intervene to silence or suppress views with which they disagree. In 2017, for example, the U.S. Holocaust Memorial Museum sponsored a careful scholarly study of the Obama administration's handling of the Syrian civil war, which questioned whether greater U.S. involvement could have significantly reduced violence there. The 193-page report had no political agenda and was carefully done, but well-placed individuals who had previously called for the United States to intervene were outraged by the study's findings and convinced the museum's directors to withdraw it.[12]

Even in a liberal democracy, therefore, there is no guarantee that unsuccessful policies will be properly assessed and the ideas that informed them permanently discredited. Not surprisingly, the same principle applies to the people who devise and defend them.

FAILING UPWARD

U.S. foreign policy would work better if the political system rewarded success and penalized failure. Ideally, people who performed well would gain greater authority and influence and those who did poorly would remain on the margins. But this straightforward management principle does not operate very consistently in the realm of politics, including foreign policy. Instead of holding officials to account and weeding out poor performers, the system often displays a remarkable indifference to accountability.

TOO BIG TO FALL?

Aversion to accountability begins at the top, where malfeasance at the highest levels of government is routinely excused. After the 9/11 attacks, for example, the Bush administration and the Republican-controlled Congress reluctantly agreed to appoint an independent, bipartisan commission to investigate the incident and make recommendations. But it was clear from the start that leading politicians did not really want a serious inquiry: the commission's initial budget was a paltry $3 million (later increased to $14 million), and Bush administration officials repeatedly stonewalled the commission's investigations.[13]

Moreover, although one of the commission's key tasks was exploring possible errors by the Clinton and Bush administrations, the co-chairs, Thomas Kean and Lee Hamilton, chose the historian Philip Zelikow as executive director, despite his long association with then–national security advisor Condoleezza Rice, his role on Bush's transition team, and his under-the-radar involvement with the administration itself.[14]

The commission eventually produced a riveting account of the 9/11 plot, but it declined to pass judgment on any U.S. officials. It was the worst attack on U.S. soil since Pearl Harbor and more than twenty-eight hundred people had died, yet apparently no one in the U.S. government was guilty of even so much as a lapse in judgment. As Evan Thomas of *Newsweek* later commented, "Not wanting to point fingers and name names . . . the 9/11 Commission shied away from holding anyone personally accountable" and "ended up blaming structural flaws for the government's failure to protect the nation." The historian Ernest May, who helped write the commission's report and defended its efforts, later acknowledged that responsibility was assigned solely to institutions (such as the FBI or CIA), described the report as "too balanced," and admitted that "individuals, especially the two presidents and their intimate advisors, received even more indulgent treatment."[15]

A similar whitewashing occurred following the revelations that U.S. soldiers abused and tortured Iraqi prisoners of war at Abu Ghraib prison. Top civilian officials were directly responsible for the migration of "enhanced interrogation" techniques from the detention facility at Guantanamo to Abu Ghraib, as well as for the lax conditions that prevailed at the latter facility. Yet even though "the lawlessness and cruelty on the ground in Iraq clearly stemmed from the policies at the top of the Bush administration,"[16] a series of internal reports—by Major General Antonio Taguba, by the U.S. Army's Office of the Inspector General, and by a team of former officials appointed by Rumsfeld and headed by former secretary of defense James Schlesinger—assigned blame entirely to local commanders or enlisted personnel.[17]

In particular, the army inspector general's report blamed the abuses on "unauthorized actions undertaken by a few individuals," a conclusion the *New York Times* editorial board termed a "300-page whitewash."[18] The Schlesinger Report referred briefly to "institutional and personal responsibility at higher levels" but exonerated all the top civilians. In fact, one member of the panel, the retired air force general Charles Horner, explicitly cautioned against assigning blame for the abuses, saying, "Any attempt by the press to say so-and-so is guilty and should resign or things of this nature, they have an inhibiting effect upon this department finding the correct way to do things in the future."[19] And at the press conference releasing the report, Schlesinger—a longtime Washington insider—openly stated that Secretary of Defense Donald Rumsfeld's resignation "would be a boon to all of America's enemies."[20] In the end, a handful of enlisted personnel were convicted of minor offenses, one army general received a reprimand and was retired at lower rank, and none of the civilian officials overseeing their activities were sanctioned at all. As analysts at Human Rights Watch later concluded, these reports "shied away from the logical conclusion that high-level military and civilian officials should be investigated for their role in the crimes committed at Abu Ghraib and elsewhere."[21] Instead, the officials whose careers suffered were those who tried to bring these facts to light. In particular, Major General Taguba was falsely accused of leaking his report, shunned by many of his army colleagues, and subsequently ordered to retire sooner than he had intended.[22]

The Obama administration's decision not to investigate or prosecute Bush administration officials accused of violating U.S. domestic laws regarding torture and committing war crimes fits this pattern as well. Despite considerable evidence that President Bush and Vice President Cheney authorized torture, the Justice Department declined to appoint a special prosecutor to investigate whether they or other top officials had violated U.S. or international law.[23]

President Obama justified this decision by saying "we need to look forward as opposed to looking backward," and the political costs of such an investigation might well have outweighed the gains.[24] Nonetheless, his decision to defer the day of reckoning for perpetrators of torture makes future recurrences more likely and casts doubt on America's professed commitment to defend human rights and the rule of law.[25]

At this late date, pointing out that U.S. officials were never held accountable for serious violations of U.S. and international law is not exactly a revelation. The more important point is that such occurrences are part of a larger pattern.

THE NINE LIVES OF NEOCONSERVATISM

When it comes to U.S. foreign policy, the unchallenged world record holders for "second chances" and "failing upward" are America's neoconservatives. Beginning in the mid-1990s, this influential network of hard-line pundits, journalists, think tank analysts, and government officials developed, purveyed, and promoted an expansive vision of American power as a positive force in world affairs. They conceived and sold the idea of invading Iraq and toppling Saddam Hussein and insisted that this bold move would enable the United States to transform much of the Middle East into a sea of pro-American democracies.

What has become of the brilliant strategists who led the nation into such a disastrous debacle? None of their rosy visions have come to pass, and if holding people to account were a guiding principle inside the foreign policy community, these individuals would now be marginal figures commanding roughly the same influence that Charles Lindbergh enjoyed after making naïve and somewhat sympathetic statements about Adolf Hitler in the 1930s.

That's not quite what happened to the neocons. Consider the fate of William Kristol, for instance, who argued tirelessly for the Iraq War in his capacity as editor of the *Weekly Standard* and as cofounder of the Project for the New American Century. Despite a remarkable record of inaccurate forecasts and questionable political advice (including the notion that Sarah Palin would be an ideal running mate for John McCain in 2008), Kristol is still editor of the *Weekly Standard* and has been at various times a columnist for *The Washington Post* and *The New York Times* and a regular contributor to Fox News and ABC's *This Week*.[26]

Similarly, although Deputy Secretary of Defense Paul Wolfowitz misjudged both the costs and the consequences of invading Iraq and helped bungle the post-invasion occupation, President Bush subsequently nominated him to serve as president of the World Bank in 2005. His tenure at the bank was no more successful, and he resigned two years later amid accusations of ethical lapses.[27] Wolfowitz decamped to a sinecure at the American Enterprise Institute and was appointed chair of the State Department's International Security Advisory Board during Bush's last year as president.

The checkered career of Elliott Abrams is if anything more disturbing for those who believe that officials should be accountable and advancement should be based on merit. Abrams pleaded guilty to withholding information from Congress in the 1980s, after giving false testimony about the infamous Iran-Contra affair. He received a pardon from President George H. W. Bush in December 1992, and his earlier misconduct did not stop George W. Bush from appointing him to a senior position on the National Security Council, focusing on the Middle East.[28]

Then, after failing to anticipate Hamas's victory in the Palestinian legislative elections in 2006, Abrams helped foment an abortive armed coup in Gaza by Mohammed Dahlan, a member of the rival Palestinian faction Fatah. This harebrained ploy backfired completely: Hamas soon learned of the scheme and struck first, easily routing Dahlan's forces and expelling Fatah from Gaza. Instead of crippling Hamas, Abrams's machinations left it in full control of the area.[29]

Despite this dubious résumé, Abrams subsequently landed a plum job as a senior fellow at the Council on Foreign Relations, where his questionable conduct continued. In 2013 he tried to derail the appointment of the decorated Vietnam veteran and former senator Chuck Hagel as secretary of defense by declaring that Hagel had "some kind of problem with Jews." This baseless smear led the CFR president Richard Haass to publicly distance the council from Abrams's action, but Haass took no other steps to reprimand him.[30] Yet, apparently, the only thing that stopped the neophyte secretary of state Rex Tillerson from appointing Abrams as deputy secretary of state in 2017 was President Donald Trump's irritation at some critical comments Abrams had voiced during the 2016 campaign.[31]

In an open society, neoconservatives and other proponents of liberal hegemony should be as free as anyone else to express their views on contemporary policy issues. But exercising that freedom doesn't require the rest of society to pay attention, especially not to individuals who have made repeated and costly blunders. Yet neoconservatives continue to advise prominent politicians and occupy influential positions at the commanding heights of American media, including the editorial pages of *The Wall Street Journal, The New York Times,* and *The Washington Post.* This continued prominence is even more remarkable given that hardly any of them have been willing to acknowledge past errors or reconsider the worldview that produced so many mistakes.[32]

MIDDLE EAST PEACE PROCESSORS: A REVOLVING DOOR

Accountability has been equally absent from U.S. stewardship of the long Israeli-Palestinian "peace process." Ending the long and bitter conflict between Israel and the Palestinians would be good for the United States, for Israel, and for the Palestinians, but the two-state solution Washington has long favored is now moribund despite repeated and time-consuming efforts by Republican and Democratic administrations alike. Yet presidents from both parties continued to appoint the same familiar faces to key positions and got the same dismal results each time.

During the first Bush administration, for example, Secretary of State James Baker's primary advisors on Israel-Palestine issues were Dennis Ross, Aaron David Miller, and Daniel Kurtzer. Baker and his team did convene the 1991 Geneva Peace Conference—a positive step that laid the groundwork for future negotiations—but they failed to halt Israeli settlement construction or begin direct talks for a formal peace deal. Together with Martin Indyk and Robert Malley, these same individuals formed the heart of the Clinton administration's Middle East team and were responsible for the fruitless effort to achieve a final status agreement between 1993 and 2000.

As Miller later acknowledged, in these years the United States acted not as an evenhanded mediator, but rather as "Israel's lawyer." U.S. peace proposals were cleared with Israel in advance, and Israeli proposals were often presented to the Palestinians as if they were American initiatives.[33] Small wonder that Palestinian leaders had little confidence in U.S. bona fides and little reason to believe U.S. assurances that their interests would be protected.

This unsuccessful past was prologue to an even less successful future. After spending the Bush years as counselor for the Washington Institute for Near East Policy (WINEP), a prominent pro-Israel think tank, Dennis Ross joined Obama's presidential campaign in 2008 and returned to the National Security Council during Obama's first term. Originally assigned to work on U.S. policy toward Iran, over time Ross became more and more heavily involved in Israel-Palestine issues, reportedly clashing with Obama's designated Middle East envoy, former senator George Mitchell.[34] Ross was also deeply skeptical about a possible nuclear deal with Iran, and significant progress toward the 2015 agreement took place only after he left the White House at the end of Obama's first term.[35]

Similarly, Indyk spent the Bush years as founding director of the Saban Center for Middle East Policy at Brookings, where he openly backed the Iraq War in 2003.[36] When Secretary of State John Kerry decided to make a new push for an agreement in 2013, he picked not a fresh face with new ideas, but the well-worn Indyk, who in turn chose as his deputy David Makovsky, a hawkish neoconservative from WINEP who had coauthored a book with Ross in 2008.[37]

Revealingly, the one member of Clinton's Middle East team who had trouble returning to government service was Robert Malley, who was also the most skeptical of the traditional U.S. approach. Malley was briefly affiliated with Obama's campaign in 2008, only to be dropped after it was revealed that he had met with representatives of Hamas in the context of his duties at the nongovernmental International Crisis Group (ICG). These activities should not have disqualified him from advising a candidate—he was not serving in the U.S. government at that time, and communicating with Hamas was an integral part of his work at ICG—but the political liability was too great, and Obama quickly distanced himself. Malley returned to the NSC during Obama's second term, but his duties were confined to Iran and the Gulf.

Resolving this long, bitter conflict would be a challenging task for anyone, and an entirely different set of U.S. officials might have failed to achieve an agreement between 1993 and 2016. One might also argue that only experienced diplomats with deep knowledge of the issues and the key players would stand any chance at all of reaching an agreement. Even so, the willingness of presidents and secretaries of state to recycle the same unsuccessful negotiators is troubling. The individuals who repeatedly failed to make peace were hardly the only people in America with intimate knowledge of these issues, and had Clinton, Bush, or Obama put this problem in the hands of experts who had a fresh and more evenhanded outlook, America's long stewardship of the peace process might have been more successful. Given where the conflict was in 1993 and where it is today, and given the potential leverage the United States had over the protagonists, Washington could hardly have done worse.

INSIDERS ON INTELLIGENCE

The same reluctance to hold individuals and organizations accountable can also be found in the management and oversight of America's vast intelligence community. By 2016 it was obvious to even casual observers that oversight of the intelligence agencies had gone badly awry. These organizations not only failed to detect or prevent the 9/11 attacks—despite numerous warning signs—they also played a supporting role in the Bush administration's fairy tales about Iraq's WMD programs and Saddam Hussein's supposed connections to Al Qaeda.[38] U.S. intelligence agencies suffered a further blow when a supposed informant (who turned out to be a double agent) detonated a suicide bomb that killed seven CIA employees and contractors in Afghanistan in December 2009. It took U.S. intelligence nine years to find Osama bin Laden, and it also failed to anticipate the Arab Spring, the Maidan uprising in Ukraine, or Russia's seizure of Crimea in 2013. And in January 2018 *The New York Times* revealed that a former CIA officer had been arrested for providing China with the names of more than a dozen CIA informants, in what it called "one of the American government's worst intelligence failures in recent years."[39]

Last but not least, the vast trove of information on the NSA's electronic surveillance programs leaked by former contractor Edward Snowden revealed serious security lapses within the agency and numerous violations of U.S. law. Subsequent revelations about NSA foreign surveillance activities (such as the hacking of German chancellor Angela Merkel's cell phone) suggested that the NSA was now acting with scant regard for the potential risks or political fallout.

Yet despite these repeated lapses and abuses of power, no one in the intelligence community was held to account. In 2011, in fact, a lengthy investigation of CIA personnel policies by the Associated Press revealed "a disciplinary system that takes years to make decisions, hands down reprimands inconsistently, and is viewed inside the agency as prone to favoritism and manipulation." Among other things, the investigation found that even after an internal review board had recommended disciplinary action for an analyst whose mistaken identification had led to an innocent German being kidnapped and held at a secret prison in Afghanistan for five months, the employee in question was promoted to a top job at the CIA's counterterrorism center. Other officials involved in the deaths of prisoners in Afghanistan went undisciplined and received promotions instead. On the rare occasions when agency personnel were forced to resign, they sometimes returned to work as independent contractors.[40]

Immunity increases as one rises to the top. In March 2013 the director of national intelligence James Clapper told a congressional oversight committee that the NSA was not "willingly" collecting data on U.S. citizens, a statement he later conceded was false after Snowden's files revealed that the NSA had been doing exactly that.[41] Lying to Congress is a criminal offense, but Clapper was not investigated. On the contrary, a White House spokesperson soon confirmed that President Obama had "full confidence" in him.

The career of former CIA director John Brennan exhibited a similar

Teflon-like quality. Brennan was reportedly Obama's first choice as CIA director in 2009 but was passed over because his prior involvement in Bush-era interrogation and detention practices made Senate confirmation questionable. He joined the White House staff instead, where he managed the administration's "kill list" of individuals deemed eligible for lethal "signature strikes."[42] In that capacity, Brennan gave a well-publicized speech in June 2011 defending the administration's policy, claiming, in response to a question from the audience, that "for nearly the past year there hasn't been a single collateral death [from counter-terrorist drone strikes] due to the exceptional proficiency, precision of the capabilities we've been able to develop."[43]

According to the independent Bureau of Investigative Journalism, however, a CIA drone strike in Pakistan had killed forty-two people attending a tribal meeting just three months earlier. The Pakistani government had issued a strong public protest, casting serious doubt on Brennan's claim that he "had no information" about civilians being killed. Nonetheless, Obama nominated him to head the CIA in January 2013, and the Senate promptly confirmed his appointment.

Then, in March 2014, the Senate Intelligence Committee chair-woman Dianne Feinstein accused the CIA of monitoring the computers used by congressional staff members who were investigating the CIA's role in the detention and torture of terrorist suspects and in other illegal activities. Such shenanigans were not entirely new, insofar as CIA officials had previously destroyed ninety-two videotapes documenting acts of torture, a move almost certainly intended to protect the perpetrators from further investigation or prosecution.[44] Other reports suggested that CIA officials were also monitoring emails between Daniel Meyer, the intelligence community official responsible for whistle-blower cases, and Senator Chuck Grassley, a leading advocate of whistle-blower protection.[45]

The obvious intent behind these actions was to keep Senate investigators from holding the CIA accountable for acts of torture or other illegal conduct. Brennan vehemently denied the accusations and the

Department of Justice declined to investigate them, but a subsequent investigation by the CIA's own inspector general confirmed the bulk of Feinstein's original charges.[46]

In response, Brennan made a limited apology and appointed an internal review board to consider disciplinary actions.[47] A few months later, the review board attributed the problem to "miscommunication" and exonerated all CIA personnel involved of any wrongdoing.[48] Despite these well-founded concerns about Brennan's truthfulness, as well as the evidence that reliance on "enhanced interrogation (i.e., torture) had done considerable damage to America's reputation and strategic position," Obama reaffirmed his "full confidence" in him, just as he had previously done with DNI Clapper.[49]

Because secrecy is pervasive, maintaining effective oversight and accountability over the intelligence community is a perennial challenge. Although the Senate and House Select Committees on Intelligence are supposed to provide this oversight, they lack the resources, staff, or electoral incentive to perform this task on a consistent basis. Instead, Congress tends to get seriously involved only after significant abuses come to light, and it inevitably faces stiff resistance from the agencies it is supposed to be monitoring. Under the circumstances, effective oversight and genuine accountability are bound to be rare to nonexistent.[50]

Adding to the difficulty is the incestuous nature of the intelligence community itself. Clapper was a former U.S. Air Force officer who subsequently worked for the Defense Intelligence Agency, directed the National Geospatial-Intelligence Agency (NGA), and served as undersecretary of defense for intelligence, overseeing the NSA, the NGA, and the National Reconnaissance Office (NRO). Brennan was a twenty-five-year CIA veteran who had held top jobs under Republicans and Democrats and ran the interagency National Counterterrorism Center before working at the White House and being appointed CIA director. One of Brennan's predecessors at the CIA, Michael Hayden, was a retired air force general and had also been director of the National Security Agency and the U.S. Cyber Command. Former NSA director Keith Alexander held a variety of intelligence posts in the army and ran the Central Security Service and the U.S. Cyber Command. And former secretary of defense Robert Gates spent most of his career at the CIA, eventually rising to the post of deputy director before moving to the Pentagon under George W. Bush.[51]

There are obvious benefits to having experienced hands in these positions, and replacing veteran intelligence experts with untrained amateurs could easily make things worse. But relying so heavily on "company men" (and women) inevitably creates a cadre of leaders who are strongly inclined to protect the organization and opposed to strict accountability. Thus, Gina Haspel, who replaced CIA director Mike Pompeo following the latter's appointment as secretary of state, helped oversee the Bush-era torture program and reportedly authorized the shredding of videotapes documenting these illegal activities. As one associate later described her: "She went to bat for the agency and the bottom line is her loyalty is impeccable."[52] The inbred and self-protective nature of the intelligence world may have its virtues, but it is not without significant vices as well.

The combination of pervasive secrecy and a semipermanent caste of national security managers goes a long way to explaining the remarkable continuity between the Bush and Obama administrations, as well as the latter's reluctance to hold Bush or his lieutenants responsible for possible transgressions and failures. When the same people are making policy and advising both Republican and Democratic presidents, when the public has little independent information about their activities, and when congressional oversight is resisted at every turn, bad judgment and serious misconduct can go undetected and unpunished for a long time. This failing might not be a serious problem if these agencies and their top leaders were as omniscient as they pretend to be, and if they were reliably committed to genuine external oversight and rigorous internal accountability, but the history of the past several decades suggests otherwise. As with the rest of the foreign policy community, accountability in the world of intelligence is the exception rather than the rule.

THE MILITARY

Lives are on the line whenever the United States goes to war. We might therefore expect the U.S. military to be a highly meritocratic enterprise that does not tolerate poor performance and holds its members strictly accountable. There are clearly cases where this principle holds true, as in the U.S. Navy's recent decision to discipline the commander and a dozen crew members of the USS *Fitzgerald* after a collision with a merchant ship cost the lives of seven crew members.[53]

Unfortunately, like the rest of the foreign policy establishment, the U.S. military has become less accountable over time, and this trend has compromised its ability to fulfill its assigned missions.[54] Secretaries of defense are fond of saying that the United States "has the best military in the world," but this well-trained and well-equipped fighting force has compiled a mostly losing record since the 1991 Gulf War. The United States has fought half a dozen wars since 1990, and apart from some gross mismatches (Iraq in 1990 and 2003 and Kosovo in 1999), its performance has not been impressive.[55] The historian and retired army colonel Andrew Bacevich sums it up well: "Having been 'at war' for virtually the entire twenty-first century, the United States military is still looking for its first win."[56]

For starters, consider the number of scandals that have embarrassed the armed services in recent years. Official Pentagon reports have revealed an epidemic of sexual assault inside military ranks, with an estimated nineteen thousand cases of rape or unwanted sexual contact (against both male and female personnel) occurring *every year*.[57] This same period also saw several prominent cheating scandals, as when thirty-four ICBM launch control officers colluded to falsify scores on their proficiency exams. The abuses at Abu Ghraib prison are well-known, but U.S. military personnel have also committed other war crimes and atrocities, including the killing of sixteen Afghan civilians by Staff Sergeant Robert Bales in 2012.[58]

Moreover, for all the technological sophistication, tactical proficiency, and individual gallantry displayed by U.S. personnel in recent decades, they have repeatedly failed to achieve victory. The United States did not achieve its stated goal of either a stable, democratic Iraq or a stable, democratic Afghanistan, despite spending trillions of dollars and losing thousands of soldiers' lives. It has been unable to create effective security forces in Afghanistan despite devoting years of effort and spending billions of dollars. A daring U.S. raid eventually found and killed bin Laden, but a decade of drone strikes and targeted killings in more than half a dozen countries has not eliminated the terrorist threat—and may have made it worse.[59]

Yet, as Thomas Ricks points out, "despite these persistent problems with leadership, one of the obvious remedies—relief of poor commanders—remained exceedingly rare."[60] Instead, the most frequent reason for relieving military officers of command is sexual misconduct, affecting roughly one out of every three commanders fired after 2005.[61] But the armed forces' losing record in its recent wars suggests that its commanders are either not leading well or not advising their civilian counterparts to end wars of choice that cannot be won.

Nor are they being held accountable. During the initial phases of the Afghan War, for example, the commanding general Tommy Franks failed to commit U.S. Army Rangers at the Battle of Tora Bora, a blunder that allowed Osama bin Laden—the key target of the entire U.S. invasion—to escape into Pakistan.[62] A few months later, a similar error during Operation Anaconda allowed several hundred Al Qaeda members to evade capture as well. Yet Franks was subsequently chosen to command the invasion of Iraq in 2003. His performance there was no better: the outmatched Iraqis were quickly defeated, but Franks's failure to prepare for the post-invasion phase contributed to the full-blown insurgency that erupted after 2004.[63]

Even worse, the military has sometimes failed to hold officers and enlisted personnel fully accountable for more serious misconduct. In January 2004, troops under the command of the army lieutenant colonel Nathan Sassaman forced two handcuffed Iraqi prisoners to jump into the Tigris River, where one of them drowned. Sassaman was not present when the incident occurred, but he later ordered soldiers under his command to obstruct the army investigation of the incident. When the truth surfaced, the divisional commander Ray Odierno issued a written reprimand describing Sassaman's conduct as "wrongful" and "criminal," but did not relieve him of command. Although his once-promising career soon ended, Sassaman "was allowed to retire quietly."[64]

Similarly, even after Staff Sergeant Frank Wuterich, the Marine Corps squad leader whose troops killed twenty-four unarmed Iraqi civilians at Haditha, admitted he had told his men to "shoot first and ask questions later," a deal with army prosecutors led to his pleading guilty to a single charge of "neglectful dereliction of duty." His rank was reduced to private, but he served no time in the brig and eventually received a "general discharge under honorable conditions" that left him eligible for full veterans' benefits. None of the other eight marines charged in the case were ever tried.[65]

Even the careers of such highly decorated commanders as Generals David Petraeus and Stanley McChrystal illustrate a certain reluctance to hold prominent commanders fully accountable. A talented soldier with a flair for public relations, Petraeus enjoyed a glowing reputation as the driving force behind the 2007 "surge" in Iraq. McChrystal was also hailed as a hard-charging counterinsurgency expert whose leadership had helped turn the tide in Iraq and was going to do the same in Afghanistan. Both generals eventually suffered embarrassing personal setbacks: McChrystal was relieved of command after a *Rolling Stone* article described him and his staff making disparaging remarks about President Obama and Vice President Joe Biden; and Petraeus later resigned as director of the CIA after an extramarital affair with his biographer became public. He later pleaded guilty to charges of having given his paramour classified information and lying to the FBI, but he was given probation and a fine and served no jail time.

These missteps did not hold either man back for long. Petraeus joined a private equity firm, became a nonresident senior fellow at Harvard's Kennedy School, cochaired a task force at the Council on Foreign Relations, and taught a course at the City University of New York. By 2016 he was back in the public eye: making regular media appearances, testifying on Capitol Hill, appearing in the *Financial Times'* weekly profile "Lunch with the *FT*," and being interviewed as a potential candidate for secretary of state in the Trump administration. McChrystal decamped to Yale, where he taught courses on leadership to carefully screened undergraduates. Both men also received lucrative speakers' fees in retirement, as other former officers have.

What went largely unnoticed in the glare of their individual indiscretions were their limited accomplishments as military leaders. Like the other U.S. commanders in Iraq and Afghanistan, Petraeus and McChrystal failed to achieve victory. The much-heralded surge in Iraq in 2007 was a tactical success but a strategic failure, for the political reconciliation it was intended to foster never materialized.[66] No workable political order could be created absent that reconciliation, and so the ramped-up U.S. effort was largely for naught.[67] Similarly, McChrystal's short-lived tenure in Afghanistan did not reverse the course of the war, and the escalation he helped force on a reluctant Obama did not produce a stable Afghanistan either.

To be sure, it is doubtful that any strategy could have brought the United States victory in Iraq or in Afghanistan after 2004, and neither Petraeus nor McChrystal bears primary responsibility for these failures. As Bacevich notes, holding commanders accountable during protracted counterinsurgency wars is more difficult "because traditional standards for measuring generalship lose their salience."[68] But like their predecessors in Vietnam, Petraeus, McChrystal, and other U.S. commanders do bear responsibility for not explaining these realities to their civilian overseers or to the American people. On the contrary, both men consistently presented upbeat (if carefully hedged) assessments of the U.S. effort in both countries and repeatedly advocated continuing the war, offering assurances that victory was achievable provided the United States did not withdraw prematurely.[69]

More recent events suggest that little has changed. In November 2017, the current U.S. commander in Afghanistan, General John Nicholson, announced that the United States had finally "turned the corner," even though the Taliban were now in control of more territory than at any time since the original U.S. invasion.[70] Unfortunately, that corner had been turned many times previously: commanding general Dan K. McNeill had spoken of "great progress" in 2007, and David Petraeus, Barack Obama, and Secretary of Defense Leon Panetta had all claimed that the United States had "turned the corner" back in 2011 and 2012.[71] Meanwhile, the U.S. Special Inspector General for Afghanistan Reconstruction reported that military officials in Kabul had begun classifying performance data on Afghan casualties and military readiness, making it harder for outsiders to determine if the war was going well and even more difficult to determine if commanders in the field are performing well or not.[72]

These anecdotes—and the larger pattern that they illustrate—do not mean that accountability is completely absent. Former secretary of defense Robert Gates relieved his first commander two months after taking office and continued to fire incompetent military leaders throughout his tenure.[73] More recently, the commander of the U.S. Seventh Fleet, Admiral Joseph Aucoin, was relieved after a series of collisions and accidents involving U.S. warships. Senior military officials have also expressed their own concerns about eroding ethical standards and are said to be trying to address them.[74] On the whole, however, the U.S. military exhibits the same reluctance to hold leaders accountable as the rest of the foreign policy community.

This combination of chronic failure and lack of accountability has repeatedly compromised the nation-building efforts that liberal hegemony encourages. As of 2016, for example, the United States has spent more than $110 billion on assorted reconstruction projects in Afghanistan, as part of the broader effort to help the Afghan people, strengthen the Kabul government, and marginalize the Taliban. Unfortunately, audits by the Pentagon's own Special Inspector General for Afghan Reconstruction (SIGAR) documented a depressing record of waste, fraud, and mismanagement, along with numerous projects that failed to achieve most of their stated objectives.[75] Yet as Special Inspector John Sopko told reporters in 2015, "nobody in our government's been held accountable, nobody's lost a pay raise, nobody's lost a promotion. That's a problem."[76]

In fairness, these failures are not due primarily to those who have commanded or fought in America's recent wars, and the U.S. Armed Forces are still capable of impressive military operations. Rather, this poor record reflects the type of wars that liberal hegemony requires—namely, long counterinsurgency campaigns in countries of modest strategic value. The fault lies not with the men and women who were sent to fight, but with the civilian leaders and pundits who insisted that these wars were both necessary and winnable.

ACCOUNTABILITY IN THE MEDIA

As discussed in previous chapters, a vigorous marketplace of ideas depends on a vigilant, skeptical, and independent media to ensure that diverse views are heard and to inform the public about how well their government is performing. This mission requires journalists and media organizations to be held accountable as well, so that errors, biases, or questionable journalistic practices do not corrupt public understanding of key issues.

One might think that the explosion of new media outlets produced by the digital revolution would multiply checks on government power and that increased competition among different news outlets might encourage them to adopt higher standards. The reverse seems to be true, alas: instead of an ever-more vigilant "fourth estate," the growing role of cable news channels, the Internet, online publishing, the blogosphere, and social media seems to be making the media environment *less* accountable than ever before. Citizens can choose which version of a nearly infinite number of "realities" to read, listen to, or watch. Anonymous individuals and foreign intelligence agencies disseminate "fake news" that is all too often taken seriously, and such "news" sites as Breitbart, the Drudge Report, and InfoWars compete for viewers not by working harder to ferret out the truth, but by trafficking in rumors, unsupported accusations, and conspiracy theories. Leading politicians—most notoriously, Donald Trump himself—have given these outlets greater credibility by repeating their claims while simultaneously disparaging established media organizations as biased and unreliable.[77]

The net effect is to discredit any source of information that challenges one's own version of events. If enough people genuinely believe "*The New York Times* is fake news," as former congressman Newt Gingrich said in 2016, then all sources of information become equally valid and a key pillar of democracy is effectively neutered.[78] When all news is suspect, the public has no idea what to believe, and some people will accept whatever they are told by the one with the biggest megaphone (or largest number of Twitter followers).

Unfortunately, the commanding heights of American journalism have contributed to this problem by making major errors on some critical foreign policy issues and by failing to hold themselves accountable for these mistakes. These episodes have undermined their own credibility and opened the door for less reliable and more unscrupulous rivals.

The most prominent recent example of mainstream media malfeasance is the role prestigious news organizations played in the run-up to the 2003 Iraq War. Both *The Washington Post* and *The New York Times* published false stories about Iraq's alleged WMD programs, based almost entirely on fictitious material provided by sources in the Bush administration. As the *Times'* editors later acknowledged, the stories were poorly reported and fact-checked, containing numerous errors, and they undoubtedly facilitated the Bush administration's efforts to sell the war.[79]

But the *Times* and the *Post* were not alone: the vaunted *New Yorker* magazine also published a lengthy article by the journalist Jeffrey Goldberg describing supposed links between Osama bin Laden and the Iraqi dictator Saddam Hussein, connections that turned out to be wholly imaginary.[80] A host of other prominent media figures—including Richard Cohen, Fred Hiatt, and Charles Krauthammer of *The Washington Post*;

Bill Keller and Thomas L. Friedman of *The New York Times*; Paul Gigot of *The Wall Street Journal*; and Fred Barnes, Sean Hannity, and Joe Scarborough of Fox News—all jumped on the pro-war bandwagon along with mass-market radio hosts like Rush Limbaugh.

Yet with the sole exception of the *Times* reporter Judith Miller—who wrote several of the false stories and eventually left the newspaper in 2005 with her reputation in tatters—none of the reporters or pundits who helped sell the war paid any price for their blunders.[81] Goldberg switched from hyping the threat from Iraq to issuing equally inaccurate warnings about a coming war with Iran, but these and other questionable journalistic acts did not prevent him from becoming editor in chief of *The Atlantic* in 2016.[82] Other pro-war journalists continued to defend the war for years from lofty positions within the media hierarchy, apparently feeling no responsibility or guilt for having helped engineer a war in which thousands died.[83] And in the rare cases where one of them did admit they were wrong—as managing editor Bill Keller of the *Times* eventually did—the mea culpa was accompanied by a cloud of excuses and a reminder that lots of other people got it wrong too.[84]

The situation was no better at *The Washington Post*. After taking over the editorial page in 2000, Fred Hiatt hired a string of hard-line neoconservatives and transformed it, in the words of James Carden and Jacob Heilbrunn, into "a megaphone for unrepentant warrior intellectuals."[85] The *Post* enthusiastically promoted the invasion of Iraq in 2003 (by one count printing twenty-seven separate editorials advocating the war), and it described Secretary of State Colin Powell's tendentious and error-filled presentation to the UN Security Council as "irrefutable." Its editorial writers saw the invasion as a triumph, writing in May 2004, "It's impossible not to conclude that the United States and its allies have performed a great service for Iraq's 23 million people," and expressing confidence that Iraq's nonexistent WMD would eventually be found.[86] The *Post* defended the decision to invade for years afterward, with the deputy editorial page editor Jackson Diehl opining that the real cost of the war wasn't the lives lost or the trillions of dollars squandered, but rather the possibility that the experience might discourage Washington from intervening elsewhere in the future.[87]

Yet the *Post*'s disturbing record was not confined to Iraq. The editorial board led the successful campaign to derail the nomination of Ambassador Chas W. Freeman to head the National Intelligence Council in 2009 and the unsuccessful effort to block Chuck Hagel's nomination as secretary of defense in 2012, in both cases by distorting Freeman's and Hagel's past records and present views. A 2010 editorial scorned Obama for believing "the radical clique in Tehran will eventually agree to negotiate" over its nuclear program, which is precisely what Iran eventually did.[88] The *Post* columnist Marc Thiessen denied that waterboarding was torture and said it was permissible under Catholic teachings, and Thiessen later received "Three Pinocchios" from the *Post*'s own in-house fact-checker for a 2012 column falsely accusing President Obama of skipping his daily intelligence briefings. Then, in 2014, Thiessen wrote an alarmist column suggesting that terrorists might inoculate themselves with Ebola and fly to the United States in order to infect Americans, a claim quickly dismissed by knowledgeable experts.[89]

As the most prominent newspaper in the nation's capital, the *Post* has significant impact on elite opinion. If there were even a modest degree of accountability in the leading newspaper in the nation's capital, or even a commitment to publishing a more representative range of opinion, Hiatt's performance in this important gatekeeper's role would have led to his dismissal long ago. And if the *Post*'s leadership were genuinely interested in publishing a diverse range of opinion on its op-ed pages, its stable of regular columnists would be rather different from its current lineup. But that is not how major news organizations operate in the Land of the Free.

What does get prominent media figures into trouble? As the cases of Jayson Blair, Stephen Glass, and Janet Cooke reveal, outright fabrication of stories or sources can end a journalist's career. Similarly, the NBC newscaster Brian Williams lost his job after falsely claiming that he had been embedded with a U.S. helicopter crew in Iraq (though he was eventually given a news slot on the MSNBC cable channel), and the Fox

News host Bill O'Reilly, the *Today* show host Matt Lauer, and the MSNBC political analyst Mark Halperin were all dismissed after reliable accounts of persistent sexual harassment came to light.[90] Making openly racist, sexist, homophobic, or obscene comments can be grounds for dismissal, and so can statements that are overly critical of Israel, as UPI's Helen Thomas and CNN's Jim Clancy and Octavia Nasr all learned to their sorrow.[91]

Being overtly committed to peace and skeptical of military intervention may be a problem too. In 2002, for example, the talk show legend Phil Donahue was fired by MSNBC, allegedly for giving airtime to antiwar voices, thereby creating anxiety for executives who believed the network should do more "flag-waving" in the wake of 9/11.[92] But being consistently wrong or flagrantly biased does not seem to be a barrier to continued employment and professional advancement, even at some of America's most prestigious publications.

As some of the sources I have relied upon in this book demonstrate, many contemporary journalists produce reportage and commentary that challenges official policy and tries to hold government officials to account. Yet accountability in the media remains erratic, and questionable journalistic practices continue to this day. When combined with the emergence of alternative media outlets such as Breitbart, not to mention even more extreme sources of "fake news," it is no wonder that public trust in regular media outlets is at an all-time low.[93] This situation is a serious threat to our democratic order, for if citizens do not trust information gleaned from outside official circles, it will be even easier for those in power to conceal their mistakes and manipulate what the public believes.

PROPHETS WITHOUT HONOR: WHAT HAPPENS WHEN YOU'RE RIGHT?

The failure to hold error-prone people accountable has a flip side—namely, a tendency to ignore or marginalize those outside the consensus even when their analysis or policy advice is subsequently vindicated by events. Being repeatedly wrong carries few penalties, and being right often brings few rewards.

In September 2002, for example, thirty-three international security scholars paid for a quarter-page advertisement on *The New York Times'* op-ed page, declaring "War with Iraq Is Not in the U.S. National Interest."[94] Published at a moment when most of the inside-the-Beltway establishment strongly favored war, the ad warned that invading Iraq would divert resources from defeating Al Qaeda and pointed out that the United States had no plausible exit strategy and might be stuck in Iraq for years. In the sixteen-plus years since the ad was printed, none of its signatories have been asked to serve in government or advise a presidential campaign. None are members of elite foreign policy groups such as the Aspen Strategy Group, and none have spoken at the annual meetings of the Council on Foreign Relations or the Aspen Security Forum. Many of these individuals hold prominent academic positions and continue to participate in public discourse on international affairs, but their prescience in 2002 went largely unnoticed.

The case of U.S. Army colonel Paul Yingling teaches a similar lesson. Yingling served two tours in Iraq, the second as deputy commander of the 3rd Armored Cavalry Regiment. His experiences there inspired him to write a hard-hitting critique of senior army leadership, which was published in the *Armed Forces Journal* in March 2007 under the title "A Failure of Generalship." As Yingling put it in a subsequent article, "Bad advice and bad decisions are not accidents, but the results of a system that rewards bad behavior." The article identified recurring command failures in Iraq and became required reading at the Army War College, the Command and General Staff College, and a number of other U.S. military institutions, but Yingling barely received promotion to full colonel in 2010. After being passed over for assignment to the Army War College (a sign that his prospects for further promotion were bleak), he retired from the army to become a high school teacher.[95]

The career trajectories of Flynt and Hillary Mann Leverett illustrate the same problem in a different guise. Until 2003 the Leveretts were well-placed figures in the foreign policy establishment. Armed with a Ph.D. from Princeton, Flynt Leverett was the author of several well-regarded scholarly works and had worked as a senior analyst at the CIA, as a member of the State Department's Policy Planning Staff, and as senior director for Middle East affairs on the National Security Council from 2002 to 2003. After leaving government, he worked briefly at the Saban Center at Brookings before moving to the American Strategy Program at the New America Foundation. Hillary Mann graduated from Brandeis and Harvard Law School, worked briefly at AIPAC, and held a number of State Department posts during the 1990s. The two met during their government service and were married in 2003.

Disillusioned by the Iraq War and the general direction of U.S. Middle East policy, the Leveretts soon became forceful advocates for a fundamentally different U.S. approach to Iran. In addition to making frequent media appearances and starting a website that dealt extensively with events in Iran, in 2013 they published a provocative book entitled *Going to Tehran: Why America Must Accept the Islamic Republic.*[96]

Going to Tehran recommended that the United States abandon the goal of regime change and make a sustained effort to reach out to Iran. It challenged the prevailing U.S. belief that Iran's government had scant popular support and that tighter economic sanctions would compel it to give up its entire nuclear research program. Most controversial of all, their analysis of public opinion polls and voting results led them to conclude that incumbent president Mahmoud Ahmedinejad had won the disputed Iranian presidential election of 2009, and that the anti-Ahmedinejad Green Movement that emerged in the wake of the election did not have majority support.

The Leveretts did not deny that there were irregularities in the election or that many Iranians opposed the clerical regime, and they described the suppression of the Greens (in which roughly a hundred people died) as involving "criminal acts" by the regime in which opponents were "physically abused" or in some cases deliberately murdered. Yet they insisted that the election results were consistent with a wide array of preelection polls and that Ahmedinejad would still have won had no fraud occurred—albeit by a smaller margin.

As one might expect, the Leveretts' departure from Washington orthodoxy provoked a furious response. Critics denounced them as apologists for Tehran, accused them of being in its pay, and portrayed the pair as callously indifferent to the fate of the protesters who were killed or arrested in the postelection demonstrations. Yet the backlash against the Leveretts occurred not because they had made repeated analytic or predictive errors; they became pariahs because they had challenged the consensus view that the Islamic Republic was deeply unpopular at home and therefore vulnerable to U.S. pressure.

In 2010, for example, an otherwise critical profile of the pair in *The New Republic* conceded that "it's not obvious that [the Leveretts'] analysis is wrong," and another critic, Daniel Drezner of the Fletcher School, later acknowledged that they had correctly anticipated that the Green Movement would not succeed.[97] The Leveretts also argued that Iran would never agree to dismantle its entire nuclear enrichment capability—and it didn't—and their insistence that the regime was not on the brink of collapse despite increasingly strict sanctions has been borne out as well. They correctly questioned whether the outcome of Iran's 2013 election was preordained and suggested that the eventual victor—Hassan Rouhani—had a real chance, even though other prominent experts had downplayed his prospects.[98]

The point is not that the Leveretts are always right or that their critics are always wrong.[99] Rather, it is that they are now marginal figures even though their record as analysts is no worse than that of their critics, and in some cases better, largely because they had the temerity to challenge the pervasive demonization of Iran's government. The Leveretts' own combativeness may have alienated potential allies and contributed to their outsider status as well, though they are hardly the only people in Washington with sharp elbows.[100] Meanwhile, those who have remained within the familiar anti-Iran consensus are viewed as reliable authorities despite repeated analytical errors, and they still enjoy prominent positions at mainstream foreign policy organizations and remain eligible for government service should the political winds blow their way.

A world that took accountability seriously—instead of preferring people who were simply loyal and adept at staying "within the lines"— would look for people who had the courage of their convictions, were willing to challenge authority when appropriate, and had expressed views that were subsequently vindicated by events. In such a world, a reluctant dissident such as Matthew Hoh might have had a rather different career. A former Marine Corps captain and State Department official who had served two tours in Iraq, Hoh first attracted public notice when he resigned his position as the senior civilian authority in Afghanistan's Zabul province in 2009, having become convinced that the U.S. effort there could not succeed. In his words: "I have lost understanding of and confidence in the strategic purposes of the United States' presence in Afghanistan . . . my resignation is based not upon how we are pursuing this war, but why and to what end." His superiors viewed Hoh as a talented and dedicated officer and tried to persuade him to stay on, but he held firm to his decision and eventually landed a short-term post as staff director at the New America Foundation's Afghanistan Study Group, which favored a rapid U.S. disengagement from the war.

Subsequent events have shown that Hoh's skepticism about U.S. prospects in Afghanistan was correct. The Council on Foreign Relations highlighted his resignation letter as an "essential document" about the Afghan War, and Hoh received the Nation Institute's Ridenhour Prize for Truth-Telling in 2010. But instead of being rewarded for his foresight and political courage, he found the "Washington national security and foreign policy establishment" effectively closed to him—"no matter how right he was."[101] Beset by lingering post-traumatic stress disorder and other problems from his combat experience, Hoh ended up unemployed for several years. Meanwhile, those who had promoted and defended the unsuccessful Afghan "surge"—thereby prolonging the war to little purpose—received prestigious posts in government, think tanks, the private sector, and academia.

In some ways, Hoh's case parallels that of other recent dissenters and whistle-blowers, including Jesselyn Radack, Peter Van Buren, Thomas Drake, John Kyriakou, and, most famous of all, Edward Snowden and Chelsea Manning. But unlike Snowden or Manning, whose actions broke the law, Hoh's only "error" was having the courage to go public with his doubts about U.S. strategy.[102]

These (and other) examples raise a fundamental question: If the people who repeatedly get important foreign policy issues wrong face little or no penalty for their mistakes while those who get the same issues right are largely excluded from positions of responsibility and power, how can Americans expect to do better in the future?

CONCLUSION

To be clear, U.S. foreign policy would not become foolproof if a few editors and pundits were replaced, if more generals were relieved for poor performance, or if advisors whose advice had proved faulty were denied additional opportunities to fail. Foreign policy is a complicated and uncertain activity, and no one who wrestles with world affairs ever gets everything right.

Moreover, the desire to hold people accountable could be taken too far. We do not want to oust government officials at the first sign of trouble or fire a reporter because he or she gets some elements of a complicated story wrong. No one is infallible, and people often learn from their mistakes and get better over time. Moreover, if we want to encourage public officials to innovate, to take intelligent chances, and to consider outside-the-box initiatives, we need to accept that sometimes they are going to fail. Instead of ostracizing people at the first mistake, a better course would be to identify the ideas, individuals, or policies that led to trouble and acknowledge the mistakes openly. But when blunders occur repeatedly and the people who make them cannot or will not admit it, we should look to someone else to do the job.

Unfortunately, the present system does not encourage systematic learning, and it does not hold people to account even when mistakes recur with depressing frequency. As discussed in chapter 2, a permissive condition for the absence of accountability is America's fortuitous combination of power and security, insulating the country from policy mistakes and allowing follies to go uncorrected.

But perhaps the greatest barrier to genuine accountability is the self-interest of the foreign policy establishment itself. Its members are reluctant to judge one another harshly and are ready to forgive mistakes lest they be judged themselves. Even when prominent insiders break the law, they have little trouble getting prominent friends and former associates to organize campaigns for acquittal or clemency.[103]

"To get along, go along" is an old political adage, and it goes a long way to explain why the foreign policy establishment tolerates both honest mistakes and less innocent acts of misconduct. Strict accountability would jeopardize friendships—especially in a town as inbred as Washington, D.C.—and going public with criticisms or blowing the whistle on serious abuses carries a high price in a world where loyalty counts for more than competence or integrity. Provided they don't buck the consensus, challenge taboos, or throw too many elbows, established members of the foreign policy community can be confident of remaining on the inside no matter how they perform.

The neophyte senator Elizabeth Warren (D-MA) offered us a revealing look at this phenomenon in her 2014 book *A Fighting Chance*. Newly elected and preparing to head to Washington, she asked her Harvard colleague Lawrence Summers, a former Treasury secretary with a lengthy Washington résumé, for advice on how to be effective. As she recounts: "He teed it up this way: I had a choice. I could be an insider or I could be an outsider. Outsiders can say whatever they want. But people on the inside don't listen to them. Insiders, however, get lots of access and a chance to push their ideas. People—powerful people—listen to what they have to say. But insiders also understand one unbreakable rule: *They don't criticize other insiders.*"[104]

Until Trump. A wealthy New York real estate developer and reality show host who inherited a fortune is hardly a genuine outsider, but Trump's campaign, transition period, and early months in office showed scant respect for established figures in either political party and displayed particular contempt for the foreign policy establishment and many of its core beliefs. Trump's skepticism was understandable, perhaps, even if his own ideas seemed ill-informed and his own character deeply worrisome.

But a critical question remained unanswered: Could an impulsive, Twitter-wielding president and a group of untested advisors make a clean break with liberal hegemony? Would they be able to overcome the reflexive opposition of the foreign policy community, or would it eventually contain and co-opt them? If Trump tried to challenge the foreign policy Blob, would he be able to put a better strategy in place or just make things worse? The next chapter describes what Trump did and how he fared.

Spoiler alert: the results are not pretty.

6. How *Not* to Fix U.S. Foreign Policy

H AD HILLARY CLINTON become president in January 2017, the central elements of U.S. foreign policy would have remained firmly in place. Clinton would have embraced America's self-proclaimed role as the world's "indispensable" power, continued "rebalancing" U.S. strategic attention toward Asia, been quick to counter a more assertive Russia, and remained fully committed to NATO. Relations with America's traditional Middle Eastern clients would have continued unaltered, and Clinton would have undoubtedly sought to preserve the 2015 nuclear deal with Iran while opposing Tehran's regional activities. She would have staffed her administration with experienced liberal internationalists and carefully vetted newcomers who shared her mainstream views. Clinton might have taken a harder line on some issues—such as the civil war in Syria—than Barack Obama had, but her overall approach to foreign policy would have been consistent with the previous quarter century of American conduct abroad. Under Hillary Clinton, liberal hegemony would have remained intact and unquestioned, despite its many short-comings.

But Donald Trump became president instead, in part because he had campaigned against the failed grand strategy that Clinton was defending and had promised to take on the establishment that Clinton personified. And enough Americans agreed with his broad-brush indictment of past failures to power him to victory in the electoral college and into the Oval Office.

As president, Trump had a golden opportunity to place U.S. foreign policy on a sounder footing. As shown in chapter 3, there is a persistent gap between the foreign policy community's views on foreign policy and the views of most Americans. The general public rejects isolation-ism, but it favors a more restrained grand strategy than most members of the foreign policy community do. In theory, Trump could have built on that base of support, sought out members of the foreign policy community who recognized that the pursuit of liberal hegemony had gone astray, and worked with America's partners to bring U.S. interests and commitments into better balance without destabilizing key regions. On some issues—such as international trade—Trump could have pressed for the judicious updating of existing institutions and trade arrangements, at the same time preserving an open economic order and defending America's central position within it. Properly implemented, a carefully managed shift to a more realistic grand strategy would have kept the United States secure and prosperous while freeing up the resources needed to address pressing domestic priorities.

It was not to be. Having promised to "shake the rust off American foreign policy," Trump's presidency began with a flurry of unconventional moves that reinforced the skepticism of the foreign policy establishment and united key elements of it against him even more strongly. Global realities and resistance from the foreign policy "Blob" began to rein Trump in, and the opportunity for a positive shift in strategy was lost. A year later, many of the policies Trump inherited were still in place and key elements of liberal hegemony were intact. In the war between Trump and tradition, tradition won most of the initial battles.[1]

Which is not to say that Trump had no impact. Modern presidents enjoy considerable latitude in the conduct of foreign policy, and what they say and how they say it—whether in person or on Twitter—can be as important as what they do. These powers allowed Trump to have a significant effect on U.S. foreign policy and on America's standing in the world, despite the opposition he faced.

Unfortunately, Trump's impact has been almost entirely negative. The United States is still pursuing a misguided grand strategy, but the captain of the ship of state is an ill-informed and incompetent skipper lacking accurate charts, an able crew, or a clear destination. The United States is still overcommitted around the world, with its military forces fighting active insurgencies in many countries. It continues to spend far more on national security than any other country does, despite recurring fiscal problems and compelling domestic needs. Long the linchpin of the global economy, its commitment to an open trading order is in serious doubt. Meanwhile, Trump's erratic, combative, self-indulgent, and decidedly unpresidential behavior has alarmed key allies and created inviting opportunities for America's rivals. Instead of orchestrating a well-designed move away from liberal hegemony and toward a more sensible strategy, Trump has abandoned hard-won positions of influence for no discernible gains and has cast doubt on whether the United States can be relied upon to carry out a successful foreign policy. Instead of "making America great again," Trump has accelerated its decline.

As president, Trump ended up embracing the worst features of liberal hegemony—overreliance on military force, disinterest in diplomacy, and a tendency toward unilateralism—while turning his back on its positive aspirations, such as support for human rights and the preservation of an open, rules-based world economy. When combined with his ignorance, chaotic management style, and impulsive decision-making, the result was a steady erosion in America's global position.

WHAT TRUMP PROMISED

In his Inaugural Address, Trump stuck to the core themes of his campaign. "From this day forward," he pledged, "it's going to be only America First." No longer would the United States underwrite the security of its allies in Europe or Asia; from now on "the countries we are defending must pay for the cost of this defense, and if not, the U.S. must be prepared to let these countries defend themselves."[2]

As described in the introduction to this book, Trump had gone even further during the 2016 campaign, at one point calling NATO "obsolete" and condemning longtime allies such as Saudi Arabia for supporting terrorism and various other sins.[3] On his watch, he promised, the United States would "get out of the nation-building business," convince Mexico to pay for a wall along the border, and take a tougher line against "radical Islamic extremism." Trump had said that he would withdraw from the Trans-Pacific Partnership (TPP), tear up the North American Free Trade Agreement (NAFTA), label China a currency manipulator, and prevent it and other trading partners from "stealing" American jobs. Trump vowed to abandon the landmark Paris Agreement on climate change and leave the agreement halting Iran's nuclear program, which he called the "worst deal ever." He pledged to move the U.S. embassy from Tel Aviv to Jerusalem, and he spoke of a desire to resolve the Israeli-Palestinian conflict—calling it "the ultimate deal." Trump also held out hope for an improved relationship with Russia and China and repeatedly expressed his admiration for Russian president Vladimir Putin, calling him a "strong leader" and telling supporters, "We're going to have a great relationship with Putin and Russia."[4]

Viewed as a whole, Trump's initial approach to foreign policy revealed a highly nationalistic, zero-sum worldview, where the United States would pursue its own interests with little or no regard for others.

Some of his pronouncements also reflected a nostalgic vision of America as a predominantly white, Anglo-Saxon, and Judeo-Christian culture that faced a growing threat from foreign influences, immigrants, and especially Islam.[5] Such instincts may explain Trump's apparent affinity for such xenophobic nationalists as Putin, Viktor Orbán of Hungary, and Marine Le Pen in France and his disdain for defenders of multicultural tolerance, including many politicians in the European Union.[6]

Thus, Trump's arrival seemed to herald a sharp break with the bipartisan consensus behind liberal hegemony. The United States would no longer use its power to spread democracy or promote liberal values and would distance itself from the multilateral institutions it had helped create, nurture, and expand in the past. Instead of trying to strengthen and expand a rules-based international order, the United States would be out for itself alone. Henceforth, relations with other states would be judged solely by whether the United States benefited from them as much or more than others did.[7] As Trump told the United Nations General Assembly in September 2017, in a speech that repeatedly stressed the importance of national sovereignty, "I will always put America first, just like you, as the leaders of your countries will always, and should always, put your countries first."[8]

What Trump Did

Trump's early appointments suggested that he fully intended to shake up the status quo. Although he briefly considered such familiar figures as retired army general and former CIA director David Petraeus and the 2012 GOP presidential nominee Mitt Romney for top foreign policy posts, many of his early appointments went to outsiders. Ignoring an explicit warning from President Obama, Trump chose a controversial retired general, Michael Flynn, as his first national security advisor.[9] Trump made Michael Anton, a far-right critic of the liberal world order, director of communications for the National Security Council, and his White House staff included several assistants with minimal experience and dubious qualifications—such as former Breitbart commentator and self-styled terrorism expert Sebastian Gorka.[10]

For his cabinet, Trump picked Exxon president Rex Tillerson for the post of secretary of state, despite Tillerson's lack of governmental or diplomatic experience. Trump also proposed a 30 percent cut in the State Department budget and was slow to submit nominees for top policy jobs there, telling Fox News in April, "I don't want to fill many of these appointments . . . they're unnecessary."[11] He was true to his word: after a year in office many top foreign policy positions were still vacant or being handled by interim officials.[12]

Instead of placing a civilian atop the Pentagon, as every president since Truman had done, Trump asked retired Marine Corps general James Mattis to serve as his secretary of defense. He chose another retired general, John Kelly, to head the Department of Homeland Security, and gave his thirty-six-year-old son-in-law, the real estate heir Jared Kushner, several high-profile administrative diplomatic assignments despite Kushner's lack of political experience or foreign policy credentials.

In another departure from past practice, Trump at first excluded the director of national intelligence and the chairman of the Joint Chiefs of Staff from the National Security Council's "principals committee" and put his chief political strategist, former Breitbart News head Stephen Bannon, on the committee instead. The economist Peter Navarro (author of the China-bashing tract Death by China) brought a protectionist outlook to Trump's new National Trade Council, the hard-line trade lawyer Robert Lighthizer became U.S. trade representative, and former Republican governor of South Carolina Nikki Haley became ambassador to the United Nations despite her own limited background in foreign affairs.

Yet a number of these unorthodox arrangements turned out to be remarkably short-lived, and Trump's foreign policy team soon took on a more normal character. Flynn resigned as national security advisor after only twenty-four days in the job, having lied about earlier meetings with Russian officials; and his deputy, former Fox News commentator K. T. McFarland, followed suit a few days later. Flynn's replacement was army lieutenant general H. R. McMaster, whose foreign policy views lay firmly within the establishment consensus. McMaster soon brought in Fiona Hill of the Brookings Institution, the author of a highly critical biography of Vladimir Putin, to handle Russian affairs at the NSC, a move that signaled a more conventional approach toward this critical relationship. In April the White House announced that the political strategist Stephen Bannon would no longer attend NSC "principals committee" meetings and that the director of national intelligence Dan Coats and chairman of the Joint Chiefs of Staff Joseph Dunford would resume their usual roles on this body.[13]

The major shake-up that repopulated Trump's White House staff in the summer of 2017 represented a further step toward Beltway orthodoxy. The beleaguered White House press secretary Sean Spicer resigned in July, and Trump installed former hedge fund manager Anthony Scaramucci as his new White House director of communications, only to fire him ten days later.[14] The homeland security secretary Kelly replaced Reince Priebus as White House chief of staff, and he and McMaster proceeded to clean house at the NSC, dismissing a number of Trump's initial appointees and bringing in experienced mainstream experts.[15] Increasingly isolated, Bannon departed the White House shortly thereafter, removing the administration's most prominent proponent for a radical shift in grand strategy.

Not surprisingly, these personnel shifts helped attenuate many of Trump's more radical inclinations. Although his behavior and rhetoric continued to defy traditional norms and expectations, the substance of U.S. policy was increasingly familiar. A new round of personnel changes occurred in early 2018—NEC director Cohn resigned and Tillerson and McMaster were dismissed and replaced by CIA director Mike Pompeo and former U.N. ambassador John Bolton respectively—but even this latest upheaval did not alter the broad direction of U.S. foreign policy, save in the area of trade policy and Iran. And as discussed below, even these shifts were not a 180-degree turn in the broad outlines of U.S. policy.

NATO ISN'T "OBSOLETE" AFTER ALL

Trump had described NATO as "obsolete" and "outdated" during the election campaign, but he reversed himself in April 2017 and said this was no longer the case "because they had changed."[16] Moreover, Vice President Pence, Secretary of State Tillerson, and Secretary of Defense Mattis all journeyed to Europe during the first half of 2017 in a coordinated effort to reassure U.S. allies. Trump prompted new concerns at the NATO summit in May, refusing to endorse the mutual defense clause (Article 5) of the NATO Treaty and berating the other heads of state attendees for failing to pull their weight, but he reversed course again the following month, telling reporters, "I'm committing the U.S. to Article 5 . . . absolutely." Driving the point home, he repeated this pledge on visits to Germany and Poland in June.[17] Efforts to bolster NATO's defenses against Russia—including the European Reassurance Initiative (ERI) and the joint military exercise Operation Atlantic Resolve—continued through 2017, and the administration's FY2018 budget called for a $1.4 billion increase in U.S. funding for ERI, a rise of roughly 40 percent. After a rocky start, the U.S. commitment to defend Europe was intact, if on increasingly thin ice.[18]

Moreover, Trump's main complaint about NATO—that its European members were not contributing their fair share—was nothing new. Disputes about burden-sharing are as old as the alliance itself, and many previous presidents, secretaries of defense, and congressional leaders had raised this issue, often in language as blunt as Trump's. In 2011, for example, Secretary of Defense Robert Gates predicted in his farewell speech at NATO headquarters that the alliance would face a "dim if not dismal future" if its European members did not increase spending, warning that "there will be dwindling appetite and patience in the U.S. Congress—and in the American body politic writ large—to expend increasingly precious funds on behalf of nations that are apparently unwilling to devote the necessary resources or . . . be serious and capable partners in their own defense." Barack Obama issued a similar rebuke during a visit to Poland in June 2014 and repeated it at the Warsaw Summit in July 2016.[19] National Security Advisor McMaster described Trump's approach to NATO as a form of "tough love," and Trump was quick to claim that his hard-nosed approach was working.[20] In terms of substance, therefore, Trump's approach to NATO was not very different from that of his predecessors.

CONFRONTING RUSSIA AND CHINA

Although Trump had stated that he wanted the United States to have positive relations with Russia and China, U.S. policy toward both states remained as wary and competitive as it had been under Obama and Bush. The White House's 2017 *National Security Strategy* placed Russia and China front and center among the long-term challenges facing the United States, declaring that the two countries "challenge American power, influence and interests, attempting to erode American security and prosperity."[21] Trump was unable to prevent the Republican-controlled Congress from imposing new economic sanctions on Russia in August 2017, which led Russian president Vladimir Putin to order the closing of two American facilities in Russia, and Trump subsequently approved a State Department recommendation to close three additional Russian diplomatic facilities (including its consulate in San Francisco). And in December, with former NATO ambassador Kurt Volker in place as special envoy to Ukraine and A. Wess Mitchell, former CEO of the hard-line Center for European Policy Analysis, serving as assistant secretary of state for Europe and Eurasian affairs, Trump authorized a $41.5 million sale of lethal arms—including Javelin antitank missiles—to Ukraine, earning kudos from former Obama officials and an angry condemnation from Moscow.[22]

The rift between Moscow and Washington widened in 2018, after a clash between Russian mercenaries and U.S.-backed militias in Syria and revelations that Russian agents had used chemical weapons in an attempt to murder a former Russian spy now living in Great Britain. The White House released a joint statement with Britain, France, and

Germany condemning the attack, while the Treasury Department imposed new sanctions to punish Russia for interfering in the 2016 election.[23] Although Trump and Putin sought to mend fences at a summit meeting in July 2018, U.S. policy toward Russia during Trump's first eighteen months in office was if anything more confrontational than it had been under Obama.

Like his predecessors (and especially the Obama administration) Trump also saw China as a major long-term rival. Trump met with Chinese president Xi Jinping on two occasions in 2017 and claimed to have established a "good relationship" with him, and the two leaders authorized annual "strategic dialogues" on critical bilateral issues just as previous U.S. administrations had done.[24] But Trump was disappointed by Xi's refusal to put more pressure on North Korea and remained troubled by the unbalanced Sino-American trade relationship. Xi's confident and proudly nationalist speech at the 19th Party Congress in October 2017 left little doubt about Beijing's growing ambitions, and both the White House *National Security Strategy* and the Pentagon's *National Defense Strategy* labeled China a "strategic competitor," criticized its efforts to expand its influence and "undermine regional stability," and declared that a "geopolitical competition between free and repressive visions of world order is taking place in the Indo-Pacific region." The *National Security Strategy* also stressed the importance of U.S. allies (including Taiwan) and said that the United States "would redouble our commitment to established alliances and partnerships."[25]

The Defense Department continued to see China as its principal long-term military rival, just as it had under Bush and Obama.[26] The U.S. Navy increased the pace of "freedom of navigation" patrols in the South China Sea during 2017, making it clear that the United States still rejected China's territorial claims in this important international waterway and echoing a point Secretary of State Tillerson had made in his own confirmation hearings.[27] The perception of China as a serious long-term competitor also drove Trump's March 2018 decision to impose targeted tariffs and investment restrictions in retaliation for China's violations of WTO trade rules and theft of U.S. intellectual property.[28] His tactics were different, but the effort to confront a rising China began long before Trump.

NORTH KOREA: THE ONCE AND FUTURE ENEMY

North Korea had been a vexing problem for Clinton, Bush, and Obama, and it remained a headache for Trump as well. The United States had worried about Pyongyang's nuclear weapons program since the early 1990s, and U.S. leaders had seriously considered preventive military action on more than one occasion. Yet North Korea's nuclear and long-range missile capabilities continued to grow, leading Barack Obama to warn President-elect Trump that North Korea would be the "most urgent problem" he would face as president.[29]

On the eve of his first meeting with Chinese president Xi Jinping, Trump threw down the gauntlet by declaring, "If China is not going to solve North Korea, we will!"[30] Trump then engaged in a provocative war of words with the North Korean leader Kim Jong-un throughout his first year in office, labeling Kim "Little Rocket Man" and warning that if North Korea continued to threaten the United States, it would be "met with fire and fury like the world has never seen." In December 2017, after Kim boasted that "the whole territory of the U.S. is within the range of our nuclear strike and a nuclear button is always on the desk of my office," Trump took to Twitter to respond, saying, "I too have a Nuclear Button, but it is a much bigger & more powerful one than his, and my Button works!"[31]

Yet bluster and saber rattling aside, Trump eventually chose to rely on sanctions and diplomacy, just as his predecessors had.[32] Trump had initially declared that additional North Korean missile tests "would not happen," but the administration responded to the new round of tests not by taking military action, but by sponsoring a unanimous UN Security Council resolution that imposed a new round of sanctions on Pyongyang.[33] U.S. officials continued to warn that "time is running out," hinting that the United States did have feasible military options, but Trump still declined to roll the iron dice of war.[34]

The problem for Trump, as for other presidents, was that there was no way to eliminate North Korea's nuclear arsenal or destroy its missile test facilities without risking an all-out war that might kill hundreds of thousands of people in South Korea, trigger open conflict with China, and cast doubt throughout Asia about the value of U.S. protection.[35] As a result, by the end of 2017 Trump had agreed to delay joint military exercises with South Korea until after Seoul had hosted the Winter Olympics and endorsed a South Korean initiative for face-to-face talks with its counterparts from the North. As Trump told reporters in January 2018, "I'd like to see [North Korea] getting involved in the Olympics and maybe things go from there."[36]

Where they went was wholly unexpected: in March, a summit meeting between Kim Jong-un and South Korean President Moon Jae-in led to an invitation from Kim to Trump for a summit meeting to address the nuclear issue and the other points of contention between the two states. Trump promptly accepted the offer, despite widespread doubts about the wisdom of such a meeting and the lack of any preparations for it.[37] The president's impulsive response was typical, perhaps, but it also underscored his own reluctant recognition that differences with North Korea were best handled via diplomacy.

The two leaders held a brief meeting in Singapore in June and signed a vague agreement to "work toward denuclearization." Trump subsequently claimed the threat from North Korea was over, but Pyongyang's actual capabilities had not changed and the meeting was largely a triumph of style over substance.

Nonetheless, the priority Trump now placed on addressing the danger from North Korea differed sharply from the stance he had taken during the 2016 campaign. Before becoming president, Trump had suggested that it might be better for South Korea and Japan to develop their own nuclear weapons rather than continuing to rely on U.S. guarantees.[38] Trump now recognized the United States should take the lead in finding a solution.

ON COURSE IN THE MIDDLE EAST

Trump's approach to the Middle East did not contain major departures either.[39] Trump met with the leaders of Egypt, Israel, Jordan, and Saudi Arabia shortly after taking office and reaffirmed U.S. support for each of these long-standing allies. Beginning his first foreign trip in Saudi Arabia in May 2017, he abandoned his harsh attacks on Islam and his earlier criticisms of the kingdom and called instead for a unified Arab front against radicalism, terrorism, and Iran. Trump embraced the ambitious reform campaign of the Saudi crown prince Mohammed bin Salman with particular enthusiasm while turning a blind eye toward the prince's reckless and unsuccessful attempts to counter Iranian influence in Yemen, Lebanon, and Qatar.[40] But this was not a new policy either: Obama had done little to rein in Saudi adventurism either, and any U.S. president would have welcomed efforts to relax religious restrictions and diversify the Saudi economy.

Trump's forceful response to the renewed use of chemical weapons by the Assad regime in April was also a revealing reversion to the familiar Beltway playbook. Trump had previously said that the United States should not get involved in Syria—even with airpower alone—but he surprised everyone by ordering cruise missile strikes on the airfield from which the chemical attacks had been conducted.[41] This embrace of Beltway orthodoxy had no impact on the war itself—indeed, Assad's position continued to improve throughout the year—but it won Trump enthusiastic plaudits from Republicans, Democrats, and prominent media pundits. As CNN's Fareed Zakaria put it, "I think Donald Trump became president of the United States [last night]."[42]

Similarly, Trump's policy toward Iran fits comfortably within the broad and deep anti-Iran consensus that has guided U.S. policy since the fall of the shah in 1979. The president's opposition to and withdrawal from the 2015 multilateral agreement that blocked Iran from acquiring nuclear weapons is an obvious departure from Obama's approach, but it is not a radical position within the U.S. foreign policy community, despite the extensive criticism it has received from the other parties to the agreement and from many Democrats.[43]

It is important to remember that the Joint Comprehensive Plan of Action (JCPOA) was extremely controversial from the start, and the Obama administration had to wage an uphill fight to win grudging acceptance from Congress. A number of well-funded groups and influential individuals inside the Beltway had worked relentlessly to overturn it, and even many supporters of the deal viewed Iran as an especially dangerous adversary that the United States had to work harder to contain.[44] Nor should we forget that Bill Clinton, George W. Bush, and Barack Obama had all imposed sanctions on Iran, backed its regional opponents, authorized covert actions against it, and either flirted with or openly embraced the goal of "regime change" in Tehran.[45] Trump's decision to unilaterally abandon the deal may have been foolish, but it is hardly a radical break with prior U.S. policy. In fact, it was the JCPOA that was the real exception, and Trump's decision to jettison it was simply a return to the policy of confrontation aimed at regime change that has long defined U.S. policy toward Iran.[46]

The most obvious difference between Trump and his predecessors was his approach to the Israeli-Palestinian conflict. Trump chose an unapologetic defender of the Israeli settler movement, David Friedman, as his ambassador to Israel, a clear signal that he was not going to press Israel on this issue.[47] And unlike Clinton, Bush, or Obama, Trump was not personally committed to the idea of the "two-state" solution. As he told an interviewer in February 2017, "I'm looking at two-state and one-state, and I like the one that both parties like."[48] Then, in December, Trump made good on a campaign pledge to recognize Jerusalem as Israel's capital. When Palestinian leaders protested, he accused them of failing to show "appreciation or respect" for the United States and threatened to cut off U.S. aid to the Palestinian Authority.[49]

The Jerusalem decision broke sharply with the international consensus that the city's status should be determined through negotiations rather than by unilateral Israeli action, which is why previous presidents had all ignored their own campaign pledges to do something similar.[50]

Yet Trump's uncritical embrace of Israel and his disinclination to oppose Israel's settlements was more a shift in appearances than a sea change in U.S. policy.[51] Previous presidents had complained about the settlements on numerous occasions and had tried to nudge Israel toward a peace agreement, but none had ever tried to force Israel to comply by threatening to reduce U.S. aid or diplomatic protection. On the contrary, Clinton, Bush, and Obama had all gone to considerable lengths to demonstrate that U.S. support for the Jewish state was "unshakable."[52]

Furthermore, there was no "peace process" to speak of in 2017, and the two-state solution that past presidents had favored was on life support, if not completely dead.[53] And in the unlikely event that it got miraculously revived, Trump's largely symbolic action on Jerusalem would not preclude the Palestinians from eventually having a capital of their own in East Jerusalem as well. Overall, Trump's approach to this issue merely made plain what sophisticated observers already knew: the U.S. government was firmly on Israel's side and was never going to use the leverage it possessed to bring about a fair settlement. At worst, his actions simply removed the pretense of American evenhandedness, a facade that no longer fooled anyone.[54]

DEFENSE POLICY AND COUNTERTERRORISM

As a candidate, Trump had charged the Obama administration with neglecting America's defenses and had insisted that the United States had become a "weak country," even though U.S. defense spending equaled the next dozen or so countries combined and was nearly three times that of China. Insisting that "our military dominance must be unquestioned," Trump promised to "spend what was necessary to rebuild our military."[55]

Once in office, he immediately proposed a 10 percent increase in base military spending, and the House of Representatives eventually authorized an even bigger budget than the president had requested.[56] As noted above, senior military officers occupied key policymaking positions—including secretary of defense, national security advisor, and White House chief of staff—and Trump gave regional commanders greater latitude to initiate combat operations without White House approval. The Pentagon responded by ramping up combat activities in several theaters, and U.S. forces launched six times more air strikes in Trump's first 142 days in office than they had by Obama's last 142.[57] Trump also tried to reverse the Obama administration's decision to permit transgender Americans to serve in uniform—apparently without consulting senior military officers or his secretary of defense—only to have his executive order struck down in federal court.[58]

Even so, these actions hardly added up to a significant shift in defense policy. Neither Trump nor Secretary of Defense Mattis proposed major shifts in U.S. overseas commitments, military strategy, or the day-to-day management of the vast Pentagon bureaucracy. And though Trump tried to portray his budget hike as an unprecedented move to strengthen the armed forces, a careful comparison by the nonpartisan Center for Strategic and Budgetary Assessments showed that it was smaller than ten previous defense buildups and "far short of an historic increase."[59]

Nor did Trump alter the broad outlines of the ongoing war on terror. The U.S. military campaign against ISIS continued to follow the strategy conceived and implemented under Obama—albeit at a slightly accelerated pace—and Trump also approved slight increases in U.S. force levels in Somalia, Syria, and several other theaters.[60] In most respects, however, U.S. counterterror policy stuck closely to the blueprint Trump had inherited: the Defense Department continued to conduct training missions for foreign military forces, perform air and drone strikes on suspected extremists, and launch occasional raids by U.S. Special Forces. According to Joshua Rovner of American University's School of International Service, "the Trump administration's approach to counter-terrrorism resembles that of its predecessors."[61] Hal Brands of Johns Hopkins University agreed, saying, "the military component of Trump's counterterrorism strategy is not fundamentally different than what President Barack Obama pursued in the final stages of his administration." Or as Bill Roggio, the editor of the counterterrorism publication *Long War Journal*, put it, "[Trump] has basically done what President Obama has done, maybe just a little bit more forcefully."[62]

In any case, unwavering support for America's armed forces was hardly a novel political stance for a U.S. president. Every president since Truman had pledged to maintain U.S. military primacy, and uncritical support for "the troops" had become de rigueur for American politicians ever since 9/11 (if not before). As noted in previous chapters, the military role in the conduct of U.S. foreign policy had been expanding for decades; one might even see the overabundance of generals in Trump's inner circle as the culmination of trends that have been under way for some time.[63] On the whole, therefore, Trump's handling of defense policy was simply "business as usual," with a bit more money and a few more bombs.

PROTECTING THE BORDER

After making lurid warnings about foreign terrorists, criminals, and other "bad hombres" during the campaign and repeatedly promising to build a wall on the Mexican border, it was no surprise that Trump took a hard line on immigration and the need to protect the U.S. homeland from unwanted foreign entrants. It took the administration three tries to come up with an executive order to restrict travel from six Muslim-majority countries that could survive judicial review, but the Supreme Court eventually agreed to let the administration's third attempt stand, pending its own examination of the issue.[64] Trump pushed the Justice Department to accelerate deportations of illegal immigrants and rescinded a 2001 program that granted "temporary protected status" to some two hundred thousand people from El Salvador admitted under humanitarian visas, making them eligible for deportation as well.[65] And in January 2018 Trump ignited a new furor when he referred to several developing nations as "shithole countries" and questioned whether the United States should admit immigrants from any of them.[66]

Yet with the exception of his controversial "zero tolerance" policy (which sought to deter migration by separating detained children from their parents), Trump's actions were not substantially different from those of his predecessors. Homeland security had been an overriding priority since 9/11—as every air traveler knows—and the federal budget for customs and border security had increased by 91 percent from 2003 to 2014. Barack Obama had expanded the ranks of the Immigration and Customs Enforcement service significantly, and his last Department of Homeland Security budget had called for hiring more than two thousand additional customs and border patrol officers. Indeed, Obama had deported more than five million people during his two terms, and the pace of deportations in Trump's first year was actually lower than in 2016.[67] After reviewing Trump's policies on immigration and border security, Peter Dombrowski and Simon Reich conclude, "When judged against U.S. operations since 9/11, [Trump's] goals and language alike do not represent a fundamental change in U.S. strategy."[68]

Nor was Trump the first president to propose a border wall with Mexico, or the first to have trouble getting it built. George W. Bush had also sought to build a barrier along the Mexican border, but Congress balked at the multibillion-dollar expense, and only seven hundred miles of fencing were ever constructed. Trump's experience was much the same: neither Mexico nor the GOP-controlled Congress agreed to provide funds for the wall, forcing Trump to assert, unconvincingly, that Mexico would pay "eventually, but at a later date."[69] By January 2018 Trump was telling congressional leaders that the wall would not be needed, with White House chief of staff John Kelly explaining that the president had not been "fully informed" when he originally promised to build a wall and that his views had "evolved."[70]

On a wide variety of important foreign policy issues, therefore, Trump's actions did not constitute a sharp break with the past. There were several areas where he did depart from the establishment consensus, but even here, the shifts may not be as far-reaching as he had originally promised.

GLOBALIZATION ON PROBATION

The United States had long sought to promote a rules-based international order, largely by bringing other states into multilateral institutions in which the United States played a central role. Consistent with his "America First" mantra, Trump had repeatedly questioned the value of these institutions—especially in the economic realm—which he saw not as tools of American influence, but as "bad deals" that limited Washington's freedom of action, undermined U.S. sovereignty, and crippled the U.S. economy.

Trump did not hesitate to put this new agenda into action. On his third day in office he announced that the United States was withdrawing from the Trans-Pacific Partnership (TPP), the ambitious multilateral trade pact that had been a key element of the Obama administration's "rebalancing" strategy in Asia. He followed this step by taking the United States out of the multilateral Paris Agreement on climate change in April, a move that left the United States as the only country in the world that rejected the accord.[71] The final communiqué from the G20 summit in March 2017 dropped its previous vow to "resist all forms of protectionism" at U.S. insistence, and Treasury Secretary Steven Mnuchin reminded reporters afterward, "We do have a new administration and a different view on trade."[72]

Trump continued to rail against the NAFTA trade treaty with Canada and Mexico, calling it a "one-sided deal" that had caused a $60 billion trade deficit. Claiming that "the [World Trade Organization] was set up for the benefit [of] everybody but us," Trump blocked new nominees to the WTO's seven-person appeals board, a move that threatened to cripple the organization's ability to resolve future trade disputes.[73] In July 2017, Trump overruled his advisors and rejected a Chinese offer to voluntarily cut steel capacity, reportedly urging U.S. officials to find reasons to impose broader tariffs.[74] Threats to abrogate the 2011 Korea-U.S. trade agreement forced Seoul to agree to a minor revision, and by September 2017 the Commerce Department had opened up more than sixty investigations of alleged import subsidies, preparing the ground for possible imposition of punitive tariffs.[75] The official *National Security Strategy* released in December 2017 said that the United States would still "pursue bilateral trade and investment agreements with countries that commit to fair and reciprocal trade," but it made no mention of broader multilateral agreements.

Even so, Trump's initial retreat from globalization was more tenta-tive than his fiery campaign rhetoric had promised. Trump declined to label China a "currency manipulator" or to eliminate the Export-Import Bank (as he had promised to do during the campaign), and he ultimately chose to renegotiate both NAFTA and the Korea-U.S. Free Trade Agree-ment instead of simply abandoning them. These shifts were partly due to opposition from the U.S. Chamber of Commerce and from business interests that benefited directly from these agreements (including agri-culture producers in key "red states"), but it also reflected deep divisions within the administration itself. Although Bannon, Lighthizer, and Na-varro had continued to push a more protectionist agenda, Treasury Sec-retary Mnuchin, Secretary of State Tillerson, and National Economic Council chair Gary Cohn were wary of sparking a punishing trade war and disrupting ties with key U.S. allies.[76]

Trump's "America First" economic agenda suffered another setback in December, when the Senate Banking Committee rejected his nomi-nee to head the Export-Import Bank, Scott Garrett, a longtime oppo-nent of the bank who was vehemently opposed by the Chamber of Commerce, the National Association of Manufacturers, and other busi-ness interests.[77] And then, in January 2018, Trump struck a moderate tone in a speech at the World Economic Forum in Davos, the high temple of the globalist internationalism he had previously scorned, saying "America First is not America alone," reiterating his support for free but fair trade, and emphasizing that "America is open for business."[78]

Trump had not become a convert to unfettered globalization or an unabashed proponent of free trade, however, and he no doubt under-stood that supporters expected him to deliver on his promises to bring lost jobs back from overseas. These instincts returned to the fore in Feb-ruary 2018, when Trump rejected Cohn and Tillerson's advice and an-nounced stiff tariffs on steel and aluminum imports, tweeting out that "trade wars are good and easy to win."[79] Cohn resigned in protest and Tillerson was fired several weeks later, giving trade representative Robert Lighthizer and National Trade Council head Peter Navarro—both staunch economic nationalists—greater influence.[80] Their ascendance opened the way for a more direct assault on the existing trade order, beginning with the March 2018 imposition of punitive tariffs on China for its alleged trade violations and theft of U.S. intellectual property, followed by stiff tariffs on steel and aluminum imports from the EU, Mexico, and Canada in June. By midsummer, the possibility of an all-out trade war could not be ruled out.

Yet even here, Trump's growing assault on the existing trade order must be seen in a broader context. The decision to impose steel and aluminum tariffs prompted a widespread outcry at home and abroad, and the administration soon announced that the measures would be administered "selectively," sparking a frantic wave of lobbying for exclusions and making it clear that the initiative was not as far-reaching as it initially appeared.[81] Nor was Trump the first president in recent times to play this card: George W. Bush had also imposed tariffs on imported steel back in 2002 and Richard Nixon had imposed a 10 percent surcharge on foreign imports in 1970.

It is also important to recognize that free trade has always been somewhat controversial in the United States. Although most members of the foreign policy establishment support reducing barriers to foreign trade and investment, this principle is the one component of liberal hegemony that faces well-organized and politically potent opposition. Domestic industries and labor unions whose positions are threatened by foreign competition have long been wary of free trade and eager for government protection, and they can usually win support from members of Congress whose districts might be adversely affected by a specific trade agreement. For this reason, major acts of trade liberalization—such as NAFTA or TPP—have always been a hard sell. It is not surprising, therefore, that this element of liberal hegemony was under more or less constant pressure under Trump despite the pushback he faced from some of his advisors. Even so, Trump's first year and a half in office showed that reversing globalization was neither as easy nor as painless as he had promised.

DEMOCRACY PROMOTION, HUMAN RIGHTS,
AND NATION-BUILDING

Trump's second clear departure from liberal hegemony was his minimal commitment to promoting democracy or human rights and his closely related aversion to nation-building. Trump had said little about democracy and human rights during the 2016 campaign, and he declined to raise these issues when meeting with such leaders as King Salman of Saudi Arabia, Xi Jinping of China, and Rodrigo Duterte of the Philippines. The 2017 *National Security Strategy* mentioned human rights but once, going so far as to say "the American way of life cannot be imposed upon others."[82]

Moreover, Trump's sometimes scathing attacks on the free press and his disregard for established democratic norms suggested that his personal commitment to traditional liberal values was paper-thin, and a number of foreign autocrats were quick to invoke Trump's frequent denunciations of what he called "fake news" to justify their own illiberal practices.[83] Overall, his diminished interest in actively spreading U.S. ideals and institutions was perhaps Trump's most obvious break with the core principles of liberal hegemony. As Barry Posen suggests, Trump's grand strategy might be termed one of "illiberal hegemony": the United States still sought primacy and its global military role was undiminished, but it was no longer strongly committed to promoting liberal values.[84]

Yet even here, Trump did not accomplish a 180-degree reversal of U.S. policy or lead Washington to abandon these concerns completely. The 2017 *National Security Strategy* insisted that the United States would continue to "champion American values" and maintained that "governments that respect the rights of their citizens remain the best vehicle for prosperity, human happiness, and peace." Indeed, in a passage that could just as easily have been written for Clinton, Bush, or Obama, it declared that the United States "will always stand with those who seek freedom" and remain "a beacon of liberty and opportunity around the world."[85]

These universal principles would be applied selectively, however.

As an internal memo written for Secretary of State Tillerson made clear, as far as human rights were concerned, the administration believed that "allies should be treated differently—and better—than adversaries."[86] In other words, human rights was an issue the United States could use to undermine and embarrass rivals such as China, Russia, North Korea, and Iran, but one it should downplay when dealing with friendly regimes that denied citizens full democratic rights or were guilty of significant human rights abuses.

This selective approach was clearly in evidence in December 2017, when antigovernment demonstrations broke out in Iran. Suddenly an administration that had paid scant attention to these issues rediscovered them with a vengeance. Trump launched his usual blizzard of tweets, saying the "great Iranian people had been oppressed for years" and denouncing the government's "numerous violations of human rights."[87] The State Department issued an official statement condemning the arrest of "peaceful protestors" and included in it congressional testimony by Secretary Tillerson declaring his support for "those elements inside of Iran that would lead to a peaceful transition of government."[88] Other administration officials, most notably the CIA director Mike Pompeo (who later succeeded Tillerson as Secretary of State) also favored continued efforts to foster regime change in Iran.

Regime change and democracy promotion remained the ultimate U.S. objective in Syria as well. In a public address at Stanford University in January 2018, Secretary of State Tillerson announced that U.S. troops would remain in Syria for an indefinite period following the final defeat of ISIS, noting that "a stable, unified and independent Syria ultimately requires post-Assad leadership in order to be successful."[89]

Moreover, Trump's personal indifference to human rights or democracy did not stop other arms of the government from continuing to promote them.[90] The State Department suspended nearly $200 million worth of economic and military aid to Egypt in August 2017, citing human rights concerns, and its annual report on religious freedom offered blunt criticisms of China, Bahrain, Turkey, Saudi Arabia, and several other countries. Members of Congress and U.S. diplomats openly criticized the ongoing assault on press and academic freedoms in Hungary, and the White House itself issued a statement condemning rising political repression in Cambodia, despite Cambodian prime minister Hun Sen's blatant attempt to curry favor with Trump at the summit of the Association of Southeast Asian Nations (ASEAN) in November 2017.[91]

Democracy promotion and human rights had been downgraded, but these goals had not vanished entirely from the U.S. foreign policy agenda. Neither had regime change, at least when dealing with acknowledged adversaries such as Iran or the Assad regime in Syria. The administration's public stance was clearly at odds with the idealistic rhetoric of Bill Clinton's commitment to democratic "enlargement" or George W. Bush's "Freedom Agenda," but it was also a reasonably accurate description of what the United States had done in the past. In fact, earlier administrations had often been embarrassingly inconsistent in defending these principles, and one could argue that Trump's appointees were merely stating openly what their predecessors had tried to obscure.

Perhaps the most dramatic sign of Trump's capture by the status quo was his decision to increase U.S. troop levels in Afghanistan in August 2017. Despite his repeated insistence that the United States needed to "get out of the nation-building business," a reluctant Trump bowed to military pressure and agreed to increase U.S. force levels in Afghanistan to more than fifteen thousand troops. In his speech announcing the decision, Trump insisted that U.S. forces would focus on counterterrorism rather than on nation-building, and he justified the increased troop presence as necessary to prevent a vacuum that terrorists "would instantly fill."[92] Preventing Afghanistan from again becoming a safe haven for terrorists was the same rationale Barack Obama had invoked to justify his own "surge" there back in 2009.

Trump claimed that U.S. military commanders had a "new strategy" for the seventeen-year-old conflict, one that would be guided by conditions in the field rather than by arbitrary deadlines. There was no new strategy, however, and no way to deny terrorists a "safe haven" in the absence of an effective and legitimate Afghan government. As Shadi Hamid of the Brookings Institution observed after Trump's speech, "It's fine to oppose 'nation-building,' but you can't have it both ways . . . There's no way to 'defeat' the Taliban without much-improved governance." In any case, the United States was still committed to providing several billion dollars in annual aid to the Afghan military and central government, much of it devoted to "capacity building."[93] Under Trump, therefore, the United States was still trying to use military power, economic aid, and political advice to create a workable democracy in Afghanistan. However reluctant Trump was to admit it, "nation-building" was still occurring on his watch.

WHY TRUMP FAILED

In several key respects, therefore, Trump's intended revolution in U.S. foreign policy was stillborn. Although his conduct as president defied convention and raised eyebrows at home and abroad, his impact on the substance of policy was more limited. Unfortunately, to the extent that Trump did initiate real change, he weakened the U.S. position instead of strengthening it.

What had gone wrong? To be fair, Trump faced an inescapable dilemma from the moment he won the election. His strident criticisms of liberal hegemony had alienated most of the foreign policy community, leaving him with few powerful or experienced allies inside or outside government. If he had tried to staff his administration solely with people who shared his worldview, dozens of jobs would have been left unfilled and the people he did appoint would undoubtedly make lots of rookie mistakes. But if he turned to more experienced foreign policy experts who knew how to make the machinery of government work, they would still be committed to most aspects of liberal hegemony, and the foreign policy revolution Trump had promised would never get off the ground.

And that is in fact what happened: once Trump's more extreme foreign policy appointees had flamed out and been replaced, the people around him worked overtime to tame his worst instincts. As Thomas Wright of the Brookings Institution observed as Trump's first year in office neared its end, "It's the first time, maybe in history, key advisors have gone into the administration to stop the president, not to enable him."[94]

Nor was Trump able to win over skeptics or play "divide and rule" within the foreign policy community. This failure was not surprising, as he did not hesitate to malign key elements of the foreign policy and national security bureaucracy—including the intelligence agencies, the State Department, and the Federal Bureau of Investigation—whenever it suited him. Not surprisingly, this approach kept much of the inside-the-Beltway "Blob" united against him.

For example, Trump repeatedly disparaged the intelligence community's nearly unanimous conclusion that Russia had tried to influence the 2016 election by promoting false news stories and releasing a trove of embarrassing emails hacked from the Democratic National Committee's computers. Trump believed that these reports tarnished his victory over Clinton, cast doubt on his legitimacy as president, and were fueling the growing suspicions of collusion between his campaign and Russia. Angered by the persistent rumors, Trump told reporters before his inauguration that "it was disgraceful that the intelligence agencies allowed any information [out] that turned out to be so false and fake. That's something that Nazi Germany would have done and did." Needless to say, his suggestion that the CIA or other intelligence agencies were acting like Nazis provoked a furious response, with former CIA director John Brennan denouncing Trump's remarks as "outrageous."[95]

Trump's visit to CIA headquarters the day after his inauguration made a bad situation worse. Speaking in front of the memorial wall honoring CIA personnel who had died in service, Trump offered a brief statement of support for the agency and its mission but devoted much of his speech to a rambling attack on the media and a defense of his claim that the crowd attending his inauguration was larger than that of Obama. A senior intelligence official later described it as "one of the most disconcerting speeches I've ever seen."[96]

Trump's handling of the State Department didn't help either. Proposals for steep budget cuts and Tillerson's decision to launch a protracted, top-to-bottom reorganization led to a wave of resignations, and morale within the department quickly hit rock bottom. A bipartisan chorus of critics began lambasting Trump for gutting a critical department, and former State Department counselor (and prominent Trump critic) Eliot A. Cohen judged Tillerson to be "the worst Secretary of State in living memory."[97] The president seemed unconcerned, however; when asked by reporters in November about the raft of diplomatic positions still waiting to be filled, Trump replied, "Let me tell you: the one that matters is me. I'm the only one that matters."[98]

Yet Trump's failure to fully staff the State Department with likeminded disciples may have crippled his efforts to shake up U.S. foreign policy, for it left key policy areas in the hands of interim officials from the career civil service rather than being guided by outsiders who shared Trump's views. Ironically, Trump and Tillerson had managed to weaken a critical instrument of U.S. foreign policy while failing to convert it to Trump's own worldview. Nor was Tillerson's replacement by CIA director Mike Pompeo, a hawkish former congressman, likely to restore the department's fortunes, given Pompeo's own fondness for military responses and apparent disregard for traditional diplomacy.

Not surprisingly, well-placed neoconservative and liberal internationalists lost no time in bemoaning the waning of U.S. global leadership, and media outlets such as *The New York Times* and *The Washington Post* offered consistently critical views of Trump's foreign policy initiatives.[99] By the summer of 2017, even the more sympathetic *Wall Street Journal* was publishing hard-hitting articles and commentaries questioning Trump's handling of foreign policy and his overall leadership style.[100] Trump's approval rating fell steadily throughout his first year despite decent economic growth and a sky-high stock market, at one point hitting the lowest levels recorded by any first-year president since the advent of modern polling.[101]

HIS OWN WORST ENEMY

Orchestrating a major shift in U.S. grand strategy would have challenged the political gifts of a Roosevelt or a Lincoln, and Trump was a far cry from these canny, subtle, and farsighted leaders. He had come to high office late in life, after an up-and-down business career roiled by lawsuits and bankruptcies, with a long list of disgruntled clients and former partners and what might charitably be described as a flexible attitude toward truth.[102] These traits were all on full view once he became president, and a management style that may have worked tolerably well in a family-run real estate business proved to be poorly suited to the Oval Office. More than anything else, Trump turned out to be his own worst enemy.

For starters, he was a poor judge of talent. He had repeatedly promised that he would hire "the best people," but no previous president had to fire his first choice as national security advisor after twenty-four days, replace his handpicked White House communications director after less than two weeks on the job, or remove his "chief political strategist" after less than eight months. Five months into his first term, Trump had earned a reputation as the "worst boss in Washington," and numerous insider accounts described him as uninformed, capricious, disinterested in detailed policy discussions, acutely sensitive to criticism, and having an inexhaustible need for adulation.[103] His own secretary of state, Rex Tillerson, reportedly referred to Trump as a "moron" during a meeting with senior national security officials, and Tillerson refused to explicitly deny the story.[104] One senior Republican insider described the White House as a "snake pit," and an unnamed White House staffer called it "the most toxic work environment on the planet." By the end of Trump's first year, turnover among senior aides was a remarkable 34 percent, an all-time record.[105]

The turmoil continued into Trump's second year: Tillerson was fired by tweet in March; National Economic Council chair Gary Cohn was replaced by Lawrence Kudlow, a conservative TV pundit with a checkered past and minimal policy experience; and national security advisor McMaster was eventually removed in favor of former U.N. ambassador John Bolton, a hard-line senior fellow at the American Enterprise

Institute. Trump defended the revolving door of departures and new appointments by saying "there will always be change. I think you want to see change." Having described his initial team as "one of the finest groups of people ever assembled as a Cabinet," Trump now claimed the various dismissals meant he was "close to having the Cabinet he wanted" after more than a year on the job.[106]

Moreover, Trump was embroiled in potential scandals even before he took the presidential oath, some involving conflicts of interest with his business holdings and others revolving around the possibility that Trump, his sons, or members of his campaign staff had colluded with Russia's efforts to influence the 2016 election. Whatever the merits of the accusations, Trump's defensive responses made things worse. In particular, his decision to fire FBI director James Comey in May 2017—after Comey refused to halt an FBI investigation of former national security advisor Michael Flynn—led Deputy Attorney General Rod J. Rosenstein to appoint a special counsel, former FBI chief Robert Mueller, to investigate possible connections between Russia and the Trump campaign.[107] Trump's political opponents may have rushed to judgment on this tangled set of issues, but the president and some of his closest associates had stoked the accusations by consistently behaving as if they had something to hide.[108] The end result was a persistent distraction that further undercut Trump's ability to govern effectively.[109]

Furthermore, while Trump's compulsive, boastful, insulting, juvenile, and frequently inaccurate tweets may have helped him retain support among his political base, they reinforced concerns about his judgment and lent credence to continuing concerns about his fitness for office.[110] So did his penchant for lying; by one estimate, Trump made six times as many false statements in his first ten months in office as Barack Obama had in eight years.[111] Making matters worse, Trump later boasted openly about having lied to Canadian prime minister Justin Trudeau, an admission not likely to encourage other politicians to trust him.[112] No one expects politicians to tell the whole truth all of the time, but how could foreign leaders have any confidence in assurances given by a man who lied with such facility and frequency?[113]

Trump's unguarded comments sometimes undercut other U.S. officials, as when he tweeted in October that Secretary of State Tillerson was
"wasting his time" trying to negotiate with North Korea.[114] At other
times, they simply sowed doubt, as no one could tell when Trump's
tweets were genuine statements of U.S. policy or when he was just blowing off steam. Over time, these unpresidential antics had a decidedly
negative effect on U.S. credibility. As Pierre Vimont, former French ambassador to the United States and former aide to the EU commissioner for
foreign affairs, put it in January 2018, Trump's tweets made it harder to
grasp "the real policy line from Washington . . . we have difficulty understanding where U.S. leadership is, what they are really looking for."[115]

Compounding these problems was Trump's reflexively combative
personality. As he had with his domestic opponents, Trump did not hesitate to insult or demean foreign leaders who disagreed with him. For
example, what were intended as friendly "get-acquainted" phone calls
with Mexican president Enrique Peña Nieto and Australian prime minister Malcolm Turnbull quickly degenerated into testy arguments over
trade and immigration policy, with Trump telling Turnbull that their
conversation "was the most unpleasant call all day . . . This is ridicu-
lous."[116] An early meeting with British prime minister Theresa May went
smoothly, but Trump lashed out after May said he had been wrong to
retweet a set of inflammatory anti-Muslim videos, telling May to "focus
on the destructive Radical Islamic Terrorism that is taking place within
the United Kingdom!"[117] Britons were equally incensed when Trump
misrepresented a statement by London mayor Sadiq Khan following a
terrorist attack there and used it to falsely accuse Khan of being compla-
cent about terrorism.[118]

Trump's petulant disregard for allied leaders reached new heights at
the G-7 meeting in June 2018, where he reportedly tossed candy on the
table in front of German chancellor Angela Merkel and told her, "Don't
say I never give you anything." He left the meeting early, removed his
signature from the official communiqué, and called Canadian prime
minister Justin Trudeau "very dishonest" after Trudeau expressed disap-
pointment with the new U.S. tariffs on Canadian aluminum and steel.[119]

Finally, although Trump may have instinctively grasped the worst flaws of liberal hegemony, he did not have a well-thought-out alternative to offer in its stead. He saw world politics as a purely zero-sum contest in which there are only winners and losers, but he seemed to have no clear sense of (1) what America's core strategic interests are, (2) what regions matter most (and why), or (3) why a world of sovereign states still needs effective rules to manage key areas of joint activity. And some of his deepest convictions about international affairs—such as his neo-mercantilist views on international trade or his denial of climate change—were simply wrong.

By contrast, the foreign policy community (aka "the Blob") that Trump had disparaged during the 2016 campaign did have a worldview: liberal hegemony. It also had the capacity to defend it. As Patrick Porter notes, "The Blob enjoys a number of advantages. As well as influence within the security bureaucracy, it can attack the legitimacy of measures that offend tradition. It can act through the courts and the quiet resistance of civil servants, and articulate alternatives through well-funded think-tanks. It has strong institutional platforms in Congress, links to a powerful business community, and a network of Nongovernmental Organizations." The "Blob" could not prevent Trump from altering policy in certain areas—sometimes significantly—but it was a constant brake on his worst instincts.[120]

Together with Trump's limitations as a manager and leader, these features produced a parade of blunders large and small. Some of the mistakes were minor ones, such as getting names and titles of foreign leaders wrong in official communiqués or releasing official statements with elementary spelling mistakes, factual errors, or displays of ignorance.[121] In July 2017, for example, a White House press release at the G20 summit mistakenly identified Chinese president Xi Jinping as the leader of Taiwan and erroneously referred to Prime Minister Shinzo Abe of Japan as "president."[122] Trump also made some embarrassing slips of his own, such as his unwitting disclosure of sensitive classified information in a May 2017 meeting with Russian foreign minister Sergei Lavrov and Russian ambassador Sergey Kislyak.[123]

Other mistakes were more consequential. Trump clearly saw China as a serious economic and military rival, for example, as did the other top U.S. officials, and he understood that the United States needed to counter China's rising power and growing ambitions. But if so, then abandoning TPP was an enormous misstep that undermined the U.S. position with key Asian allies, gave Beijing inviting opportunities to expand its influence, and brought the United States nothing in return. It was also a mistake on purely economic grounds, as TPP's remaining members went ahead with the agreement, depriving U.S. exporters of more open access to a large and growing market and giving Washington no say over the health, regulatory, or labor standards embedded within the agreement.[124]

Similarly, Trump and his advisors correctly understood that North Korea's nuclear and missile programs were a serious problem that required close attention, but his bluster, empty threats, and childish tweets were unlikely to persuade North Korea that it had no need for a powerful deterrent. Instead, Trump's saber rattling merely alarmed U.S. allies in the region unnecessarily. Furthermore, given the importance of maintaining a united front against Pyongyang, it made no sense for Trump to quarrel with South Korea over trade or over who would pay for a missile defense system that Washington had previously agreed to provide. It was equally foolish to renege on the nuclear agreement with Iran (which had never built a nuclear weapon), while at the same time trying to persuade North Korea to agree to give up the nuclear bombs it had already produced.

And, though encouraging America's Middle East allies to do more to combat extremism or to counter Iran was a reasonable objective, Trump's handling of this complicated task was inept. In particular, giving the reformist crown prince Mohammed bin Salman of Saudi Arabia unconditional support was a mistake, as the young Saudi leader's reckless gambits undermined the united front Trump said he wanted to create. To make matters worse, Trump's tweeted suggestion that he had inspired the Saudi boycott of Qatar in June 2017 jeopardized U.S. access to a critical air base in the emirate and forced Secretaries Mattis and Tillerson to step in to smooth things over.[125]

For that matter, if Trump genuinely believed that Iran was a loom-ing threat that had to be contained, then his decision to violate the multi-national deal that had rolled back its nuclear program was a strategic blunder. In addition to sowing broader concerns about the reliability of American promises, tearing up the nuclear deal (or even chipping away at the spirit of the agreement) would eventually dissolve the coali-tion of major powers whose pressure on Iran had helped convince its leaders to compromise. Doing so would strengthen hard-line factions within Iran, give Tehran more reason to want its own nuclear deterrent, and ultimately leave Washington with the choice of accepting a nuclear-armed Iran or starting a preventive war. From the purely self-interested "America First" perspective that Trump supposedly championed, his ap-proach made little sense.

Finally, Trump's controversial decision on Jerusalem (reportedly made to fulfill a pledge to Sheldon Adelson, a passionate Zionist who was also the largest contributor to Trump's presidential campaign) did nothing to make the United States safer or richer, or to advance U.S. values.[126] Previous presidents understood that recognizing Jerusalem as Israel's capital and moving the U.S. embassy there was a valuable carrot that might one day be used to clinch a final peace agreement, but Trump gave it up for nothing. All the United States got in return for Trump's move was nearly universal international criticism, including a UN Gen-eral Assembly resolution condemning the move, which passed 135–9 even after UN ambassador Haley threatened a reduction in U.S. funding were the resolution to be approved.[127]

Some observers have seen the reshuffling of Trump's foreign policy team that began in February 2018 as evidence of a desire to escape the constraints his more mainstream advisors had imposed on him and to return to the more radical approach he had articulated as a candidate.[128] This assessment is clearly correct regarding trade policy, but the de-partures of Tillerson, Cohn, McMaster, etc., and the appointments of Pompeo, Haspel, and Bolton were hardly a rejection of establishment thinking or a radical alteration in U.S. strategy. Each of these individuals occupied respected positions within the mainstream foreign policy community, and their views on key foreign policy issues, while clearly from the hawkish end of the spectrum, were still within the "acceptable" Washington consensus.[129] None of them were likely to favor less reliance on military force, greater emphasis on multilateral diplomacy, or a significant reduction in U.S. commitments abroad.

If anything, these appointments were less a triumph of Trumpism in its original form than a return to the confrontational unilateralism of George W. Bush, Dick Cheney, and the neoconservatives. As such, these appointments offer additional evidence to support the claims made in the previous chapter: the United States frequently fails to learn from past errors and tends to forget any lessons it may temporarily absorb. Hardly anyone is held accountable, and officials with abysmal track records often receive new chances to repeat past mistakes.[130]

THE IMPACT OF INCOMPETENCE

Viewed as a whole, Trump's efforts to "shake the rust off of U.S. foreign policy" turned out to be a giant step backward. Instead of lessening the burden on America's overstretched armed forces and reducing the nation's overseas obligations, he had kept every one of America's existing commitments, increased troop levels in Afghanistan, accelerated the pace of operations in several distant theaters, and stoked fears of new wars with North Korea and possibly Iran.

Trump's handling of U.S. foreign economic policy was equally inept. He raised fears of a trade war but brought scant positive results: the "beautiful" trade deals he promised had yet to materialize, and by the end of his first year the trade deficit he had vowed to reverse had reached its highest level since 2012.[131] And while Trump was correct in wanting to get tough with China over its predatory trade and investment practices, his approach to the problem was incoherent. As Ely Ratner of the Council on Foreign Relations observed, "Trump is right to be saying enough is enough. But his administration is going about it all wrong." Instead of relying solely on unilateral U.S. sanctions, it would have made more sense to assemble a coalition of other major world economies to press China and work within the existing WTO system. But Trump had already abandoned TPP (which was designed in part to counter Chinese trade practices) and then alienated potential partners by threatening to impose tariffs and quotas on them too. He also repeatedly criticized the WTO and took steps to weaken it, thereby making it a less powerful tool for challenging China. Trump may have been serious about wanting China to change its behavior, but his bumbling approach to the issue was far less effective than it might have been.[132]

Trump had long portrayed himself as a hard-nosed negotiator who had mastered the "art of the deal," but his approach to foreign policy was, in the words of the *New York Times* columnist Thomas L. Friedman, more accurately described as "the art of the giveaway."[133] His decisions on Jerusalem and the TPP withdrawal were obvious examples, as was his impulsive decision to accept Kim Jong-un's invitation to a summit meeting without first establishing terms for the discussions. Simply by meeting with Kim, Trump had given him a status and legitimacy that North Korea's leaders had long craved. Trump went even further at the meeting itself, agreeing to cancel annual military exercises with South Korea without first informing Seoul. And what did Trump get in return for these twin concessions? Only a vague promise to "work toward" eventual denuclearization.

Trump and his supporters believe that increased U.S. pressure—in the form of ever-tightening sanctions and threats of military action— have forced Kim to change his behavior. Finally getting tough with North Korea, they think, caused Kim to offer to meet with President Trump, stop testing missiles that can hit the United States, pursue a peace agreement with South Korea, and abandon his nuclear weapons. North Korea has agreed to talks on many occasions in the past, how- ever, and Kim's willingness to do so in 2018 is more likely the result of the progress North Korea has recently made in refining its nuclear war- head designs (including testing a hydrogen bomb) and long-range mis- sile capabilities, which give the regime a more potent nuclear deterrent. In any case, it is hard to imagine Kim ever accepting the United States' definition of "complete denuclearization," which means a rapid, irreversible, and fully verified dismantling of North Korea's entire nuclear infrastructure.

Moreover, even if the two sides reached a more modest interim deal—such as a temporary halt in long-range missile tests—it would still leave America's allies in Asia vulnerable to a North Korean nuclear attack and raise doubts about the U.S. commitment to their security. North Korea has long insisted that meaningful reductions in its arsenal have to be accompanied by the removal of external threats to the regime, which implies substantial cuts in the U.S. military presence in South Korea and perhaps the complete withdrawal of U.S. forces from the peninsula. Even if accompanied by a formal end to the Korean War, an agreement of this sort would undermine the U.S. role in Asia and constitute a major victory for North Korea and its Chinese patron. Trump's handling of North Korea has definitely succeeded in stirring things up, but the net effect is a further weakening of the U.S. position in Asia.

Worst of all, Trump almost singlehandedly squandered the remaining confidence other states had in America's judgment. Reasons to doubt U.S. wisdom and competence had increased since the end of the Cold War, as the quest for liberal hegemony foundered and the financial crisis tarnished Wall Street's reputation for integrity and acumen. Partisan wrangling and political gridlock at home had raised further doubts about America's ability to address problems at home and challenges abroad, doubts only partially allayed by the Obama administration's relatively successful management of the postcrisis economic recovery. But Trump raised these nagging concerns to unprecedented heights: suddenly leaders and publics all over the world had reason to question whether the American president had any idea what he was doing. And the contrast with some other countries—especially China—was hard to miss.[134]

Near the end of Obama's second term, for example, a survey of thirty-seven countries found that roughly 64 percent of respondents still had confidence in U.S. leadership. After less than six months under Donald Trump, the percentage with "confidence" had fallen to 22 and countries like Japan and South Korea showed especially sharp declines. Even more remarkably, more people around the world believed that Chinese president Xi Jinping and Russian president Vladimir Putin were "more likely to do the right thing in world affairs" than the current president of the United States.[135] The results one year in were no better: a Gallup poll of 134 countries released in January 2018 showed that "global approval of U.S. leadership" had dropped from an average of 48 percent in 2016 to only 30 percent in 2017, a historic low, with some of the biggest declines occurring among longtime U.S. allies.[136]

As the wobbles and inconsistencies and embarrassing episodes multiplied, other countries started hedging their bets and making deals with each other that excluded the United States. The EU and Japan signed a major trade pact in July 2017, and leaders from Germany to Canada spoke openly about their lack of confidence in the United States and the need to take responsibility for their own fates.[137] Meanwhile, China continued to advance its ambitious One Belt, One Road initiative in Central Asia and to negotiate a Regional Comprehensive Economic Partnership (RCEP) with sixteen Asian countries (but not the United States). RCEP was China's original response to the U.S.-led TPP, but Trump's decision to withdraw from the latter gave China "an irresistible opportunity."[138] And the blame for all of these worrisome developments lay squarely with Donald J. Trump.

Conclusion

Looking back on Trump's first year, one could easily imagine Hillary Clinton pursuing many of the same policies if she were in the White House. Clinton almost certainly would have used military force when the Assad regime used chemical weapons, and she undoubtedly would have reaffirmed U.S. support for NATO and for America's traditional Middle Eastern allies, just as Trump did. Unlike Trump, she would have kept the nuclear deal with Iran in place, but she would have taken a hard line toward Iran in other respects and no doubt would have kept up the military campaign against ISIS and continued America's far-flung counterterror operations. Clinton would have been highly critical of

North Korea's missile tests but open to negotiations, and there is little reason to think she would have opposed increased defense spending or rejected military requests to increase U.S. troop levels in Afghanistan.[139] She would have spoken more openly about the importance of democracy and human rights but looked the other way when close U.S. allies fell short. One suspects that Clinton would have walked back her own opposition to TPP in order to balance more effectively against China, but one can easily see her pushing for minor changes in that agreement, as well as seeking to update NAFTA and reform the WTO.

But it is much harder to imagine Clinton pursuing these goals as ineptly as Trump has. She would never have used Twitter to pick fights with adversaries, allies, the media, and entire agencies of the U.S. government, as he has done repeatedly. She would have staffed her administration with experienced insiders from the beginning and avoided the intense and ceaseless turmoil that characterized the Trump White House from Day One.[140] The United States would still have pursued a flawed grand strategy under Clinton and there would have been few successes, but there is no question that she and her colleagues would have done a much better job of implementing that misguided approach.

As this chapter shows, Trump's rhetoric and outlook were in many ways at odds with with liberal hegemony, but his administration's actual policies were a continuation of its worst tendencies. The United States continues to embrace a flawed grand strategy, but its implementation is now in the hands of the least competent president in modern memory. The results of this deadly combination of foolish policy and inept statecraft are already apparent: U.S. influence and status is declining, but its global burdens are not. And he may yet provoke a global trade war that would inflict additional harm on the United States and almost every other country in the world.[141]

Sadly, Trump's presidency thus far provides a textbook case for how *not* to fix U.S. foreign policy. It also reminds us that no matter how bad things might be, they can always get worse. In the final chapter, I explain what must be done to turn things around.

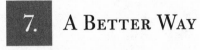

7. A BETTER WAY

A MERICA'S RECENT EFFORTS to manage and shape world politics have not made the United States safer or richer, and they have not advanced its core political values. On the contrary, U.S. foreign policy has multiplied enemies and destabilized key regions of the world, wasted thousands of lives and trillions of dollars in failed wars, led to serious human rights abuses abroad, and compromised important civil liberties.

This book has sought to explain why. These failures occurred and persisted because both Democrats and Republicans have pursued a misguided strategy of liberal hegemony. The strategy has repeatedly failed to deliver as promised, yet the foreign policy establishment remains deeply committed to it.

Donald Trump challenged this consensus when he ran for office and tried—however haphazardly—to change course. But he lacked the acumen, discipline, and political support to pull off a judicious revision in U.S. foreign policy, and his inept handling of these issues has undermined U.S. influence without lightening America's burdens. Trump may have been largely correct when he called U.S. foreign policy "a complete and total disaster," but he failed to develop a coherent alternative to liberal hegemony, and his errors in judgment, poor personnel choices, and ill-advised decisions only made things worse.

COUNTERARGUMENTS

Even those who recognize that U.S. foreign policy has been less than perfect might object to my indictment of America's recent efforts and my explanation for these failings. One could argue, for example, that U.S. foreign policy is no worse today than it was in the past. The United States was slow to recognize the dangers of fascism in the 1940s, and then it overreacted to the threat of communism after World War II. The "best and the brightest" in the old Eastern establishment led the country into a futile war in Indochina and stayed there far too long, simultaneously mismanaging events in the Middle East and backing assorted unsavory dictators solely because they claimed to be anticommunist. From this perspective, U.S. foreign policy is as good (or bad) as it ever was, and its recent missteps have little to do with America's dominant position or the foreign policy community's commitment to liberal hegemony.

There is an element of truth in this position, insofar as past U.S. leaders made their own share of blunders. But the overall performance of some previous administrations was still impressive, especially when one considers that they were dealing either with formidable expansionist powers (Germany or Japan in the two world wars) or confronting a continent-size, nuclear-armed superpower whose revolutionary ideology attracted considerable support around the globe. U.S. leaders may have exaggerated the danger that international communism posed, but the threat was hardly imaginary. For more than forty years, both Republicans and Democrats focused laserlike on containing and eliminating the Soviet rival while avoiding all-out war, and they used a combination of economic, military, and diplomatic tools to achieve a peaceful victory. They made their full share of mistakes—of which Vietnam was the worst—but they also got many big things right. For all their failings, the record is better than the parade of missed opportunities and self-inflicted wounds recorded by the four post–Cold War presidents.

Defenders of U.S. foreign policy might also argue that other countries have done even worse. U.S. officials may have mishandled the Israeli-Palestinian peace process, walked open-eyed into quagmires in Afghanistan and Iraq, and failed to build constructive relations with Russia, etc., but they still did a lot better than Muammar Gaddafi of Libya (who was overthrown by a foreign intervention and eventually killed), Saddam Hussein of Iraq (who lost three wars and was eventually executed by his successors), or Recep Erdogan of Turkey (whose country went from "zero problems with neighbors" a decade ago to problems with virtually all of them today). America's foreign policy mandarins may stumble with some frequency, but maybe that is because they keep trying to solve so many difficult problems.

This line of argument sounds compelling at first, but it does not stand up to close scrutiny. If a nation's foreign policy is judged by whether it makes that country safer and richer, and whether it promotes certain core values, then there are plenty of countries that have been doing at least as well as the United States and some that have done considerably better. By remaining aloof from most quarrels and concentrating on economic development, for example, China has improved the lives of its people dramatically and gained substantially more international influence than it had thirty years ago. Iran is hardly the regional colossus depicted in some hard-liners' alarmist fantasies, but it has taken full advantage of America's missteps to shore up its regional position, even in the face of powerful opposition from the United States and others. Russia may be a declining power for both economic and demographic reasons, but it is not the basket case it was in the 1990s, and Vladimir Putin has played a weak hand well over the past fifteen years.[1]

Similarly, America's many wealthy allies have enjoyed considerable "free" security over the past few decades, largely because Washington bore a disproportionate share of global security burdens and allowed its allies to spend their money on other goals. Nor should we forget the thousands of foreign and American lives lost as a result of Washington's recent missteps. A few states have caused more harm to others in recent years than the United States has, but not very many.

Moreover, even if U.S. foreign policy had consistently outperformed all other countries, that is not the real issue. The real question is whether U.S. foreign policy is as good as one might reasonably expect, or whether the choices U.S. leaders have made forced the American people to bear costs or run risks they could have avoided. Being better than some other countries is not a compelling defense when there's still enormous room for improvement.

Skeptics might also concede that key foreign policy institutions were not performing very well yet still maintain that military, diplomatic corps, intelligence services, and other parts of the foreign policy community outperform other public policy sectors. U.S. foreign policy might be inept, but does the government do a better job of educating the public, preventing crime, managing the economy, or maintaining the nation's public infrastructure? If not, perhaps the indictment offered in this book is too harsh and we should judge those responsible for America's relations with the outside world more gently.

This excuse misses the point as well. There are no benchmarks or performance measures available to rank different government sectors, making precise comparisons among them largely meaningless. But it is not hard to identify areas of public policy—such as Social Security, Medicare, inoculation campaigns, or federal support for scientific research—that are more successful and popular than many recent foreign policy initiatives.[2] And even if the federal government was in fact better at conducting foreign policy than it was at maintaining infrastructure, policing, or controlling firearms, it might still be pursuing the wrong goals and thus failing to make Americans as safe or as prosperous as they could be.

Lastly, one could argue that my indictment of recent U.S. foreign policy depends on a small number of events—especially the failures in Iraq and Afghanistan—and that the overall record is actually quite positive. Were it not for those missteps, some defenders of liberal hegemony now argue, U.S. global leadership would be looking pretty darn good. For them, the obvious lesson is to maintain U.S. "deep engagement" and continue to pursue liberal hegemony while avoiding stupid blunders such as the Iraq War.[3]

There are two obvious problems with this line of defense. First, the failures of liberal hegemony are not confined to Iraq, but also include the fallout from NATO expansion, the consequences of regime change in Afghanistan, Yemen, Libya, and elsewhere, the open-ended "war on terror," the mismanagement of the Middle East peace process, the continuing spread of weapons of mass destruction, and the antidemocratic backlash that has occurred since the 2008 financial crisis. The United States would undoubtedly be in a better position today if it had "kept Saddam in a box" in 2003 and after, but other aspects of U.S. foreign policy would still have been disappointing.

Second, pinning the blame on the Iraq War overlooks how liberal hegemony makes mistakes of this sort far more likely. Once the United States is committed to spreading its values, turning dictatorships into democracies, and disarming autocrats who seek WMD, and once it declares itself to be the "indispensable power" whose leadership is essential for international stability, it will inevitably be drawn toward the use of force whenever other tools fail to achieve these ends.[4] Americans may be reluctant to repeat the Iraq experience at the moment, but as we saw in chapter 5, that lesson is already being challenged by those who now defend the decision to invade and maintain that the United States should simply have stayed there longer.

In sum, none of these alibis can absolve recent U.S. leaders from responsibility for the recent parade of foreign policy failures or vindicate the strategy of liberal hegemony that Presidents Clinton, Bush, and Obama all pursued, albeit in slightly different ways, and that Donald Trump has been unable to abandon. U.S. foreign policy is unlikely to improve, therefore, until U.S. leaders adopt a new approach—a new grand strategy—for dealing with the outside world. What should that strategy be, and what might convince the country to adopt it?

AN ALTERNATIVE: OFFSHORE BALANCING

Given the repeated failures of the past two decades, it is hardly surprising that Americans are more receptive to the idea of a different grand strategy than at any time in recent memory.[5] As noted at the beginning of this book, Trump's triumph in November 2016 was itself evidence of considerable discontent. The American people want their country to maintain a "shared leadership" role, but far fewer want it to be a "dominant" world power, and there is only modest support for using military force in a wide array of scenarios.[6] Indeed, a survey in early 2018 found that more than 70 percent of Americans would support legislation that required "clearly defined goals to authorize military action overseas, including what constitutes victory or success, and a clear timeline."[7]

Furthermore, the "millennial" generation now entering active political life sees engagement with the outside world very differently than prior generations did. Millennials perceive fewer foreign dangers, are less reflexively patriotic, and are decidedly less supportive of military solutions to contemporary global problems.[8] In the 2016 campaign, both Trump on the right and Bernie Sanders on the left found receptive audiences on the campaign trail whenever they questioned the U.S. penchant for promoting democracy, subsidizing its allies' defense, and intervening with military force, leaving only Hillary Clinton—whose foreign policy "brain trust" was the living embodiment of the mainstream foreign policy community—to defend the status quo.[9]

Fortunately, a superior alternative is available—offshore balancing—which is America's traditional grand strategy. Instead of trying to remake the world in America's image, offshore balancing is principally concerned with America's position in the global balance of power and focuses on preventing other states from projecting power in ways that might threaten the United States. Accordingly, it calls for the United States to deploy its power abroad only when there are direct threats to vital U.S. interests.

In particular, offshore balancers believe that only a few areas of the globe are of vital importance to U.S. security or prosperity and thus worth sending Americans to fight and die for. The first vital region is the Western Hemisphere itself, where America's dominant position ensures that no neighbor can pose a serious threat to the U.S. homeland. This fortuitous situation is a luxury no other major power has ever enjoyed.[10]

But unlike isolationists, offshore balancers believe that three distant regions also matter to the United States: Europe, Northeast Asia, and the Persian Gulf. Europe and Asia are vital because they contain key centers of industrial power and military potential. The Persian Gulf is also important—at least for now—because the area produces roughly 30 percent of the world's oil and holds about 55 percent of its proven reserves, and oil and gas are still critical for the world economy.

For offshore balancers, the primary concern would be the rise of a local hegemon that dominated one of these regions in the same way that the United States now dominates the Western Hemisphere. Such a state in Europe or Northeast Asia would have considerable economic clout, the ability to develop sophisticated weaponry, and the potential to project power and influence around the globe. It might eventually control greater economic resources than the United States and be able to outspend it in an arms race. If it wished, such a state could even ally with countries in the Western Hemisphere and interfere close to American soil, as its own homeland would not be in serious danger from its immediate neighbors.

Thus, America's principal aim in Europe and Northeast Asia should be to maintain the local balance of power so that the strongest state in these regions has to worry about one or more of its neighbors and is not free to roam into the Western Hemisphere, or any other area deemed vital to the United States. A hegemon in the Persian Gulf would be undesirable, for example, because it might interfere with the flow of oil from that region, thereby damaging the world economy and threatening U.S. prosperity. The United States does not need to control any of these regions directly, however; it can achieve its core strategic aims merely by helping to ensure that these regions do not fall under the control of another major power, especially not a peer competitor.

HOW WOULD OFFSHORE BALANCING WORK?

Under a strategy of offshore balancing, the proper role and size of the U.S. national security establishment depends on the distribution of power in the key regions. If there is no potential hegemon in sight in Europe, Northeast Asia, or the Gulf, there is little reason to deploy U.S. ground or air forces there and little need for a national security establishment that dwarfs those of the major powers.

If a potential hegemon does appear, the United States should turn to local forces as the first line of defense. It should expect them to uphold the regional balance of power out of their own self-interest and to deal with local security challenges themselves. Washington might provide material assistance and pledge to support certain regional powers if they were in danger of being conquered, but it should refrain from deploying significant U.S. forces under most conditions. In some circumstances it might be prudent to maintain small military contingents, intelligence-gathering facilities, or pre-positioned equipment overseas, but in general Washington would "pass the buck" to local powers because they have a greater interest in preventing any state from dominating their region.

If local actors cannot contain a potential hegemon on their own, however, the United States must deploy enough military force to the region to shift the local balance in its favor. American forces might be needed before war broke out, if the local actors could not uphold the balance by themselves. The United States kept large ground and air forces in Europe throughout the Cold War, for example, because U.S. leaders believed the countries of Western Europe could not contain the Soviet Union on their own.[11]

At other times, the United States might intervene after a war starts if one side seems likely to emerge as a regional hegemon. American intervention in both world wars fits this pattern. The United States came in late both times, when it appeared that Germany might win and end up dominating Europe.

In essence, this strategy aims to keep U.S. forces "offshore" for as long as possible while recognizing that sometimes the United States will have to come onshore even before a conflict starts. If that happens, the United States should get its allies in the region to do as much of the heavy lifting as possible and go back offshore once the threat has been defeated.

THE VIRTUES OF OFFSHORE BALANCING

Offshore balancing has a number of obvious benefits. First and foremost, it reduces the resources Washington must devote to defending distant regions and allows for greater investment and consumption at home. And by limiting the areas of the world the United States is committed to defend, this strategy puts fewer Americans in harm's way.

Second, offshore balancing would prolong America's current position of primacy, as it avoids costly and counterproductive crusades and allows for greater investment in the long-term ingredients of power and prosperity: education, infrastructure, and research and development. The United States became a great power in the nineteenth century by staying out of distant wars and building the world's largest and most advanced economy, much as China has been attempting to do over the past three decades. And as China has built power at home, the United

States has wasted trillions of dollars pursuing liberal hegemony, placing its position of primacy at risk. Returning to offshore balancing would help remedy that problem.

Offshore balancing would also reduce the tendency for other states to "free-ride" on U.S. protection, a problem that has grown in scope since the end of the Cold War. U.S. GDP is less than 50 percent of NATO's total, for example, yet it accounts for about 75 percent of the alliance's military spending.[12] In Asia, local efforts to strengthen defense capabilities remain modest, with key U.S. allies such as Japan—the world's third largest economy—and Australia spending less than 2 percent of GDP on defense. As MIT's Barry Posen observes, America's willingness to subsidize its allies' defense often amounts to "welfare for the rich."[13]

America's terrorism problem would be less worrisome under offshore balancing as well. Liberal hegemony commits the United States to spreading democracy in unfamiliar places, which sometimes requires military occupation and always involves trying to dictate local political arrangements. Such efforts invariably foster nationalist resentment in these societies and sometimes trigger violent resistance, including terrorism.[14] At the same time, trying to spread American values via regime change undermines local institutions and creates ungoverned spaces where violent extremists can operate. Thus, liberal hegemony both inspires terrorists and facilitates their operations.

Offshore balancing alleviates this problem by eschewing large-scale social engineering and minimizing the U.S. military footprint. U.S. troops would be stationed on foreign soil only when a given state is in a vital region and threatened by a potential hegemon. Under these conditions, the potential victim will be grateful for U.S. protection and will not view its military forces as occupiers. And once the threat is gone, U.S. military forces would go back over the horizon and not stay behind to meddle in local politics. By respecting the sovereignty of other states, offshore balancing is less likely to foster the nationalist anger that is a powerful source of anti-American extremism. It would not eliminate the terrorism problem overnight, but it would almost certainly reduce it over time.

A REASSURING HISTORY

Offshore balancing may seem like a radical idea today, but it provided the guiding logic for U.S. foreign policy for many decades. During the nineteenth century, the U.S. government was preoccupied with building a powerful state and establishing hegemony in the Western Hemisphere. It achieved these goals around 1900 but continued to let the great powers check each other, and Washington intervened militarily only when the balance of power broke down in one or more of the key strategic regions, as it did during the two world wars.

The same logic drove U.S. policy during the Cold War, but circumstances required a different response. Because its allies in Europe and Northeast Asia could not contain the Soviet Union by themselves, the United States had no choice but to go "onshore" in Europe and Northeast Asia. Accordingly, Washington forged alliances and stationed significant military forces in both regions, and it entered the Korean War to preserve the balance of power in Northeast Asia and prevent the Soviet Union from posing a greater threat to Japan.

In the Persian Gulf, however, the United States stayed offshore. Until 1968, Washington relied on Great Britain to prevent any state from dominating that oil-rich region. As Britain withdrew, America turned to the shah of Iran and to Saudi Arabia to achieve that same end. When the shah fell in 1979, Washington built the Rapid Deployment Force (RDF) to keep Iran or the Soviet Union from dominating the Gulf. The Reagan administration also helped thwart an Iranian victory in the Iran-Iraq War (1980–88) by giving Saddam Hussein military intelligence and other forms of assistance.

The United States kept the RDF offshore until 1990, when Saddam Hussein's seizure of Kuwait threatened to increase Iraq's power and place Saudi Arabia and other Gulf oil producers at risk. Consistent with offshore balancing, the Bush administration assembled a large coalition and sent a powerful expeditionary force to liberate Kuwait and smash Saddam's military machine.

For nearly a century, in short, offshore balancing prevented the emergence of dangerous regional hegemons and preserved a global balance of power that maximized U.S. security. Moreover, whenever Washington abandoned that strategy and tried a different approach, the result was a costly failure. The Vietnam War was a clear violation of offshore balancing, for example, as Indochina was not a vital strategic interest and Vietnam's fate had no impact on the global balance of power.[15]

As we have seen throughout this book, events since the end of the Cold War offer a similar warning. In Europe, open-ended NATO expansion poisoned relations with Russia, helped spark the frozen conflicts in Georgia and Ukraine, and drove Moscow closer to China. In the Middle East, "dual containment" kept thousands of U.S. troops in the Gulf after the 1991 Gulf War, where their presence helped inspire the September 11 attacks. Subsequent U.S. efforts at regime change in Afghanistan, Iraq, and Libya led to costly debacles as well, and U.S. support for antigovernment forces in Yemen and Syria failed to produce stable, pro-American governments. None of these wars were fought to uphold the balance of power in a vital region; instead, each involved trying to topple an unsavory regime and replace it with one more to America's liking. None of these efforts were successful. Abandoning offshore balancing after the Cold War has been a recipe for disaster.

Indeed, imagine how the world might look today had the United States embraced offshore balancing when the Cold War ended. For starters, there would have been no NATO expansion; instead, the United States would have pursued its original idea—the so-called Partnership for Peace—and done more to integrate Russia into a pan-European security framework. With no state threatening to become a hegemon in Europe, the U.S. role in European security would have decreased steadily and Washington could have actively supported Anglo-French efforts to build a common foreign and security policy.

In fairness, this approach might have prolonged the Balkan conflicts of the 1990s and left leaders such as Slobodan Milosevic in power. That outcome would have been objectionable on moral grounds, but it would not have affected U.S. security or prosperity very much, if at all. Nor should we forget that the Rube Goldberg solutions devised at Dayton in 1995 and after the Kosovo War in 2000 are far from ideal and remain fragile.

More important, reducing the U.S. role and eschewing NATO expansion would have avoided triggering long-term Russian security fears, thereby removing its incentive to maintain "frozen conflicts" in Georgia, seize Crimea, and destabilize Ukraine. Nor would the United States now be committed to defending weak and vulnerable allies in the Baltic region. The European security environment would likely still be tranquil, and relations with Russia—a declining but still influential regional power—would be much better than they are today.

In the Persian Gulf, a Clinton administration that embraced offshore balancing would have recognized the folly of dual containment and let Iran and Iraq continue to check each other. If U.S. forces had left Saudi Arabia after the first Gulf War, as offshore balancing would have prescribed, Osama bin Laden might never have decided to attack the "far enemy." One cannot be sure that 9/11 (or something like it) would not have occurred, but it would have been substantially less likely.

Needless to say, there would have been no Iraq War had offshore balancing prevailed. Instead of trying to "transform" the region into a sea of pro-American democracies, Washington would have intervened with military force only if Iran or Iraq (or some other state) attacked a U.S. ally or seemed likely to dominate the Gulf. This policy would have saved the United States trillions of dollars and spared the lives of thousands of U.S. soldiers and tens of thousands of innocent Iraqis. Iran's influence in the region would be substantially less today.

Moreover, an offshore balancer would have responded more sensibly to Iran's repeated efforts to pursue some sort of détente with the United States. Tehran reached out to Washington on several occasions

after the 1990s but was ultimately spurned each time.[16] A hateful buf-
foon such as Mahmoud Ahmedinejad would have less likely been chosen
as Iran's president, and Iran would probably have agreed to cap its nuclear
enrichment capacity earlier and at even lower levels. It is impossible to
know for certain if U.S.-Iranian relations would be significantly better
today had a different strategy been adopted, but the odds favor it.

Offshore balancing is not a miracle drug, so it might have failed to
overcome the many obstacles to a two-state solution between Israel and
the Palestinians. But eschewing the "special relationship" between the
United States and Israel in favor of a normal one would have forced
Israeli leaders to think more carefully about the long-term consequences
of continued settlement growth. A lasting final status agreement might
still have proved elusive, but a different U.S. strategy would have made it
more likely.

Offshore balancing would have also left the United States better
prepared to deal with a rising China. Instead of being distracted by conflicts in Central Asia and Iraq, U.S. leaders would have devoted more
time and attention to managing relations with Beijing and reinforcing
America's Asian alliances. The money squandered in Iraq and Afghanistan
would have been available to enhance the U.S. force posture, maintain
its technological edge, and invest in key regional partnerships. In retro-
spect, the failed pursuit of liberal hegemony was one of the greatest
gifts Beijing has received in recent decades.

Finally, and more speculatively, offshore balancing would have
been better for the U.S. economy. The United States could have enjoyed a
longer and larger "peace dividend," rebuilt its eroding infrastructure,
kept the federal budget balanced, and avoided the burgeoning deficits
and easy-money policies that followed 9/11 and fueled the pre-2008
housing bubble and the subsequent financial crisis. Wall Street might
have gone off the rails anyway, but a different grand strategy might
have made it less likely.

Counterfactuals such as these cannot be proved, of course, and a
strategy of offshore balancing might have produced a few unintended

consequences that policymakers would have been forced to address. Nonetheless, it is hard to imagine that it would have performed worse than liberal hegemony did, and there are good reasons to think it would have done substantially better.

OFFSHORE BALANCING TODAY

What would offshore balancing look like today? The good news is that a serious challenge to American hegemony in the Western Hemisphere is unlikely and there are presently no potential hegemons in Europe or the Persian Gulf. Now for the bad news: if China's impressive rise continues, it is likely to seek a dominant position in Asia. The United States should make a major effort to prevent it from succeeding, for Chinese hegemony in Asia would give Beijing the latitude to project power around the world—much as the United States does today—including in the Western Hemisphere. From the standpoint of U.S. national security, it is better if China has to focus its attention and effort closer to home.

In an ideal world, Washington would rely on local powers to contain China, but that strategy may not work. Not only is China likely to be much more powerful than its neighbors, but these states are located far from each other and do not always get along, making it more difficult for them to maintain an effective balancing coalition. The United States will almost certainly have to coordinate their efforts and may have to throw its considerable weight behind them. In the years ahead, Asia may be the one place where U.S. leadership is indeed "indispensable."[17]

In Europe, the United States should gradually draw down its military presence and turn NATO over to the Europeans. The United States entered both world wars in good part to keep Germany from controlling the continent, but there is no prospect of something similar happening today. Germany and Russia are going to get relatively weaker over time because their populations are gradually declining and becoming considerably older, and no other potential hegemon is in sight. Leaving European security to the local powers could increase the potential for trouble somewhat, but a conflict there, while obviously undesirable, would not lead to one state dominating all of Europe and thus would not pose a serious threat to vital U.S. interests. The United States should use its good offices to help resolve disagreements among the European powers and to encourage them to cooperate on a variety of issues, but there is no compelling strategic need for the United States to spend billions each year (and pledge its own citizens' lives) to keep the peace there.

Regarding the Persian Gulf, the United States should return to the strategy that served it well from 1945 to 1993. No local power is presently able to dominate the region, so the United States can keep most of its forces offshore and over the horizon. U.S. leaders should respect the principle of state sovereignty when dealing with the Middle East and should abandon its misguided efforts at regime change and social engineering. The Middle East will remain unstable for many years to come, and the United States has neither the need nor the ability to resolve the complex conflicts now roiling the region.

For the present, Washington should also pursue better relations with Iran. It is not in America's interest for Iran to abandon, or not renew, the current nuclear agreement and to race for the bomb. Iran is more likely to do so if it fears an American attack, which is why Washington should try to mend fences with Tehran in the interim. Moreover, China is likely to want allies in the Gulf in the future, and Iran will probably be at the top of its list.[18] The United States has an obvious interest in discouraging Sino-Iranian security cooperation, and that requires détente with Iran. Talking to Tehran is also a good way to remind America's other Middle East allies that Washington has many options, thereby giving them an incentive to act in ways that will secure U.S. backing if needed.

Iran has a significantly larger population and greater economic potential than its Persian Gulf neighbors, and it may eventually be in a position to dominate the region.[19] If Iran begins to move in this direction, the United States should help the other local powers balance Tehran, calibrating its own efforts and local military presence to the magnitude of the danger.

Taken together, these steps would allow the United States to reduce its national security expenditures to a percentage of GDP similar to that of the other major powers.[20] U.S. policymakers would focus primarily on Asia, curtail spending on counterterrorism, end the Afghanistan war, and cease most of its other overseas interventions. The United States would maintain substantial naval and air assets along with modest but capable ground forces and would spend enough to ensure that its military technology and personnel are the best in the world. It should also be prepared to expand its capabilities should circumstances require. For the foreseeable future, however, the U.S. government could spend more money on urgent domestic needs or leave it in the taxpayers' pockets.

BRINGING DIPLOMACY BACK IN

By design and by necessity, offshore balancing would shift the focus of U.S. foreign policy away from its present emphasis on military power and coercion and back toward diplomacy. Over the past two decades Washington has repeatedly tried to compel weaker powers to do its bidding by issuing threats, imposing sanctions, and, if necessary, unleashing its unmatched armada of drones, Special Forces, cruise missiles, stealthy aircraft, and conventional ground forces. At the same time, the Defense Department's vastly greater resources allowed it to usurp many functions previously performed by other government agencies.[21]

As noted repeatedly in previous chapters, these efforts have mostly failed to achieve the stated objectives. Even so, whenever some new problem arises—a civil war in Syria, fighting in Ukraine, a ballistic missile test by North Korea or Iran, or new Chinese efforts to "reclaim" shoals and reefs in the South China Sea—the reflexive U.S. response is to sell arms to local allies, ramp up economic sanctions, send an aircraft carrier, ship weapons and trainers to indigenous forces, issue threats and warnings, create a "no-fly" zone, or launch air strikes by manned aircraft, cruise missiles, and drones. Foreign policy pundits endlessly debate the merits of these (and other) initiatives, rarely asking what the United States could do to ameliorate or remove the underlying causes of the problem through persuasion and accommodation. Diplomacy has not disappeared entirely from the nation's foreign policy tool kit, but it routinely takes a back seat to the use of force and coercion.

Yet as former ambassador and assistant secretary of defense Chas W. Freeman reminds us, "diplomacy is how a nation advances its interests and resolves problems with foreigners with minimal violence."[22] Putting diplomacy first does not eliminate the need for military power, but sees it as the last resort rather than the first, and as a tool of statecraft rather than an end in itself. Prioritizing diplomacy means striving to reach mutually acceptable solutions with others rather than simply dictating to them. A nation that privileges diplomacy empowers its representatives to listen carefully to others, seeks to understand their views even when they are at odds with ours, tries to empathize with others' perspectives though we do not share them, and searches for creative agreements that can advance our interests along with theirs, ideally making a resort to force unnecessary.[23]

Under offshore balancing, diplomacy takes center stage. To implement the strategy successfully, U.S. leaders need a sophisticated understanding of strategic trends and must be familiar with the interests, goals, and likely responses of key regional states. Washington has to spot potential hegemons as they emerge and coordinate responses with the rising power's local rivals. Far from encouraging isolationism or disengagement, offshore balancing depends first and foremost on intelligent and adroit diplomacy in the service of America's broader strategic objectives.

It also places a premium on flexibility. Like Great Britain, the original "offshore balancer," the United States has "no eternal friends or enemies," but rather interests that are "eternal and perpetual."[24] Because its overriding goal is to maintain local balances of power in the key regions, the United States must have the agility to shift sides as needed. Flexibility of alignment can also help contain dangerous regional rivalries, as local actors will be less inclined to challenge the status quo if they know that doing so could lead the United States to bring its considerable power to bear against them.

When there is no potential hegemon in sight, however, Washington should strive to be on cordial terms with as many local states as possible. Cultivating businesslike relations with all states makes it easier to cooperate where interests overlap and would enhance U.S. diplomatic leverage. In short, instead of having "special relationships" with some countries and treating others as pariahs, offshore balancers keep the lines of communication open with everyone.

Among other benefits, this approach reminds current partners not to take U.S. support for granted, discourages free-riding, and gives both rivals and partners an incentive to compete for Washington's attention and support. The United States will be very powerful for many years to come, its support is still an enormous asset, and other states will be more attentive to U.S. concerns if they know that Washington has a decent working relationship with them but also with their rivals. Rather than bending over backward to convince local allies that its pledges are 100 percent reliable, the United States would take advantage of its favorable geopolitical position and play "hard to get" instead.

Ideally, a renewed emphasis on diplomacy would include a major effort to reform and professionalize America's diplomatic ranks. The United States is the only major power that routinely allows inexperienced amateurs to hold key diplomatic positions and frequently places individuals with little governmental experience in influential foreign policy positions. No president would appoint a wealthy campaign donor to command an armored division or a warship—let alone serve as a regional combatant commander—but roughly a third of U.S. ambassadorial appointments are doled out to campaign contributors rather than to trained professional diplomats, with sometimes embarrassing results.[25]

When the Ukraine crisis erupted in 2013, for example, the Russian ambassador in Germany, Vladimir Grinin, was in his fourth ambassadorship in a diplomatic career that began in 1971, including seventeen years in Germany itself. He speaks fluent German and English and is intimately acquainted with key German officials. By contrast, the U.S. ambassador in Berlin, John B. Emerson, was a former entertainment lawyer from Los Angeles who had been a major fundraiser for Barack Obama's presidential campaigns. He had no prior diplomatic experience and spoke no German. Emerson's political skills may have been exceptional, but which of these individuals was better prepared to represent his country's interests and perspective to his German counterparts and to explain their views to his superiors back home?[26]

America's diplomats also suffer from a haphazard personnel system and the lack of a systematic and well-funded program of career development. The U.S. military starts by training many of its officers at the three service academies, and career officers routinely receive additional professional training at one of many staff colleges (such as the Naval War College or the Command and General Staff College) or by earning advanced academic degrees at government expense. This commitment to career-long learning creates more effective military leaders and enhances their connection to other key parts of the foreign policy establishment.

By comparison, options for professional career development for U.S. diplomats consist mostly of language training undertaken prior to postings abroad. According to former ambassador Charles Ray, a typical military officer might receive a year or more of advanced training on roughly four occasions in a twenty-year career; a typical Foreign Service officer may be lucky to receive a single full year of training over a similar period.[27] The heavy reliance on political appointees also limits avenues for experienced Foreign Service officers to rise within the department and leaves fewer senior diplomats available to mentor their junior colleagues.

These problems are compounded by the peculiar manner in which the United States staffs key positions in the executive branch. When a new president is inaugurated, the transition team must fill several thousand government positions, from cabinet secretaries on down. Hundreds of these posts require Senate confirmation, which often takes months and sometimes more than a year. Some appointees will be serving in government for the first time, and many will remain in their posts for only a year or two. This situation is akin to having Apple, General Electric, or IBM replace their entire senior management team every four years and leaving key positions unfilled for months if not years at a time.

These pathologies would not be a problem if the United States had modest foreign policy goals. Instead, Washington has been trying to conduct a breathtakingly ambitious foreign policy with a combination of amateurs and short-timers and with many key positions unfilled. As Secretary of State John Kerry complained in 2016, "The United States is today more deeply engaged in more parts of the world on more consequential issues than ever before in history all at one time . . . And it just doesn't make sense . . . to leave open for sometimes more than a year vacant, important positions for our nation."[28] No other major power has such vast ambitions yet staffs a vast and complicated foreign policy apparatus in such a haphazard way.

Reforms such as these would also reverse the creeping militarization of U.S. foreign policy that has been under way for many years, and they would restore politics and diplomacy to their rightful place. A wise nation uses all instruments of national power to promote desired political ends, but in recent years politics and diplomacy have frequently been subordinated to narrow military objectives, including the endless "war on terror."

None of this is to deny the importance of military power. The diplomat and historian George F. Kennan was hardly a reflexive proponent of military solutions, but he once told an audience, "You have no idea how much it contributes to the general politeness and pleasantness of diplomacy when you have a little quiet armed force in the background."[29] Kennan's reflection also reveals the right way to think about these instruments: military power is a tool that must be harnessed to broader diplomatic and political ends, not the other way around.

Needless to say, the approach just described is the exact opposite of the one Donald Trump has pursued as president. In addition to appointing military officers to positions normally reserved for civilians, Trump has increased the already bloated Pentagon budget while simultaneously gutting the State Department. But this approach makes sense only if one wants to go on fighting lots of protracted wars. Or as Secretary of Defense James Mattis warned, "If you don't fully fund the State Department, then I need to buy more ammunition."[30]

MAKE PEACE A PRIORITY

Returning to offshore balancing would also allow U.S. leaders to focus less on issuing threats, imposing change, or demonstrating credibility and to focus more on promoting peace. Not just for idealistic or moral reasons, but because promoting peace is in the U.S. national interest.

One could argue that the United States has done well from war in the past. Conquering North America involved considerable violence and a "war of choice" with Mexico, and conflicts elsewhere in the world weakened or distracted potential rivals and improved America's relative position. But that was when the United States was a rising power and the European great powers still held sway in the rest of the world. Today, the United States is in exceptionally good shape: no other power is as strong, as far removed from potential enemies, as immune to violent internal upheaval, or as insulated from other dangers. Its position is not perfect, but it would be hard to ask for much more.

When a country sits atop the global pyramid, as the United States has for decades, the last thing it should do is embark on risky ventures that might dislodge it from its lofty perch. Instead of an exciting, thrill-a-minute foreign policy where glorious victory or shocking defeat may lurk around every corner, a dominant power like the United States should above all seek tranquility. For a power in America's privileged position, fomenting conflicts overseas will rarely if ever be a good idea, as "the iron dice of war" are inherently unpredictable. The United States has little to gain and much to lose from war, and even campaigns that appear to be smashing successes can easily become costly quagmires. Unless war is forced upon them, Americans should seek peace.

Peace is also good for business. Lockheed Martin, Boeing, United

Technologies, and Raytheon may have an obvious commercial interest in international insecurity, but such firms are actually a rather small and declining fraction of America's $17 trillion-plus economy.[31] More important, peace facilitates economic interdependence and thus fosters greater global growth. When peace prevails and security concerns are low, states worry less about being intertwined with potential rivals, and corporations won't worry about building factories abroad or sending capital off to far-away destinations. By contrast, when rivals abound and war looms on the horizon, states and private investors will worry more about foreign exposure and be less inclined to put their wealth at risk.[32]

Peace also tends to elevate individuals who are committed to and skilled at promoting human welfare, whether in the form of cool new products, improved health care, better government services, inspiring books, art, and music, or any of the other things that promote broader human well-being. War, by contrast, privileges those who are good at inspiring or using violence and who stand to gain from the hatred of others: the very people who readily become warlords, terrorists, revolutionaries, xenophobes, and the like. Many people who take up arms are motivated by a larger sense of duty and eagerly lay down their swords as soon as they are able, but some of them have a genuine taste for violence and an interest in their own glory and gain. Enduring peace should be a central goal of U.S. foreign policy, with a premium put on leaders who are better at building things than blowing them up.

Lastly, peace is morally preferable. War inevitably creates an enormous amount of death, destruction, and human suffering, and alleviating it when we can is intrinsically desirable. Putting peace at the top of America's foreign policy agenda is hardly something for which U.S. leaders need apologize.

From a selfish, hardheaded, flag-waving, red-white-and-blue perspective, therefore, peace is a goal to proclaim, to pursue, and to prize. Yet in the threat-driven, credibility-obsessed, overly militarized world of contemporary U.S. foreign policy, one is hard-pressed to find a prominent politician, pundit, or national security expert who will

talk unapologetically about their passion for peace, their commitment to pursuing it in office, or the specific strategies they would pursue
to further this goal.

This situation is surely odd, for some of America's greatest foreign
policy triumphs were won not by raw military power, but by the persistent, patient, and creative use of diplomatic and other nonmilitary tools.
Furthermore, many of these success stories were explicitly guided by a
desire to establish and enhance peace. Fear of communism may have
inspired the Marshall Plan, for example, but this diplomatic and economic masterstroke did as much to preserve U.S. interests in Europe as
the formation of NATO or the Berlin Airlift. It was diplomacy that produced the Egypt-Israeli peace treaty (1979), resolved the 1999 Kargil
crisis between India and Pakistan, midwifed the democratic transitions
in South Korea, the Philippines, and Myanmar, and made the Good Fri-
day Agreement in Northern Ireland happen. And lest we forget: the reunification of Germany and the peaceful conclusion to the Cold War was
a diplomatic achievement, won not by soldiers on the battlefield, but by
politicians and diplomats facing one another across a negotiating table.[33]

THE EMPIRE BUILDERS STRIKE BACK

Needless to say, the bulk of the foreign policy community will be dead
set against the more restrained policy of offshore balancing. The interest groups, corporations, and lobbies that have long shaped U.S. foreign
policy will oppose such a shift for fear that it would reduce the attention
the United States devotes to their particular agendas. Most members of
the foreign policy establishment will be similarly skeptical, in part
because they hold benevolent views of U.S. leadership but also because
their roles, status, and power would diminish were the United States to
adopt a less interventionist foreign policy.[34]

Indeed, an active campaign to discredit offshore balancing is already under way, with a cottage industry of prominent pundits, former
U.S. officials, and academics offering up spirited defenses of the status

quo and attacking any suggestion that the United States might modify
or reduce its global ambitions even slightly.[35] Not surprisingly, they invoke all the familiar arguments about the indispensability of America's
current world role and the adverse consequences that will supposedly
occur should the United States try a different approach. And whenever
Donald Trump even hinted that he might move toward a more restrained approach, a chorus of critics quickly attacked him for igno-
rantly abandoning America's supposedly essential leadership role.[36]

Once again, Americans are being told that they face a world filled with
threats both near and far, and that U.S. power must be deployed around
the world in order to keep those dangers at bay. If the United States were
to shift to offshore balancing, they warn, important allies would lose
confidence in U.S. security guarantees, adversaries would be embold-
ened, and renewed great power competition would erupt, undermining today's globalized world economy and threatening U.S. prosperity.
States accustomed to U.S. protection would be tempted to acquire nuclear
weapons, and curtailing active efforts to spread democracy and human
rights would imperil freedom around the globe and eliminate hopes for
a broader "democratic peace."

At the same time, defenders of liberal hegemony believe that the
United States can forestall these dangers and advance its ideals at little
cost or risk. In their view, America's $17 trillion economy can easily afford
the defense and foreign affairs outlays that liberal hegemony requires
and has the capacity to spend even more if needed. The risks of this
policy are minuscule, they maintain, because spreading democracy and
extending U.S. security guarantees around the world will prevent wars
from occurring, thereby saving money in the long run. Despite its recent failures, they still see liberal hegemony as an affordable and risk-
free insurance policy, and they portray offshore balancing as a dangerous
leap in the dark. According to the blue-ribbon CNAS task force discussed
in chapter 3, offshore balancing is "a recipe for uncertainty, miscalcula-
tion and ultimately more conflict and considerably more expense."[37]

As discussed in chapter 4, none of these arguments stand up to close inspection. Deep U.S. engagement does not always produce peace, especially when the United States keeps trying to topple dictators and spread democracy. Policing the world is not as cheap as the defenders of liberal hegemony contend, either in terms of dollars spent or human lives lost. The Iraq and Afghan wars alone cost between four and six trillion dollars, along with nearly seven thousand U.S. soldiers killed and more than fifty thousand wounded. Returning veterans from these conflicts exhibit high rates of suicide and depression, and the United States has little to show for their sacrifices.

As for the problem of proliferation, no grand strategy is likely to be wholly successful at preventing the spread of nuclear weapons or other types of WMD, but offshore balancing would do a better job than liberal hegemony. After all, the latter strategy did not stop India and Pakistan from ramping up their nuclear capabilities, North Korea from testing the bomb in 2006, or Iran from becoming a nuclear threshold state. Countries usually seek nuclear weapons because they fear being attacked and want a powerful deterrent, and U.S. efforts at regime change heighten such fears. By eschewing regime change, limiting U.S. military commitments to three key regions, and reducing America's military footprint, offshore balancing would give potential proliferators less reason to seek the bomb. The nuclear agreement with Iran shows that coordinated multilateral pressure and tough economic sanctions are a better way to discourage proliferation than preventive war or regime change. This approach, needless to say, is entirely consistent with offshore balancing.

To be sure, reducing U.S. security guarantees might lead a few vulnerable states to seek their own nuclear deterrent. Such a development is not desirable, but all-out efforts to prevent it would also be costly and may not succeed. Moreover, the negative consequences may not be as severe as pessimists fear. Getting the bomb does not transform weak countries into great powers or enable them to attack or blackmail rival states. Ten states have crossed the nuclear threshold since 1945, yet the world was not turned upside down every time some new member joined the nuclear club. Nuclear proliferation will remain a concern no matter what the United States does, but offshore balancing provides a better strategy for dealing with it.

Some foreign policy experts who are skeptical of liberal hegemony nonetheless still believe that the United States should keep large military forces deployed in Europe, Asia, and the Middle East in order to preserve peace. This approach—sometimes termed "selective engagement"—sounds appealing, but it will not work either.[38]

For starters, this strategy is likely to revert back to liberal hegemony. Once committed to preserving peace in key regions, U.S. leaders will be strongly inclined to spread democracy there too, based on the widespread belief that "democracies don't fight each other." NATO expansion illustrates this tendency perfectly, as it sought to create a Europe "whole and free" that would live in peace and harmony forever. When these efforts run into difficulties—as is likely to be the case—Washington will then be tempted to use its powerful military machine to rescue the situation, and all the more so given the importance U.S. leaders typically place on credibility. In the real world, the line between selective engagement and liberal hegemony is easily erased.

The problem with "selective engagement," in short, is that it is not selective enough. Once Washington takes on full responsibility for preventing conflict all over the world, it invariably gets tempted to solve problems that are not vital to its security or prosperity, or it is drawn toward idealistic missions it does not know how to achieve. Nor does selective engagement solve the problem of free-riding, for as long as Washington continues to protect countries that are capable of defending themselves, the latter will go on letting Uncle Sam shoulder the burden and spend the money they save on themselves.

Lastly, what about the claim that the United States has both a strategic interest and a moral duty to spread democracy, protect human rights, and prevent genocide? In this view, spreading democracy—by force, if necessary—will eventually lead to a "democratic peace" where war is unlikely, human rights violations are rare, and large-scale atrocities are unknown. If Americans can just be convinced to stay the course, liberal hegemony will eventually deliver a world of tranquillity, peace, and prosperity.

In fact, no one knows if a world consisting solely of liberal democracies would be peaceful. We do know, however, that spreading democracy at the point of a gun rarely works and that fledgling democracies are prone to conflict.[39] Instead of promoting peace, the United States ends up fighting war after war and gets trapped in open-ended occupations. These conflicts have led it to torture prisoners, conduct targeted killings, expand government secrecy, and undertake vast electronic surveillance of U.S. citizens. Ironically, the attempt to spread liberal values abroad has compromised them at home.

Encouraging the spread of liberal democracy and basic human rights should be a long-term U.S. objective, but the best way to do this is by setting a good example. Other societies are more likely to embrace U.S. values if they believe the United States is a just, prosperous, peaceful, and open society and they decide they want similar things for themselves. It follows that Americans who want to spread liberal values should do more to improve conditions here at home than to manipulate politics abroad. Offshore balancing fits this prescription to a T.

WHY REFORM WILL NOT BE EASY

Offshore balancing is a grand strategy born of confidence in America's core traditions and recognition of its enduring advantages. It exploits America's providential geographic position, recognizes the powerful incentives other states have to oppose potential hegemons in their own regions, and passes the buck to other countries whenever possible. It respects the power of nationalism, does not try to impose U.S. values on foreign societies, and focuses on setting an example that others will want to emulate. It would save U.S. taxpayers a significant amount of money, allow for long-term investments in America's future wealth and power, and limit government incursions on Americans' individual freedoms. For these reasons, offshore balancing was the right strategy for most of U.S. history and would be the best grand strategy today.

Yet the foreign policy community does not see it this way, thereby making meaningful reform unlikely. Thus, Michael Glennon ends his insightful analysis of the national security establishment on a gloomy note, concluding that the traditional system of "checks and balances" is effectively impotent and that little can be done to arrest the power of the existing "Trumanite network." In his words, the U.S. government now has "the power to kill and arrest and jail, the power to see and hear and read people's every word and action, the power to instill fear and suspicion, the power to quash investigations and quell speech, the power to shape public debate or to curtail it, and the power to hide its deeds and evade its weak-kneed overseers. The Trumanite network holds, in short, the power of *irreversibility*."[40]

Similarly, the longtime congressional staffer Mike Lofgren ends his own critique of America's "deep state" by enumerating an ambitious program of reforms—eliminating private money from public elections, redirecting the peace dividend to national infrastructure, reforming tax policy, staying out of the Middle East, etc.—only to concede that his proposals are "utopian, even unworldly." He presents no plan for moving the country in the directions he favors and is left with the wan hope that "the United States has done more surprising things in its history" and might be capable of similar surprises today.[41] But as we have seen, the foreign policy community has made little or no effort to rethink its deep commitment to liberal hegemony.[42]

What might produce such a "surprising" turn? In theory, world events could trigger a serious reconsideration of U.S. grand strategy and a major effort to reform existing foreign policy institutions. A catastrophic foreign policy disaster—such as an actual nuclear attack—might discredit reigning orthodoxies once and for all and create the opportunity for meaningful change. But no patriotic American should wish for such a tragedy to befall the country, and even a major setback might not be sufficient to produce meaningful change. If the failures of the past two decades, a major financial crisis, and the consecutive elections of

Barack Obama and Donald Trump did not prompt a systematic rethinking, what could?

To be sure, the emergence of a true peer competitor would probably impose greater discipline over U.S. foreign policy, force the establishment to set clearer priorities, and make it easier to dismiss dangerous or wasteful schemes. If China continues to rise and challenge the U.S. position, the foreign policy establishment might even begin to hold more people more accountable for failures and put a greater premium on effective performance in office.

It is hard to be enthusiastic about this "solution" either, however, because a new great power rivalry entails its own costs and risks.[43] In an ideal world, a future peer competitor would be just worrisome enough to encourage meaningful reform yet not too strong for the United States to handle. Alas, there is no guarantee that this convenient "sweet spot" will be realized or that U.S. leaders would make the right choices in response. The tragedy of 9/11 was as loud a wake-up call as a nation ever gets, but the foreign policy establishment responded in ways that made the problem worse.

Given America's abundant security and the elite consensus behind liberal hegemony, external pressures are unlikely to produce meaningful reform by themselves. Bureaucratic interests are notoriously resistant to change, and far-reaching policy shifts do not occur unless there is strong and sustained political pressure behind them. Absent sustained political action at home, debates on foreign policy will continue to occur within the same familiar echo chamber and stay between the forty-eight-yard lines. And instead of considering alternatives to liberal hegemony, its acolytes will just redouble their efforts to persuade the rest of the country to let them keep searching for a way to make it work.

HOW TO BEAT THE BLOB

What is needed, therefore, is a fairer fight *within* the existing political system, so that liberal hegemony no longer enjoys pride of place and rival approaches are not confined to the margins of political discourse or a few isolated ramparts inside the Beltway. Defenders of the status quo are already well represented in government, academia, the media, and the intertwined world of think tanks and lobbies, thereby tilting discussion heavily in their favor. The only way to broaden public debate on these topics, therefore, is to create a countervailing set of organizations and institutions that can do battle in the marketplace of ideas.

In particular, those who favor offshore balancing or other more restrained approaches must build a broader political movement and organize a countervailing set of institutions that can actively work to influence public perceptions and bring pressure to bear on politicians and officials who continue to favor policies that simply don't work. Such a movement would build upon the handful of groups that already favor a different grand strategy, such as the libertarian CATO Institute, the realist Center for the National Interest, or the left-leaning Center for International Policy. At the same time, it would strive to build bridges and form coalitions with other groups whose agendas are compatible.

Needless to say, this effort will require significant financial resources drawn from Americans who worry that continuing to pursue liberal hegemony will do serious long-term damage to the United States.[44] In addition to supporting policy-relevant research on critical foreign policy issues, this network should employ the same tactics that proponents of liberal hegemony have used to build influence in Washington. In particular, supporters of offshore balancing should conduct academic research on key issues related to a more restrained U.S. grand strategy, organize conferences designed to refine and disseminate their ideas, lobby politicians and policymakers directly, and engage in a broad array of public outreach activities. It will be especially important to recruit, mentor, and support a cadre of like-minded younger experts and provide them with sustainable career paths so that aspiring foreign policy wonks do not have to embrace the current consensus in order to have successful careers.

Indeed, a movement of the sort just described is probably a necessary condition for significant strategic change. In *War and Democratic Constraint: How the Public Influences Foreign Policy*, the political scientists

Matthew Baum and Philip Potter argue that "two basic conditions must be present for citizens of mass democracies to hold their leaders accountable. First, there must be independent and politically potent opposition partisans that can alert the public when a leader missteps . . . Second, media and communication institutions must be both in place and accessible sufficiently to transmit messages from these opposition elites to the public."[45]

The United States has numerous media outlets and robust laws protecting free speech; the problem has been the absence of a "politically potent" opposition to the reigning doctrine of liberal hegemony. As a result, when mainstream media organizations cover foreign policy topics, they do so within the boundaries of the existing consensus. The sources on which they rely typically include government officials or policy experts who are committed to liberal hegemony, as indeed are most prominent members of mainstream media organizations. Given that marriage of minds, it is hardly surprising that major news organizations such as *The Wall Street Journal*, *The Washington Post*, and *The New York Times* feel little pressure to offer genuinely alternative views to the readers, except on an intermittent basis.

But if advocates of a different grand strategy can establish enduring institutions and achieve critical mass, major media organizations will take notice and provide more space for their views. Over time, debates on key foreign policy topics would feature a wider range of opinion and Americans would be more aware of the deficiencies of their present grand strategy and the virtues of alternative approaches. Should this movement gain momentum, news organizations such as the *Times* or the *Post* might even conclude that it was time to add an advocate of greater foreign policy restraint to their current roster of crusading commentators.[46]

SELLING A SENSIBLE FOREIGN POLICY

It remains to be seen whether a politically potent movement in favor of a more restrained policy can be built and sustained over time. If such a movement were established, how might it gain broad public support? What is the best way to sell a more sensible foreign policy?

EMPHASIZE PATRIOTISM

Although offshore balancers—including this author—are often critical of many past U.S. policies, the strategy itself is deeply patriotic and should always be portrayed in this light. As emphasized throughout this book, it assumes that the primary task of U.S. foreign policy is to protect and promote the interests of the American people and to help them remain secure, prosperous, and free. In other words, offshore balancers are far from "anti-American." On the contrary, they believe the American people deserve a better foreign policy than the one they have been given over the past two decades.

RESPECT THE MILITARY

Offshore balancers are wary of military intervention—except when necessary to preserve balances of power in key regions—but they are neither pacifists nor hostile to the armed services. The strategy assumes that military power is still necessary and that protecting U.S. interests sometimes requires the use of force. And though offshore balancers are mindful that the foreign policy establishment and the so-called military-industrial complex routinely inflate threats for bureaucratic or budgetary reasons, they respect the sacrifices military personnel make on behalf of the nation. They believe that proponents of liberal hegemony have used America's armed forces carelessly and with insufficient regard for the human sacrifices involved; by contrast, offshore balancers oppose risking soldiers' lives for trivial or ill-considered reasons.

Indeed, offshore balancing strives to minimize the burdens borne by men and women in uniform. Instead of viewing the American military as an obedient tool that can be used to pursue unrealistic goals, offshore balancers believe that soldiers, sailors, and pilots should be sent in harm's way only when vital interests are at stake. In particular, offshore balancers believe that the American military should never be sent to fight wars they are destined to lose, whether because vital interests were not engaged or because the stated mission—such as trying to grow new democracies on unfertile ground—is one that military force cannot accomplish.

NO MORE "UNCLE SUCKER"

Advocates of offshore balancing can enhance its appeal by stressing the need for other states to contribute their fair share to collective security efforts instead of free-riding on Uncle Sam. The foreign policy elite may relish the stature and prestige that "global leadership" gives them, but ordinary Americans rightly resent subsidizing wealthy allies, protecting states that will not or cannot contribute to U.S. security, and tolerating the reckless behavior that some U.S. allies indulge in under the mantle of American protection.

Connecting adventures abroad with conditions at home will strengthen the case for offshore balancing even more. Although the United States is still remarkably well off, the time, resources, and attention devoted to foolish adventures abroad inevitably affect the quality of life back home. It is important to explain to Americans the connection between our foreign and defense policies and the quality of life at home, the level of taxes we are asked to pay, the number of wounded veterans for whom we must care, the intrusiveness of U.S. security agencies, and the state of the federal budget and the overall economy. The more bases we garrison around the world, the fewer roads, bridges, subways, parks, museums, hospitals, schools, fiber-optic cables, and WiFi networks will be available for U.S. citizens, diminishing the quality of life for everyone. Making these connections clearer to more people is critical to winning their support for a smarter strategy.

DEFEND THE MORAL HIGH GROUND

Offshore balancing is a self-interested strategy, but it is not indifferent to moral considerations. Because the United States remains a deeply liberal society, its citizens are unlikely to embrace for long a grand strategy they believe is unethical or indifferent to morality. Accordingly, pro-

ponents of offshore balancing must also stress its positive moral qualities and its consistency with core U.S. values.[47]

In particular, offshore balancing does not preclude using American
power to try to prevent wars, halt genocides, or persuade other countries to improve their human rights performance, but it does set a high
bar for the use of force. In particular, offshore balancers would willingly
endorse disaster relief and other purely humanitarian actions and would
even countenance using force to halt mass killings when (1) the danger
was imminent, (2) the anticipated costs to the United States were modest,
(3) the ratio of foreign lives saved to U.S. lives risked was high, and (4) it
was clear that intervention would not make things worse or lead to an
open-ended commitment.

Offshore balancing is also more likely to protect these values here at
home. As the Founding Fathers understood well, no nation can remain
at war for long periods without compromising civil liberties and other
liberal institutions. Warfare, after all, is a quintessentially illiberal activity: it is violent, coercive, and hierarchical, and it privileges secrecy and
command over transparency and freedom.

In fact, offshore balancers have a powerful moral case in favor of
their preferred strategy, and they should not hesitate to make it. Offshore balancing would cause less conflict and human suffering than
liberal hegemony has, and the United States is more likely to promote
progressive change if it presents an attractive model to others and if it
promotes liberal values through patient diplomacy and moral suasion
rather than by coercion or military action. Above all, they need not cede
the moral high ground to their liberal or neoconservative opponents,
especially in light of the considerable human suffering that the latter's
policies have produced.

MIND THE MESSENGER

Last but not least, offshore balancing needs able advocates to make the
case for it. In recent years, unfortunately, the public figures whose views
on foreign policy most closely approximate the strategy of offshore

balancing have been Ron and Rand Paul, Pat Buchanan, and back in 2016, Donald Trump. Although these men have all said some sensible things about the failures of U.S. foreign policy, they also carry considerable negative baggage and hold other beliefs that are foolish, ignorant, or offensive.

In a sense, their mistakes are not surprising. It takes a degree of iconoclasm to see through the clouds of rhetoric and conventional wisdom underpinning liberal hegemony—such as the constant invocation of American "exceptionalism" or the claim that U.S. leadership is the only barrier between civilization and the abyss. It is no accident, therefore, that offshore balancing's most visible proponents have been outliers within the American political establishment. For it to reemerge as America's default grand strategy, therefore, it will need champions who are smart, sophisticated, well-informed, articulate, patriotic, and free of embarrassing skeletons.

If such a figure does emerge, however, he or she will find a ready audience. Americans remain willing to bear certain burdens abroad for the sake of their own safety and prosperity, and in some cases to help others. But they are less and less willing to undertake the same quixotic missions that have failed in the past and are doomed to fail in the future, and intelligent politicians who promise not to repeat these errors would almost certainly attract considerable popular support.

FINAL THOUGHTS

"There is a great deal of ruin in a nation," wrote Adam Smith—all the more so when a country has as many enduring advantages as the United States still enjoys. Good fortune has allowed the country to survive its haphazard, cavalier, and, in recent years, unrealistic approach to foreign policy. For all its recent mistakes, America is still a remarkably lucky country, confirming Bismarck's alleged quip that "there seems to be a special providence that looks after drunkards, fools, and the United States of America."

The real danger we face, therefore, is not a well-organized and powerful array of foreign adversaries whose clever strategems will snatch our security, prosperity, and way of life away from us. On the contrary, the problems the United States has faced abroad are mostly of its own making. As the political cartoonist Walt Kelly observed many years ago, "We have met the enemy and he is us."

At what point might America's good fortune run out? It is by no means clear that the reform movement outlined here will take root, grow and flourish, and eventually help correct some of the follies that have led the United States astray at considerable cost to ourselves and even greater cost to others. It is entirely possible that the United States will continue on its present stumbling course no matter who resides in the White House, who occupies key positions in the executive branch, or which party controls the House or Senate.

As a nation, therefore, we stand at a crossroads. Down one road lies more of the same, with similar disheartening results. Repeating past follies may be endurable but is hardly desirable, and it will pose graver risks as the "unipolar moment" recedes further into the past. Down another road lies a more realistic strategy that has served the country well in the past and would do so again if adopted. It is not the foreign policy that the current occupant of the Oval Office can deliver successfully, but it is the foreign policy most Americans want and deserve. The only question is: How long will it take before they get it?

NOTES

INTRODUCTION

1. See John Hudson, "Inside Hillary Clinton's Massive Foreign Policy Brain Trust," *Foreign Policy*, February 10, 2016; and Stephen M. Walt, "The Donald vs. the Blob," *Foreign Policy*, May 16, 2016, at http://foreignpolicy.com/2016/05/16/the -donald-vs-the-blob-hillary-clinton-election/.

2. See "Open Letter on Donald Trump from GOP National Security Leaders," March 2, 2016, at http://warontherocks.com/2016/03/open-letter-on-donald -trump-from-gop-national-security-leaders/; and "A Letter from GOP National Se- curity Officials Opposing Donald Trump," *The New York Times*, August 8, 2016, at www.nytimes.com/interactive/2016/08/08/us/politics/national-security-letter -trump.html?_r=0.

3. See "Transcript: Trump Expounds on His Foreign Policy Views," *The New York Times*, March 26, 2016, at www.nytimes.com/2016/03/27/us/politics/donald -trump-transcript.html; and "Transcript: Donald Trump on NATO, Turkey's Coup Attempt and the World," July 21, 2016, at www.nytimes.com/2016/07/22/us /politics/donald-trump-foreign-policy-interview.html.

4. When announcing his presidential bid in 2015, Trump claimed that Mexico was sending to the United States "people that have lots of problems . . . They're bringing drugs. They're bringing crime. They're rapists." See "Full Text: Trump Announces a Presidential Bid," *The Washington Post*, June 16, 2015. And in his first major foreign policy speech in April 2016, Trump said, "There are scores of recent migrants inside our borders charged with terrorism . . . We must stop importing extremism through senseless immigration policies." Ryan Teague Beckwith, "Read Donald Trump's 'America First' Foreign Policy Speech," *Time*, April 27, 2016, at http://time.com/4309786/read-donald-trumps-america-first-foreign-policy -speech/.

5. See Juliet Eilperin, "Obama Lays Out His Foreign Policy Doctrine: Singles, Doubles, and the Occasional Home Run," *The Washington Post*, April 28, 2014, at www.washingtonpost.com/world/obama-lays-out-his-foreign-policy-doctrine -singles-doubles-and-the-occasional-home-run/2014/04/28/e34ec058-ceb5-11e3 -937f-d3026234b51c_story.html.

6. See David Law and Mila Versteeg, "The Declining Influence of the U.S. Constitution," *New York University Law Review* 87, no. 3 (June 2012).

7. See Beckwith, "Read Donald Trump's 'America First' Foreign Policy Speech."

8. In a March 2016 interview with *The New York Times*, Trump said, "We're not a rich country. We were a rich country with a very strong military and tremendous capability in so many ways. We're not anymore. We have a military that's severely depleted." See "Transcript: Donald Trump Expounds on His Foreign Policy Views."

9. Trump was not alone in this view. For criticisms of recent U.S. foreign policy from a variety of perspectives, see Andrew Bacevich, *Washington Rules: America's Path to Permanent War* (New York: Metropolitan Books, 2010); Barry R. Posen, *Restraint: A New Foundation for U.S. Grand Strategy* (Ithaca, NY: Cornell University Press, 2014); Chas W. Freeman, "Militarism and the Crisis of American Diplomacy," *Epistulae*, no. 20, July 7, 2015; Michael Mandelbaum, *Mission Failure: America and the World in the Post–Cold War Era* (New York: Oxford, 2016); Robert Lieber, *Retreat and Its Consequences: American Foreign Policy and the Problem of World Order* (Cambridge: Cambridge University Press, 2015); Bret Stephens, *America in Retreat: The New Isolationism and the Coming Global Disorder* (New York: Sentinel, 2014); and Jeremy Scahill, *Dirty Wars: The World Is a Battlefield* (New York: Nation Books, 2013).

10. George H. W. Bush and Brent Scowcroft, *A World Transformed* (New York: Alfred A. Knopf, 1998), p. 564.

11. Thus, Jimmy Carter, Ronald Reagan, Bill Clinton, George W. Bush, and Barack Obama are all "liberals," in the sense that all were equally committed to the ideals of individual freedom, democracy, rule of law, and competitive markets.

12. On the foreign policy establishment, see Michael J. Glennon, *National Security and Double Government* (New York: Oxford University Press, 2014); Mike Lofgren, *The Deep State: The Fall of the Constitution and the Rise of a Shadow Government*

(New York: Viking, 2016); and Scott Horton, *The Lords of Secrecy: The National Security Elite and America's Stealth Warfare* (New York: Nation Books, 2015).

1: A DISMAL RECORD

1. For useful discussions of alternative U.S. grand strategies, see Andrew Ross and Barry R. Posen, "Competing Visions of U.S. Grand Strategy," *International Security* 21, no. 3 (Winter 1996/97); and Robert J. Art, *A Grand Strategy for America* (Ithaca, NY: Cornell University Press, 2004).

2. See Eugene Gholz, Daryl Press, and Harvey Sapolsky, "Come Home, America: The Strategy of Restraint in the Face of Temptation," *International Security* 21, no. 4 (Spring 1997); Christopher Layne, "From Preponderance to Offshore Balancing: America's Future Grand Strategy," *International Security* 22, no. 1 (Summer 1997); Eric Nordlinger, *Isolationism Reconfigured: American Foreign Policy for a New Century* (Princeton, NJ: Princeton University Press, 1996); and Ted Galen Carpenter, *Beyond NATO: Staying Out of Europe's Wars* (Washington, DC: CATO Institute, 1994).

3. See Patrick E. Tyler, "U.S. Plan Calls for Ensuring No Rivals Develop," *The New York Times*, March 8, 1992; and James Mann, *Rise of the Vulcans: The History of Bush's War Cabinet* (New York: Viking, 2004), pp. 209–15.

4. George H. W. Bush and Brent Scowcroft, *A World Transformed* (New York: Alfred A. Knopf, 1998), p. 564.

5. Richard N. Haass, "Defining U.S. Foreign Policy in a Post-Post Cold War World," Arthur Ross Lecture, Foreign Policy Association, April 22, 2002, at http://2001-2009.state.gov/s/p/rem/9632.htm.

6. See "US GDP as Percentage of World GDP," at https://ycharts.com /indicators/us _gdp_as_a_percentage_of_world_gdp.

7. See Barry Posen, "Command of the Commons: The Military Foundation of U.S. Hegemony," *International Security* 28, no. 1 (Summer 2003).

8. R & D data drawn from "Historical Trends in Federal R & D," *American Association for the Advancement of Science*, at www.aaas.org/sites/default/files/DefRD .jpg; total defense expenditure data from *The Military Balance* (London: International Institute for Strategic Studies, various years).

9. See Charles Krauthammer, "The Unipolar Moment," *Foreign Affairs* 70, no. 1 (1990).

10. See William C. Wohlforth, "The Stability of a Unipolar World," *International Security* 24, no. 1 (Summer 1999); William C. Wohlforth and Stephen Brooks, *World Out of Balance: International Relations and the Challenge of American Primacy* (Princeton, NJ: Princeton University Press, 2008).

11. This was also a recurring theme in the writings of Joseph Nye, including his *Bound to Lead: The Changing Nature of American Power* (New York: Basic Books, 1990), and more recently, *Is the American Century Over?* (New York: Polity, 2015).

12. In 1998, for example, Cuba, Serbia, Afghanistan, Iraq, Iran, Libya, and North Korea had a combined GNP of roughly $165 billion and combined defense

spending of roughly $11 billion. By contrast, U.S. GNP in 1998 was more than $10 trillion and its defense budget was more than $266 billion.

13. Quoted in "Communism's Collapse Poses a Challenge to America's Military," *U.S. News and World Report*, October 14, 1991, p. 28.

14. See Francis Fukuyama, "The End of History," *The National Interest* (Summer 1989); idem, *The End of History and the Last Man* (New York: Free Press, 1993).

15. John Mueller, *Retreat from Doomsday: The Obsolescence of Major War* (New York: Random House, 1989); and idem, *The Remnants of War* (Ithaca, NY: Cornell University Press, 2004). Hoffmann is quoted in Thomas Friedman, "Friends Like Russia Make Diplomacy a Mess," *The New York Times*, March 28, 1993.

16. For example, countries seeking to join the World Trade Organization must have "full autonomy in the conduct of its external commercial relations," provide extensive information about any national policies and economic conditions that could affect these relations, and agree to abide by WTO rules and dispute resolution procedures. See World Trade Organization, "How to Become a WTO Member," at www.wto.org/english/thewto_e/acc_e/how_to_become_e .htm.

17. Thomas Friedman, "A Manifesto for the Fast World," *The New York Times Magazine*, March 28, 1999.

18. See Paul I. Bernstein and Jason D. Wood, *The Origins of Nunn-Lugar and Cooperative Threat Reduction* (Washington, DC: National Defense University Press, 2010); and "The Nunn-Lugar Vision," at www.nti.org/analysis/articles/nunn-lugar -vision-20-years-reducing-global-dangers/.

19. The Clinton administration seriously considered preventive air strikes against North Korea's nuclear facilities in 1994, a step they would never have seriously considered had the Soviet Union still been intact. South Korea and Japan were both opposed, however, and U.S. officials ultimately chose to pursue a diplomatic deal instead. See Daniel Poneman, Joel S. Wit, and Robert Gallucci, *Going Critical: The First North Korean Nuclear Crisis* (Washington, DC: Brookings Institution, 2004); and Scott Silverstone, *Preventive War and American Democracy* (New York: Routledge, 2007), chap. 6.

20. See in particular Daniel Benjamin and Steven Simon, *The Age of Sacred Terror: Radical Islam's War Against America* (New York: Random House, 2002), pp. 407–18.

21. See Warren Christopher, "The Shifting Priorities of U.S. Foreign Policy, Peacekeeping Downgraded," Testimony to the Senate Foreign Relations Committee, November 4, 1993, *Department of State Bulletin* 4, nos. 4–5 (January–April 1994), p. 43.

22. Kennan's views are quoted at length in Thomas Friedman, "Now a Word from X," *The New York Times*, May 2, 1998.

23. In January 1990, the West German foreign minister Hans-Dietrich Genscher publicly declared that German reunification should not "lead to an impairment of Soviet security interests" and proposed that NATO rule out "an expansion of [its] territory to the east." In February, the U.S. secretary of state James Baker

met with Soviet foreign minister Eduard Shevardnadze and Soviet premier Mikhail Gorbachev and made the case for anchoring a reunified Germany in NATO, together with "iron-clad guarantees" that "NATO's jurisdiction or forces would not move eastward." In particular, Baker told Gorbachev, "If we maintain a presence in a Germany that is a part of NATO, there would be no extension of NATO's jurisdiction or forces of NATO one inch to the east." See "NATO Expansion: What Gorbachev Heard" (Washington, DC: National Security Archive, December 12, 2017), at https://nsarchive.gwu.edu/briefing-book/russia-programs /2017-12-12/nato-expansion-what-gorbachev-heard-western-leaders-early. See also Joshua Shifrinson, "Deal or No Deal?: The End of the Cold War and the U.S. Offer to Limit NATO Expansion," *International Security* 40, no. 4 (Spring 2016); and Mary Sarotte, "A Broken Promise?: What the West Really Told Moscow about NATO Expansion," *Foreign Affairs* 93, no. 5 (September/October 2014).

24. See "Russia's National Security Concept," in *Arms Control Today* 30, no. 1 (January/February 2000), p. 15.

25. As former secretary of defense Leon Panetta wrote in his memoirs, "I said what everyone in Washington knew but we couldn't officially acknowledge: that our goal in Libya was regime change." See Leon Panetta with Jim Newton, *Worthy Fights: A Memoir of Leadership in War and Peace* (New York: Penguin, 2014). For a careful sifting of the evidence showing that regime change was a U.S. objective nearly from the beginning, see Stephen R. Weissman, "Presidential Deception in Foreign Policy Making: Military Intervention in Libya 2011," *Presidential Studies Quarterly* 46, no. 3 (September 2016). See also David E. Sanger, *Confront and Conceal: Obama's Secret Wars and Surprising Use of American Power* (New York: Crown, 2012), pp. 345–55.

26. Peter Baker, "U.S.-Russian Ties Fall Short of Reset Goal," *The New York Times*, September 2, 2013.

27. See John J. Mearsheimer, "Why the Ukraine Crisis Is the West's Fault," *Foreign Affairs* 93, no. 5 (September/October 2014); Richard Sakwa, *Frontline Ukraine: Crisis in the Borderlands* (London: I. B. Tauris, 2015); and Rajan Menon and Eugene Rumer, *Conflict in Ukraine: The Unwinding of the Post–Cold War Order* (Boston: MIT Press, 2015).

28. The relevant passage read "in pursuing advanced military capabilities that can threaten its neighbors in the Asia-Pacific region, China is following an outdated path that, in the end, will hamper its own pursuit of national greatness. In time, China will find that social and political freedom is the only source of that greatness." *The National Security Strategy of the United States of America* (Washington, DC: The White House, 2002), at www.state.gov/documents/organization /63562.pdf.

29. See Bonnie S. Glaser and Matthew P. Funaiole, "The 19th Party Congress: A More Assertive Chinese Foreign Policy," *Lowy Interpreter*, October 26, 2017, at www.lowyinstitute.org/the-interpreter/19th-party-congress-more-assertive -chinese-foreign-policy.

30. For a summary, see Christopher Johnson, "President Xi Jinping's 'Belt and

Road Initiative': A Practical Assessment of the Chinese Communist Party's Road-map for Chinese Global Resurgence" (Washington, DC: Center for Strategic and International Studies, 2016).

31. See Charlie Campbell, "Donald Trump's Pledge to Withdraw U.S. from TPP Opens Door for China," *Time*, November 22, 2016, at http://time.com/4579580/china-donald-trump-tpp-obama-asia-rcep-business-trade/.

32. See John J. Mearsheimer, *The Tragedy of Great Power Politics*, 2nd ed. (New York: W. W. Norton, 2011), chap. 10; Aaron Friedberg, *A Contest for Supremacy: China, America, and the Struggle for Mastery in Asia* (New York: W. W. Norton, 2015); and Graham T. Allison, *Destined for War: Can America and China Escape Thucydides's Trap?* (New York: Houghton Mifflin, 2017). For a Chinese perspective, see "Yan Xuetong on Chinese Realism, the Tsinghua School of International Relations, and the Impossibility of Harmony," at www.theory-talks.org/2012/11/theory-talk-51.html.

33. On the Afghan War, see Rajiv Chandrasekaran, *Little America: The War Within the War for Afghanistan* (New York: Alfred A. Knopf, 2012); Anand Gopal, *No Good Men Among the Living: America, the Taliban, and the War Through Afghan Eyes* (New York: Metropolitan Books, 2014); and Daniel P. Bolger, *Why We Lost: A General's Insider Account of the Iraq and Afghanistan Wars* (New York: Houghton Mifflin, 2014).

34. On the U.S. failure in Iraq, see especially Peter W. Galbraith, *The End of Iraq: How American Incompetence Created a War Without End* (New York: Simon & Schuster, 2007); Peter Van Buren, *We Meant Well: How I Helped Lose the Battle for the Hearts and Minds of the Iraqi People* (New York: Metropolitan Books, 2012); Thomas Ricks, *Fiasco: The American Military Adventure in Iraq, 2003 to 2005* (New York: Penguin, 2006); and Emma Sky, *The Unraveling: High Hopes and Missed Opportunities in Iraq* (New York: Public Affairs, 2015).

35. See Jeremy Scahill, *Dirty Wars: The World Is a Battlefield* (New York: Nation Books, 2013).

36. Michael Mullen, "National Security Priorities for President-Elect Trump," *Washington Ideas Festival*, November 21, 2016, at www.youtube.com/watch?v=buu9IZYzmUo&app=desktop.

37. See Martin Murphy, "The Importance of Alliances for U.S. Security," *2017 Index of Military Strength* (Washington, DC: Heritage Foundation, 2017) at http://index.heritage.org/military/2017/essays/importance-alliances-u-s-security/.

38. See Jennifer Kavanagh, *U.S. Security-Related Agreements in Force Since 1955: Introducing a New Database*, RR-736-AF (Washington, DC: The RAND Corporation, 2014), p. 22.

39. See Richard Haass, "The Unraveling," *Foreign Affairs* (November/December 2014). General Dempsey is quoted in Micah Zenko, "Most. Dangerous. World. Ever." *Foreign Policy*, February 26, 2013, at http://foreignpolicy.com/2013/02/26/most-dangerous-world-ever/. Kissinger's statement is from "Opening Statement by Dr. Henry A. Kissinger before the United States Senate Committee on Armed Services, at a Hearing to Discuss 'Global Challenges and National Security Strategy,'" January 29, 2015, at www.henryakissinger.com/speeches/012915.html.

40. See William J. Clinton, *A National Security Strategy of Engagement and En-largement* (Washington, DC: The White House, 1995); and George W. Bush, "Preface," *The National Security Strategy of the United States of America* (Washington, DC: The White House, September 2002).

41. Aides strongly committed to liberal objectives include James Steinberg, Samantha Power, Susan Rice, Michael McFaul, and Anne-Marie Slaughter. Steinberg was deputy secretary of state during Obama's first term, while Power served initially on the National Security Council and later as ambassador to the United Nations. Susan Rice was UN ambassador during Obama's first term and became national security advisor in the second term. Michael McFaul served on the NSC staff and as ambassador to Russia, and Anne-Marie Slaughter was director of policy planning in the State Department from 2009 to 2011. See James Mann, *The Obamians: The Struggle Inside the White House to Redefine American Power* (New York: Penguin, 2015).

42. Obama also told the Assembly, "[E]xperience shows us that history is on the side of liberty; that the strongest foundation for human progress lies in open economies, open societies, and open governments." See "Remarks by the President to the UN General Assembly," September 23, 2010, at https://obamawhitehouse .archives.gov/the-press-office/2010/09/23/remarks-president-united-nations -general-assembly.

43. A partial list of activities undertaken to promote democracy is in *Enduring Leadership in a Dynamic World: The 2015 Quadrennial Diplomacy and Development Review* (Washington, DC: U.S. Department of State, 2015), pp. 28–32.

44. See Eric Patterson, "Clinton Declares Religious Freedom a National Interest," *First Things*, September 12, 2012, at www.firstthings.com/web-exclusives /2012/09/clinton-declares-religious-freedom-a-national-interest.

45. "About NED," at www.ned.org/about, downloaded December 20, 2014.

46. Victoria Nuland, "Remarks at the U.S.-Ukraine Foundation Conference," December 13, 2013, at www.voltairenet.org/article182080.html.

47. Economist Intelligence Unit, *Democracy Index 2012*, p. 2; and *Democracy Index 2015: Democracy in an Age of Anxiety*, p. 9.

48. See John Nichols, "*The Economist* Just Downgraded the United States from a 'Full' to a 'Flawed' Democracy," *The Nation*, January 26, 2017.

49. See Freedom House, *Freedom in the World 2018: Democracy in Crisis*, at https://freedomhouse.org/report/freedom-world/freedom-world-2018.

50. See "A Notable Year of the Wrong Kind," at http://dartthrowingchimp .wordpress.com/2013/12/26/a-banner-year-of-the-wrong-kind/, downloaded December 26, 2013.

51. See Ty McCormick, "Unmade in the USA," *Foreign Policy*, February 25, 2015, at http://foreignpolicy.com/2015/02/25/unmade-in-the-usa-south-sudan-bush -obama/.

52. See Larry Diamond, "Democracy in Decline," *Foreign Affairs* 95, no. 4 (July/August 2016), p. 151.

53. See Klaus Armingeon and Kai Guthmann, "Democracy in Crisis?: The Declining Support for National Democracy in European Countries, 2007–2011,"

European Journal of Political Research 53, no. 2 (August 2014); see also Roberto Stefan Foa and Yascha Mounk, "The Danger of Deconsolidation: The Democratic Disconnect," *Journal of Democracy* 27, no. 3 (July 2016); and Marc Plattner, "Is Democracy in Decline?" *Democracy & Society* 13, no. 1 (Fall–Winter 2016).

54. See Thomas Carothers, "Democracy Promotion at 25: Time to Choose," *Journal of Democracy* 26, no. 1 (January 2015).

55. See Jane Mayer, *The Dark Side: The Inside Story of How the War on Terror Turned into a War on American Ideals* (New York: Doubleday, 2008); James Risen, *State of War: The Secret History of the CIA and the Bush Administration* (New York: The Free Press, 2006); James Risen, *Pay Any Price: Greed, Power, and Endless War* (New York: Houghton Mifflin Harcourt, 2014); and *The Senate Intelligence Committee Report on Torture: Committee Study of the Central Intelligence Agency's Detention and Interrogation* (New York: Melville House, 2014).

56. On U.S. policy toward Egypt, see Jason Brownlee, *Democracy Prevention: The Politics of the U.S.-Egyptian Alliance* (Cambridge: Cambridge University Press, 2012). In the case of Turkey, the United States has ignored the government's increasingly authoritarian behavior, growing limits to press freedom, and the use of politicized prosecutions and show trials to intimidate potential opponents. Regarding Israel, not only did the United States do nothing to halt Israel's attacks on Lebanon in 2006 or on Gaza in 2008–09—campaigns that killed or wounded hundreds of innocent civilians—U.S. officials protected Israel from censure by the UN Security Council and defended its actions in public.

57. See Harriet Sherwood, "Human Rights Groups Face Global Crackdown 'Not Seen in a Generation,'" *The Guardian*, August 26, 2015, at www.theguardian .com/law/2015/aug/26/ngos-face-restrictions-laws-human-rights-generation.

58. See Branko Milanovic, "Why the Global 1% and the Asian Middle Class Have Gained the Most from Globalization," *Harvard Business Review*, May 13, 2016, at https://hbr.org/2016/05/why-the-global-1-and-the-asian-middle-class-have-gained -the-most-from-globalization.

59. See Martin Wolf, "Inequality Is a Threat to Our Democracies," *Financial Times*, December 20, 2017. In 2018 the World Inequality Lab found that "Income inequality in the United States is among the highest of all rich countries" and reported that incomes for the bottom 50 percent of Americans had "stagnated" since 1980 while income growth for the middle 40 percent had been "weak." "By contrast," they write, "the average income of the top 10% doubled over this period, and for the top 1% it tripled, even on a post-tax basis." See *World Inequality Report 2018*, at http://wir2018.wid.world, pp. 78–81.

60. Technological change (e.g., the development of robotics-based manufacturing) eliminated far more U.S. jobs than expanded global trade or the emergence of low-wage states such as China or India. See Brad DeLong, "Where U.S. Manufacturing Jobs Really Went," *Project Syndicate*, May 3, 2017, at www.project -syndicate.org/commentary/manufacturing-jobs-share-of-us-economy-by-j —bradford-delong-2017-05; idem, "NAFTA and Other Big Trade Deals Have Not Gutted American Manufacturing—Period." *Vox.com*, January 24, 2017, at www.vox

.com/the-big-idea/2017/1/24/14363148/trade-deals-nafta-wto-china-job-loss-trump.

61. A nuanced and sensible analysis of the downside of contemporary globalization is Dani Rodrik, *Straight Talk on Trade: Ideas for a Sane World Economy* (Princeton, NJ: Princeton University Press, 2017), especially chap. 1 and pp. 27–29.

62. See Uri Dadush, "The Decline of the Bretton Woods Institutions," *The National Interest*, September 22, 2014, at http://nationalinterest.org/blog/the-buzz/the-decline-the-bretton-woods-institutions-11324.

63. According to Gordon I. Bradford and Johannes F. Linn, "Global institutions are not working well individually and as a group. For example, the global institutions at the core of the international system, such as the United Nations, the International Monetary Fund, the World Bank and the G8 Summit, are to varying degrees fragmented, unrepresentative, and ineffective. They generally suffer from a corrosive decline in their legitimacy. They are increasingly undemocratic and unable to address the global challenges of the 21st century." See their "Reform of Global Governance: Priorities for Action," *Brookings Policy Brief* no. 163 (Washington, DC: Brookings Institution, 2007).

64. On this point, see Rodrik, *Straight Talk on Trade*, pp. 24–29.

65. Jonathan Kirshner, "The Global Financial Crisis: A Turning Point," *Forbes*, November 8, 2014, at www.forbes.com/sites/jonathankirshner/2014/11/08/the-global-financial-crisis-a-turning-point/#7909a1a34c2f.

66. See Foundation for Middle East Peace, "Comprehensive Settlement Population, 1972–2011," at http://fmep.org/resource/comprehensive-settlement-population-1972-2010/; "Settlements," from B'tselem, at www.btselem.org/settlements/statistics; and "Israeli Settlement" at https://en.wikipedia.org/wiki/Israeli_settlement.

67. For varied accounts of this long series of failures, see Jeremy Pressman, "Visions in Collision: What Happened at Camp David and Taba?" *International Security* 28, no. 2 (Fall 2003); Hussein Agha and Robert Malley, "Camp David: The Tragedy of Errors," *New York Review of Books*, 48, no. 13 (August 9, 2001), pp. 59–65; Rashid Khalidi, *Brokers of Deceit: How the United States Has Undermined Peace in the Middle East* (Boston: Beacon Press, 2013); Dennis Ross, *The Missing Peace: The Inside Story of the Fight for Middle East Peace* (New York: Farrar, Straus & Giroux, 2004); Aaron David Miller, *The Much Too Promised Land: America's Elusive Search for Middle East Peace* (New York: Bantam, 2006); Charles Enderlin, *Shattered Dreams: The Failure of the Peace Process in the Middle East, 1995–2002*, trans. Susan Fairfield (New York: Other Press, 2003); Ron Pundak, "From Oslo to Taba: What Went Wrong?," *Survival* 43, no. 3 (Autumn 2001), pp. 31–46; Jerome Slater, "What Went Wrong?: The Collapse of the Israeli-Palestinian Peace Process," *Political Science Quarterly* 116, no. 2 (July 2001), pp. 171–99; Clayton E. Swisher, *The Truth About Camp David: The Untold Story About the Collapse of the Middle East Peace Process* (New York: Nation Books, 2004); Martin Indyk, *Innocent Abroad: An Intimate Account of American Peace Diplomacy in the Middle East* (New York: Simon & Schuster, 2014); and Ben

Birnbaum and Amir Tibon, "How the Israeli-Palestine Peace Deal Died," *The New Republic*, July 20, 2014.

68. On the pledge to Gaddafi, see Bruce W. Jentleson and Christopher A. Whytock, "Who 'Won' Libya?: The Force-Diplomacy Debate and Its Implications for Theory and Practice," *International Security* 30, no. 3 (Winter 2005/2006), pp. 70, 74, 76, and 82.

69. Barack Obama began his presidency with a well-publicized speech saying that he wanted to lead the world toward a nonnuclear future, but his administration eventually proposed a $1 trillion program to modernize the U.S. strategic nuclear arsenal and improve its ability to wage a nuclear war. See Philip Ewing, "Obama's Nuclear Paradox: Pushing for Cuts, Agreeing to Upgrades," National Public Radio, May 25, 2016, at www.npr.org/sections/parallels/2016/05/25 /479498018/obamas-nuclear-paradox-pushing-for-cuts-agreeing-to-upgrades; and also Austin Long and Brendan Rittenhouse Green, "Stalking the Secure Second Strike: Intelligence, Counterforce, and Nuclear Strategy," *Journal of Strategic Studies* 38, nos. 1–2 (2015).

70. When the United States and its allies intervened in Libya in 2011, North Korean officials called the earlier bargain over Libya's WMD programs "an invasion tactic to disarm the country," and said "the Libyan crisis is teaching the international community a grave lesson." See Mark McDonald, "North Korea Suggests Libya Should Have Kept Nuclear Program," *The New York Times*, March 24, 2011. In January 2016, North Korea's official news agency defended its latest nuclear test by saying "the Saddam Hussein regime in Iraq and the Gaddafi regime in Libya could not escape the fate of destruction after being deprived of their foundations for nuclear development and giving up nuclear programmes of their own accord." See "North Korea Cites Muammar Gaddafi's 'Destruction' in Nuclear Test Defence," *The Telegraph*, January 9, 2016, at www.telegraph.co.uk/news/worldnews/asia /northkorea/12090658/North-Korea-cites-Muammar-Gaddafis-destruction-in -nuclear-test-defence.html.

71. Bureaucratic resistance within the U.S. government and foot-dragging by key allies such as Saudi Arabia hampered efforts to develop an effective counterterrorism strategy, and major attacks took place throughout Clinton's term. On Saudi Arabia's reluctance to cooperate with U.S. counterterrorism efforts in the 1990s, see James Risen, *State of War*, pp. 180–86. The sluggish bureaucratic response to concerns about terrorism is described at length in *The 9/11 Commission Report: Final Report of the National Commission on Terrorist Attacks Upon the United States* (New York: W. W. Norton, 2004), chap. 3.

72. The Clinton administration believed that a pharmaceutical factory might be producing nerve gas for terrorist use, based on reports that bin Laden was a part owner of the facility and a soil sample taken near the factory that reportedly contained a precursor chemical for VX nerve gas. Administration officials described the evidence as compelling and said that there was little internal dissent over the attack, but other senior officials later claimed that the available information was ambiguous. For a dispassionate summary of the evidence, see Michael Barletta,

"Chemical Weapons in the Sudan: Allegations and Evidence," *The Nonproliferation Review* 6, no. 1 (Fall 1998), pp. 115–36. See also Tim Weiner and James Risen, "Decision to Strike Factory in Sudan Based Partly on Surmise," *The New York Times*, September 28, 1998; and James Risen, "To Bomb Sudan Plant, or Not: A Year Later, Debates Rankle," *The New York Times*, October 27, 1999. For a defense of the administration's decision, see Benjamin and Simon, *Age of Sacred Terror*, pp. 351–63.

73. On the motivations for the 9/11 attacks, see *9/11 Commission Report*, p. 48; Lawrence Wright, *The Looming Tower: Al Qaeda and the Road to 9/11* (New York: Alfred A. Knopf, 2006), pp. 209–10; and John J. Mearsheimer and Stephen M. Walt, *The Israel Lobby and U.S. Foreign Policy* (New York: Farrar, Straus & Giroux, 2007), pp. 65–70.

74. The Bush administration had downgraded counterterror efforts after taking office, and the FBI and other intelligence agencies failed to "connect the dots" that might have allowed them to derail the plot ahead of time. As the 9/11 Commission noted afterward, "information was not shared . . . Analysis was not pooled. Effective operations were not launched. Often the handoffs of information were lost across the divide separating the foreign and domestic agencies of government." *9/11 Commission Report*, p. 353.

75. "President Bush's Remarks at Prayer Service," *The Washington Post*, September 14, 2001. By declaring war on "terrorism"—a tactic that many states and groups had employed for decades—the United States had committed itself to an open-ended campaign that had no definable end point and therefore could never be won. On this point, see Paul R. Pillar, *Terrorism and U.S. Foreign Policy* (Washington, DC: Brookings Institution, 2001), p. 217.

76. In particular, Bergen and Cruickshank found "a stunning sevenfold increase in the yearly rate of fatal jihadist attacks . . . Even when terrorism in Iraq and Afghanistan is excluded, fatal attacks in the rest of the world have increased by more than one-third." See Peter Bergen and Paul Cruickshank, "The Iraq Effect: The War in Iraq and Its Impact on the War on Terrorism," *Mother Jones*, March 1, 2007.

77. "Inquiry Begins into Motives of Shooting Suspect Hasan," *The Washington Post*, November 7, 2009. Hasan later testified that he had intended his attack to help defend the Afghan Taliban.

78. See Bruce Hoffman and Fernando Reinares, "Conclusion," in Bruce Hoffman and Fernando Reinares, eds., *The Evolution of the Global Terrorist Threat: From 9/11 to Osama bin Laden's Death* (New York: Columbia University Press, 2014), p. 638.

79. As the International Crisis Group warned in 2005, "counter-terrorism efforts in Somalia have won a few key battles against extremists, but they have been steadily losing the war for Somali hearts and minds." See "Counter-Terrorism in Somalia: Losing Hearts and Minds?" *International Crisis Group Report No. 95*, July 11, 2005, p. 15; and for background, Jeffrey Gettleman, "The Most Dangerous Place in the World," *Foreign Policy*, September 30, 2009, at http://foreignpolicy.com/2009/09/30/the-most-dangerous-place-in-the-world/.

80. According to Nabeel Khoury, former U.S. deputy chief of mission in Yemen, "Drone strikes take out a few bad guys to be sure, they also kill a large number of innocent civilians. Given Yemen's tribal structure, the U.S. generates roughly forty to sixty new enemies for every AQAP operative killed by drones." See Nabeel Khoury, "In Yemen, Drones Aren't a Policy," *Cairo Review of International Affairs*, October 23, 2013, at www.aucegypt.edu/GAPP/CairoReview/Pages/articleDetails.aspx?aid=443#.

81. See "Feinstein, 'Terror Is Up Worldwide,'" *CNN.com*, December 1, 2013, at cnnpressroom.blogs.cnn.com/2013/12/01/feinstein-terror-is-up-worldwide/; and "Statement by Director Brennan as Prepared for Delivery to the Senate Select Committee on Intelligence," June 16, 2016, at www.cia.gov/news-information/speeches-testimony/2016-speeches-testimony/statement-by-director-brennan-as-prepared-for-delivery-before-ssci.html.

82. Quoted in Eric Schmitt, "Using Special Forces Against Terrorism, Trump Hopes to Avoid Big Ground Wars," *The New York Times*, March 19, 2017.

83. See Nick Turse, "U.S. Is Building $100 Million Drone Base in Africa," *The Intercept*, September 29, 2016, at https://theintercept.com/2016/09/29/u-s-military-is-building-a-100-million-drone-base-in-africa/; and idem, "The War You've Never Heard Of," *Vice News*, May 28, 2017, at https://news.vice.com/en_ca/article/nedy3w/the-u-s-is-waging-a-massive-shadow-war-in-africa-exclusive-documents-reveal.

84. Based on the post-9/11 record, Mueller and Stewart estimate that the chances of a U.S. citizen dying in a terrorist attack each year are roughly one in 3.5 million. See John Mueller and Mark G. Stewart, "The Terrorism Delusion: America's Overwrought Response to September 11," *International Security 37*, no. 1 (Summer 2012); and idem, *Chasing Ghosts: The Policing of Terrorism* (New York: Oxford University Press, 2015).

85. Stephen Biddle, "American Grand Strategy after 9/11: An Assessment," Strategic Studies Institute, U.S. Army War College (Carlisle, PA: 2005), p. 14.

2: WHY LIBERAL HEGEMONY FAILED

1. For a classic statement of the strategy of liberal hegemony, see William J. Clinton, *A National Security Strategy of Engagement and Enlargement* (Washington: The White House, 1994). Subsequent national security strategies issued by Clinton, George W. Bush, and Barack Obama are consistent with this approach, as were a number of prominent task force and think tank reports published between 1993 and 2017. I discuss this broad consensus in detail in chapter 3.

2. In his March 1947 speech to Congress announcing the so-called Truman Doctrine, President Harry S. Truman declared, "At the present moment in world history nearly every nation must choose between alternative ways of life . . . One way of life is based upon the will of the majority, and is distinguished by free institutions, representative government, free elections, guarantees of individual liberty, freedom of speech and religion, and freedom from political oppression. The second way of life is based upon the will of a minority forcibly imposed upon the majority. It relies upon terror and oppression, a controlled press and radio, fixed

elections, and the suppression of personal freedoms." See "President Truman's Address Before a Joint Session of Congress, March 12, 1947," at http://avalon.law .yale.edu/20th_century/trudoc.asp.

3. The intellectual case for liberal hegemony is found in G. John Ikenberry, *Liberal Leviathan: The Origins, Crisis and Transformation of American World Order* (Princeton, NJ: Princeton University Press, 2011); Robert Lieber, *The American Era: Power and Strategy for the 21st Century* (Cambridge: Cambridge University Press, 2005); Robert Kagan, *The World America Made* (New York: Vintage, 2013); Stephen G. Brooks, G. John Ikenberry, and William Wohlforth, "Don't Come Home, America: The Case Against Retrenchment," *International Security* 37, no. 3 (Autumn 2012/13); and Stephen G. Brooks and William C. Wohlforth, *America Abroad: The United States' Global Role in the 21st Century* (New York: Oxford University Press, 2017). For critiques of its core assumptions, see John J. Mearsheimer, *The Great Delusion: Liberal Dreams and International Realities* (New Haven, CT: Yale University Press, 2018); Barry Posen, *Restraint: A New Foundation for U.S. Grand Strategy* (Ithaca, NY: Cornell University Press, 2014), chap. 1; and David C. Hendrickson, *Republic in Peril: American Empire and the Liberal Tradition* (New York: Oxford University Press, 2018), chap. 1.

4. The literature on democratic peace theory is now enormous. Core works include Michael W. Doyle, "Kant, Liberal Legacies and Foreign Affairs," *Philosophy and Public Affairs*, 12, nos. 3–4 (Summer–Autumn 1983); Bruce Russett, *Grasping the Democratic Peace* (Princeton, NJ: Princeton University Press, 1993); and John M. Owen IV, *Liberal Peace, Liberal War: American Politics and International Security* (Ithaca, NY: Cornell University Press, 1998). For valuable critiques, see Sebastian Rosato, "The Flawed Logic of Democratic Peace Theory," *American Political Science Review* 97 (2003); and Miriam Elman, ed., *Paths to Peace: Is Democracy the Answer?* (Cambridge, MA: MIT Press, 1997).

5. The idea that economic interdependence will reduce conflict and prevent war goes back to the eighteenth century. Extended discussions of the logic and evidence behind this claim include Richard Rosecrance, *The Rise of the Trading State* (New York: Basic Books, 1986); and Dale C. Copeland, *Economic Interdependence and War* (Princeton, NJ: Princeton University Press, 2014).

6. See especially Robert O. Keohane, *After Hegemony: Cooperation and Discord in the World Political Economy* (Princeton, NJ: Princeton University Press, 1984).

7. See "THE 1992 CAMPAIGN; Excerpts From Speech By Clinton on U.S. Role," *The New York Times*, October 2, 1992.

8. Clinton, *National Security Strategy*, pp. i, iii.

9. See Samuel P. Huntington, "Why International Primacy Matters," *International Security* 17, no. 4 (Spring 1993), p. 83.

10. Madeleine Albright, "Interview on NBC-TV *The Today Show* with Matt Lauer," February 19, 1998, at https://1997-2001.state.gov/statements/1998/980219a .html.

11. The full quotation reads, "The land mine that protects civilization from barbarism is not parchment but power, and in a unipolar world, American power— wielded, if necessary, unilaterally." See "Democratic Realism: An American

Foreign Policy for a Unipolar World," *Irving Kristol Annual Lecture*, American Enterprise Institute, February 10, 2004, at www.aei.org/publication/democratic-realism/print/.

12. See, for example, *Rebuilding America's Defenses: Strategy, Forces and Resources for a New Century* (Washington, DC: Project for a New American Century, 2000); G. John Ikenberry and Anne-Marie Slaughter, eds., *Forging a World of Liberty Under Law: U.S. National Security in the 21st Century* (Princeton, NJ: Princeton Project on National Security, 2006); *America's National Interests* (Washington, DC: Commission on America's National Interests, 2000); *Setting Priorities for American Leadership: A New National Security Strategy for the United States* (Washington, DC: Project for a United and Strong America, 2013); and *CSIS Commission on Smart Power: A Smarter, More Secure America* (Washington, DC: Center for Strategic and International Studies, 2008).

13. That Obama held this view is hardly surprising. In 2008, a group of prominent Democratic Party officials released a report detailing how the United States could "reclaim the mantle of global leadership." See Anne-Marie Slaughter, Bruce Jentleson, Ivo Daalder, et al., *Strategic Leadership: A New Framework for National Security Strategy* (Washington, DC: Center for New American Security, 2008). The report's authors all received prominent appointments in the Obama administration.

14. "President Bush's Second Inaugural Address," at www.npr.org/templates/story/story.php?storyId=4460172.

15. The phrase "focused enmity" is that of William Wohlforth, whose 1999 essay on unipolarity argued that it was uniquely stable provided the unipolar power (i.e., the United States) did not disengage from Europe or Asia. See his "The Stability of a Unipolar World," *International Security* 24, no. 1 (Summer 1999), and also Stephen Brooks and William Wohlforth, *World Out of Balance: International Relations and the Challenge of American Primacy* (Princeton, NJ: Princeton University Press, 2008).

16. This was a central theme of Samantha Power's Pulitzer prizewinning book *"A Problem from Hell": America in the Age of Genocide* (New York: Basic Books, 2002).

17. *America's National Interests* (Washington, DC: Commission on America's National Interests, 2000). The commission's cochairs were Robert Ellsworth, Andrew Goodpaster, and Rita Hauser; its executive directors were Graham Allison of Harvard, Dmitri Simes of the Nixon Center, and James Thomson of the RAND Corporation.

18. Quoted in Patrick Porter, *The Global Village Myth* (Washington, DC: Georgetown University Press, 2015), p. 19.

19. *Leading Through Civilian Power: The First Quadrennial Diplomacy and Development Review* (Washington, DC: U.S. Department of State, 2010), p. xii.

20. Ibid., p. iii.

21. See Louis Hartz, *The Liberal Tradition in America* (New York: Harcourt Brace, 1955).

22. On the tendency for liberal states to engage in idealistic crusades, see

Mearsheimer, *Great Delusion*. Also relevant are Tony Smith, *America's Mission: The United States and the Worldwide Struggle for Democracy in the Twentieth Century* (Princeton, NJ: Princeton University Press, 1994); and *A Pact with the Devil: Washington's Bid for World Supremacy and the Betrayal of the American Promise* (New York: Rutledge, 2007).

23. This recommendation was contained in a draft of "Defense Guidance" that was leaked to *The New York Times* in early 1992. It prompted a heated response from key U.S. allies and was subsequently rewritten, but its core goals were never abandoned. See Patrick E. Tyler, "U.S. Strategy Plan Calls for Insuring No Rivals Develop," *The New York Times*, March 8, 1992; and James Mann, *Rise of the Vulcans: The History of Bush's War Cabinet* (New York: Viking, 2004), pp. 208–15.

24. See Strobe Talbott, "War in Iraq, Revolution in America," John Whitehead Lecture, Royal Institute of International Affairs, October 9, 2009; at www.brookings.edu/articles/war-in-iraq-revolution-in-america/.

25. Barack Obama, *National Security Strategy* (Washington, DC: The White House, May 2010), p. 14.

26. The United States spent a higher percentage of its GDP on defense than China did every year, and a larger percentage than Russia between 2004 and 2013. Calculated from "Military Expenditures" (Washington, DC: The World Bank, 2015), at http://data.worldbank.org/indicator/MS.MIL.XPND.GD.ZS.

27. See "Total Military Personnel and Dependent End Strength by Service, Regional Area, and Country," Defense Manpower Data Center, July 31, 2015, at www.globalsecurity.org/military/library/report/2015/drs_54601_309_report_p1506.xlsx.

28. For a map of the regional combatant commands, see www.defense.gov/About/Military_Departments/Unified-Combatant_Commands/.

29. See Michael McFaul, "The Liberty Doctrine," *Policy Review* 112 (April–May 2002).

30. See Lawrence Kaplan and William Kristol, *The War Over Iraq: Saddam's Tyranny and America's Mission* (San Francisco: Encounter Books, 2003), p. 112.

31. The invasion of Afghanistan could be seen as a direct defense of American soil insofar as the Taliban government in Kabul had refused to turn Osama bin Laden and his associates over to the United States after the 9/11 attacks. Yet the United States did not limit its goals solely to catching bin Laden and has been trying for seventeen years to create a stable and effective democracy there at a cost of more than $1 trillion and more than two thousand U.S. soldiers' lives.

32. See Micah Zenko and Jennifer Wilson, "How Many Bombs Did the United States Drop in 2016?" January 5, 2017, at www.cfr.org/blog/how-many-bombs-did-united-states-drop-2016.

33. The first wave of NATO enlargement occurred in 1999 and brought in the Czech Republic, Hungary, and Poland. Bulgaria, Estonia, Latvia, Lithuania, Romania, Slovakia, and Slovenia joined in 2004, and Albania and Croatia followed in 2009. This policy reached its apotheosis (or perhaps its nadir) in 2016, when mighty Montenegro joined the alliance.

34. See John L. Harper, "American Visions of Europe After 1989," in Christina V. Balls and Simon Serfaty, eds., *Visions of America and Europe: September 11, Iraq, and Transatlantic Relations* (Washington, DC: Center for Strategic and International Studies, 2004), chap. 2.

35. Dual containment was the brainchild of Martin Indyk, who first articulated it while working at the Washington Institute for Near East Policy and implemented it as Clinton's assistant secretary of state for Near East Affairs. According to Kenneth Pollack, who worked with Indyk at the Brookings Institution, dual containment was undertaken to reassure Israel and make it more pliable in the Oslo peace process. See Kenneth Pollack, *The Persian Puzzle: The Conflict Between Iran and America* (New York: Random House, 2004), pp. 261–65.

36. On the goal of regional transformation, see John J. Mearsheimer and Stephen M. Walt, *The Israel Lobby and U.S. Foreign Policy* (New York: Farrar, Straus & Giroux, 2007), pp. 255–57.

37. See Nick Turse, "U.S. Special Operations Numbers Surge in Africa's Shadow Wars," *The Intercept*, December 31, 2016.

38. The United States is now committed to defend sixty-nine countries, which together produce about 75 percent of global economic output and contain nearly two billion people. See Michael Beckley, "The Myth of Entangling Alliances," *International Security* 39, no. 4 (Spring 2015). Beckley argues that these commitments do not increase the risk that the United States will get dragged into unnecessary wars, but they do shape U.S. defense requirements, and some of America's recent conflicts—including the Kosovo War and the two wars against Iraq—were partly inspired by a desire to protect nearby allies.

39. During the uprising, Assistant Secretary of State Victoria Nuland handed out pastries to antigovernment demonstrators in Maidan Square and was secretly recorded telling U.S. ambassador Geoffrey Pyatt that opposition leader Vitali Klitschko should be kept out of the government and Arseniy Yatsenyuk should become acting prime minister instead. See "Ukraine Crisis: Transcript of Leaked Nuland-Pyatt Call," *BBC News Online*, at www.bbc.com/news/world-europe -26079957.

40. For Obama's speech, see "Remarks by the President on the Middle East and North Africa," May 19, 2011, at www.whitehouse.gov/the-press-office/2011/05 /19/remarks-president-middle-east-and-north-africa.

41. The Defense Department and the Central Intelligence Agency provided arms and training for various anti-Assad forces and cooperated with other foreign efforts to bolster opposition groups. See Christopher Phillips, *The Battle for Syria: International Rivalry in the New Middle East* (New Haven, CT: Yale University Press, 2016), pp. 141–43; David Ignatius, "What the Demise of the CIA's anti-Assad Program Means," *The Washington Post*, July 20, 2017; and Austin Carson and Michael Poznansky, "The Logic for (Shoddy) U.S. Covert Action in Syria," *War on the Rocks*, July 21, 2016, at https://warontherocks.com/2016/07/the-logic-for-shoddy-u-s-covert-action-in-syria/.

42. "Senator Kerry Statement at Hearing on Sudan," March 15, 2012, at www

.foreign.senate.gov/press/chair/release/chairman-kerry-statement-at-hearing-on
-sudan-.

43. According to Denise Froning of the Heritage Foundation, "Free trade helps to spread the value of freedom, reinforce the rule of law, and foster economic development in poor countries. The national debate over trade-related issues too often ignores these important benefits." See her "The Benefits of Free Trade: A Guide for Policymakers" (Washington, DC: Heritage Foundation, August 25, 2000), at www .heritage.org/trade/report/the-benefits-free-trade-guide-policymakers. See also Jeffrey Kucik, "The TPP's Real Value—It's Not Just About Trade," *The Hill*, December 7, 2016, at http://thehill.com/blogs/pundits-blog/foreign-policy/309088-the -tpps-real-value-its-not-just-about-trade.

44. See in particular Edward Mansfield and Jack L. Snyder, *Electing to Fight: Why Emerging Democracies Go to War* (Cambridge, MA: MIT Press, 2005).

45. Germany and Great Britain were each other's largest trading partners in 1914, and Japan went to war in 1941 to try to free itself from economic dependence on the United States and others. On the latter case, see Michael Barnhart, *Japan Prepares for Total War: The Search for Economic Security 1919–1941* (Ithaca, NY: Cornell University Press, 1987). A comprehensive recent study of this subject finds that interdependence reduces incentives for war when states expect close ties to continue, but not when they fear these connections could be cut off. See Dale C. Copeland, *Economic Interdependence and War* (Princeton, NJ: Princeton University Press, 2014).

46. See especially John J. Mearsheimer, "The False Promise of International Institutions," *International Security* 19, no. 3 (Winter 1994/95).

47. This argument is convincingly made in Lloyd Gruber, *Ruling the World: Power Politics and the Rise of Supranational Institutions* (Princeton, NJ: Princeton University Press, 2000).

48. See Stephen M. Walt, *Taming American Power: The Global Response to U.S. Primacy* (New York: W. W. Norton, 2005), chaps. 2–3.

49. Quoted in Craig Whitney, "NATO at 50: With Nations at Odds, Is It a Misalliance?" *The New York Times*, February 15, 1999.

50. Timothy Garton Ash, "The Peril of Too Much Power," *The New York Times*, April 9, 2002.

51. In November 2009, for example, Major Nidal Hasan, an army psychiatrist, murdered thirteen people and injured more than thirty others at Fort Hood. Hasan had been in email contact with Anwar al-Awlaki, an influential Al Qaeda cleric, and had increasingly come to see the United States as a threat to Islam. In 2014, while awaiting execution for his crimes, Hasan wrote a letter expressing his desire to become a citizen of the "Islamic State" (i.e., ISIS).

52. See Murtaza Hussain and Cora Currier, "U.S. Military Operations Are Biggest Motivation for Homegrown Terrorists, FBI Study Finds," *The Intercept*, October 11, 2016.

53. Serbia, Libya, and Iran all made concessions in the face of U.S. and/or multilateral pressure, but they also held firm on key principles, bargained hard, and eventually extracted their own concessions in exchange.

54. Quoted in Mark Landler, "The Afghan War and the Evolution of Obama," *The New York Times*, January 1, 2016.

55. Chas W. Freeman, "Militarism and the Crisis of American Diplomacy," *Epistulae*, no. 20, National Humanities Institute, July 7, 2015.

56. See "President Delivers State of the Union Speech," January 29, 2002, at http://georgewbush-whitehouse.archives.gov/news/releases/2002/01/20020129-11 .html; "Text: Bush Remarks at Prayer Service," *The Washington Post*, September 14, 2001, at www.washingtonpost.com/wp-srv/nation/specials/attacked/transcripts /bushtext_091401.html. See also Richard Jackson, *Writing the War on Terrorism: Language, Politics and Counter-Terrorism* (Manchester, UK: Manchester University Press, 2005), p. 67.

57. Critical assessments of U.S. diplomacy in the Kosovo War include Michael Mandelbaum, "A Perfect Failure: NATO's War against Yugoslavia," *Foreign Affairs* 78 (September–October 1999); Christopher Layne and Benjamin Schwarz, "Kosovo: For the Record," *National Interest* 57 (Fall 1999); and Alan Kuperman, "Botched Diplomacy Led to War," *The Wall Street Journal*, June 17, 1999. On the concessions Milosevic gained by resisting, see Stephen Hosmer, *The Conflict Over Kosovo: Why Milosevic Decided to Settle When He Did* (Washington, DC: RAND Corporation, 2001), pp. 116–17. Ivo Daalder and Michael O'Hanlon defend the Clinton administration's handling of the negotiations preceding the war, but they concede that the United States and its allies greatly exaggerated the ease with which Serbia could be compelled to accept NATO's demands. See their *Winning Ugly: NATO's War to Save Kosovo* (Washington, DC: Brookings Institution), pp. 89–90.

58. In negotiations with several European states in 2005, Iran offered to confine enrichment to LEU levels, limit its enrichment capacity to the amount needed to fuel its nuclear reactors, ratify and implement the Additional Protocol of the Nuclear Non-Proliferation Treaty, and accept enhanced IAEA monitoring of its nuclear facilities. Iran had fewer than three thousand centrifuges installed at that time, and the British foreign minister Jack Straw later maintained that "had it not been for major problems within the US administration under President Bush, we could have actually settled the whole Iran nuclear dossier back in 2005." The Bush administration pressed the Europeans to reject the proposal, and serious talks did not resume until 2009, by which time Iran had more than seven thousand centrifuges available. See David Morrison and Peter Oborne, "U.S. Scuppered Deal with Iran in 2005, says then British Foreign Minister," *OpenDemocracy.net*, September 23, 2013, at www.opendemocracy.net/david-morrison-peter-oborne/us-scuppered -deal-with-iran-in-2005-says-then-british-foreign-minister. See also Seyed Hossein Mousavian, *The Iranian Nuclear Crisis: A Memoir* (Washington DC: Carnegie Endowment for International Peace, 2012); Gareth Porter, *Manufactured Crisis: The Untold Story of the Iran Nuclear Scare* (Charlottesville, VA: Just World Books, 2014), pp. 153–59; Ali M. Ansari, *Confronting Iran: The Failure of American Foreign Policy and the Next Great Conflict in the Middle East* (New York: Basic Books, 2006), pp. 221–25; and "Communication Dated 1 August 2005 Received from the Permanent Mission of the Islamic Republic of Iran to the Agency," INFCIRC/648 (Vienna: International Atomic Energy Agency, 2005).

59. In 2010 Brazilian and Turkish mediation (the so-called Tehran Declaration) produced an agreement that would have swapped 1,200 kilograms of Iran's low-enriched uranium in exchange for 120 kilograms of fuel for the Tehran Research Reactor. The Obama administration had initially encouraged Brazil and Turkey's efforts, but it backed away when the declaration threatened to derail the fragile consensus in favor of new United Nations sanctions. See Trita Parsi, *A Single Roll of the Dice: Obama's Diplomacy with Iran* (New Haven, CT: Yale University Press, 2013), especially chap. 10.

60. In June 2012 Secretary of State Hillary Clinton rejected Iran's participation in the Geneva I talks, saying, "It is hard, for the United States certainly, to imagine that a country putting so much effort into keeping Assad in power . . . would be a constructive actor. And we think this would not be an appropriate participant at this point to include." The point, however, was that any effort to end the conflict had to include all the stakeholders, and especially those in a position to derail an agreement. See U.S. Department of State, "Remarks with Foreign Minister Ahmet Davutoglu After Their Meeting," June 2012, at www.state.gov.secretary/20092013 clinton/rm/2012/06/19138.htm.

61. See Christopher D. Kolenda, Rachel Reid, Chris Rogers, and Marte Retzius, *The Strategic Costs of Civilian Harm: Applying the Lessons from Afghanistan to Current and Future Conflicts* (New York: Open Society Foundation, June 2016), p. 9.

62. See Elisabeth Bumiller, "We Have Met the Enemy and He Is PowerPoint," *The New York Times*, April 26, 2010.

63. Among a large literature, see especially Peter W. Galbraith, *The End of Iraq: How American Incompetence Created a War Without End* (New York: Simon & Schuster, 2007); Peter Van Buren, *We Meant Well: How I Helped Lose the Battle for the Hearts and Minds of the Iraqi People* (New York: Metropolitan Books, 2012); Rajiv Chandrasekaran, *Little America: The War Within the War for Afghanistan* (New York: Alfred A. Knopf, 2012); Emma Sky, *The Unraveling: High Hopes and Missed Opportunities in Iraq* (New York: Public Affairs, 2015); Daniel P. Bolger, *Why We Lost: A General's Inside Account of the Iraq and Afghanistan Wars* (Boston: Houghton Mifflin Harcourt, 2014); Carter Malkasian, *War Comes to Garmser: Thirty Years of Conflict on the Afghan Frontier* (New York: Oxford, 2013); and Anand Gopal, *No Good Men Among the Living: America, the Taliban, and the War Through Afghan Eyes* (New York: Metropolitan Books, 2014).

64. John Spencer, "How to Rethink the U.S. Military's Troop Deployment Policy," *Politico*, July 27, 2016, at www.politico.com/agenda/story/2016/07/rethinking -us-military-troop-deployment-policy-000177.

65. See Sayed Salahuddin and Pamela Constable, "U.S. General in Afghanistan Apologizes for Highly Offensive Leaflets," *The Washington Post*, September 7, 2017.

66. As a top Afghan official told a group of senior U.S. officials, "corruption is not just a problem for the system of governance in Afghanistan; it is the system of governance." Quoted in *Corruption in Conflict: Lessons from the U.S. Experience in Afghanistan* (Washington, DC: U.S. Special Inspector-General for Afghanistan Reconstruction, September 2016), at www.sigar.mil/pdf/LessonsLearned/SIGAR-16 -58-LL.pdf, p. 4.

67. See Carlotta Gall, "Afghanistan: Obama's Sad Legacy," *New York Review of Books*, January 19, 2017, p. 32.

68. See Mohammad Samim, "Afghanistan's Addiction to Foreign Aid," *The Diplomat*, May 19, 2016, at https://thediplomat.com/2016/05/afghanistans-addiction -to-foreign-aid/; and Joel Brinkley, "Money Pit: The Monstrous Failure of U.S. Aid to Afghanistan," *World Affairs*, January/February 2013, at www.worldaffairsjournal .org/article/money-pit-monstrous-failure-us-aid-afghanistan.

69. See John Judis, "America's Failure—and Russia and Iran's Success—in Syria's Cataclysmic Civil War," *TPM Café-Opinion*, January 10, 2017, at http:// talkingpointsmemo.com/cafe/americas-failure-russia-success-in-syrias-war (emphasis added).

70. See Jonathan Monten and Alexander Downes, "FIRCed to be Free: Why Foreign-Imposed Regime Change Rarely Leads to Democratization," *International Security* 37, no. 4 (Spring 2013); Bruce Bueno de Mesquita and George W. Downs, "Intervention and Democracy," *International Organization* 60, no. 3 (Summer 2006); Jeffrey Pickering and Mark Peceny, "Forging Democracy at Gunpoint," *International Studies Quarterly* 50, no. 3 (September 2006); and Stephen Haggard and Lydia Tiede, "The Rule of Law in Post-Conflict Settings: The Empirical Record," *International Studies Quarterly* 58, no. 3 (2014).

71. See Porter, *The Global Village Myth*.

72. See Chris Heathcote, "Forecasting Infrastructure Investment Needs for 50 Countries, 7 Sectors Through 2040," August 10, 2017, at http://blogs.worldbank .org/ppps/forecasting-infrastructure-investment-needs-50-countries-7-sectors -through-2040.

73. See especially Bruce W. Jentleson and Christopher A. Whytock, "Who 'Won' Libya?: The Force-Diplomacy Debate and Its Implications for Theory and Policy," *International Security* 30, no. 3 (Winter 2005/2006), especially pp. 74–76; see also Ronald Bruce St. John, "Libya Is Not Iraq: Preemptive Strikes, WMD, and Diplomacy," *Middle East Journal* 58, no. 3 (Summer 2004); Flynt Leverett, "Why Libya Gave Up on the Bomb," *The New York Times*, January 23, 2004; and Martin Indyk, "The Iraq War Did Not Force Gaddafi's Hand," *Financial Times*, March 9, 2004.

74. I am indebted to Barry Posen for this line of argument. Fears that the post–Cold War order might collapse completely if America retrenched is explicit in Brooks, Ikenberry, and Wohlforth, "Don't Come Home, America," and Kagan, "Superpowers Don't Get to Retire."

75. For comprehensive analyses of America's dominant global position, see Brooks and Wohlforth, *America Abroad*; idem, *World Out of Balance*; Nuno Monteiro, *Theory of Unipolar Politics* (Cambridge: Cambridge University Press, 2014), pp. 116–22; and Peter Zeihan, *The Accidental Superpower: The Next Generation of American Preeminence and the Coming Global Disorder* (New York: Twelve, 2014).

76. On the "free security" produced by America's geographic location, see C. Vann Woodward, *The Age of Reinterpretation* (Washington, DC: American Historical Association, 1961), p. 2; and Campbell Craig and Fredrik Logevall, *America's*

Cold War: The Politics of Insecurity (Cambridge, MA: Harvard University Press, 2012), pp. 13–14, 19–20, 363.

77. See Jeremy Shapiro and Richard Sokolsky, "How America Enables Its Allies' Bad Behavior," April 27, 2016, at www.vox.com/2016/4/27/11497942/america-bad-allies.

3: DEFINING THE "BLOB": WHAT IS THE "FOREIGN POLICY COMMUNITY"?

1. Quoted in Eric Bradner, Elise Labott, and Dana Bash, "50 GOP National Security Experts Oppose Trump," August 8, 2016, at www.cnn.com/2016/08/08/politics/republican-national-security-letter-donald-trump-election-2016/index.html. See also Doug Bandow, "Trump Criticizes Washington's Policy Elite—With Cause," *CATO at Liberty*, May 17, 2016, at www.cato.org/blog/donald-trump-criticizes-washingtons-policy-elite-cause.

2. Thomas Oatley, *A Political Economy of American Hegemony: Buildups, Booms, and Busts* (Cambridge: Cambridge University Press, 2015), p. 29.

3. See Dan Reiter and Allan Stam, *Democracies at War* (Princeton, NJ: Princeton University Press, 2002); Jack Snyder, *Myths of Empire: Domestic Politics and International Ambition* (Ithaca, NY: Cornell University Press, 1991); idem, *From Voting to Violence: Democratization and Nationalist Conflict* (New York: W. W. Norton, 2000).

4. This idea is usually attributed to John Stuart Mill, who argued that open debate would allow democratic systems to more readily determine the best policies. Justice Oliver Wendell Holmes appears to have coined the "marketplace" metaphor, arguing in his dissent to *Abrams v. United States* (1919) that "the best test of truth is the power of thought to get itself accepted in the competition of the market."

5. For this reason, Amartya Sen argues, "no famine has ever taken place in the history of the world in a functioning democracy," in part because public officials have obvious incentives to keep voters fed, but also because democratic systems transmit information more efficiently. See his *Development as Freedom* (New York: Alfred A. Knopf, 1999).

6. See Ernest May, *American Imperialism: A Speculative Essay* (New York: Athenaeum, 1968); and idem, "American Imperialism: A Reinterpretation," *Perspectives in American History* 1 (1967), p. 187.

7. Ironically, Wilson ignored the group's recommendations and relied on his own counsel instead. According to Robert Schulzinger, Wilson "refused to take the advice of the corps [of experts] he had taken with him to Paris. Left to themselves, the experts brooded." See *The Wise Men of Foreign Affairs: The History of the Council on Foreign Relations* (New York: Columbia University Press, 1984), p. 3; also Peter Grose, *Continuing the Inquiry: The Council on Foreign Relations from 1921 to 1996* (New York: Council on Foreign Relations Press, 1996), chap. 1; and Lawrence E. Gelfand, *The Inquiry: American Preparations for Peace, 1917–1919* (New Haven, CT: Yale University Press, 1963).

8. See Inderjeet Parmar, *Foundations of the American Century: The Ford, Carnegie, and Rockefeller Foundations in the Rise of American Power* (New York: Columbia University Press, 2012); and Edward Berman, *The Influence of the Ford, Carnegie, and Rockefeller Foundations on American Foreign Policy: The Ideology of Philanthropy* (Albany, NY: State University of New York Press, 1983).

9. Joseph Kraft, *Profiles in Power: A Washington Insight* (New York: New American Library, 1966), p. 188.

10. I. M. Destler, Leslie H. Gelb, and Anthony Lake, *Our Own Worst Enemy: The Unmaking of American Foreign Policy* (New York: Simon & Schuster, 1982), p. 91.

11. For similar critiques of the foreign policy establishment and the standard view of U.S. foreign policy institutions, see Michael Glennon, *National Security and Double Government* (New York: Oxford, 2015); Mike Lofgren, *The Deep State: The Fall of the Constitution and the Rise of a Shadow Government* (New York: Viking, 2016); Tom Engelhardt, *Shadow Government: Surveillance, Secret Wars, and a Global Security State in a Single Superpower World* (Chicago: Haymarket Books, 2015); Scott Horton, *Lords of Secrecy: The National Security State and Amerca's Stealth Warfare* (New York: Nation Books, 2015); and Patrick Porter, "Why U.S. Grand Strategy Has Not Changed: Power, Strategy, and the Foreign Policy Establishment," *International Security* 42, no. 4 (Spring 2018).

12. See David Samuels, "The Aspiring Novelist Who Became Obama's Foreign Policy Guru," *The New York Times Magazine*, May 5, 2016.

13. An invaluable survey of the literature on the foreign policy establishment is Priscilla Roberts, "'All the Right People': The Historiography of the American Foreign Policy Establishment," *Journal of American Studies* 26, no. 3 (December 1992).

14. As with most social groups, the "foreign policy community" has a core of individuals and organizations whose membership is indisputable—such as the top officials of the Council on Foreign Relations, members of the U.S. Foreign Service, or the professional staff of the Arms Control Association—and a surrounding penumbra of members who are less extensively engaged.

15. See Karen DeYoung, "White House Tries for Leaner National Security Staff," *The Washington Post*, June 22, 2015.

16. See "U.S. Military Personnel End Strength," *GlobalSecurity.Org*, at www .globalsecurity.org/military/agency/end-strength.htm, downloaded July 28, 2017; U.S. Department of State, "Mission," at https://careers.state.gov/learn/what-we -do/mission/; Office of the Director of National Intelligence, *2015 Annual Report on Security Clearance Determinations*, June 5, 2016; at www.dni.gov/files/documents /Newsroom/Reports%20and%Pubs/2015-Annual_Report_on_Security _Clearance_Determinations.pdf; and Dana Priest and William Arkin, *Top Secret America: The Rise of the New American Security State* (New York: Little Brown, 2011).

17. See Glennon, *National Security and Double Government*, chap. 2.

18. As the bipartisan Project on National Security Reform noted back in 2008, "Although departments have become proficient at generating functional capabilities within their mandates, the national security system cannot rapidly develop new capabilities or combine capabilities from multiple departments for new mis-

sions. As a consequence, mission essential capabilities that fall outside the core mandate of a department receive less emphasis and fewer resources." See Project on National Security Reform, *Ensuring Security in an Unpredictable World: The Urgent Need for National Security Reform* (Washington, DC: Center for the Study of the Presidency, 2008), p. v.

19. James G. McGann, *2017 Global Go To Think Tanks Index Report* (Philadelphia: Think Tanks and Civil Society Program, University of Pennsylvania, 2017) at https://repository.upenn.edu/cgi/viewcontent.cgi?article=1012&context=think _tanks, p. 8. Two recent examinations of this evolving world are Thomas Medvetz, *Think Tanks in America* (Chicago: University of Chicago Press, 2012); and Daniel W. Drezner, *The Ideas Industry: How Pessimists, Partisans, and Plutocrats Are Transforming the Marketplace of Ideas* (New York: Oxford University Press, 2017).

20. See Janine Wedel, *Unaccountable: How Elite Power Brokers Corrupt Our Finances, Freedom, and Security* (New York: Pegasus Books, 2014), especially chap. 7.

21. This point is emphasized in James McGann, "Academics to Ideologues: A Brief History of the Public Policy Research Industry," *PS: Political Science and Politics* 25, no. 4 (1992). See also Medvetz, *Think Tanks in America*, chap. 3.

22. See Steven Clemons, "The Corruption of Think Tanks," *JPRI Critique* 10, no. 2 (February 2003) at www.jpri.org/publications/critiques/critique_X_2.html.

23. For example, former Foreign Policy Studies senior fellow Richard Betts eventually left Brookings for a tenured position at Columbia University; Yahya Sadowski moved to Johns Hopkins; Joshua Epstein joined the Santa Fe Institute, and the Foreign Policy Studies director John Steinbruner took a tenured faculty position at the University of Maryland.

24. On the impact of interest groups in American politics, see Allan J. Cigler, Burdett Loomis, and Anthony Nownes, eds., *Interest Group Politics* (Washington, DC: CQ Press, 9th ed., 2015); Frank R. Baumgartner and Beth L. Leech, *Basic Interests: The Importance of Groups in Politics and Political Science* (Princeton, NJ: Princeton University Press, 1998); Helen V. Milner and Dustin Tingley, *Sailing the Water's Edge: The Domestic Politics of American Foreign Policy* (Princeton, NJ: Princeton University Press, 2015), chap. 3; Richard L. Hall and Alan V. Deardorff, "Lobbying as Legislative Subsidy," *American Political Science Review* 100, no. 1 (2006); and Robert G. Kaiser, *So Damn Much Money: The Triumph of Lobbying and the Corrosion of American Government* (New York: Vintage, reprint ed., 2010).

25. Recent examples would include my colleagues Joseph S. Nye, Graham T. Allison, Ashton B. Carter, Nicholas Burns, Samantha Power, and Meghan O'Sullivan, among others. Condoleezza Rice was professor of political science and provost at Stanford University before serving as national security advisor and secretary of state under George W. Bush, and both Stephen Krasner and Anne-Marie Slaughter held prominent academic posts before directing the Bureau of Policy Planning at the State Department. Colin Kahl was a tenured professor at Georgetown before serving as national security advisor to Vice President Joe Biden, Paul Wolfowitz taught at Yale and was dean of the Johns Hopkins School of Advanced International Studies (SAIS) before his stint as deputy secretary of defense in the Bush administration, and one of his successors at SAIS, Vali Nasr, was an advisor to

the late Richard Holbrooke in the latter's capacity as special envoy for Afghanistan. These names are but a small sample of the academics who have served in important foreign policy positions in recent years.

26. The United Arab Emirates reportedly gave some $20 million to support the Middle East Institute, a well-known D.C. think tank, and the Brookings Institution, the Atlantic Council, and the Center for Strategic and International Studies have all received millions of dollars' worth of grants from a number of foreign countries in recent years. See Ryan Grim, "Gulf Government Gave Secret $20 Million Gift to D.C. Think Tank," *The Intercept*, August 9, 2017 at https://theintercept.com/2017/08/09/gulf-government-gave-secret-20-million-gift-to-d-c-think-tank/; Eric Lipton, Brooke Williams, and Nicholas Confessore, "Foreign Powers Buy Influence at Think Tanks," *The New York Times*, September 6, 2014; Tom Medvetz, "The Myth of Think Tank Independence," *The Washington Post*, September 9, 2014; and Tom Hamburger and Alexander Becker, "At Fast Growing Brookings, Donors May Have an Impact on Research Agenda," *The Washington Post*, October 30, 2014.

27. See Steve Horn and Allen Ruff, "How Private Warmongers and the US Military Infiltrated American Universities," *Truthout.org*, at http://truth-out.org/index.php?option=com_k2&view=item&id=4905:how-private-warmongers-and-the-us-military-infiltrated-american-universities.

28. See Greg Jaffe, "Libertarian Billionaire Charles Koch Is Making a Big Bet on National Security," *The Washington Post*, November 11, 2017. Full disclosure: I am codirecting one of these programs, which provides research fellowships for pre- and postdoctoral students working on U.S. foreign policy topics.

29. In March 2018, the foundation filed suit against the University of Chicago, claiming the university had failed to fulfill the terms of the gift and seeking the return of the funds it had already provided. See "International Security Center Receives $3.5 Million Grant," at https://al.nd.edu/news/latest-news/international-security-center-receives-3-5-million-grant/; and "$100 Million Gift Creates Institute to Confront New Era of Global Conflicts," at http://harris.uchicago.edu/news-and-events/features/student-campus-news/100-million-gift-creates-institute-confront-new-era-glo; and Dawn Rhodes, "Pearson Family Members Foundation Sues University of Chicago, Seeking to Have $100 Million Gift Revoked," *Chicago Tribune*, March 6, 2018.

30. Glennon, *National Security and Double Government*, pp. 58–59.

31. The career of Leslie H. Gelb, former president of the Council on Foreign Relations (CFR), exemplifies this pattern. After receiving a Ph.D. in government from Harvard University in the early 1960s, Gelb taught for several years at Wesleyan University before becoming an aide to Senator Jacob Javits (D-NY). Moving to the Pentagon, Gelb directed the in-house study of Vietnam decision-making (the "Pentagon Papers") before moving to the Brookings Institution in 1969. Gelb served as director of political-military affairs at the Department of State during the Carter administration and became national security correspondent for *The New York Times* in 1980. After leaving the *Times*, Gelb was a senior fellow at the Carnegie Endowment for International Peace before being chosen to head the CFR in 1993.

32. The career of Richard Holbrooke offers a different but equally viable pattern: after serving in the Foreign Service and the Peace Corps, he became managing editor of *Foreign Policy* magazine from 1972 to 1976. An inveterate networker, he served as assistant secretary of state for East Asia in the Carter administration and then joined Lehman Brothers in 1981. He was also vice chair of a private equity firm, served on corporate and nonprofit boards, and later held prominent diplomatic positions in the Clinton and Obama administrations.

33. To take a typical example: Thomas J. Christensen is simultaneously a professor at Columbia University, a nonresident fellow at the Brookings Institution, and a sometime advisor to the Department of State, where he served as deputy assistant secretary of state for East Asian Affairs from 2006 to 2008.

34. For in-depth summaries of the neoconservative policy network, see Janine Wedel, *Shadow Elite: How the World's New Power Brokers Undermine Democracy, Government, and the Free Market* (New York: Basic Books, 2009), chap. 6; Justin Vaisse, *Neoconservatism: The Biography of a Movement* (Cambridge, MA: Harvard/Belknap, 2010); and John J. Mearsheimer and Stephen M. Walt, *The Israel Lobby and U.S. Foreign Policy* (New York: Farrar, Straus & Giroux, 2007), pp. 128–32.

35. Donilon was a lawyer and lobbyist who worked primarily on domestic political issues and electoral reform before becoming chief of staff to Secretary of State Warren Christopher in 1993. He also served as assistant secretary of state for public affairs under President Clinton. See "National Security Advisor: Who Is Tom Donilon?" November 29, 2010, at www.allgov.com/news/appointments-and-resignations/national-security-advisor-who-is-thomas-donilon?news=841821. Similarly, Berger worked on domestic issues as an aide to New York mayor John V. Lindsay and two different congressmen before being appointed deputy director of policy planning in the State Department in 1977. He also worked as a lobbyist on international trade issues.

36. The apotheosis of this tendency is the recent career of Jared Kushner, whose sole qualification for an influential White House job is his marriage to Donald Trump's daughter Ivanka.

37. See "CNAS Announces 2018 Next Generation National Security Fellows" (press release, Center for a New American Security, January 2018); and see www.cnas.org/next-generation-programs/nextgeneration.

38. See http://trumanproject.org/programs/lead/fellowship/. For an insightful but critical assessment of this effort, see Kevin Baron, "Meet the Insurgency: Inside the Liberal Takeover of U.S. National Security," *Defense One*, June 2014, at www.defenseone.com/ideas/2014/06/meet-insurgency-inside-liberal-take-over-us-national-security/85966/.

39. Wedel, *Unaccountable*, p. 181.

40. Mark Leibovich, *This Town: Two Parties and a Funeral—Plus, Plenty of Free Parking!—in America's Gilded Capital* (New York: Penguin, 2013), p. 57.

41. See James Mann, *Rise of the Vulcans: The History of Bush's War Cabinet* (New York: Viking, 2004), p. 252.

42. See Elisabeth Bumiller, "Backing an Iraqi Leader, This Time for a Fee," *The New York Times*, October 29, 2007.

43. See Edward Luce, "The Untimely Death of American Statecraft," *Financial Times*, June 1, 2007.

44. After Barack Obama was reelected in November 2012, for example, the liberal Center for American Progress and the conservative American Enterprise Institute partnered to present a panel on national security featuring CAP's Brian Katulis and Rudy de Leon and AEI's Danielle Pletka and Paul Wolfowitz. See www .americanprogress.org/press/advisory/2012/11/09/44616/advisory-caps-deleon -and-katulis-and-aeis-pletka-and-wolfowitz-discuss-national-security-in-obamas -second-term/. On this general phenomenon, see Medvetz, *Think Tanks in America*, pp. 116–20.

45. See "Why War," *PBS NewsHour*, February 12, 2003, at www.pbs.org/newshour /bb/middle_east-jan-june03-why_war_2-12/.

46. The classic treatment of civilian and military views on the use of force is Richard K. Betts, *Soldiers, Statesmen, and Cold War Crises* (Cambridge, MA: Harvard University Press, 1977).

47. World Affairs Councils of America, "Our History," at www.worldaffairs councils.org/2011/main/home.cfm?Database=about_us&Category =History&Section=Main, downloaded May 25, 2014.

48. See http://nationalconference.worldaffairscouncils.org, accessed August 4, 2016.

49. Leslie H. Gelb, preface, in Grose, *Continuing the Inquiry*, p. xiv; "100 Years of Impact: A Timeline of the Carnegie Endowment," at http://carnegieendowment .org/about/timeline100/index.html.

50. See Joseph Lieberman and Jon Kyl, *Why American Leadership Still Matters: A Report of the American Internationalism Project* (Washington, DC: American Enterprise Institute, 2015), available at www.aei.org/wp-content/uploads/2015/12/Why -American-Leadership-Still-Matters_online.pdf.

51. See Richard Fontaine and Michèle Flournoy, "America: Beware the Siren Song of Disengagement," *The National Interest*, August 14, 2014, at http:// nationalinterest.org/feature/america-beware-the-siren-song-disengagement -11078.

52. On the relationship between CAP and CNAS, see Mann, *The Obamians*, pp. 52–53.

53. Brian Katulis, "Against Disengagement," *Democracy*, no. 32 (Spring 2014).

54. See "Introduction," in Will Marshall, ed., *With All Our Might: A Progressive Strategy for Defeating Jihadism and Defending Liberty* (New York: Rowman and Littlefield, 2006). Marshall also signed several open letters advocating the overthrow of Saddam Hussein, was a member of the pro-war Committee for the Liberation of Iraq, and called the invasion "undoubtedly a triumph for President Bush." For his views on Libya, see Will Marshall, "Lessons of Libya," *Huffington Post*, October 28, 2011, at www.huffingtonpost.com/will-marshall/gaddafi-al-assad_b_1063832 .html.

55. See "Where We Stand," at http://newdemocracy.net/about/; and Ryan

Cooper, "When Will Centrist Democrats Account for Their Foreign Policy Failures?" *This Week*, August 16, 2017.

56. See Zack Beauchamp, "Why Democrats Have No Foreign Policy Ideas," *Vox.com*, September 5, 2017, at www.vox.com/world/2017/9/5/16220054/democrats-foreign-policy-think-tanks.

57. Examples include Michael Ignatieff, Anne-Marie Slaughter, Fareed Zakaria, Leon Wieseltier, and the celebrity "philosopher" Bernard Henri-Lévy.

58. See Tony Smith, *Foreign Attachments: The Power of Ethnic Groups in the Making of U.S. Foreign Policy* (Cambridge, MA: Harvard University Press, 2000).

59. Not surprisingly, the founder of the U.S. Committee on NATO, one of the main groups pushing NATO expansion, was Bruce Jackson, who also happened to be vice president of strategic planning at Lockheed Martin, the country's largest defense contractor. See Stephen Gowans, "War, NATO Expansion, and the Other Rackets of Bruce P. Jackson," *What's Left?* November 25, 2002, at http://www3.sympatico.ca/sr.gowans/jackson.html.

60. On May 29, 2003, Friedman appeared on Charlie Rose's eponymous PBS show and said, "I think it [the invasion of Iraq] was unquestionably worth doing, Charlie . . . What they needed to see was American boys and girls going house to house, from Basra to Baghdad, um and basically saying, 'Which part of this sentence don't you understand?' You don't think, you know, we care about our open society, you think this bubble fantasy, we're just gonna let it grow? Well, Suck. On. This." Available at www.youtube.com /watch?v=ZwFaSpca_3Q.

61. See Michael Hirsh, *At War with Ourselves: Why America Is Squandering Its Chance to Build a Better World* (New York: Oxford University Press, 2003), pp. 39–40, 254.

62. See Bret Stephens, *America in Retreat: The New Isolationism and the Coming Global Disorder* (New York: Sentinel, 2015). Stephens's hiring by the *Times* in 2017 added scant intellectual diversity to its roster of regular columnists, insofar as his worldview was already well-represented by Brooks.

63. Cohen was a consistent advocate of U.S. military intervention in Ukraine and especially the Syrian civil war, declaring Obama's failure to act there to be the "greatest blot" on his presidency. See his "Intervene in Syria," *The New York Times*, February 4, 2013; "Make Assad Pay," *The New York Times*, August 29, 2013; "The Diplomacy of Force," *The New York Times*, June 19, 2014; "Western Illusions Over Ukraine," *The New York Times*, February 9, 2015; and "Obama's Syrian Nightmare," *The New York Times*, September 10, 2015.

64. See George Will, "On Libya, Too Many Questions," *The Washington Post*, March 8, 2011; and "McChrystal Had to Go," *The Washington Post*, June 24, 2010.

65. G. John Ikenberry and Anne-Marie Slaughter, *Forging a World of Liberty Under Law: U.S. National Security in the 21st Century* (Final Report, Princeton Project on National Security, 2006), downloaded from www.princeton.edu/~ppns/report/FinalReport.pdf.

66. In fact, the only way Iran will dominate the Middle East in the near future is if the United States keeps toppling its rivals, as it did when it foolishly invaded Iraq in 2003 (a step most of the signatories of the report supported).

67. One could say the same for the American Enterprise Institute's 2015 report *Why American Leadership Still Matters.*

68. See Lawrence R. Jacobs and Benjamin I. Page, "Who Influences U.S. Foreign Policy?" *American Political Science Review* 99, no. 1 (Feb. 2005), pp. 113, 121.

69. See Benjamin Page and Jason Barabas, "Foreign Policy Gaps Between Citizens and Leaders," *International Studies Quarterly* 44, no. 3 (September 2000), p. 344. Similarly, Daniel Drezner concludes his own comparison of U.S. mass and elite attitudes in foreign policy by saying "the elite public is more liberal internationalist than the mass public." See his "The Realist Tradition in American Public Opinion," *Perspectives on Politics* 6, no. 1 (March 2008), p. 63.

70. See Benjamin I. Page with Marshall M. Bouton, *The Foreign Policy Disconnect: What Americans Want from Our Leaders but Don't Get* (Chicago: University of Chicago Press, 2006), pp. 201–02, 240.

71. The Chicago Council on Global Affairs has posed this question repeatedly in its annual surveys of public opinion. See Dina Smeltz et al., *America Divided: Political Partisanship and U.S. Foreign Policy* (Chicago: Chicago Council on Global Affairs, 2016), p. 10.

72. Eighty-three percent favored the United States "doing its share in effort to solve international problems," and 82 percent supported a "shared leadership role." See Program for Public Consultation, *Americans on the U.S. Role in the World: A Study of U.S. Public Attitudes* (College Park, MD: University of Maryland, January 2017), p. 3.

73. See "Worldviews 2002: American Public Opinion and Foreign Policy" (Chicago: Chicago Council on Foreign Relations, 2002), p. 26.

74. See Public Agenda, "America in the World," September 2006, at www.americans-world.org/digest/overview/us_role/concerns.cfm.

75. Pew Research Center, *Public Sees U.S. Power Declining as Support for Global Engagement Slips*, December 3, 2013, at www.people-press.org/2013/12/03/public-sees-u-s-power-declining-as-support-for-global-engagement-slips/.

76. *Americans on the U.S. Role in the World*, p. 4.

77. Pew Research Center, "U.S. Seen as Less Important, China as More Powerful," December 3, 2009, at www.people-press.org/2009/12/03/us-seen-as-less-important-china-as-more-powerful/.

78. Pew Research Center, *America's Place in the World 2013* (December 2013), at www.people-press.org/files/legacy-pdf/12-3-2013%20APW%20VI.pdf, p. 67.

79. "American Views on Intervention in Syria," *The New York Times* online, at www.nytimes.com/interactive/2013/09/10/world/middleeast/american-views-on-intervention-in-syria.html?_r=0.

80. CNN/ORC poll, September 6–8, 2013, downloaded at http://i2.cdn.turner.com/cnn/2013/images/09/09/6a.poll.syria.pdf.

81. "WSJ/NBC Poll," April 27, 2014, *The Wall Street Journal* (online), at http://graphics.wsj.com/wsjnbcpoll/.

82. See "Public Uncertain, Divided Over America's Place in the World," Pew Research Center, May 5, 2016, at www.people-press.org/2016/05/05/public-uncertain-divided-over-americas-place-in-the-world/.

83. See Andrew Kohut, "American International Engagement on the Rocks," Pew Research Center, July 11, 2013, at www.pewglobal.org/2013/07/11/american-international-engagement-on-the-rocks/.

84. In September 2013, shortly after President Obama announced a campaign of air strikes and military training to counter ISIL, 61 percent of Americans said that military action against ISIL "was in America's national interest." See "WSJ/NBC Poll: Almost Two-Thirds Back Attacking Militants," *The Wall Street Journal* (online), September 10, 2014, at http://online.wsj.com/articles/wsj-nbc-poll-finds-that-almost-two-thirds-of-americans-back-attacking-militants-1410301920.

85. See Adam J. Berinsky, "Assuming the Costs of War: Events, Elites, and American Public Support for Military Conflict," *Journal of Politics* 69, no. 4 (November 2007); and Jon Western, *Selling Intervention and War: The Presidency, the Media, and the American Public* (Baltimore: Johns Hopkins University Press, 2005).

4: SELLING A FAILING FOREIGN POLICY

1. He added: "Why forgo the advantages of so peculiar a situation? Why quit our own to stand on foreign ground?" See "Washington's Farewell Address, 1796," at http://avalon.law.yale.edu/18th_century/washing.asp.

2. Quoted in Stephen Kinzer, *The True Flag: Theodore Roosevelt, Mark Twain, and the Birth of American Empire* (New York: Henry Holt, 2016), p. 6.

3. See George Stephanopoulos, *All Too Human: A Political Education* (Boston: Little Brown., 1999), p. 214.

4. See John A. Thompson, "The Exaggeration of American Vulnerability: The Anatomy of a Tradition," *Diplomatic History* 16, no. 1 (1992), p. 38.

5. Prominent examples of this argument are Jack Snyder, *Myths of Empire: Domestic Politics and International Ambition* (Ithaca, NY: Cornell University Press, 1991); and Dan Reiter and Allan Stam, *Democracies at War* (Princeton, NJ: Princeton University Press, 2002).

6. One 2010 source estimated that the U.S. government has classified more than a trillion pages of material since the late 1970s. See Peter Grier, "WikiLeaks' Trove Is a Mere Drop in Ocean of U.S. Classified Documents," *Christian Science Monitor*, December 21, 2010; at www.csmonitor.com/USA/DC-Decoder/Decoder-Buzz/2010/1221/WikiLeaks-trove-is-a-mere-drop-in-ocean-of-US-classified-documents. A 2012 report by the Public Interest Declassification Board found that "the current classification system is fraught with problems . . . [I]t keeps too many secrets and keeps them too long; it is overly complex; it obstructs desirable information sharing inside of government and with the public." See *Transforming Classification: Report to the President* (Washington, DC: Public Interest Declassification Board, 2012), p. 2.

7. See Mark Mazzetti and Matt Apuzzo, "Classified Report on the C.I.A.'s Secret Prisons Is Caught in Limbo," *The New York Times*, November 9, 2015.

8. See Chaim Kaufmann, "Threat Inflation and the Failure of the Marketplace of Ideas: The Selling of the Iraq War," *International Security* 29, no. 1 (Summer

2004); Frank Rich, *The Greatest Story Ever Sold: The Decline and Fall of Truth in Bush's America* (New York: Penguin, 2006); John Schuessler, *Deceit on the Road to War: Presidents, Politics, and American Democracy* (Ithaca, NY: Cornell University Press, 2015), pp. 105–09; and John J. Mearsheimer, *Why Leaders Lie: The Truth about Lying in International Politics* (New York: Oxford University Press, 2011), pp. 49–55. See also Eric Alterman, *When Presidents Lie: A History of Official Deception and Its Consequences* (New York: Penguin, 2004).

9. For a devastating chronology of the Bush administration's false statements (along with evidence showing that they were aware that their assertions were untrue), see "Lie by Lie by Lie: A Timeline of How We Got Into Iraq," *Mother Jones*, at www.motherjones.com/politics/2011/12/leadup-iraq-war-timeline/.

10. See John Schuessler, *Deceit on the Road to War*, p. 3.

11. See Bob Woodward, "McChrystal: More Forces or Mission Failure," *The Washington Post*, September 21, 2009, at www.washingtonpost.com/wp-dyn/content/article/2009/09/20/AR2009092002920.html.

12. In addition to the well-known case of Chelsea Manning, the army corporal who gave *WikiLeaks* a trove of diplomatic documents, the U.S. government has also prosecuted the journalist James Risen of *The New York Times* (who allegedly disclosed classified information about the NSA), former NSA official William Drake, former CIA official John Kiriakou (who served a prison term for confirming to journalists that the agency had tortured prisoners), former State Department employee Peter Van Buren (who put a link to a previously released *WikiLeaks* report on his blog), former TSA air marshal Robert MacLean (who gave reporters unclassified information about a TSA decision to cancel heightened security measures), and former vice chair of the Joint Chiefs of Staff General James "Hoss" Cartwright (who pleaded guilty to confirming the U.S. cyber campaign against Iran to a journalist and lying to the FBI and was subsequently pardoned by President Obama). On these various cases, see Peter Van Buren, "Leaking War: How Obama's Targeted Killings, Leaks, and the Everything-Is-Classified State Have Fused," *Tom-Dispatch*, at www.tomdispatch.com/archive/175554/; idem, "Least Transparent Administration Ever: A New Front in the Obama Administration's War on Whistleblowers," www.juancole.com/2014/03/transparent-administration-whistleblowers.html; and Charlie Savage, "James Cartwright, Ex-General, Pleads Guilty in Leak Case," *The New York Times*, October 17, 2016.

13. David Pozen argues that this behavior is an "adaptive response to key external liabilities—such as the mistrust generated by presidential secret-keeping and media manipulation—and internal pathologies—such as overclassification and fragmentation across a sprawling bureaucracy—of the modern administrative state." See David Pozen, "The Leaky Leviathan: Why the Government Condemns and Condones Unlawful Disclosures of Information," *Harvard Law Review* 127 (December 2013), p. 518.

14. See Benjamin I. Page with Marshall Bouton, *The Foreign Policy Disconnect: What Americans Want from Our Leaders but Don't Get* (Chicago: University of Chicago Press, 2006), p. 220.

15. As Page and Bouton put it, "[E]ven electorally mindful politicians [may] slight the preferences of the mass public and instead respond to the intense preferences of well-organized interest groups, activists, and money givers. The diffuse and uncertain threat posed by foreign policy–oriented voters may often be less intimidating . . . than concentrated pressure and tangible threats of retribution from party activists, interest groups, financial contributors, and business threatening disinvestment from the United States," *Foreign Policy Disconnect*, p. 221.

16. Groups opposing the deal were far better funded (with the American Israel Public Affairs Committee and its allies reportedly spending upward of $40 million to counter the deal), but pro-agreement organizations such as the antinuclear Ploughshares Fund were able to organize a potent coalition of experts and former officials to support it. See Elizabeth Drew, "How They Failed to Block the Iran Deal," *New York Review of Books*, October 22, 2015.

17. See Cindy Boren, "Report: At Least 50 Teams Were Paid by Department of Defense for Patriotic Displays," *The Washington Post*, November 15, 2015; and John McCain and Jeff Flake, *Tackling Paid Patriotism: A Joint Oversight Report*, at www .mccain.senate.gov/public/_cache/files/12de6dcb-d8d8-4a58-8795-562297f948c1 /tackling-paid-patriotism-oversight-report.pdf.

18. Walter Lippmann, *The Stakes of Diplomacy* (New York: Henry Holt, 1915), p. 51.

19. Until very recently, anyone who questioned the U.S. embargo on Cuba or called for a sustained rapprochement with Iran was likely to be treated as a pariah as well.

20. A good example of this kind of misrepresentation is Richard Haass's op-ed "The Isolationist Temptation," *The Wall Street Journal*, August 6, 2016.

21. See Stephen M. Walt, "Give Peace a Chance," *Foreign Policy*, October 10, 2015, at http://foreignpolicy.com/2015/10/02/give-peace-a-chance-president -republican-democrat-clinton/.

22. See Leslie H. Gelb with Jeanne Paloma-Zelmati, "Mission Not Accomplished," *Democracy* 13 (Summer 2009).

23. Between 2009 and 2013 McCain and Graham were the two most frequent guests on *Meet the Press, Face the Nation, This Week, Fox News Sunday*, and *State of the Union*, appearing ninety-seven and eighty-five times respectively. Senator Mitch McConnell (R-KY) and Rogers were the fifth and sixth most frequent guests. The only frequent guest who consistently represented a noninterventionist perspective was *The Nation* editor Katrina vanden Heuvel, but she appeared a mere twenty-two times. See David Leonhardt, "The Upshot: Sunday Talk Show Guests," at www.nytimes.com/interactive/2014/09/05/upshot/05up-sundayguests.html?_ r=0. See also: Derek Willis, "Congressional Conservatives Tip Scales to the Right on the Sunday Shows," at www.nytimes.com/2014/09/20/upshot/congressional -conservatives-tip-scales-to-the-right-on-the-sunday-shows.html; and Steve Benen, "The Great 2013 Sunday Show Race," December 30, 2013, at www.msnbc.com /rachel-maddow-show/the-great-2013-sunday-show-race.

24. It is revealing, for example, when a trio of *New York Times* columnists—

Roger Cohen, David Brooks, and former managing editor Bill Keller—take to the
op-ed pages to warn of the perils of isolationism, and the contributing writer Sam
Tanenhaus hosts a video on the *Times* website comparing critics of U.S. intervention today to such isolationists as Charles Lindbergh and the antiwar presidential
candidate George McGovern. See Bill Keller, "Our New Isolationism," *The New
York Times*, September 8, 2013; Roger Cohen, "An Anchorless World," *The New York
Times*, September 12, 2013; David Brooks, "The Leaderless Doctrine," *The New
York Times*, March 10, 2014; and "Think Back: America and Isolationism," at
www.nytimes.com/video/us/politics/100000002448238/think-back-america
-and-isolationism.html.

25. See Patrick Porter, "Why U.S. Grand Strategy Has Not Changed: Power,
Habit, and the Foreign Policy Establishment," *International Security* 42, no. 4
(Spring 2018). Porter's discussion of this point is based on Elliott Negin, "News
Media Coverage of the Defense Budget," in Leon V. Sigal, ed., *The Changing
Dynamics of U.S. Defense Spending* (London: Praeger, 1999).

26. Michael Glennon, *National Security and Double Government* (New York:
Oxford University Press, 2015), p. 93.

27. David Barstow, "Behind TV Analysts, Pentagon's Hidden Hand," *The New
York Times*, April 20, 2008, and idem, "One Man's Military-Industrial Complex," *The
New York Times*, November 30, 2008. See also Lee Fang, "Who's Paying the Pro-
War Pundits?" *The Nation*, September 12, 2014.

28. There is good evidence that embedded reporters portray the military
more favorably than non-embedded reporters do, subtly reinforcing public support for military campaigns that may or may not be going as planned. See Michael
Pfau, Elaine M. Wittenberg, Carolyn Jackson, Phil Mehringer, Rob Lanier, Michael Hatfield, and Kristina Brockman, "Embedding Journalists in Military Combat Units: How Embedding Alters Television News Stories," *Mass Communication
and Society* 8, no. 3 (2005); and Michael Pfau, Michel Haigh, Mitchell Gettle, Michael
Donnelly, Gregory Scott, Dana Warr, and Elaine Wittenberg, "Embedding Journalists in Military Combat Units: Impact on Newspaper Story Frames and Tone,"
Journalism and Mass Communication Quarterly 81, no. 1 (Spring 2004).

29. See Paul Farhi, "At the Times, A Scoop Deferred," *The Washington Post*,
December 17, 2005; David Folkenflik, "New York Times' Editor: Losing Snowden
Scoop 'Really Painful,'" *NPR Online*, June 5, 2014, at www.npr.org/2014/06/05/319233332
/new-york-times-editor-losing-snowden-scoop-really-painful.

30. Prominent examples include James Risen, Ken Silverstein, Glenn Greenwald, Jane Mayer, Jeremy Scahill, and Dana Priest.

31. See Thompson, "Exaggerating American Vulnerability"; and Campbell
Craig and Fredrik Logevall, *America's Cold War: The Politics of Insecurity* (Cam-
bridge, MA: Harvard University Press, 2009). On this general phenomenon, see
Peter Scoblic, *Us vs. Them: How a Half-Century of Conservatism Has Undermined Ameri-
ca's Security* (New York: Viking, 2008); Christopher Preble and John Mueller, eds., *A
Dangerous World?: Threat Perception and U.S. National Security* (Washington, DC:
CATO Institute, 2014); and Trevor Thrall and Jane Cramer, eds., *American Foreign
Policy and the Politics of Fear: Threat Inflation since 9/11* (New York: Routledge, 2009).

"Threat-mongering" is also discussed in Mearsheimer, *Why Leaders Lie*; and Schuessler, *Deceit on the Road to War*.

32. See Samuel Wells, "Sounding the Tocsin: NSC-68 and the Soviet Threat," *International Security* 4, no. 2 (1979).

33. The phrase was that of Richard Nixon, who justified the invasion of Cambodia in 1970 by saying, "If, when the chips are down, the world's most powerful nation, the United States of America, acts like a pitiful, helpless giant, the forces of totalitarianism and anarchy will threaten free nations and free institutions throughout the world."

34. NSC-68 ("U.S. Objectives and Programs for National Security"), reprinted in John Lewis Gaddis and Thomas Etzold, eds., *Containment: Documents on American Policy and Strategy, 1945–1950* (New York: Columbia University Press, 1978), p. 404; also pp. 389, 414, and 434. I discuss balancing and bandwagoning at length in *The Origins of Alliances* (Ithaca, NY: Cornell University Press, 1987), especially chap. 5.

35. See Max Fisher, "The Credibility Trap," *Vox.com*, at www.vox.com/2016/4 /29/11431808/credibility-foreign-policy-war.

36. To be precise, Obama said that he would not strike Syria without congressional authorization. Prior to the vote, Senator John McCain (R-AZ) warned that a "vote against the resolution . . . would be catastrophic, because it would undermine the credibility of the United States of America and of the President of the United States." See Zeke J. Miller, "McCain: Vote Against Syria Strike Would Be 'Catastrophic,'" *Time*, September 2, 2013, at http://swampland.time.com/2013/09 /02/mccain-blocking-syria-strike-would-be-catastrophic/.

37. See in particular Daryl Press, *Calculating Credibility: How Leaders Assess Military Threats* (Ithaca, NY: Cornell University Press, 2005); and Jonathan Mercer, *Reputation and International Politics* (Ithaca, NY: Cornell University Press, 1996).

38. The domino theory is perhaps the most obvious example of this type of reasoning: it argued that a single setback (or even a voluntary U.S. withdrawal) might trigger a lengthy cascade of defections and defeat and eventually leave the United States isolated and beleaguered. On its flaws, see Jerome Slater, "The Domino Theory and International Politics: The Case of Vietnam," *Security Studies* 3, no. 2 (1993); idem, "Dominos in Central America: Will They Fall? Does It Matter?" *International Security* 12, no. 2 (Fall 1987).

39. See Walt, *Origins of Alliances*, chap. 8.

40. Nan Tian et al., "Trends in Military Expenditure 2016," Stockholm International Peace Research Institute (2017), at www.sipri.org/sites/default/files/Trends -world-military-expenditure-2016.pdf.

41. Given prior U.S. actions in the region and its repeated threats to overthrow the clerical regime, it is hardly surprising that Iranian leaders have contemplated acquiring a nuclear deterrent. Iran could not do so as long as the JCPOA remained in force, however, and it would take upward of a year for it to build a nuclear bomb if it tried.

42. See Stephen M. Walt, "The Islamic Republic of Hysteria," *Foreign Policy* (January/February 2018), at http://foreignpolicy.com/2018/01/16/the-islamic

-republic-of-hysteria-iran-middle-east-trump/; and Michael Wahid Hanna and Dalia Dassa Kaye, "The Limits of Iranian Influence," *Survival* 57, no. 5 (September 2015).

43. See John Mueller and Mark G. Stewart, *Terror, Security, and Money: Balancing the Costs and Risks of Homeland Security* (New York: Oxford University Press, 2011); idem, *Chasing Ghosts: The Policing of Terrorism* (New York: Oxford University Press, 2015).

44. "Hagel: 'ISIS Beyond Anything We've Seen, U.S. Must Get Ready,'" Fox News, August 22, 2014, www.foxnews.com/politics/2014/08/22/isis-beyond-anything-that-weve-ever-seen-hagel-says//; "FBI: ISIS Is Biggest Threat to U.S.," *Daily Beast*, July 22, 2015, at www.thedailybeast.com/cheats/2015/07/22/fbi-isis-bigger-threat-than-al-qaeda.html.

45. "Statement by Director Brennan as Prepared for Delivery Before the Senate Select Committee on Intelligence," June 16, 2016, at www.cia.gov/news-information/speeches-testimony/2016-speeches-testimony/statement-by-director-brennan-as-prepared-for-delivery-before-ssci.html.

46. Since 2014, "ISIS-related" attacks outside its home base have killed roughly two thousand people worldwide, mostly in the Middle East, and only sixty-five in North America. See "ISIS Goes Global: 143 Attacks in 29 Countries Have Killed 2,043," at www.cnn.com/2015/12/17/world/mapping-isis-attacks-around-the-world/index.html. By contrast, there were more than thirty thousand murders in the United States in that same period. On the Islamic State's limited capabilities, see Stephen M. Walt, "ISIS as a Revolutionary State: New Twist on an Old Story," *Foreign Affairs* 94, no. 6 (November/December 2015).

47. See Sam Mullins, "The Road to Orlando: Jihadist-Inspired Violence in the West, 2012–2016," *CTC Sentinel* 9, no. 6 (2016).

48. See Kenneth Pollack, *The Threatening Storm: The Case for Invading Iraq* (New York: Random House, 2002). Pollack also wrote several op-eds and made numerous media appearances supporting the invasion. For a critique, see John J. Mearsheimer and Stephen M. Walt, "An Unnecessary War," *Foreign Policy*, November–December 2002.

49. See "Ex-CIA Head: Iran Is Genocidal, Theocratic, Imperialistic, Totalitarian," June 5, 2105, at www.clarionproject.org/news/join-our-conference-call-iran-james-woolsey; Bret Stephens, "Iran Cannot Be Contained," *Commentary*, July 1, 2010; and Michael Rubin, "Can Iran Be Deterred or Contained?" August 5, 2008, at www.aei.org/publication/can-a-nuclear-iran-be-contained-or-deterred/. For a convincing rebuttal, see Matt Duss, "The Martyr State Myth," *Foreign Policy*, August 24, 2011, at http://foreignpolicy.com/2011/08/24/the-martyr-state-myth/.

50. Bernard Lewis, "August 22," *The Wall Street Journal*, August 6, 2006.

51. For examples, see Walt, *Taming American Power*, pp. 83–98.

52. Quoted in Leslie H. Gelb, "In the End, Every President Talks to the Bad Guys," *The Washington Post*, April 27, 2008.

53. For an overview, see Robert S. Litwak, *Rogue States and U.S. Foreign Policy: Containment After the Cold War* (Washington, DC: Woodrow Wilson Center Press, 2000).

54. W. Anthony Lake, "Confronting Backlash States," *Foreign Affairs* 73, no. 2 (March–April 1994).

55. See David Frum, *The Right Man: The Surprise Presidency of George W. Bush* (New York: Random House, 2003), pp. 232–33.

56. See in particular Norman Podhoretz, *World War IV: The Long Struggle Against Islamofascism* (New York: Vintage, 2008).

57. See Carl Conetta and Charles Knight, "Post–Cold War US Military Expenditure in the Context of World Spending Trends," Briefing Memo No. 10, *Project on Defense Alternatives* (1997), at www.comw.org/pda/bmemo10.htm.

58. See, for example, Matthew Kroenig, "Time to Attack Iran," *Foreign Affairs* 91, No. 1 (January-February 2012).

59. During its initial campaign to oust the Taliban and capture Osama bin Laden, for example, the Bush administration preferred to run the war on its own and reject proffered help from NATO. This decision was rooted in the experience of the Kosovo War, when many U.S. commanders felt their ability to prosecute the war was undermined by the need to obtain approval from America's NATO allies. As one Pentagon official put it in 2002, "The fewer allies you have, the fewer permissions you have to get." See Elaine Sciolino and Steven Lee Myers, "Bush Says 'Time Is Running Out': U.S. Plans to Act Largely Alone," *The New York Times*, October 7, 2001.

60. The situation reverses balance-of-power logic: the more (weak) allies the United States acquires, the more places it has to protect and the more its military requirements grow. Nowhere is this clearer than with NATO's new Baltic members, who are militarily weak and difficult to defend. The pledge to defend them was undertaken on the assumption that it would never have to be honored. Let us hope so.

61. See Erich Lichtblau, "FBI Steps Up Use of Stings in ISIS Cases," *The New York Times*, June 7, 2016; Glenn Greenwald, "Why Does the FBI Have to Manufacture Its Own Plots If Terrorism and ISIS Are Such Grave Threats?" *The Intercept*, February 26, 2015; Risa Brooks, "Muslim 'Homegrown' Terrorism in the United States," *International Security* 36, no. 2 (Fall 2011); John Mueller and Mark G. Stewart, "How Safe Are We?" *Foreign Affairs* 95, no. 5 (September/October 2016); and idem, "Misoverestimating ISIS: Comparisons with Al Qaeda," *Perspectives on Terrorism* 10, no. 4 (August 2016).

62. In 2012, Secretary of Defense Leon Panetta warned that a cyberattack could "shut down the power grid across large parts of the country," and other experts warned of a "cyber Pearl Harbor" and other devastating attacks that could damage key civilian infrastructure or inflict a decisive military defeat. See Ted Koppel, "Where Is America's Cyberdefense Plan?" *The Washington Post*, December 7, 2015; Nicole Perlroth, "Infrastructure Armageddon," *The New York Times*, October 15, 2015; and Richard Clarke and Robert Knake, *Cyberwar: The Next Threat to National Security and What to Do About It* (New York: Ecco, 2010).

63. Benjamin Wittes and Gabriella Blum, *The Future of Violence: Robots and Germs, Hackers and Drones, Confronting a New Age of Threat* (New York: Basic Books, 2015), pp. 6–7.

64. For a sober and serious analysis of the cyber domain and its impact on world politics, see Lucas Kello, *The Virtual Weapon and International Order* (New Haven, CT: Yale University Press, 2017).

65. See Scott Shane, "The Fake Americans Russia Created to Influence the Election," *The New York Times*, September 7, 2017; Mike Isaac and Daisuke Wakabayashi, "Russian Influence Reached 126 Million Through Facebook Alone," *The New York Times*, October 30, 2017.

66. See Alexis Madrigal, "What Facebook Did to American Democracy (and why it was so hard to see it coming)," *The Atlantic*, October 12, 2017, at www .theatlantic.com/technology/archive/2017/10/what-facebook-did/542502/.

67. Paul Pillar, "Russia Had a Lot to Work With: The Crisis in American Democracy," *The National Interest*, January 9, 2017, at http://nationalinterest.org/blog /paul-pillar/russia-had-plenty-work-the-crisis-american-democracy-18999?page=3.

68. This incident provided the title for Ronald Suskind's *The One-Percent Doctrine: Deep Inside America's Pursuit of Its Enemies Since 9/11* (New York: Simon & Schuster, 2006).

69. See Jack L. Goldsmith, *The Terror Presidency: Law and Judgment Inside the Bush Administration* (New York: W. W. Norton, 2007), p. 72.

70. See Chase Madar, "The Anti-Warrior," *The American Conservative*, March 18, 2014.

71. Steven Erlanger, "Saudi Prince Criticizes Obama Administration, Citing Indecision in Mideast," *The New York Times*, December 15, 2013.

72. As one Japanese defense expert put it, "The Obama administration is not doing such a good job maintaining its credibility . . . [Obama's blurred "red line" in Syria showed] "a lack of commitment, determination, coherence and consistency . . . If you are a superpower symbolism is very important." See John Lash, "Calling America, from Asia," *Star-Tribune*, April 18, 2014, at www.startribune.com /opinion/commentaries/255827891.html.

73. He added, "I think the Saudis, the Emirates, the Egyptians, many in that part of the world no longer have confidence in the United States." See ABC News, "This Week Transcript with Former Vice-President Dick Cheney," October 27, 2013, at http://abcnews.go.com/ThisWeek/week-transcript-vice-president-dick -cheney/story?id=20687048. Yet all these states continued to rely on U.S. support and protection.

74. See Haass, "Isolationist Temptation."

75. According to the Obama administration's 2015 *National Security Strategy*, "there is no shortage of challenges that demand continued American leadership. The potential proliferation of weapons of mass destruction . . . poses a grave risk . . . [M]ore diffuse networks of al-Qa'ida, ISIL, and affiliated groups threaten U.S. citizens, interests, allies, and partners . . . Fragile and conflict-affected states incubate and spawn infectious disease, illicit weapons and drug smugglers, and destabilizing refugee flows . . . The danger of disruptive and even destructive cyber-attack is growing, and the risk of another global economic slowdown remains . . . These complex times have made clear the power and centrality of

America's indispensable leadership in the world." See *National Security Strategy 2015*, pp. 1–2.

76. Drezner notes several other discredited rationales for military predominance, including claims that it can provide a Keynesian stimulus, that military R & D is an efficient source of technological innovation, or that dominant powers can extract wealth by controlling an "informal empire." In his words, these arguments "can be dispatched quickly." See his "Military Dominance Doesn't Pay (Nearly as Much as You Think)," *International Security* 38, no. 1 (Summer 2013), pp. 57–58.

77. Thus, the 2010 trade agreement between the United States and South Korea is no more favorable than South Korea's trade deal with the EU, even though South Korea is a formal U.S. ally and protected (in part) by thousands of U.S. troops. See Drezner, "Military Dominance Doesn't Pay," pp. 64–65.

78. An exception is Carla Norrlof, *America's Global Advantage: U.S. Hegemony and International Cooperation* (Cambridge: Cambridge University Press, 2010), which argues that U.S. security commitments have "purchased goodwill and provided Great Powers with an interest in preserving an American-centered world order" (p. 10).

79. See in particular G. John Ikenberry, *Liberal Leviathan: The Origins, Crisis, and Transformation of the American World Order* (Princeton, NJ: Princeton University Press, 2012); and Stephen G. Brooks, G. John Ikenberry, and William C. Wohlforth, "Don't Come Home, America: The Case against Retrenchment," *International Security* 37, no. 3 (Winter 2012/13).

80. See Robert Gilpin, *The Political Economy of International Relations* (Princeton, NJ: Princeton University Press, 1987).

81. The academic theory of "hegemonic stability" argues that open economic orders require a single dominant power that can provide liquidity or generate demand after a slump, but subsequent research has cast significant doubt on this theory. See Charles P. Kindleberger, *The World in Depression, 1929–1939* (Berkeley: University of California Press, 1973); and Robert O. Keohane, *After Hegemony: Cooperation and Discord in the World Political Economy* (Princeton, NJ: Princeton University Press, 1984). For various critiques see Duncan Snidal, "The Limits of Hegemonic Stability Theory," *International Organization* 39, no. 4 (1985), and Timothy McKeown, "Hegemonic Stability Theory and 19th Century Tariff Levels in Europe," *International Organization* 37, no. 1 (Winter 1983). Drezner concludes that "the literature rejects the notion that hegemony is a necessary condition for an open global economy," and adds "the existence of a liberal hegemon alone is not a sufficient condition" either. See "Military Primacy Doesn't Pay," p. 70.

82. In recent years the United States has devoted as much effort to sanctioning oil producers such as Iraq, Libya, Iran, and Russia as it has to keeping oil and gas flowing. These policies remind us that there is still ample slack in global energy markets and suggest that U.S. officials were not very concerned about access to Middle East energy supplies.

83. On this general point, see Eugene Gholz and Daryl G. Press, "Protecting the Prize: Oil and the U.S. National Interest," *Security Studies* 19, no. 3 (2010).

84. On the role of liberal ideology in shaping U.S. foreign policy goals, see Tony Smith, *America's Mission: The United States and the Worldwide Struggle for Democracy in the 20th Century* (Princeton, NJ: Princeton University Press, 1994).

85. The evolution of Francis Fukuyama's views on this subject is instructive. A learned and influential public intellectual, Fukuyama argued in the early 1990s that the entire world would eventually converge on some version of liberal democratic capitalism. By 2016 he was writing increasingly dark and sober essays on U.S. political dysfunction and suggesting that addressing the ills of U.S. democracy would require far-reaching reforms. See in particular "America in Decay: The Sources of Political Dysfunction," *Foreign Affairs* 93, no. 5 (September/October 2014).

86. Brooks, Ikenberry, and Wohlforth, "Don't Come Home, America"; Steve Coll, "Global Trump," *The New Yorker*, April 11, 2016.

87. See Sarah E. Kreps, *Taxing Wars: The American Way of War Finance and the Decline of Democracy* (New York: Oxford University Press, 2018).

88. See Thomas Oatley, *The Political Economy of American Hegemony: Buildups, Booms, and Busts* (Cambridge: Cambridge University Press, 2014).

89. Fareed Zakaria, "The New American Consensus: Our Hollow Hegemony," *The New York Times Magazine*, November 1, 1998.

90. See "The Obama Doctrine," *The Atlantic*, April 2016.

91. "An Oral History of the Bush White House," *Vanity Fair* (February 2009); Eric Schmitt, "Threats and Responses: Pentagon Contradicts Army General on Iraq Occupation Force's Size," *The New York Times*, February 28, 2003.

92. Joseph Stiglitz and Linda Bilmes, *The Three Trillion Dollar War: The True Cost of the Iraq War* (New York: W. W. Norton, 2008); and Linda Bilmes, "The Financial Legacy of Iraq and Afghanistan: How Wartime Spending Decisions Will Constrain Future National Security Budgets," HKS Faculty Research Working Paper Series RWP13-006, March 2013 at https://research.hks.harvard.edu/publications/workingpapers/citation.aspx?PubId=8956&type=WPN.

93. Dwight D. Eisenhower, "The Chance for Peace," Speech to the American Association of Newspaper Editors, April 16, 1953.

94. Haass admits that a smarter foreign policy would yield domestic benefits, but the central focus of his book is the need to preserve the foundations of U.S. global power. He also points out that focusing on the need for domestic reform "borders on heresy" within the foreign policy establishment. See *Foreign Policy Begins at Home: The Case for Putting America's House in Order* (New York: Basic Books, 2013), pp. 1, 8.

95. See *The All-Volunteer Military: Issues and Performance* (Washington, DC: Congressional Budget Office, 2007), pp. 8–9.

96. See Pew Research Center, "The Military-Civilian Gap: War and Sacrifice in the Post 9/11 Era" (Washington, DC: Pew Social and Demographic Trends, October 5, 2011).

97. See Michael C. Horowitz and Matthew S. Levendusky, "Drafting Support for War: Conscription and Mass Support for War," *Journal of Politics* 73, no. 2 (April 2011).

98. See Jeffrey Record, "Force Protection Fetishism: Sources, Consequences, and (?) Solutions," *Aerospace Power Journal* 14, no. 2 (Summer 2000).

99. See Tim Harper, "Pentagon Keeps War Dead Out of Sight," *Toronto Star*, November 5, 2003; and "Pentagon Lifts Media Ban on Coffin Photos," Associated Press, February 26, 2009. Harper's original story mistakenly claimed that the Pentagon had replaced the term "body bag" with the euphemistic "transfer tube"; see Ben Zimmer, "How Does the Pentagon Say 'Body Bag'?" *Slate.com*, April 4, 2006, at www.slate.com/articles/life/the_good_word/2006/04/how_does_the_pentagon _say_body_bag.html.

100. See Christopher Gelpi, Peter Feaver, and Jason Reifler, *Paying the Human Costs of War: American Public Opinion and Casualties in Military Conflicts* (Princeton, NJ: Princeton University Press, 2009).

101. U.S. Department of Army, *Field Manual 100-5 (Operations)*, pp. 1-2; downloaded from www.fs.fed.us/fire/doctrine/genesis_and_evolution/source_materials /FM-100-5_operations.pdf.

102. General Tommy Franks's failure to deploy sufficient U.S. troops at the Battle of Tora Bora in Afghanistan, which allowed Osama bin Laden to escape, is an obvious example. See Senator John Kerry, *Tora Bora Revisited: How We Failed to Get Bin Laden and Why It Matters Today*, Report to Members of the Committee on Foreign Relations, United States Senate, 111th Congress, 1st sess. (Washington, DC: U.S. G.P.O., 2009); and Peter Bergen, "The Account of How We Nearly Caught Bin Laden in 2001," *The New Republic*, December 30, 2009.

103. See Mearsheimer and Walt, *Israel Lobby and U.S. Foreign Policy*, pp. 65–67.

104. The published report mentions bin Laden's oft-repeated complaints about U.S. support for Israel, the U.S. military presence in Saudi Arabia, and U.S.-led sanctions against Iraq, but it suggests that his opposition "may have started in reaction to specific U.S. policies but quickly became far deeper." The cochairs of the commission, Thomas Kean and Lee Hamilton, later admitted that protests from other commission members led them to downplay the connection between U.S. support for Israel and bin Laden's anti-Americanism. Moreover, by linking bin Laden and Al Qaeda to anti-Western thinkers such as Sayyid Qutb and tracing its emergence to broader social, economic, and political trends in the Arab world, the report minimizes the extent to which the 9/11 plot was a direct response to specific U.S. policy choices. See *The 9/11 Commission Report* (New York: W. W. Norton, 2004), pp. 48–54; Thomas Kean and Lee Hamilton, *Without Precedent: The Inside Story of the 9/11 Commission* (New York: Knopf, 2006), pp. 284–85; and Ernest May, "When Government Writes History: The 9/11 Commission Report," *History News Network*, at http://historynewsnetwork .org/article/11972.

105. See Murtaza Hussain and Cora Currier, "U.S. Military Operations Are Biggest Motivation for Homegrown Terrorists, FBI Study Finds," *The Intercept*, October 11, 2016, at https://theintercept.com/2016/10/11/us-military-operations-are -biggest-motivation-for-homegrown-terrorists-fbi-study-finds/.

106. Chalmers Johnson, *Blowback: The Costs and Consequences of American Empire* (New York: Metropolitan Books, 2000), pp. 8–11.

107. As Tim Arango and Eric Schmitt of *The New York Times* noted in August 2014, "Mr. Baghdadi's rise has been shaped by the United States' involvement in Iraq—most of the political changes that fueled his fight, or led to his promotion, were born directly from some American action." See Tim Arango and Eric Schmitt, "U.S. Actions in Iraq Fueled Rise of a Rebel," *The New York Times*, August 10, 2014. On the origins of the Islamic State, see Will McCants, *The ISIS Apocalypse: The History, Strategy, and Doomsday Vision of the Islamic State* (New York: St. Martin's, 2015).

108. See John Tirman, *The Deaths of Others: The Fate of Civilians in America's Wars* (New York: Oxford University Press, 2011).

109. See Phil Stewart and Warren Strobel, "U.S. to Halt Some Arms Sales to Saudi, Citing Civilian Deaths in Yemen Campaign," Reuters, December 13, 2016.

110. See John M. Broder, "A Nation at War: The Casualties; U.S. Military Has No Count of Iraqi Dead in Fighting," *The New York Times*, April 2, 2003; and Mark Thompson, "Should the Military Return to Counting Bodies?" *Time*, June 2, 2009.

111. Quoted in Anna Badkhen, "Critics Say 600,000 Iraqi Dead Doesn't Tally," *San Francisco Chronicle*, October 12, 2006.

112. See Sabrina Tavernise and Andrew Lehren, "A Grim Portrait of Civilian Deaths in Iraq," *The New York Times*, October 22, 2010.

113. Gilbert Burnham et al., "Mortality After the 2003 Invasion of Iraq: A Cross-Sectional Cluster Sample Survey," *The Lancet*, October 11, 2006. For a summary of conflicting totals, see C. Tapp et al., "Iraq War Mortality Estimates: A Systematic Review," *Conflict and Health* 2, no. 1 (2008).

114. See Azmat Khan and Anand Gopal, "The Uncounted," *The New York Times Magazine*, November 16, 2017.

115. See Rob Malley and Stephen Pomper, "An Accounting for the Uncounted," *The Atlantic*, December 16, 2017, at www.theatlantic.com/international/archive/2017/12/isis-obama-civilian-casualties/548501/.

116. See Tim McGurk, "Collateral Damage or Civilian Massacre in Haditha," *Time*, March 19, 2006. One U.S. Marine was eventually prosecuted for the incident; he was convicted of "dereliction of duty" but served no jail time. See Tirman, *Deaths of Others*, pp. 302–07.

117. Washington also rejected a demand by Médicins sans Frontières for an independent international inquiry into the incident. See Siobhan O'Grady, "Washington and Kabul Stand in the Way of International Probe into Kunduz Attack," *Foreign Policy*, October 14, 2015, at https://foreignpolicy.com/2015/10/14/washington-and-kabul-stand-in-the-way-of-international-probe-into-kunduz-attack/.

118. See Matthew Rosenberg, "Pentagon Details Chain of Errors in Strike on Afghan Hospital," *The New York Times*, April 29, 2016.

5: IS ANYONE ACCOUNTABLE?

1. Quoted in Eric Bradner, Elise Labott, and Dana Bash, "50 GOP National Security Experts Oppose Trump," August 8, 2016, at www.cnn.com/2016/08/08

/politics/republican-national-security-letter-donald-trump-election-2016/index
.html.

2. As Kenneth Waltz pointed out in 1967, "We are misled by the vision of dominoes. States in the area of the fighting lack the solidity, shape, and cohesion that the image suggests. Externally ill-defined, internally fragile and chaotic, they more appropriately call to mind sponges; and sponges, whatever their other characteristics, do not from the transmission of impulses neatly fall down in a row." See his "The Politics of Peace," *International Studies Quarterly* 11, no. 3 (September 1967), p. 205.

3. See Jerome Slater, "The Domino Theory and International Politics: The Case of Vietnam," *Security Studies* 3, no. 2 (1993); idem, "Dominos in Central America: Will They Fall? Does it Matter?" *International Security* 12, no. 2 (Fall 1987); and Ted Hopf, *Peripheral Visions: Deterrence Theory and American Foreign Policy in the Developing World, 1965–1990* (Ann Arbor: University of Michigan Press, 1994).

4. Thus the pro-war *Wall Street Journal* approvingly quoted Pakistani foreign minister Shah Mehmood Qureshi's 2009 prediction that a U.S. withdrawal from Afghanistan "will be disastrous . . . you will lose credibility . . . Who is going to trust you again? . . . Why did you send so many billions of dollars and lose so many lives? And why did we ally with you?" U.S. troops were still fighting in Afghanistan when Obama left office. See "U.S. Credibility and Pakistan," *The Wall Street Journal*, October 1, 2009, at www.wsj.com/articles/SB10001424052748704471504574443352072071822.

5. See Elliott Abrams, "Haunted by Syria," *Weekly Standard*, January 13, 2014. Barack Obama used military force in many countries throughout his presidency, yet François Heisbourg maintains that his decision not to intervene in Syria did "enormous, perhaps irretrievable" damage to U.S. credibility. Quoted in Celestine Bohlen, "A Turning Point for Syria, and for U.S. Credibility," *The New York Times*, February 22, 2016.

6. See Carmen M. Reinhart and Kenneth S. Rogoff, *This Time Is Different: Eight Centuries of Financial Folly* (Princeton, NJ: Princeton University Press, 2009).

7. As enunciated by former JCS chairman and secretary of state Colin Powell, the Powell Doctrine consists of a series of eight questions that must be answered in the affirmative before committing U.S. forces to battle: (1) Is a vital national security interest threatened? (2) Do we have a clear attainable objective? (3) Have the risks and costs been fully and frankly analyzed? (4) Have all other nonviolent policy means been fully exhausted? (5) Is there a plausible exit strategy to avoid endless entanglement? (6) Have the consequences of our action been fully considered? (7) Is the action supported by the American people? and (8) Do we have genuine broad international support?

8. See Paul D. Miller, "Obama's Failed Legacy in Afghanistan," *The American Interest* 11, no. 5 (February 2016); Rick Brennan, "Withdrawal Symptoms," *Foreign Affairs* 93, no. 6 (November/December 2014); and Danielle Pletka, "What Obama Has Wrought in Iraq," *U.S. News and World Report*, June 13, 2014.

9. Not to be outdone, Jeb Bush said that "the premature withdrawal was the

334   NOTES TO PAGES 186–189

fatal error"; former New York mayor Rudy Giuliani called withdrawal "the worst decision so far of the 21st century"; and the neoconservative pundit Max Boot, an outspoken advocate of the original invasion, termed the decision to withdraw "tragic." See "Rubio: Iraq Invasion 'Was Not a Mistake,'" *The Hill*, May 17, 2015, at http://thehill.com/policy/defense/242339-rubio-iraq-invasion-was-not-a-mistake; "Lindsay Graham Calls for 10,000 Troops in Iraq," CNN, May 18, 2015, at http://cnn.com/2015/05/18/politics/lindsay-graham—iraq-not-a-mistake-election-2016/index.html; "Giuliani: Obama's Iraq Withdrawal 'Worst Decision of the 21st Century,'" *The Hill*, June 10, 2015, at http://thehill.com/blogs.blog-briefing-room/244548-giuliani-obamas-iraq-withdrawal-worst-decision-of-21st-century; and Max Boot, "Obama's Tragic Iraq Withdrawal," *The Wall Street Journal*, October 31, 2011.

10. See in particular Alexander Downes and Jonathan Monten, "FIRCed to be Free: Why Foreign-Imposed Regime Change Rarely Leads to Democratization," *International Security* 37, no. 4 (Spring 2013); and Stephen M. Walt, "Why Is the US So Bad at Promoting Democracy in Other Countries?" *Foreign Policy*, April 25, 2016; at http://foreignpolicy.com/2016/04/25/why-is-america-so-bad-at-promoting-democracy-in-other-countries/.

11. See John Judis's interview with Landis, "America's Failure—And Russia and Iran's Success—in Syria's Cataclysmic Civil War," *TPMCafe*, January 10, 2017, at http://talkingpointsmemo.com/cafe/americas-failure-russia-success-in-syrias-war.

12. See Sopan Deb and Max Fisher, "Seeking Lessons on Syria, but Taken to Task Instead," *The New York Times*, September 18, 2017.

13. See Philip Shenon, *The Commission: The Uncensored Story of the 9/11 Commission* (New York: Hachette, 2008), pp. 25–26, 29–30, 214–19.

14. Rice and Zelikow worked together on the NSC staff under George H. W. Bush and later coauthored a book on their experience. Zelikow attended briefings on U.S. counterterror policy as a member of Bush's transition team, and Rice hired him to draft the White House's *National Security Strategy* in 2002. After Rice was appointed secretary of state in 2005, she picked Zelikow as her counselor at the State Department. Given these close professional ties, Zelikow was hardly the ideal person to help determine if Rice, Bush, or other administration officials bore significant responsibility for failing to prevent the September 11 attacks.

15. Ernest May, "When Government Writes History: The 9/11 Commission Report," *History News Network*, June 24, 2005, at http://historynewsnetwork.org/article/11972.

16. See Jane Mayer, *The Dark Side: The Inside Story of How the War on Terror Turned into a War on American Ideals* (New York: Doubleday, 2008), p. 245.

17. The key reports are: *Article 15-6 Investigation of the 800th Military Police Brigade*, available at https://fas.org/irp/agency/dod/taguba.pdf; Department of the Army, The Inspector General, *Detainee Operations Inspection* (July 21, 2004), at www1.umn.edu/humanrts/OathBetrayed/Mikolashek%20Report.pdf; and *Final Report of the Independent Panel to Review DoD Detention Operations* (Washington,

DC: August 2004). On Rumsfeld's role in approving harsher interrogation methods, see Mayer, *The Dark Side*, pp. 220, 240–41.

18. "Abu Ghraib, Whitewashed," editorial, *The New York Times*, July 24, 2004.

19. Eric Rosenburg, "Abu Ghraib Is Like 'Animal House,' but Rumsfeld Should Not Resign," *Deseret News*, August 25, 2004, at www.deseretnews.com/article /595086544/Abu-Ghraib-like-Animal-House-but-Rumsfeld-should-not-resign .html.

20. "Pentagon Panel: Top Brass Was Lax in Abu Ghraib Oversight," NBC News, August 8, 2004, at www.nbcnews.com/id/5807013/ns/world_news-mideast _n_africa/t/pentagon-panel-top-brass-was-lax-abu-ghraib-oversight/# .U9aZglYQf0A.

21. "Getting Away with Torture: Command Responsibility for the U.S. Abuse of Detainees," *Human Rights Watch*, April 2005, p. 21.

22. See Seymour M. Hersh, "The General's Report," *The New Yorker*, June 25, 2007.

23. Bush admitted approving the waterboarding of Khalid Sheikh Mohammed, and Vice President Cheney said publicly that he had been a "big supporter" of the same technique. See David Cole, "Obama's Torture Problem," *NYRBlog*, November 18, 2010, at www.nybooks.com/blogs/nyrblog/2010/nov/18/obamas-torture -problem/.

24. Charlie Savage, "Obama Reluctant to Look into Bush Programs," *The New York Times*, January 11, 2009.

25. See especially Mark Danner, *Spiral: Trapped in the Forever War* (New York: Simon & Schuster, 2016), and Mayer, *The Dark Side*.

26. See Paul Farhi, "Bill Kristol Knows His Predictions Have Been Bad, but He's Going to Keep Making Them," *The Washington Post*, February 17, 2016; and Stephen M. Walt, "The Shattered Kristol Ball," *The National Interest* 97 (September/ October 2008).

27. See Steven R. Weisman, "Wolfowitz Resigns, Ending Long Fight at World Bank," *The New York Times*, May 18, 2007.

28. In that role Abrams frequently colluded with Israeli officials seeking to derail peace initiatives pushed by Secretary of State Condoleezza Rice and others. See Jim Lobe, "US/Mideast: Rice Faces Formidable Mideast Foe," *InterPress News*, February 21, 2007, at www.ipsnews.net/2007/02/us-mideast-rice-faces-formidable -white-house-foe/; and Shahar Smooha, "All the Dreams We Had Are Now Gone," *Ha'aretz*, July 19, 2007.

29. See David Rose, "The Gaza Bombshell," *Vanity Fair*, April 2008; "Hamas Coup in Gaza," International Institute for Strategic Studies, *Strategic Comments* 13, no. 5 (June 2007); and "Elliot Abrams' Uncivil War," *Conflicts Forum* (2007), at www .conflictsforum.org/2007/elliot-abrams-uncivil-war/.

30. See Eric Alterman, "The Rehabilitation of Elliott Abrams," *The Nation*, March 13, 2013. Tellingly, Alterman writes, "What does it say about our most influential and important institutions that this lifelong embarrassment to American democracy can be embraced as one of their own?"

31. See Maggie Haberman, Jonathan Weisman, and Eric Lichtblau, "Trump Overrules Tillerson, Rejecting Elliott Abrams for Deputy Secretary of State," *The New York Times*, February 10, 2017.

32. See Stephen M. Walt, "So Wrong for So Long: Why Neoconservatives Are Never Right," *Foreign Policy* (online) at http://foreignpolicy.com/2015/08/21/neoconservatives-so-wrong-for-so-long-iraq-war-iran-deal/.

33. Miller, Malley, Indyk, Kurtzer, and Ross have all written conflicting accounts of the Oslo process, placing blame for its failure on a number of culprits (including the Palestinians). See Robert Malley and Hussein Agha, "Camp David: The Tragedy of Errors," *New York Review of Books*, August 9, 2001; Dennis Ross, *The Missing Peace: The Inside Story of the Fight for Middle East Peace* (New York: Farrar, Straus & Giroux, 2004); Aaron D. Miller, *The Much Too Promised Land: America's Elusive Search for Arab-Israeli Peace* (New York: Bantam, 2008); Martin Indyk, *Innocent Abroad: An Intimate Account of American Peace Diplomacy in the Middle East* (New York: Simon & Schuster, 2009); and Daniel B. Kurtzer et al., *The Peace Puzzle: America's Quest for Israeli-Palestinian Peace 1989–2011* (Ithaca, NY: Cornell University Press, 2013).

34. The Israeli journalist Barak Ravid called Ross "one of the most central people in the White House in everything that has to do with the Israeli-Palestinian peace process. He has whispered in the ear of U.S. President Barack Obama, maintained a secret and direct channel with Prime Minister Benjamin Netanyahu and his envoy Isaac Molho, and undermined U.S. Mideast envoy George Mitchell . . . Despite the fact that he is considered to be Netanyahu's man in the White House, he did not manage to get almost anything from the Israeli prime minister. In Ramallah, his status is even worse. Palestinian President Mahmoud Abbas pushed him aside and effectively declared him a persona non grata. As far as Washington was concerned, he had a far greater impact: mainly a negative one." See "Dennis Ross Discovers Palestine," *Ha'aretz*, January 9, 2009, at www.haaretz.com/blogs/diplomania/dennis-ross-discovers-palestine-1.406290.

35. Ross believed that the United States should be ready to use force to prevent Iran from obtaining nuclear weapons, and he cosigned a public letter expressing doubts about the emerging agreement in June 2015. See "Public Statement on U.S. Policy Toward the Iran Nuclear Negotiations," *Washington Institute for Near East Policy*, June 24, 2015, at www.washingtoninstitute.org/policy-analysis/view/public-statement-on-u.s.-policy-toward-the-iran-nuclear-negotiations. Ross continued to push a hard-line approach toward Iran after the agreement was signed, recommending that the United States give Israel bombs designed to destroy Iran's buried nuclear facilities "and the aircraft needed to carry it." See Dennis B. Ross, "How to Make Iran Keep Its Word," *Politico*, July 29, 2015.

36. On Indyk's support for the Iraq War, see Martin S. Indyk and Kenneth M. Pollack, "How Bush Can Avoid the Inspections Trap," *The New York Times*, January 25, 2003; and Martin S. Indyk and Kenneth M. Pollack, "Lock and Load," *Los Angeles Times*, December 19, 2002.

37. Dennis Ross and David Makovsky, *Myths, Illusions, and Peace: Finding a New Direction for America in the Middle East* (New York: Viking, 2009).

38. Experts disagree on whether the relevant agencies failed to do an adequate job of collection and analysis in the run-up to war in Iraq, or whether they allowed themselves to be politicized and manipulated by a White House determined to go to war. Either way, it was a significant analytic failure. For alternative perspectives, see Joshua Rovner, *Fixing the Facts: National Security and the Politics of Intelligence* (Ithaca, NY: Cornell University Press, 2011); Robert Jervis, *Why Intelligence Fails: Lessons from the Iranian Revolution and the Iraq War* (Ithaca, NY: Cornell University Press, 2011); Paul R. Pillar, *Intelligence and U.S. Foreign Policy: Iraq, 9/11, and Misguided Reform* (New York: Columbia University Press, 2011); Thomas Powers, "How They Got Their Bloody War," *New York Review of Books*, May 27, 2010; and Fulton Armstrong (with reply by Thomas Powers), "The CIA and WMDs: The Damning Evidence," *New York Review of Books*, August 19, 2010.

39. See Adam Goldman, "Ex-C.I.A. Officer Suspected of Compromising Chinese Informants Is Arrested," *The New York Times*, January 16, 2018.

40. See Adam Goldman and Matt Apuzzo, "CIA Officers Make Grave Mistakes, Get Promoted," *NBC News*, February 9, 2011, at www.nbcnews.com/id/41484983/ns/us_news-security/t/cia-officers-make-grave-mistakes-get-promoted/#.U9uvFFYQf0C. See also Matthew Schofield, "CIA Knew It Had the Wrong Man, but Kept Him Anyway," *McClatchy News Service*, June 30, 2016, at www.mcclatchydc.com/news/nation-world/world/article86890087.html.

41. Clapper later told NBC's Andrea Mitchell that his answer was the "least untruthful" he could give in an open hearing.

42. A signature strike is an attack on a suspect whose behavior fits the assumed profile of terrorist activity, even if the identity of the target is not known. See Amy Davidson, "John Brennan's Kill List," *The New Yorker*, January 7, 2013.

43. www.c-span.org/video/?300266-1/obama-administration-counterterrorism-strategy.

44. Carrie Johnson and Joby Warrick, "CIA Destroyed 92 Interrogation Tapes, Probe Says," *The Washington Post*, March 3, 2009.

45. See Marisa Taylor and Jonathan Landay, "After CIA Gets Secret Whistleblower Email, Congress Worries About More Spying," July 25, 2014, at www.mcclatchydc.com/2014/07/25/234484/after-cia-gets-secret-whistleblower.html.

46. See Jonathan S. Landay and Ali Watkins, "CIA Admits It Broke into Senate Computers; Senators Call for Spy Chief's Ouster," at www.mcclatchydc.com/news/nation-world/national/national-security/article24771274.html#storylink=cpy.

47. After the initial reports of CIA monitoring, Brennan accused lawmakers of making "spurious allegations about C.I.A. actions that are wholly unsupported by the facts." He subsequently added, "I think a lot of people who are claiming that there has been this tremendous sort of spying and monitoring and hacking will be proved wrong." See Mark Mazzetti and Carl Hulse, "CIA Admits Penetrating Senate Intel Committee Computers," *The New York Times*, July 31, 2014.

48. Dustin Volz and Lauren Fox, "CIA Review Clears Its Spies of Wrongdoing," *National Journal*, January 15, 2015.

49. Carl Hulse and Mark Mazzetti, "President Expresses Confidence in CIA Director," *The New York Times*, August 1, 2014. On the negative effects of the torture regime, see Douglas Johnson, Alberto Mora, and Averell Schmidt, "The Strategic Costs of Torture," *Foreign Affairs* 95, no. 5 (September/October 2016).

50. On the pervasive weakness of congressional oversight, see Michael Glennon, *National Security and Double Government* (New York: Oxford University Press, 2015), pp. 52–57.

51. Glennon, *National Security and Double Government*, pp. 61–64.

52. See Katrina Manson, "The Undercover Spy Picked as CIA Chief," *Financial Times*, March 17, 2018.

53. See Dan Lamothe, "Top Two Officers and Other Sailors Aboard the USS Fitzgerald to Be Disciplined Following Deadly Collision at Sea," *The Washington Post*, August 17, 2017.

54. See Thomas Ricks, "Whatever Happened to Accountability?" *Harvard Business Review*, October 2012; James Fallows, "The Tragedy of the American Military," *The Atlantic*, January/February 2015; William Astore, "An Army of None," *Salon .com*, March 23, 2016; at www.salon.com/2016/03/23/an_army_of_none_the_u_s _military_is_more_powerful_less_accountable_and_more_dangerous_than _ever_before/.

55. Thomas E. Ricks, *The Generals: American Military Command from World War II to Today* (New York: Penguin, 2012), pp. 388–94.

56. See Andrew Bacevich, "Winning: Trump Loves to Do It, but American Generals Have Forgotten How," *TomDispatch.com*, at www.tomdispatch.com /blog/176215/tomgram%3A_andrew_bacevich%2C_the_swamp_of_war.

57. The Defense Department defines "unwanted sexual contact" as "completed and attempted oral, anal, and vaginal penetration with any body part or object, and the unwanted touching of genitalia and other sexually-related areas of the body." Based on surveys, the Pentagon estimates that at least nineteen thousand servicemen or -women experienced an incident of this type in recent years. Total *reported* assaults are much lower, but still exceed three thousand cases per year. See *Department of Defense Annual Report on Sexual Assault in the Military, FY 2012* at www.sapr.mil/public/docs/reports/FY12_DoD_SAPRO_Annual_Report _on_Sexual_Assault-VOLUME_ONE.pdf.

58. The perpetrators of the Haditha massacre received light sentences under a plea agreement; Sergeant Bales was given a life sentence. See Charlie Savage and Elisabeth Bumiller, "An Iraqi Massacre, a Light Sentence, and a Question of Military Justice," *The New York Times*, January 27, 2012; and Michael E. Miller, "U.S. Army Mass Murderer: 'The Hate Grows Not Only for Insurgents, but Towards Everyone Who Isn't American,'" *The Washington Post*, June 8, 2015.

59. "Beginning in 2010," notes Seth Jones of the RAND Corporation, "there was a rise in the number of Salafi-jihadist groups and fighters, particularly in Syria and North Africa. There was also an increase in the number of attacks perpetrated by al Qa'ida and its affiliates." See Seth G. Jones, *A Persistent Threat: The Evolution of*

Al Qa'ida and Other Salafi Jihadists (Washington, DC: RAND Corporation, 2014), p. x. See also International Human Rights and Conflict Resolution Clinic at Stanford Law School and Global Justice Clinic at NYU School of Law, *Living under Drones: Death, Injury and Trauma to Civilians from U.S. Drone Practices* (2012); and Hassan Abbas, "How Drones Create More Terrorists," *The Atlantic*, August 20, 2013.

60. Ricks, *The Generals*, p. 392; Barton Gellman and Thomas E. Ricks, "U.S. Concludes Bin Laden Escaped at Tora Bora Fight; Failure to Send More Troops Termed Major Error," *The Washington Post*, April 17, 2002.

61. Associated Press, "Sex Is Major Reason Military Commanders Are Fired," January 21, 2013; at www.military.com/daily-news/2013/01/21/sex-is-major-reason -military-commanders-are-fired.html.

62. For a careful campaign analysis suggesting that deploying U.S. troops would have worked, see Peter John Paul Krause, "The Last Good Chance: A Reassessment of U.S. Operations at Tora Bora," *Security Studies* 17, no. 4 (2008).

63. Civilians in the Pentagon and the White House bear primary responsibility for failing to plan the occupation, but Franks did not challenge their rosy assessments or inadequate preparations. See Ricks, *The Generals*, chap. 27.

64. See Dexter Filkins, "The Fall of the Warrior King," *The New York Times Magazine*, October 23, 2005; Ricks, *The Generals*, pp. 422–25.

65. See "Marine to Serve No Time in Haditha, Iraq Killings Case," *USA Today*, January 24, 2012; and "Squad Leader in Haditha Killings Discharged from Marine Corps," *Los Angeles Times*, February 21, 2012.

66. Nor is it clear how innovative the surge really was, insofar as many of the tactical innovations Petraeus adopted had been developed by units serving in the field. On this point, see James A. Russell, *Innovation, Transformation, and War: Counterinsurgency Operations in Anbar and Ninewa Provinces, Iraq, 2005–2007* (Stanford, CA: Stanford University Press, 2011).

67. When he announced the "surge," President Bush said its aim was "to put down sectarian violence and bring security to the people of Baghdad" to "help make reconciliation possible . . . these [U.S.] teams bring together military and civilian experts to help local Iraqi communities pursue reconciliation." See "President's Address to the Nation," January 10, 2007; at http://georgewbush-whitehouse .archives.gov/news/releases/2007/01/20070110-7.html. See also Peter Beinart, "The Surge Fallacy," *The Atlantic*, September 2015; and Peter W. Galbraith, *Unintended Consequences: How War in Iraq Strengthened America's Enemies* (New York: Simon & Schuster, 2008), chap. 1.

68. Bacevich explains: "Without pertinent standards, there can be no accountability. Absent accountability, failings and weaknesses escape notice. Eventually, what you've become accustomed to seems tolerable. Twenty-first-century Americans inured to wars that never end have long since forgotten that bringing such conflicts to a prompt and successful conclusion once defined the very essence of what generals were expected to do." See "Winning."

69. See Petraeus's testimony in "The Status of the War and Political Developments in Iraq," Hearing before the Committee on Armed Services, 110th Congress, 1st sess., September 10, 2007 (Washington, DC: U.S. Government Printing Office,

2008). In a December 2009 hearing on Afghanistan, McChrystal told a congressional committee, "The next eighteen months will likely be decisive and ultimately enable success," adding that "we can and will accomplish this mission." The following month, he told ABC's Diane Sawyer that he "believed we had turned the tide." Petraeus issued a similarly optimistic assessment a year later, though it was at odds with U.S. intelligence assessments and followed by a major increase in the overall level of violence. See "Afghanistan," Hearings Before the Committee on Armed Services, U.S. Senate, 111th Congress, 1st sess., December 2 and 8, 2009 (Washington, DC: U.S. Government Printing Office, 2010), p. 103; "Top General Optimistic About Afghanistan," ABC News, January 11, 2010, at www.youtube.com/watch?v=ABdm3bdUeDE; and Josh Rogin, "Petraeus's Optimism About Afghanistan Not Shared at CIA," *Foreign Policy*, April 27, 2011, at http://thecable.foreignpolicy.com/posts/2011/04/27/petraeuss_optimism_about_afghanistan_not_shared_at_cia_0.

70. See Ellen Mitchell, "Top General in Afghanistan Says Taliban Fight Has 'Turned the Corner,'" *The Hill*, November 28, 2017, at http://thehill.com/policy/defense/362205-top-us-general-in-afghanistan-says-taliban-fight-has-turned-the-corner; and Andrew Bacevich, "Still Waiting: A Harvey Weinstein Moment for America's Wars?" TomDispatch, December 10, 2017, at www.tomdispatch.com/post/176361/tomgram%3A_andrew_bacevich%2C_a_country_addicted_to_war/.

71. See Paul McCleary, "U.S. Has 'Turned the Corner' in Afghanistan, Top General Says," *Foreign Policy*, November 28, 2017, at http://foreignpolicy.com/2017/11/28/u-s-has-turned-the-corner-in-afghanistan-top-general-says/.

72. See Shawn Snow, "Report: US Officials Classify Crucial Metrics on Afghan Casualties, Readiness," *Army Times*, October 20, 2017, at www.armytimes.com/flashpoints/2017/10/30/report-us-officials-classify-crucial-metrics-on-afghan-casualties-readiness/; and Thomas Gibbons-Neff, "Afghan War Data, Once Public, Is Censored in U.S. Military Report," *The New York Times*, October 30, 2017.

73. See Noah Shachtman, "Gates Has a Long, Loooong Record of Firing Generals," *Wired*, June 11, 2010, at www.wired.com/2010/06/gates-has-a-long-record-of-firing-generals/.

74. See Thom Shanker, "Concern Grows Over Top Military Officers' Ethics," *The Washington Post*, November 12, 2012.

75. These audits are available at www.sigar.mil. See also Andrew deGrandpre and Alex Horton, "Here Are Six Costly Failures from America's Longest War. No. 1: Cashmere Goats," *The Washington Post*, August 22, 2017.

76. He added: "We also don't appreciate and enforce personal accountability in the U.S. government. It takes a hell of a lot of screw-ups for someone to get fired. And I dare anybody to show me somebody who's gotten fired in Afghanistan for wasting 100 million dollars, 300 million dollars, or failing to accomplish a program he or she was given." See Priyanka Boghani, "'Nobody's Been Held Accountable' for Wasteful Spending in Afghanistan, Says U.S. Watchdog," *Frontline*, October 9, 2015, at www.pbs.org/wgbh/frontline/article/nobodys-been-held-accountable-for-wasteful-spending-in-afghanistan-says-u-s-watchdog/.

77. See Sapna Maheshwari, "10 Times Trump Spread Fake News," *The New York Times*, January 18, 2017, at www.nytimes.com/interactive/2017/business/media/trump-fake-news.html?_r=0.

78. See Ruth Marcus, "When All News Is 'Fake,' Whom Do We Trust?" *The Washington Post*, December 12, 2016.

79. See "From the Editors: The *Times* and Iraq," May 26, 2004.

80. See Jeffrey Goldberg, "The Great Terror," *The New Yorker*, March 25, 2002; and Daniel Lazare, "*The New Yorker* Goes to War," *The Nation*, May 15, 2003.

81. Miller's coauthor on several of these articles, Michael Gordon, remains in a prominent senior post at the *Times*. On Miller's departure, see Katharine Seelye, "*Times* and Reporter Reach Agreement on Her Departure," *The New York Times*, November 9, 2005.

82. In 2010 Goldberg published an alarming cover story suggesting that Israel was likely to launch a preventive strike on Iran's nuclear program within a year. See his "The Point of No Return," *The Atlantic* (September 2010). The deadline passed, and no attack occurred, but Goldberg recycled the same warning in a 2012 Bloomberg View column, saying, "I'm highly confident that Netanyahu isn't bluffing." Goldberg seems to have been taken in by a well-orchestrated Israeli campaign to convince the United States that it was prepared to use force, in order to persuade Washington to impose harsher sanctions on Iran and either reject or toughen up the agreement capping Iran's nuclear program. See Daniel Sobelman, "Signaling Credibility in IR," unpublished ms. (2016), which describes the Israeli effort in detail.

83. See especially Eric Hananoki, "Where Are the Media's Iraq War Boosters 10 Years Later?" *Media Matters for America*, March 19, 2013, at www.mediamatters.org/research/2013/03/19/where-are-the-medias-iraq-war-boosters-10-years/193117.

84. See Bill Keller, "My Unfinished 9/11 Business," *The New York Times Magazine*, September 6, 2011; also Stephen M. Walt, "How Not to Learn from Past Mistakes," *Foreign Policy*, September 12, 2011, at http://foreignpolicy.com/2011/09/12/how-not-to-learn-from-past-mistakes/.

85. See James Carden and Jacob Heilbrunn, "The Washington Post: The Most Reckless Editorial Page in America," *The National Interest*, January/February 2015.

86. "An Unfinished Mission," *The Washington Post*, May 4, 2003.

87. Jackson Diehl, "What the Iraq War Taught Me About Syria," *The Washington Post*, March 31, 2013.

88. Subsequent editorials falsely described Iran as actively seeking a nuclear weapon and falsely attributed Iran's decision to divert some of its stockpile of enriched uranium to an accusatory speech by Israeli prime minister Benjamin Netanyahu (the diversion had actually taken place several years before Netanyahu's speech). See Matt Duss, "Washington Post Editors Get Mixed Up on Iran's Nuclear Program," http://thinkprogress.org/security/2013/04/09/1838431/washington-post-iran/?mobile=nc.

89. Marc Thiessen, "A Dark Winter of Ebola Terrorism," *The Washington Post*, October 20, 2014; see also Louis Jacobson, "Could Terrorists Use Ebola to Attack

the United States?" *Politifact*, October 23, 2014, at www.politifact.com/truth-o -meter/article/2014/oct/23/could-terrorists-use-ebola-attack-united-states.

90. On Williams, see Elliot Hannon, "NBC Suspends Brian Williams Without Pay for Six Months," *Slate.com*, February 10, 2015, at www.slate.com/blogs/the _slatest/2015/02/10/nbc_news_suspends_brian_williams_for_fabricated_stories .html. On O'Reilly, see Emily Steel and Michael S. Schmidt, "Bill O'Reilly Is Forced Out at Fox News," *The New York Times*, April 19, 2017.

91. After a pioneering career as a White House correspondent, the eighty-nine-year-old Thomas was fired after she was recorded saying, "Jews should get out of Palestine," and "go home" to Europe. For an eyewitness account, see Paula Cruickshank, "42 Seconds That Sullied Helen Thomas—and New Media," *Real Clear Politics*, July 31, 2013. Clancy was fired after a Twitter exchange in which he accused an online critic from the pro-Israel Foundation for Defense of Democracies of being "part of a campaign to do PR for #Israel . . . Nothing illegal—but PR not HR: Human Rights." Nasr was dismissed for a single tweet expressing sympathy after the death of the Hezbollah cleric Sayyed Fadlallah. Despite apologizing for her tweet and clarifying that she sought only to acknowledge Fadlallah's support for women's rights and opposition to honor killings, Nasr was promptly terminated.

92. See Gabriel Sherman, "Chasing Fox," *New York Magazine*, October 10, 2010; Elias Isquith, "Phil Donahue's Vindication," *Salon.com*, July 10, 2014.

93. See Art Swift, "Americans' Trust in Mass Media Sinks to New Low," Gallup Organization, September 14, 2016, at www.gallup.com/poll/195542/americans -trust-mass-media-sinks-new-low.aspx.

94. Full disclosure: I helped draft the text and recruit signatories for the ad.

95. Yingling's original article—which he forthrightly chose not to publish anonymously—was "A Failure in Generalship," *Armed Forces Journal* (May 2007). See also Paul Yingling, "Why an Army Colonel Is Retiring Early—To Become a High School Teacher," *The Washington Post*, December 2, 2011; and Ricks, *The Generals*, pp. 441–44.

96. Flynt Leverett and Hillary Mann Leverett, *Going to Tehran: Why America Must Accept the Islamic Republic* (New York: Metropolitan Books, 2011).

97. Michael Crowley, "Iran Contrarians," *The New Republic*, February 10, 2010; and Daniel B. Drezner, "Your Humble Blogger Was So Wrong," *Foreign Policy*, August 30, 2010, at http://foreignpolicy.com/2010/08/30/your-humble-blogger-was -so-wrong/.

98. See Flynt Leverett and Hillary Mann Leverett, "Iran's Presidential Election Will Surprise America's So-Called 'Iran Experts,'" *Huffington Post*, June 6, 2013, at www.huffingtonpost.com/flynt-and-hillary-mann-leverett/iran-presidential-elec tion_b_3431154.html.

99. For example, the Leveretts were too pessimistic about the Obama administration's ability to negotiate a nuclear deal with Iran.

100. In particular, picking fights with political opponents does not seem to have hurt many neoconservatives.

101. See Kelley Vlahos, "Washington Doesn't Forgive Whistleblowers," *The American Conservative*, July 30, 2014.

102. Hoh's story has a happy ending, as he was eventually appointed a senior fellow at the left-leaning Center for International Policy. See www.ciponline.org /about-us/experts-staff/matthew_hoh.

103. After Irving "Scooter" Libby was convicted of lying to the FBI and to a grand jury regarding his role in exposing the identity of CIA agent Valerie Plame, a veritable "who's who" of influential insiders—including Henry Kissinger, Leonard Garment, Donald Rumsfeld, Eric Edelman, Christopher DeMuth, Leon Wieseltier, Robert Blackwill, and many more—wrote letters to the presiding judge, urging clemency. See Sidney Blumenthal, "The Libby Lobby's Pardon Campaign," *Salon .com*, June 7, 2007. A few years later a similar campaign may have helped David Petraeus secure a plea bargain after admitting that he had given his mistress classified information and lied to the FBI about it. See Andrew V. Pestano, "Report: Government Elite Officials Wrote to Keep Petraeus Out of Prison," UPI, June 9, 2015, at www.upi.com/Top_News/US/2015/06/09/Report-Government-elite-officials -wrote-to-keep-Gen-Petraeus-out-of-prison/6141433857287/.

104. Elizabeth Warren, *A Fighting Chance* (New York: Metropolitan Books, 2014), p. 106. Ironically, Summers has ignored his own advice of late, accusing Treasury Secretary Steven Mnuchin of making "irresponsible" statements about tax reform and at one point tweeting that Mnuchin "may be the greatest sycophant in Cabinet history." Summers's "insider status" is probably safe, however, and he may no longer aspire to hold a top job in Washington. If so, then criticizing a fellow "insider" carries fewer negative consequences.

6: HOW *NOT* TO FIX U.S. FOREIGN POLICY

1. See Patrick Porter, "Tradition's Quiet Victories: Trump's National Security Strategy," *War on the Rocks*, December 22, 2017, at https://warontherocks.com /2017/12/traditions-quiet-victories-trumps-national-security-strategy/; and idem, "Why U.S. Grand Strategy Has Not Changed: Power, Habit, and the Foreign Policy Establishment," *International Security* 42, no. 4 (Spring 2018).

2. "Trump's Inauguration: Full Text of New President's Speech," *BBC News*, January 20, 2017, at www.bbc.com/news/world-us-canada-38697653.

3. In a presidential debate in 2016, Trump said that the Saudis were "people that push gays off buildings" and "kill women and treat women horribly." See Adam Taylor, "Trump Once Denounced Saudi Arabia as Extremist; Now He's Heading There to Promote Moderate Islam," *The Washington Post*, May 19, 2017.

4. Andrew Kaczynski, Chris Massie, and Nathan McDermott, "80 Times Trump Talked About Putin," *CNN.com*, March 2017, at www.cnn.com/interactive /2017/03/politics/trump-putin-russia-timeline/.

5. An expression of this view was Trump's speech in Poland in July 2017, when he warned darkly of the threat from "radical Islamic extremism" and said "the fundamental question of our time is whether the West has the will to survive." See "Remarks by President Trump to the People of Poland," July 6, 2017, at www

.whitehouse.gov/the-press-office/2017/07/06/remarks-president-trump-people
-poland-july-6-2017.

6. Trump's chief political strategist, former Breitbart News chief Stephen Bannon, believed that the Judeo-Christian world was in great peril from a multifaceted and growing threat from Islam, whether in the form of increased immigration or violent extremism. See Paul Blumenthal, "Steve Bannon Believes the Apocalypse Is Coming and War Is Inevitable," *Huffington Post*, February 8, 2017; Frances Stead Sellers and David A. Fahrenthold, "'Why let 'em in?': Understanding Bannon's Worldview and the Politics That Follow," *The Washington Post*, January 21, 2017; Daniel Kreiss, "Trump, Breitbart, and the Rejection of Multicultural Democracy," *Medium.com*, January 29, 2017; Steve Reilly and Brad Heath, "Steve Bannon's Own Words Show Sharp Break on Security Issues," *USA Today*, January 31, 2017; and Nahal Toosi, "The World According to Breitbart," *Politico*, November 28, 2016.

7. See the controversial op-ed by National Security Advisor H. R. McMaster and White House Economic Council director Gary Cohn, "America First Doesn't Mean America Alone," *The Wall Street Journal*, May 30, 2017, at www.wsj.com /articles/america-first-doesnt-mean-america-alone-1496187426. Despite its title, the central theme of the essay is the zero-sum nature of international politics and the conditional nature of U.S. support for other countries.

8. "Remarks by President Trump to the 72nd Session of the United Nations General Assembly," at www.whitehouse.gov/briefings-statements/remarks-president -trump-72nd-session-united-nations-general-assembly/.

9. Barack Obama had removed Flynn from his post as head of the Defense Intelligence Agency for managerial failings, and Flynn joined Trump's campaign team in 2016.

10. Anton's views on Trump's agenda can be found in his article "America and the Liberal International Order," *American Affairs*, March 2017. On Gorka's questionable qualifications, see Andrew Reynolds, "Stop Calling Him 'Doctor': The Academic Fraud of Sebastian Gorka, Trump's Terrorism 'Expert,'" *Ha'aretz*, April 27, 2017; Daniel Nexon, "Sebastian Gorka May Be a Far-Right Nativist, but for Sure He's a Terrible Scholar," *Foreign Policy*, March 17, 2017, at http:// foreignpolicy.com/2017/03/17/dr-sebastian-gorka-may-be-a-far-right-nativist-but -for-sure-hes-a-terrible-scholar-trump-radical-islam/; and Mitch Prothero, "The Hungarian Rise and Fall of Sebastian Gorka," *Buzzfeed*, April 26, 2017, at www .buzzfeed.com/mitchprothero/how-a-trump-adviser-failed-upwards-from -hungary-to-the?utm_term=.yxRY298V5#.svnlZ69jQ. Gorka was not the only example of an early Trump hire with dubious qualifications; see Jeff Stein, "Ezra Cohen-Watnick: Inside the Rise of Trump's Invisible Man in the White House," *Newsweek*, April 13, 2017, at www.newsweek.com/ezra-cohen-watnick-donald-trump -devin-nunes-russia-barack-obama-wiretap-susan-583904.

11. See Nancy Cook, Josh Dawsey, and Andrew Restuccia, "Why the Trump Administration Has So Many Vacancies," *Politico*, April 11, 2017, at www.politico .com/story/2017/04/donald-trump-white-house-staff-vacancies-237081; and "Trump: No Plans to Fill 'Unnecessary' Unfilled Positions," Fox News, February 28, 2017, at

www.foxnews.com/politics/2017/02/28/trump-no-plans-to-fill-unnecessary
-appointed-positions.html.

12. See Laura Koran, Aaron Kessler, and Joyce Tseng, "Map: Trump Continues to Leave Key State Department Posts Unfilled," *CNN.com*, December 8, 2017, at
www.cnn.com/2017/12/07/politics/trump-ambassador-vacancies/index.html.

13. See Peter Baker, Maggie Haberman, and Glenn Thrush, "Trump Removes
Stephen Bannon from National Security Council Post," *The New York Times*, April 5,
2017; and Robert Costa, Abby Phillip, and Karen DeYoung, "Bannon Removed
from Security Council as McMaster Asserts Control," *The Washington Post*,
April 5, 2017.

14. Scaramucci resigned after giving an indiscreet and vulgar interview to the
reporter Ryan Lizza of *The New Yorker*. See "Ryan Lizza Revisits His Phone Call
with Anthony Scaramucci," *The New Yorker Radio Hour*, August 3, 2017, at www
.newyorker.com/podcast/the-new-yorker-radio-hour/ryan-lizza-revisits-his
-phone-call-with-anthony-scaramucci.

15. NSC staffers Ezra Cohen-Watnick, Rich Higgins, and Derek Harvey
were all dismissed during the shake-up. See Rosie Gray, "H. R. McMaster Cleans
House at the NSC," *The Atlantic*, August 2, 2017, at www.theatlantic.com/politics
/archive/2017/08/hr-mcmaster-cleans-house-at-the-national-security-council
/535767/.

16. "Trump Says NATO Not Obsolete, Reversing Campaign Stance," Reuters,
April 12, 2007, at www.reuters.com/article/us-usa-trump-nato-idUSKBN17E2OK.

17. See Rosie Gray, "Trump Declines to Affirm NATO's Article 5," *The Atlantic*, May 25, 2017, at www.theatlantic.com/international/archive/2017/05/trump-
declines-to-affirm-natos-article-5/528129; Robbie Gramer, "Trump Discovers Article
5 After Disastrous NATO Summit," *Foreign Policy*, June 9, 2017, at http://
foreignpolicy.com/2017/06/09/trump-discovers-article-5-after-disastrous-nato
-visit-brussels-visit-transatlantic-relationship-europe; and Louis Nelson, "Trump
Publicly Commits to NATO Mutual Defense Provision," *Politico*, June 9, 2017, at
www.politico.com/story/2017/06/06/trump-nato-article-five-239632.

18. See Peter J. Dombrowski and Simon Reich, "Does Donald Trump Have a
Grand Strategy?" *International Affairs*, 93, no. 5 (2017), pp. 1026–30.

19. See Thom Shanker, "Defense Secretary Warns NATO of 'Dim' Future,"
The New York Times, June 10, 2011; "Remarks by President Obama and President
Komorowski of Poland in a Joint Press Conference," June 3, 2014, at https://
obamawhitehouse.archives.gov/the-press-office/2014/06/03/remarks-president
-obama-and-president-komorowski-poland-joint-press-conf; and Ayesha Rascoe
and Yeganah Torbati, "Burden Sharing Woes to Cloud Obama's Trip to NATO
Summit," Reuters, July 6, 2016, at www.reuters.com/article/us-nato-summit-obama
/burden-sharing-woes-to-cloud-obamas-trip-to-nato-summit-idUSKCN0ZM2KX.

20. In June 2017 Trump told reporters, "Because of our actions, money was
starting to pour into NATO." In fact, pledges to increase defense spending preceded Trump's tirade at the NATO summit and were largely a response to perceptions of a growing threat from Russia. See Ryan Browne, "NATO Members to

Increase Defense Spending," June 29, 2017, at www.cnn.com/2017/06/29/politics/nato-members-increase-defense-spending/index.html; and Robbie Gramer, "Thank Putin, Not Trump, for NATO's New Defense Spending Boost," *Foreign Policy,* June 28, 2017, at http://foreignpolicy.com/2017/06/28/thank-putin-not-trump-for-natos-new-defense-spending-boost-transatlantic-relations-military-europe/.

21. *National Security Strategy* (Washington, DC: The White House, December 2017), p. 2, at www.whitehouse.gov/wp-content/uploads/2-17/12/NSS-Final-12-18-2017-0905.pdf.

22. See Felicia Schwartz, "U.S. to Send Anti-Tank Weaponry to Ukraine, Entering New Phase of Conflict," *The Wall Street Journal,* December 24, 2017; and Diana Stancy Correll, "Ex-Obama Official Lauds Jim Mattis 'for Arming Ukraine,'" *Washington Examiner,* December 20, 2017. On Mitchell's background, see "Bureau of Europe and Eurasian Affairs: Who Is A. Wess Mitchell?" August 15, 2017, at www.allgov.com/news/top-stories/bureau-of-european-and-eurasian-affairs-who-is-a-wess-mitchell-170815?news=860276; see also CEPA's website at http://cepa.org/home.

23. On these events, see Ivan Nechepurenko, Neil MacFarquhar, and Thomas Gibbons-Neff, "Dozens of Russians Are Believed Killed in U.S.-Backed Syrian Attack," *The New York Times,* February 13, 2018; "Trump: 'It looks like' Russia Was Behind Poisoning of Former Spy," *The Guardian,* March 15, 2018, at www.theguardian.com/us-news/video/2018/mar/15/trump-it-looks-like-russia-was-behind-poisoning-of-former-spy-video; Alex Ward, "The US and Three Allies Are Blaming Russia for Nerve Agent Attack on Ex-Spy," *Vox.com,* March 15, 2018, at www.vox.com/2018/3/15/17124062/usa-russia-uk-france-germany-statement-full-text; U.S. Department of the Treasury, "Treasury Sanctions Russian Cyber Actors for Interference in the U.S. Elections and Malicious Cyberattacks," March 15, 2018, at https://home.treasury.gov/news/press-releases/sm0312.

24. See Jeffrey A. Bader, David Dollar, and Ryan Hass, "U.S.-China Relations, Six Months into the Trump Presidency," Brookings Institution, August 16, 2017, at www.brookings.edu/blog/order-from-chaos/2017/08/14/u-s-china-relations-6-months-into-the-trump-presidency/.

25. *National Security Strategy,* pp. 45–46; and U.S. Department of Defense, *Summary of the 2018 National Defense Strategy of the United States of America: Sharpening the American Military's Competitive Edge,* at www.defense.gov/Portals/1/Documents/pubs/2018-National-Defense-Strategy-Summary.pdf, pp. 1–2, 8–9.

26. See, for example, U.S. Department of Defense, *Annual Report to Congress: Military and Security Developments Involving the People's Republic of China* (Washington, DC, May 2017), at www.defense.gov/Portals/1/Documents/pubs/2017_China_Military_Power_Report.PDF.

27. See Ankit Panda, "South China Sea: Fourth US FONOP in Five Months Suggests a New Operational Rhythm," *The Diplomat,* October 12, 2017. At his confirmation hearing in January 2017 Tillerson said, "We're going to have to send China a clear signal that, first, the island-building stops, and second, your access to those islands also is not going to be allowed." See Michael Forsythe, "Rex Tiller-

son's South China Sea Remarks Foreshadow Possible Foreign Policy Crisis," *The New York Times*, January 12, 2017.

28. Ana Swanson, "Trump Readies Sweeping Tariffs and Investment Restrictions on China," *The New York Times*, March 15, 2018; Mark Landler and Jim Tankersley, "U.S. Sets $60 Billion in Punitive Tariffs on Chinese Goods," *The New York Times*, March 23, 2018.

29. See David E. Sanger and William J. Broad, "Trump Inherits a Secret Cyber-War against North Korean Missiles," *The New York Times*, March 4, 2017.

30. "Trump Says U.S. Will Act Alone on North Korea If China Fails to Help," *The Guardian*, April 3, 2017, at www.theguardian.com/us-news/2017/apr/02/donald-trump-north-korea-china.

31. See https://twitter.com/realDonaldTrump/status/948355557022420992; and Peter Baker and Michael Tackett, "Trump Says His 'Nuclear Button' Is 'Much Bigger' than North Korea's," *The New York Times*, January 2, 2018.

32. See Jacqueline Klimas, "Trump's North Korea Strategy: A Lot Like Obama's," *Politico*, August 8, 2017, at www.politico.com/story/2017/08/08/trump-obama-north-korea-241389.

33. The resolution took aim at North Korea's $3 billion export earnings and would have reduced them by about one-third if fully implemented. See Adam Taylor, "What the New UN Sanctions on North Korea Mean," *The Washington Post*, August 7, 2017.

34. See Connor Finnegan, "North Korea Crisis Becoming Unsolvable, Experts Warn, as Trump Heads to Asia," *ABC News*, November 2, 2017, at http://abcnews.go.com/International/north-korea-crisis-unsolvable-experts-warn-trump-heads/story?id=50872436; Kori Schake, "The North Korea Debate Sounds Eerily Familiar," *The Atlantic*, December 8, 2017, at www.theatlantic.com/international/archive/2017/12/north-korea-iraq-war-george-w-bush-trump/547796/; and Helene Cooper, "Mattis Leaves the Door Open to Military Options in North Korea," *The New York Times*, September 18, 2017.

35. A good discussion of the limited options and the continued relevance of deterrence is Scott Sagan, "The Korean Missile Crisis: Why Deterrence Is Still the Best Option," *Foreign Affairs* 96, no. 6 (November/December 2017).

36. Quoted in Choe-Sang Hun and David E. Sanger, "North Korea Moves Toward Détente with Seoul," *The New York Times*, January 9, 2018.

37. See Robin Wright, "Trump Accepts North Korea's Audacious Invitation—But Then What?" *The New Yorker*, March 9, 2015, at www.newyorker.com/news/news-desk/trump-accepts-north-koreas-audacious-invitation-but-then-what.

38. See Zack Beauchamp, "Donald Trump: Make America Great Again by Letting More Countries Have Nukes," *Vox.com*, March 30, 2016, at www.vox.com/2016/3/30/11332074/donald-trump-nuclear-weapons-japan-south-korea-saudi-arabia; and David E. Sanger and Maggie Haberman, "Transcript: Donald Trump Expounds on His Foreign Policy Views," *The New York Times*, March 26, 2016, at www.nytimes.com/2016/03/27/us/politics/donald-trump-transcript.html.

39. For a similar assessment, see Marc Lynch, "Trump's Middle East Policies

Are Boorish and Belligerent, but Surprisingly Normal," *War on the Rocks*, April 3, 2017, at http://warontherocks.com/2017/04/trumps-middle-east-policies-boorish-and-belligerent-but-surprisingly-normal/.

40. Saudi Arabia had conducted a brutal air war in Yemen since 2015 but failed to defeat its Houthi opponents. With Trump's apparent approval, bin Salman launched an economic boycott of Qatar in June 2017, demanding that the emirate cut its ties with Iran, expel the Muslim Brotherhood, and curtail the satellite news service Al Jazeera. He followed up by forcing Lebanese prime minister Saad Hariri to resign during his visit to Riyadh in November, in an attempt to weaken Hezbollah and reduce Iran's influence, but the heavy-handed ploy backfired, Hariri reversed his decision to resign as soon as he returned home, and Hezbollah's position was unaffected. On bin Salman's blunders, see Aaron David Miller and Richard Sokolsky, "Saudi Arabia's New Crown Prince Is a Bumbling Hothead. Trump Needs to Treat Him Like One," *Politico*, June 29, 2017; and Anne Barnard and Maria Abi-Habib, "Why Saad Hariri Had That Strange Sojourn in Riyadh," *The New York Times*, December 24, 2017.

41. On Trump's earlier opposition, see "Trump's View of Syria: How It Evolved, in 19 Tweets," *The New York Times*, April 7, 2007, at www.nytimes.com/2017/04/07/us/politics/donald-trump-syria-twitter.html.

42. On the media response to the attacks, see Margaret Sullivan, "The Media Loved Trump's Show of Military Might: Are We Really Doing This Again?" *The Washington Post*, April 8, 2017; and Adam Johnson, "Five Top Papers Run 18 Opinion Pieces Praising Syria Strikes—Zero Are Critical," *FAIR.org*, April 7, 2017, at http://fair.org/home/five-top-papers-run-18-opinion-pieces-praising-syria-strikes-zero-are-critical/.

43. For a comprehensive critique of Trump's decision, see Paul R. Pillar, "Hold the Deal-Killers Accountable," *Lobelog*, May 8, 2018, at https://lobelog.com/hold-the-deal-killers-accountable/.

44. See, for example, Nicholas Burns, "The Deal Is Historic, but the US Must Now Act to Contain Iran," *Financial Times*, July 14, 2015; and William J. Burns and Jake Sullivan, "The Iranian Protests Are an Opportunity for Trump—Just Not the One He Wants," *The Washington Post*, January 8, 2017.

45. For example, the United States and Israel had conducted a sophisticated cyberattack on Iran's nuclear enrichment facilities that destroyed a large number of Iranian centrifuges. See David Sanger, *Confront and Conceal: Obama's Secret Wars and the Surprising Use of American Power* (New York: Crown, 2012), chap. 8.

46. See Stephen M. Walt, "The Art of the Regime Change," *Foreign Policy*, May 8, 2018, at http://foreignpolicy.com/2018/05/08/the-art-of-the-regime-change/.

47. Among other things, Friedman once claimed that Barack Obama was an anti-Semite and said that supporters of the liberal, pro-peace lobby J Street were "far worse" than Nazi collaborators. See Eric Levitz, "Trump Picks Lawyer Who Says Liberal Jews Are Worse Than Nazi Collaborators as Ambassador," *New York*, December 16, 2016, at http://nymag.com/daily/intelligencer/2016/12/trumps-israel-ambassador-likens-left-wing-jews-to-kapos.html.

48. Nicole Gaouette and Elise Labott, "Trump Backs Off Two-State Framework for Israel-Palestinian Deal," *CNN.com*, February 16, 2017.

49. See Tracy Wilkinson, "Trump Threatens to Cut Off Aid to Palestinians," *Los Angeles Times*, January 2, 2018.

50. Clinton, Bush, and Obama all promised to move the U.S. embassy to Jerusalem while campaigning for the presidency; none did so once in office.

51. See Jason Horowitz, "U.N., European Union, and Pope Criticize Trump's Jerusalem Decision," *The New York Times*, December 6, 2017.

52. See, for example, "Statement by the President on the Memorandum of Understanding Reached with Israel," September 14, 2016, at https://obamawhitehouse.archives.gov/the-press-office/2016/09/14/statement-president-memorandum-understanding-reached-israel.

53. Trump's son-in-law Jared Kushner was supposed to lead the peace process, and Kushner told a group of congressional interns in July 2017 that no new peace initiative was in the works. See Ashley Feinberg, "Kushner on Middle East Peace: 'What Do We Offer That's Unique? I Don't Know,'" *Wired*, August 1, 2017, at www.wired.com/story/jared-kushner-middle-east/.

54. As Randa Slim of the Middle East Institute put it, "Donald Trump's decision at least clarifies the situation—declares the peace process officially over and removes any remaining doubt about the US third party role as a fair mediator." Quoted in Joyce Karam, "Experts React to Trump's Jerusalem Decision: A Diplomatic Upgrade or End of the Peace Process?" *The National*, December 7, 2017, at www.thenational.ae/world/the-americas/experts-react-to-trump-s-jerusalem-decision-a-diplomatic-upgrade-or-end-of-the-peace-process-1.682188.

55. Ryan Teague Beckwith, "Read Trump's 'America First' Foreign Policy Speech," *Time*, April 27, 2016, at http://time.com/4309786/read-donald-trumps-america-first-foreign-policy-speech/.

56. See Karoun Demirjian, "House Passes Nearly $700 Billion Defense Authorization Bill," *The Washington Post*, November 14, 2017.

57. Based on data from the U.S. Air Forces Central Command at www.afcent.af.mil/About/Airpower-Summaries/. I am grateful to Micah Zenko for providing this information; see https://twitter.com/MicahZenko/status/873899992901185536.

58. Trump announced the shift in policy via Twitter on July 26, catching the Pentagon by surprise. The White House issued an official order to discharge all transgender troops by March 2018, but Secretary of Defense Mattis subsequently announced that transgender troops would continue to serve pending a policy review, and a federal court struck down Trump's proposed ban in October. See Helene Cooper, "Mattis Says Military Panel Will Study Trump's Transgender Ban," *The New York Times*, August 29, 2017; and Dave Philipps, "Judge Blocks Trump's Ban on Transgender Troops in Military," *The New York Times*, October 30, 2017.

59. See Katherine Blakeley, "The Trump Administration's FY2018 Defense Budget in Context," Center for Strategic and Budgetary Assessments, August 3, 2017, at http://csbaonline.org/reports/the-trump-administrations-fy-2018-defense-budget-in-context.

60. See Nicole Gaouette and Ryan Browne, "Trump Changes Tune, Flexes U.S. Muscle Overseas," *CNN.com*, July 17, 2017, at www.cnn.com/2017/07/17/politics /trump-world-policeman/index.html.

61. See Joshua Rovner, "The War on Terror as Imperial Policing," *War on the Rocks*, November 2, 2017, at https://warontherocks.com/2017/11/the-war-on-terrorism-as-imperial-policing/.

62. See Hal Brands, "The Problem with Trump's Counterterrorism Strategy? Trump," *Bloomberg View*, October 25, 2017, at www.bloomberg.com/view/articles /2017-10-25/the-problem-with-trump-s-terrorism-strategy-trump. Roggio is quoted in Nick Miriello, "Trump's Military Strategy Is a Lot Like Obama's, but with a Lot More Bombs," *Vice News*, April 26, 2017, at https://news.vice.com/en_us /article/ywnj4v/trumps-military-strategy-is-just-like-obamas-but-with-a-lot-more -bombs.

63. Jason Dempsey and Amy Schafer, "Is There Trouble Brewing for Civil-Military Relations in the U.S.?" *World Politics Review*, May 23, 2017, at www .worldpoliticsreview.com/articles/22222/is-there-trouble-brewing-for-civil -military-relations-in-the-u-s. See also Rosa Brooks, *How Everything Became War and the Military Became Everything: Tales from the Pentagon* (New York: Simon & Schuster, 2016); James Fallows, "The Tragedy of the American Military," *The Atlantic* (January/February 2015), at www.theatlantic.com/magazine/archive/2015/01 /the-tragedy-of-the-american-military/383516/; Gordon Adams and Shoon Murray, eds., *Mission Creep: The Militarization of U.S. Foreign Policy?* (Washington, DC: Georgetown University Press, 2014); and Eliot A. Cohen, "The Downsides of John Kelly's Ascension," *The Atlantic*, July 31, 2017, at www.theatlantic.com/politics /archive/2017/07/the-downsides-of-john-kellys-ascension/535383/.

64. The order imposed a variety of restrictions on visitors from Chad, Iran, Libya, Somalia, Syria, Venezuela, and North Korea. See Adam Liptak, "Supreme Court Wipes Out Travel Ban Appeal," *The New York Times*, October 24, 2017.

65. Miriam Jordan, "Trump Administration Says 200,000 Salvadorans Must Leave," *The New York Times*, January 9, 2018.

66. For a sense of the international reaction, see Laignee Barron, "'A New Low': The World Is Furious at Trump for His Remark About 'Shithole Countries,'" *Time*, January 12, 2018, at http://time.com/5100328/shithole-countries-trump-reactions/.

67. See Muzaffar Chishti, Sarah Pierce, and Jessica Bolter, "The Obama Record on Deportations: Deporter in Chief or Not?" Migration Policy Institute, January 26, 2017, at www.migrationpolicy.org/article/obama-record-deportations -deporter-chief-or-not; and Dara Lind, "Fewer Immigrants Are Being Deported Under Trump Than Under Obama," *Vox.com*, August 10, 2017, at www.vox.com /policy-and-politics/2017/8/10/16119910/trump-deportations-obama.

68. See Dombrowski and Reich, "Does Donald Trump Have a Grand Strategy?" pp. 1023–26.

69. See "Trump Says Mexico 'Eventually' Will Pay for Border Wall," Reuters, April 23, 2017, at www.reuters.com/aticle/us-usa-budget-trump-mexico/trump -says-mexico-eventually-will-pay-for-border-wall-idUSKBN17POQG.

70. See Julie Hirshfeld Davis, Sheryl Gay Stolberg, and Thomas Kaplan, "Trump Was Not 'Fully Informed' in 2016 Vows on Wall, Kelly Says," *The New York Times*, January 17, 2018.

71. See Lisa Friedman, "Syria Joins Paris Climate Accord, Leaving Only U.S. Opposed," *The New York Times*, November 7, 2017, at www.nytimes.com/2017/11/07/climate/syria-joins-paris-agreement.html.

72. Clare Jones and Sam Fleming, "G20 Drops Vow to Resist All Forms of Protectionism," *Financial Times*, March 18, 2017.

73. Trump falsely claimed, "We lose the lawsuits, almost all of the lawsuits in the WTO." In fact, the United States has won roughly 90 percent of the disputes it has taken to the WTO, although it has usually lost the disputes brought against it by others. Rather than being evidence of WTO bias, this pattern confirms that states generally bring disputes to the WTO only when they have a strong case. See Shawn Donnen, "Fears for Global Trade as Trump Fires First Shots to Kneecap WTO," *Financial Times*, November 9, 2017.

74. See Demetri Sevastopulo and Shawn Donnan, "Donald Trump Rejected China Steel Offer That His Officials Backed," *Financial Times*, August 28, 2017.

75. See David Lawder, "U.S. Commerce Dept 'Self-Initiates' Dumping Probe of Chinese Aluminum," Reuters, November 28, 2017; at www.reuters.com/article/us-usa-trade-china-aluminum/u-s-commerce-dept-self-initiates-dumping-probe-of-chinese-aluminum-idUSKBN1DS2S9; and Robert Zoellick, "Trump Courts Economic Mayhem," *The Wall Street Journal*, January 7, 2018.

76. See John Cassiday, "Trump's NAFTA Reversal Confirms the Globalists Are in Charge—For Now," *The New Yorker*, April 27, 2017, at www.newyorker.com/news/john-cassidy/trumps-nafta-reversal-confirms-the-globalists-are-in-charge-for-now; and Bill Scher, "Why Bannon Lost and Globalists Won," *Politico*, August 18, 2017, at www.politico.com/magazine/story/2017/08/18/why-bannon-lost-globalists-won-215506.

77. Ana Swanson and Thomas Kaplan, "Senate Panel Rejects Trump Nominee to Head Export-Import Bank," *The New York Times*, December 19, 2017.

78. "Full Text: Trump Davos Speech Transcript," *Politico*, January 28, 2018, at www.politico.com/story/2018/01/26/full-text-trump-davos-speech-transcript-370861.

79. Damian Paletta, "Trump Insists 'Trade Wars Are Good, and Easy to Win' after Vowing New Tariffs," *The Washington Post*, March 2, 2018.

80. See Ana Swanson, "Peter Navarro, a Top Trade Skeptic, Is Ascendant," *The New York Times*, February 29, 2018.

81. See Jim Tankersley and Natalie Kitroeff, "U.S. Exempts Some Allies from Tariffs, but May Impose Quotas," *The New York Times*, March 22, 2018; see also Ana Swanson and Kenneth P. Vogel, "Trump's Tariffs Set Off Storm of Lobbying," *The New York Times*, March 16, 2018; and Jack Ewing, "U.S. Allies Jostle to Win Exemptions from Trump Tariffs," *The New York Times*, March 9, 2018.

82. *National Security Strategy* (2017), p. 4.

83. See Steven Erlanger, "'Fake News,' Trump's Obsession, Is Now a Cudgel for Strongmen," *The New York Times*, December 12, 2017.

84. See Barry R. Posen, "The Rise of Illiberal Hegemony: Trump's Surprising Grand Strategy," *Foreign Affairs* 97, no. 2 (March/April 2018).

85. *National Security Strategy*, p. 41.

86. The memorandum to Tillerson was written by the senior aide Brian Hook in May 2017 and leaked to *Politico* in December 2017. It can be found at www .politico.com/f/?id=00000160-6c37-da3c-a371-ec3f13380001.

87. Amanda Erickson, "Trump Rails Against Iran Over Its Human Rights Record. But He Spares Allies," *The Washington Post*, January 4, 2018.

88. See "Press Statement: Peaceful Protests in Iran," U.S. Department of State, December 29, 2017, at www.state.gov/r/pa/prs/ps/2017/12/276811.html.

89. See Alex Shashkevich, "U.S. Wants Peace, Stability in Syria, Secretary of State Rex Tillerson Says in Policy Speech at Stanford," *Stanford News*, January 18, 2018, at https://news.stanford.edu/2018/01/18/secretary-state-rex-tillerson-discusses -u-s-strategy-syria-stanford/.

90. See "Donald Trump's Administration Is Promoting Democracy and Human Rights," *The Economist*, December 6, 2017.

91. In his speech to the conference, Sen referred to Trump as "a great person who I respect the most," praised his "non-interference policy," and called upon the president to rebuke U.S. diplomats, whom he accused of trying to topple his government. In response, the White House expressed "strong concerns over recent steps that challenged the country's democratic progress." See David Boyle, "Cambodian Strongman's Trump Outreach Falls Flat," *Voice of America News*, November 14, 2017, at www.voanews.com/a/cambodia-strongman-trump-outreach-falls -flat/4114717.html.

92. See "Remarks by President Trump on the Strategy in Afghanistan and South Asia," August 21, 2017, at www.whitehouse.gov/briefings-statements /remarks-president-trump-strategy-afghanistan-south-asia/; and John Haltiwanger, "The Forever War: U.S. Military Now Has 15,000 Troops in Afghanistan and That Number Could Soon Increase," *Newsweek*, November 9, 2017, at www .newsweek.com/forever-war-us-military-now-has-15000-troops-afghanistan -706573.

93. See Laura King, "No Nation-Building in Afghanistan? Easier Said Than Done, Experts Say," *Los Angeles Times*, August 22, 2017, at www.latimes.com/nation /la-fg-afghanistan-nation-building-20170822-story.html.

94. Quoted in Susan Glasser, "Donald Trump's Year of Living Dangerously," *Politico* (January/February 2018).

95. See Doyle McManus, "Trump Just Compared the U.S. Intelligence Community to Nazi Germany. Just Let That Sink In," *Los Angeles Times*, January 11, 2017; Cristiano Lima, "CIA Chief Called Trump Nazi Germany Comparison 'Outrageous,'" *Politico*, January 15, 2017, at www.politico.com/story/2017/01/cia -brennan-trump-nazi-germany-233636.

96. Philip Wagner, John Rucker, and Greg Mitchell, "Trump, in CIA Visit, Attacks Media for Coverage of His Inaugural Crowds," *The Washington Post*, January 21, 2017.

97. See Eliot A. Cohen, "The Worst Secretary of State in Living Memory," *The Atlantic*, December 1, 2017. See also Julia Ioffe, "The State of Trump's State Department," *The Atlantic*, March 1, 2017; Roger Cohen, "The Desperation of Our Diplomats," *The New York Times*, July 28, 2017; Max Bergmann, "Present at the Destruction: How Rex Tillerson Is Wrecking the State Department," *Politico*, June 29, 2017, at www.politico.com/magazine/story/2017/06/29/how-rex-tillerson-destroying-state-department-215319; and Nicholas Burns and Ryan Crocker, "Dismantling the Foreign Service," *The New York Times*, November 27, 2017.

98. See Bill Chappell, "'I'm the Only One That Matters,' Trump Says of State Dept. Job Vacancies," *NPR.org*, November 3, 2017, at www.npr.org/sections/thetwo-way/2017/11/03/561797675/im-the-only-one-that-matters-trump-says-of-state-dept-job-vacancies.

99. See for example Eliot A. Cohen, "The Rudderless Ship of State," *The Atlantic*, February 14, 2017, at www.theatlantic.com/politics/archive/2017/02/no-one-at-the-helm-of-the-ship-of-state/516591/; G. John Ikenberry, "The Plot Against American Foreign Policy: Can the Liberal Order Survive?" *Foreign Affairs* 96, no. 3 (May/June 2017); and Hal Brands, *American Grand Strategy in the Age of Trump* (Washington, DC: Brookings Institution, 2018). The critical stance of the *Times* and the *Post* is described in James Warren, "Is the *New York Times* vs. the *Washington Post* vs. Trump the Last Great Newspaper War?" *Vanity Fair*, July 30, 2017, at www.vanityfair.com/news/2017/07/new-york-times-washington-post-donald-trump.

100. See, for example, Aaron David Miller and Richard Sokolsky, "Donald Trump's Foreign Policy Is 'America Only,' Not 'America First,'" *The Wall Street Journal*, January 24, 2017; Bret Stephens, "The Vertigo Presidency," *The Wall Street Journal*, March 6, 2017; and Peggy Noonan, "Trump Is Woody Allen Without the Humor," *The Wall Street Journal*, July 27, 2017.

101. See Jen Kirby, "Trump Has Lowest Approval Rating of Any Modern President at the End of His First Year," *Vox.com*, December 21, 2017, at www.vox.com/policy-and-politics/2017/12/21/16798432/trump-low-approval-december-first-year.

102. During his business career, Trump admitted to engaging in what he called "truthful hyperbole." See David Barstow, "Trump's Business Dealings Rely on Being Creative with the Truth," *The New York Times*, July 16, 2016.

103. In early June 2017, for example, the White House released a video of cabinet secretaries and top White House aides telling Trump that he was doing a wonderful job and it was a "blessing" to serve him. See Julie Hirschfeld Davis, "Trump's Cabinet, with a Prod, Extols the 'Blessing' of Serving Him," *The New York Times*, June 12, 2017; and Chris Cillizza, "Trump Just Held the Weirdest Cabinet Meeting Ever," *CNN.com*, June 13, 2017, at www.cnn.com/2017/06/12/politics/donald-trump-cabinet-meeting/index.html.

104. See Julian Borger, "Rex Tillerson Says He Won't Quit but Doesn't Deny Calling Trump a 'Moron,'" *The Guardian*, October 4, 2017, at www.theguardian.com/us-news/2017/oct/04/rex-tillerson-trump-moron.

105. See Glasser, "Donald Trump's Year of Living Dangerously"; Jonathan Swan and Mike Allen, "The Most Toxic Work Environment on the Planet," *Axios*, March 14, 2018, at www.axios.com/the-most-toxic-working-environment-on-the -planet-1521061118-87211185-63b7-468b-aa1b-880f3dcaf524.html; Britt Peterson, "Donald Trump Is the Worst Boss in Washington," *The New York Times*, June 9, 2017; and Jeff Shesol, "A Year into the Trump Era, White House Turnover Is 'Off the Charts,'" *The New Yorker*, December 15, 2017, at www.newyorker.com/news/news-desk/a -year-into-the-trump-era-white-house-staff-turnover-is-off-the-charts.

106. Michael D. Shear and Maggie Haberman, "'There Will Always Be Change,' Trump Says as More Personnel Shake-Ups Loom," *The New York Times*, March 15, 2018; Associated Press, "Cabinet Chaos: Trump's Team Battles Scandal, Irrelevance," March 14, 2018, at www.nytimes.com/aponline/2018/03/14/us/ap-us -chaos-in-the-cabinet.html.

107. Trump fired Comey after he failed to pledge his "loyalty" to Trump in a one-on-one meeting at the White House and refused to curtail the FBI investigation into Russia's role in the election. Detailed accounts of Russia's alleged activities include Evan Osnos, David Remnick, and Joshua Yaffa, "Trump, Putin, and the New Cold War," *The New Yorker*, March 6, 2017; and Greg Miller, Ellen Nakashima, and Adam Entous, "Obama's Secret Struggle to Punish Russia for Putin's Election Assault," *The Washington Post*, June 23, 2017.

108. A useful guide to these events is Philip Bump, "An Interactive Guide to Key Moments in the Trump Russia Investigation," *The Washington Post*, July 19, 2017, at www.washingtonpost.com/news/politics/wp/2017/07/19/an-interactive -timeline-of-key-moments-in-the-trump-russia-investigation/?utm_term= .04939963181b.

109. On the latter point, see Micah Zenko, "Trump's Russia Scandal Is Already Swallowing His Foreign Policy," *Foreign Policy*, June 6, 2017, at http:// foreignpolicy.com/2017/06/06/trumps-russia-scandal-is-already-swallowing-his -foreign-policy/.

110. In January 2018, for example, when the journalist Michael Wolff published *Fire and Fury: Inside the Trump White House,* an unflattering portrait of Trump that questioned the president's intelligence and mental stability, the White House first tried to block the book's publication (which raised public interest in it even more). The administration then released a statement declaring that former chief strategist Stephen Bannon (one of Wolff's inside sources) had "lost his job, and then lost his mind," and Trump took to Twitter to proclaim "my two greatest assets have been mental stability and being, like, really smart . . . I went from VERY successful businessman, to top T.V. Star to President of the United States (on my first try). I think that would qualify as not smart, but genius . . . and a very stable genius at that!" Unfortunately, the tweet contradicted the message it sought to send and lent credence to the embarrassing anecdotes in Wolff's book.

111. See David Leonhardt, Ian Prasad Philbrick, and Stuart A. Thompson, "Trump's Lies vs. Obama's," *The New York Times*, December 14, 2017, at www .nytimes.com/interactive/2017/12/14/opinion/sunday/trump-lies-obama-who-is -worse.html.

112. See Bess Levin, "Trump Openly Brags about Lying to Justin Trudeau's Face," *Vanity Fair*, March 15, 2018, at www.vanityfair.com/news/2018/03/trump-openly-brags-about-lying-to-justin-trudeaus-face.

113. On this point, see Keren Yarhi-Milo, "After Credibility: American Foreign Policy in the Trump Era," *Foreign Affairs* 97, no. 1 (January/February 2018).

114. See https://twitter.com/realdonaldtrump/status/914497877543735296.

115. Quoted in Steven Erlanger, "Trump's Twitter Threats Put American Credibility on the Line," *The New York Times*, January 7, 2017.

116. The transcripts of the two calls were leaked in August 2017 and can be found at www.washingtonpost.com/graphics/2017/politics/australia-mexico-transcripts/?utm_term=.07b5af8a2b68/.

117. See "Donald Trump Hits Back at Theresa May after Re-Tweeting British Far-Right Group's Anti-Muslim Videos," *The Telegraph*, November 30, 2017, at www.telegraph.co.uk/news/2017/11/29/trump-shared-muslim-crimes-videos-tweeted-british-far-right/.

118. Khan had told Londoners not to be alarmed by the heightened security presence following the attacks. Taking his remark out of context, Trump tweeted, "7 dead and 48 wounded in terror attack. Mayor of London Says 'there's no reason to be alarmed!'" See Martin Pengelly, "Donald Trump Berates London Mayor Over Response to Terror Attacks," *The Guardian*, June 4, 2017, at www.theguardian.com/uk-news/2017/jun/04/trump-berates-london-mayor-sadiq-khan-terror-attacks.

119. See Christina Maza, "Donald Trump Threw Starburst Candies at Angela Merkel, Said 'Don't Say I Never Give You Anything,'" *Newsweek*, June 20, 2018, at www.newsweek.com/donald-trump-threw-starburst-candies-angela-merkel-dont-say-i-never-give-you-987278.

120. See Porter, "Why U.S. Grand Strategy Has Not Changed."

121. In January 2017 the White House issued a press release that misspelled the name of British prime minister Theresa May. In April, Press Secretary Sean Spicer suggested that the Syrian leader Bashar al-Assad was worse than Hitler because the latter "hadn't used chemical weapons." Shortly thereafter, Secretary of Commerce Wilbur Ross told an interviewer that Trump's visit to Saudi Arabia was going well because there had been no public protests there, Ross apparently being unaware that the kingdom suppresses such forms of dissent.

122. See Nicole Lewis and Kristine Phillips, "The Trump White House Keeps Mixing Up the Names of Asian Countries and Their Leaders' Titles," *The Washington Post*, July 10, 2017, at www.washingtonpost.com/news/the-fix/wp/2017/07/08/white-house-press-office-misidentifies-japanese-prime-minister-abe-as-president/?utm_ term= .fe4eafac8774.

123. The information was highly sensitive intelligence about ISIS obtained from an Israeli double agent operating inside the terrorist group. See Carole E. Lee and Shane Harris, "Trump Shared Intelligence Information in Meeting with Russians in Oval Office," *The Wall Street Journal*, May 16, 2017; and Jack L. Goldsmith, "Bombshell: Initial Thoughts on the *Washington Post*'s Game-Changing Story," *Lawfare*,

May 15, 2017, at https://lawfareblog.com/bombshell-initial-thoughts-washington -posts-game-changing-story.

124. See Jeffrey Kucik, "The TPP's Real Value—It's Not Just About Trade," *The Hill*, December 7, 2016, at http://thehill.com/blogs/pundits-blog/foreign -policy/309088-the-tpps-real-value-its-not-just-about-trade; and Robert D. Black- will and Theodore Rappleye, "Trump's Five Mistaken Reasons for Withdrawing from the Trans-Pacific Partnership," *Foreign Policy*, June 22, 2017, at http:// foreignpolicy.com/2017/06/22/trumps-five-mistaken-reasons-for-withdrawing -from-the-trans-pacific-partnership-china-trade-economics/.

125. On this incident, see E. A. Crunden, "Trump, Tillerson Offer Conflicting Statements on Qatar Crisis Within 90 Minutes," *ThinkProgress.org*, June 9, 2017, at https://thinkprogress.org/qatar-tillerson-trump-saudi-incoherent-8d7e180d650d; and also Noah Feldman, "Fixing Trump's Qatar Blunder (He's Not Helping)," *Bloomberg View*, June 11, 2017.

126. On Trump's promise to Adelson, see Mark Landler, "For Trump, an Em- bassy in Jerusalem Is a Political Decision, Not a Diplomatic One," *The New York Times*, December 6, 2017.

127. In addition to the United States and Israel, the only countries that opposed the resolution were Micronesia, Nauru, Togo and Tonga, Palau, the Marshall Is- lands, Guatemala, and Honduras. Thirty-five countries abstained. See Nicole Gaou- ette, "Despite Haley Threat, UN Votes to Condemn Trump's Jerusalem Decision," *CNN.com*, December 22, 2017, at www.cnn.com/2017/12/21/politics/haley-un -jerusalem/index.html.

128. See Toluse Olorunnipa and Nick Wadhams, "Trump Moves Closer to a Presidency of One with Tillerson Firing," *Bloomberg News*, March 14, 2018, at www .bloomberg.com/news/articles/2018-03-14/trump-moves-closer-to-presidency-of -one-with-tillerson-firing.

129. The appointment of John Bolton provoked considerable alarm, but he is hardly a fringe figure in contemporary America. He is a graduate of Yale Univer- sity and Yale Law School, worked at Covington & Burling, a venerable D.C. law firm, and has spent many years as a senior fellow at the conservative but main- stream American Enterprise Institute. He served as Ambassador to the United Na- tions under George W. Bush and writes for such "radical" publications as *The Wall Street Journal*, *The New York Times*, and *Foreign Policy*. See Stephen M. Walt, "Wel- come to the Dick Cheney Administration," *Foreign Policy*, March 23, 2018, at http:// foreignpolicy.com/2018/03/23/welcome-to-the-dick-cheney-administration/.

130. See Joshua Keating, "John Bolton and Gina Haspel are the Consequences of Our Failure to Reckon with the Bush Years," *Slate*, March 23, 2018, at https:// slate.com/news-and-politics/2018/03/john-bolton-and-gina-haspel-are-the -consequences-of-our-failure-to-reckon-with-the-bush-years.html.

131. See "U.S. Trade Gap Highest Since 2012," at https://tradingeconomics .com/united-states/balance-of-trade. For a critical evaluation of Trump's handling of U.S. trade policy, see Phil Levy, "2017: Trump's Troubled Year in Trade Policy," *Forbes*, December 29, 2017, at www.forbes.com/sites/phillevy/2017/12/29/2017 -trade-year-in-review/#6f74ad7a482b.

132. Ely Ratner, "Trump Could be Bumbling Into a Trade War with China," *The Atlantic*, March 22, 2018, at www.theatlantic.com/international/archive/2018/03/trump-china-trade-war/556238/; Paul Krugman, "Bumbling into a Trade War," *The New York Times*, March 22, 2018.

133. Thomas L. Friedman, "Trump, Israel, and the Art of the Giveaway," *The New York Times*, December 6, 2017.

134. See Evan Osnos, "Making China Great Again," *The New Yorker*, January 9. 2018.

135. These results are especially striking insofar as Xi and Putin were not especially well-regarded in most countries. See "U.S. Image Suffers as Publics Around the World Question Trump Leadership," *Pew Research Center*, June 26, 2017, at www.pewglobal.org/2017/06/26/u-s-image-suffers-as-publics-around-world-question-trumps-leadership/; and "Publics Worldwide Unfavorable Toward Putin, Russia," Pew Research Center, August 16, 2017, at www.pewglobal.org/2017/08/16/publics-worldwide-unfavorable-toward-putin-russia/.

136. Julie Ray, "World's Approval of U.S. Leadership Drops to New Low," Gallup News, January 18, 2018, at http://news.gallup.com/poll/225761/world-approval-leadership-drops-new-low.aspx?g_source=WORLD_REGION_WORLDWIDE&g_medium=topic&g_campaign=tiles.

137. After the NATO summit in May, German chancellor Angela Merkel and Canadian foreign minister Chrystia Freeland both gave speeches indicating diminished confidence in the United States and the need to act more independently. See James Masters, "Merkel Reiterates Call for Europe to Take Fate into Our Own Hands," *CNN.com*, May 31, 2017, at www.cnn.com/2017/05/30/europe/merkel-europe-fate-modi-india/index.html; and Paul Vieira, "Canada Says It Will Chart Own Course, Apart from U.S.," *The Wall Street Journal*, June 6, 2017, at www.wsj.com/articles/canada-says-it-will-chart-its-own-course-apart-from-u-s-1496780439.

138. See Osnos, "Making China Great Again."

139. On Clinton's hawkish tendencies and habitual deference to the military, see Mark Landler, "How Hillary Became a Hawk," *The New York Times Magazine*, April 21, 2016.

140. Clinton's presidential campaigns were not well-managed affairs, but they still fell well short of the feuds and backstabbing that have been commonplace between Trump and his present and former aides.

141. See Tom Nichols, "Trump's First Year: A Damage Assessment," *The Washington Post*, January 19, 2018, at www.washingtonpost.com/outlook/trumps-first-year-a-damage-assessment/2018/01/19/0b410f3c-fa66-11e7-a46b-a3614530bd87_story.html?hpid=hp_no-name_opinion-card-d%3Ahomepage%2Fstory&utm_term=.ade2121af895.

7: A BETTER WAY

1. In particular, Russian intervention in Georgia and Ukraine has put an effective end to NATO expansion.

2. Peter Schuck explains why government performs well in some areas but

poorly in others in his *Why Government Fails So Often: And How It Can Do Better* (Princeton, NJ: Princeton University Press, 2014).

3. Thus Stephen Brooks, John Ikenberry, and William Wohlforth argue that the Iraq War was an outlier that is unlikely to be repeated. See their "Don't Come Home, America: The Case Against Retrenchment," *International Security* 37, no. 3 (Winter 2012/13), pp. 31–33.

4. See especially John J. Mearsheimer, *The Great Delusion: Liberal Dreams and International Realities* (New Haven, CT: Yale University Press, 2018).

5. In April 2016 a survey by the Pew Research Center found that 57 percent of Americans believe that the United States should "deal with its own problems and let others deal with theirs the best they can." Forty-one percent thought their country did "too much" in world affairs, and only 27 percent felt the United States did "too little." Pew Research Center, "Public Uncertain, Divided Over America's Place in the World," May 5, 2016, at www.people-press.org/2016/05/05/public-uncertain-divided-over-americas-place-in-the-world/.

6. See Michael C. Desch, "How Popular Is Peace?" *American Conservative*, November/December 2015.

7. The same survey showed equal support for legislation giving Congress "oversight and accountability regarding where troops are stationed around the world" and requiring recipients of U.S. military aid to adhere to the Geneva Convention. See "Press Release," Committee for Responsible Foreign Policy, January 2, 2018, at http://responsibleforeignpolicy.org/wp-content/uploads/2018/01/Press-Release-One_Final.pdf; and James Carden, "A New Poll Shows the Public Is Overwhelmingly Opposed to Endless US Military Interventions," *The Nation*, January 9, 2018.

8. See A. Trevor Thrall and Erik Goepner, "Millennials and U.S. Foreign Policy: The Next Generation's Attitudes Toward Foreign Policy and War (and Why They Matter)," Washington, DC: CATO Institute, June 16, 2015, at http://object.cato.org/sites/cato.org/files/pubs/pdf/20150616_thrallgoepner_millennialswp.pdf.

9. On Clinton's establishment-heavy team of advisors, see Stephen M. Walt, "The Donald vs. the Blob," *Foreign Policy*, May 16, 2016, at http://foreignpolicy.com/2016/05/16/the-donald-vs-the-blob-hillary-clinton-election/. On her interventionist proclivities, see Mark Landler, "How Hillary Became a Hawk," *The New York Times Magazine*, April 21, 2016.

10. Great Britain faced the prospect of a cross-Channel invasion on several occasions, but the United States has not faced a similar danger for more than two centuries.

11. U.S. leaders did not intend to keep several hundred thousand troops in Europe during the Cold War, and President Dwight D. Eisenhower tried to find a reliable way to reduce U.S. force levels during the 1950s. But in the end, U.S. leaders concluded that America's NATO partners could not balance the U.S.S.R. on their own. See Marc Trachtenberg, *A Constructed Peace: The Making of the European Settlement, 1945–1963* (Princeton, NJ: Princeton University Press, 1999).

12. For GDP and defense spending figures, see *The Military Balance, 2015–2016* (London: International Institute for Strategic Studies, 2016).

13. Barry R. Posen, "Pull Back: The Case for a Less Activist Foreign Policy," *Foreign Affairs* (January/February 2013).

14. It is worth remembering that both Osama bin Laden and the Taliban were motivated in good part by opposition to a foreign military presence in their respective homelands.

15. Unlike Korea, which occupied a critical location in close proximity to the Soviet Union and Japan, Indochina was neither a center of industrial might nor near to Soviet territory.

16. Iranian presidents Akbar Hashemi Rafsanjani and Mohammad Khatami made repeated efforts at détente in the 1990s. The Clinton administration responded with some modest positive gestures, but Iran's initiative was thwarted when Clinton backed the AIPAC-inspired Iran and Libya Sanctions Act in 1996. A new Iranian initiative in 2003 was spurned by the Bush administration, and Iranians subsequently elected Mahmoud Ahmedinejad president in 2005. Ahmedinejad's offensive beliefs made a rapprochement infeasible, and genuine dialogue did not occur until Obama was elected in 2008 and Hassan Rouhani became president of Iran in 2013. See Trita Parsi, *Treacherous Alliance: The Secret Dealings of Israel, Iran, and the United States* (New Haven, CT: Yale University Press, 2007); and John J. Mearsheimer and Stephen M. Walt, *The Israel Lobby and U.S. Foreign Policy* (New York: Farrar Straus & Giroux, 2007), pp. 286–91.

17. See Kurt H. Campbell, *The Pivot: The Future of American Statecraft in Asia* (New York: Twelve, 2016).

18. In a harbinger of things to come, Chinese president Xi Jinping visited Iran in 2016 and signed seventeen separate agreements with the Islamic Republic. See also James Dorsey, "China and the Middle East: Venturing into the Maelstrom," Working Paper No. 296, S. Rajaratnam School of International Studies, March 2016.

19. Some observers maintain that Tehran already "dominates" the region, but this view greatly exaggerates Iran's present capabilities or its capacity to dictate events there. For useful correctives see Justin Logan, "How Washington Has Inflated the Iran Threat," *Washington Examiner*, August 4, 2015; John Bradshaw and J. Dana Stuster, "Iran Is Hardly on the March," *Defense One*, July 15, 2015, at www .defenseone.com/ideas/2015/07/iran-hardly-march/117835/; and Thomas Juneau, "Iran's Failed Foreign Policy: Dealing from a Position of Weakness," *Policy Paper*, Middle East Institute, May 2015, at www.mei.edu/content/article/iran's-failed -foreign-policy-dealing-position-weakness.

20. If the United States spent 2.5 percent of GDP on defense, for example, the Pentagon's budget would be approximately $425 billion, an amount more than twice the amount spent by China, the world's number two military power.

21. On the militarization of U.S. foreign policy, see Rosa Brooks, *How Everything Became War and the Military Became Everything: Tales from the Pentagon* (New York: Simon & Schuster, 2016); Gordon Adams and Shoon Murray, eds., *Mission*

Creep: The Militarization of U.S. Foreign Policy (Washington, DC: Georgetown University Press, 2014); and Andrew Bacevich, *The New American Militarism: How Americans Are Seduced by War*, 2nd rev. ed. (New York: Oxford University Press, 2013).

22. Chas W. Freeman, "Militarism and the Crisis of American Diplomacy," *Epistulae*, no. 20, July 7, 2015.

23. On these points, see Stephen M. Walt, "The Power of a Strong State Department," *The New York Times*, May 12, 2017.

24. This sentiment is attributed to Lord Palmerston, who told the House of Commons in 1848, "We have no eternal allies, and we have no perpetual enemies. Our interests are eternal and perpetual, and those interests it is our duty to follow."

25. During his February 2014 confirmation hearings to serve as ambassador to Norway, for example, the Obama campaign bundler and hotel executive George Tsunis admitted that he had never been to Norway and erroneously referred to Norway's Progress Party as a "fringe" movement (it was then part of the ruling government coalition). See Juliet Eilperin, "Obama Ambassador Nominees Prompt an Uproar with Bungled Answers, Lack of Ties," *The Washington Post*, February 14, 2014.

26. See James Bruno, "Russian Diplomats Are Eating America's Lunch," *Politico*, April 16, 2014, at www.politico.com/magazine/story/2014/04/russias-diplomats-are-better-than-ours-105773.

27. Charles Ray, "America Needs a Professional Foreign Service," *Foreign Service Journal*, July/August 2015. See also "American Diplomacy at Risk," *American Academy of Diplomacy* (Washington, DC: April 2015), at www.academyofdiplomacy.org/wp-content/uploads/2016/01/ADAR_Full_Report_4.1.15.pdf.

28. Secretary of State John Kerry, "Remarks to the Press," U.S. Department of State, Office of the Spokesperson, January 7, 2016.

29. Quoted in Barton Gellman, *Contending with Kennan: Toward a Philosophy of American Power* (New York: Praeger, 1984), pp. 126–27.

30. Nicole Gaouette, "Retired Generals: Don't Cut State Department," CNN, February 27, 2017, at www.cnn.com/2017/02/27/politics/generals-letter-state-department-budget-cuts/index.html. For a list of additional ways to rebuild the State Department, see Stephen M. Walt, "The State Department Needs Rehab," *Foreign Policy*, March 5, 2018, at http://foreignpolicy.com/2018/03/05/the-state-department-needs-rehab/.

31. See William J. Lynn, "The End of the Military-Industrial Complex," *Foreign Affairs*, November/December 2014.

32. See Barry Buzan, "Economic Structure and International Security: The Limits of the Liberal Case," *International Organization* 38 (Autumn 1984).

33. See Mary Sarrotte, *1989: The Struggle to Create Postwar Europe*, updated ed. (Princeton, NJ: Princeton University Press, 2014).

34. See Michael Glennon, *National Security and Double Government* (New York: Oxford University Press, 2014).

35. See Richard Haass, "The Isolationist Temptation," *The Wall Street Journal*, August 5, 2016; Brooks, Ikenberry, and Wohlforth, "Don't Come Home, America"; Robert Kagan, "Superpowers Don't Get to Retire," *The New Republic*, May 26, 2014; Richard Fontaine and Michèle Flournoy, "Beware the Siren Song of Disengagement," *The National Interest*, August 14, 2014; *Extending American Power: Strategies to Expand U.S. Engagement in a Competitive World Order* (Washington, DC: Center for a New American Security, 2016); Zbigniew Brzezinski, "Toward a Global Realignment," *The American Interest*, April 17, 2016; Kenneth M. Pollack, "Security and Public Order: A Working Group Report of the Middle East Strategy Task Force" (Washington, DC: The Atlantic Council, 2016); and "Strengthening the Liberal World Order," White Paper, Global Agenda Council on the United States, World Economic Forum, April 2016.

36. See, for example, David Frum, "The Death Knell for America's Global Leadership," *The Atlantic*, May 31, 2017, at https://www.theatlantic.com/international/archive/2017/05/mcmaster-cohn-trump/528609/; G. John Ikenberry, "The Plot Against American Foreign Policy," *Foreign Affairs* 96, no. 3 (May/June 2017); and Robin Wright, "Why Is Donald Trump Still So Horribly Witless About the World?" *The New Yorker*, August 4, 2017.

37. *Extending American Power*, p. 14.

38. The case for selective engagement is made in Robert J. Art, *A Grand Strategy for America* (Ithaca, NY: Cornell University Press, 2004).

39. On this point, see Edward D. Mansfield and Jack Snyder, *Electing to Fight: Why Emerging Democracies Go to War* (Cambridge, MA: MIT Press, 2005).

40. Glennon, *National Security and Double Government*, p. 118.

41. Mike Lofgren, *The Deep State: The Fall of the Constitution and the Rise of a Shadow Government* (New York: Viking 2016), pp. 269–77.

42. See Patrick Porter, "Why U.S. Grand Strategy Has Not Changed: Power, Habit, and the Foreign Policy Establishment," *International Security* 42, no. 4 (Spring 2018).

43. See in particular John. J. Mearsheimer, *The Tragedy of Great Power Politics* (New York: W. W. Norton, 2013), chap. 9.

44. Whatever one thinks of David and Charles Koch's broader political agenda, the support the Charles Koch Institute has given to proponents of offshore balancing or "restraint" is an encouraging development. See the program summary of "Advancing American Security: the Future of U.S. Foreign Policy," at www.charleskochinstitute.org/advancing-american-security-future-u-s-foreign-policy/. Even so, the resources devoted to groups espousing liberal hegemony or its cousins are still vastly greater than the money supporting advocates of greater restraint.

45. See Matthew A. Baum and Philip B. K. Potter, *War and Democratic Constraint: How the Public Influences Foreign Policy* (Princeton, NJ: Princeton University Press, 2015), p. 4.

46. As of 2017, the only editorial columnists at major U.S. newspapers who espouse a noninterventionist view of U.S. foreign policy are Steve Chapman of

the *Chicago Tribune* and Stephen Kinzer of *The Boston Globe*. See Stephen M. Walt, "America Needs Realists, Not William Kristol," *Salon.com*, January 16, 2008; and "What Would a Realist World Have Looked Like?" *Foreign Policy*, January 8, 2016.

47. See Michael C. Desch, "It's Kind to Be Cruel: The Humanity of American Realism," *Review of International Studies* 29 (2003); and idem, "America's Illiberal Liberalism: The Ideological Origins of Overreaction in U.S. Foreign Policy," *International Security* 32, no. 3 (Winter 2007/08).

ACKNOWLEDGMENTS

I HAVE INCURRED MANY DEBTS in writing this book, and it is a pleasure to acknowledge them here. Ironically, one of my debts is to the foreign policy establishment itself. I have been part of that community for much of my professional life, as a young researcher at the Center for Naval Analyses; a member of the Council on Foreign Relations; a guest scholar at think tanks like the Carnegie Endowment for International Peace and the Brookings Institution; a faculty member at Princeton's Woodrow Wilson School, the University of Chicago, and Harvard's Kennedy School of Government; and a participant in numerous other "establishment" activities. I am surely something of an outlier within this world, but I have learned a great deal from the friends, colleagues, and former students I have met along the way. I have benefited greatly from the opportunities that my role within this world has provided, and remain deeply grateful to all who have helped me.

I wish to thank the following individuals for their comments and suggestions on the manuscript: Andrew Bacevich, Ian Bremmer, Ilene Cohen, Michael Desch, Michael Glennon, Stephen Kinzer, Fredrik Logevall, Ramzy Mardini, Tarek Masoud, Steven E. Miller, Moisés Naím, Barry Posen, and Richard Sokolsky. My father, Martin Walt IV, read an early draft with particular care and made many useful suggestions, and John Mearsheimer deserves special thanks for his comments and advice through the entire process. I am also grateful to Steve Clemons, Chas W. Freeman, Carla Robbins, Jeremy Shapiro, and Tara McKelvey for useful conversations about different aspects of U.S. foreign policy–making. Orga Cadet, Gabriel Costa, Kyle Herman, Enea Gjoza, and Jason Kwon provided able research assistance, and Leah Knowles kept the rest of my professional life in order.

Over the past two years, students in my course on U.S. foreign policy took up the challenge of reading draft chapters and did not hesitate to tell me where my arguments were either confusing or just plain wrong. My editor at FSG, Eric Chinski, performed his usual wise, masterful (and when necessary, ruthless) job of improving the manuscript, and my agent, Bill Clegg, was supportive from start to finish. And it is a pleasure to offer a special shout-out to the chefs and staff at Cutty's sandwich shop in Brookline, Massachusetts, whose addictive creations fueled countless afternoons of research and writing.

Some portions of the book appeared in slightly different form as "The Case for Offshore Balancing: A Superior U.S. Grand Strategy" (coauthored with John Mearsheimer), in *Foreign Affairs* 95, no. 4 (July/August 2016); and "The Donald vs. the Blob," in Robert Jervis, Francis Gavin, Joshua Rovner, and Diane Labrosse, eds., *Chaos in the Liberal Order: The Trump Presidency and International Politics in the Twenty-First Century* (New York: Columbia University Press, 2018). I thank the Council on Foreign Relations and Columbia University Press for permission to use these materials here.

Finally, my greatest thanks and admiration go to my wife, Rebecca Stone, for acting locally while I was thinking globally. Together with my now-adult children, Gabriel and Katherine, her example is a constant reminder of the good that people can do if they don't worry about who gets credit.

Stephen Walt
Brookline, Massachusetts

INDEX

Gaza, 192

Gelb, Leslie, 115, 143, 316n31

Geneva Peace Conference (1991), 193

geography, xi, 132

Georgia, 32, 67, 73, 266, 267

Germany, 24, 35, 72, 157, 196, 224, 253, 256, 263, 269, 273, 309n45; Nazi, 156, 242

Gerson, Michael, 120

Gigot, Paul, 207

Gingrich, Newt, 206

Giuliani, Rudy, 334n9

Glass, Stephen, 208

Glasser, Susan, 104, 114

Glennon, Michael, 97, 103, 144, 283

globalization, 6, 17, 27–28, 30, 44–46, 67, 84, 128, 234–37, 301n63; economy, 27–28, 38, 42–46, 56, 67–68, 70, 87, 90, 158, 165–67, 219, 234–37, 253, 261–62, 278, 279, 295n12; failures of, 44–46; "global village" myth, 84; immigration and, 45; Trump opposition to, 6, 10, 234–37

Goldberg, Jeffrey, 206, 207

Goldgeier, James, 123, 127

Goldsmith, Jack, 161

Goodman, Amy, 122

Gorbachev, Mikhail, 297n23

Gorka, Sebastian, 222, 344n10

Graham, Lindsay, 144, 185, 323n23

Grassley, Chuck, 197

Great Britain, 8, 24, 35, 55, 84, 165, 225, 246, 272, 309n45, 355n118, 355n121; Brexit decision, 8, 44; colonialism, 265

Greece, 147, 168

Greenpeace, 98

Greenspan, Alan, 28

Greenwald, Glenn, 114, 121–22

Grinin, Vladimir, 273

Grossman, Marc, 113

G20, 167, 235, 247

Guantanamo, 43, 189–90

Gulf War (1991), 23, 26, 28, 47, 151, 200, 265–66

Haass, Richard, 22, 38, 105, 163–64, 172, 192, 330n94; *Foreign Policy Begins at Home*, 172

Haditha, 202, 338n58

Hadley, Stephen, 114, 130

Hagel, Chuck, 152, 192, 208

Hague, The, 34

Haiti, 233

Haley, Nikki, 222, 249

Halperin, Mark, 209

Hamas, 73, 192, 194

Hamid, Shadi, 241

Hamilton, Lee, 188

Hannity, Sean, 101, 207

Harriman, Averell, 107

Hartz, Louis, 61

Harvard University, 103, 108, 109, 122, 202–203

Hasan, Nidal, 74, 309n51

Haspel, Gina, 199, 249

Hastings, Michael, 121

Hayden, Michael, 5, 198

hegemonic stability theory, 329n81

Heilbrunn, Jacob, 207

Heritage Foundation, 98, 100, 115

Hertog, Roger, 103

Hewlett Foundation, 102

Hezbollah, 73, 151

Hiatt, Fred, 120, 206, 207, 208

Hill, Fiona, 223

Hirsh, Michael, 119

Hitler, Adolf, 191, 355n121

Hoagland, Jim, 120

Hoffman, Bruce, 49

Hoffmann, Stanley, 27

Hoh, Matthew, 213–14, 343n102

Holbrooke, Richard, 111, 317n32

Holmes, Oliver Wendell, 313n4

homeland security, Trump policy on, 233–34

Hoover Institution, 42

Horner, Charles, 189–90

House, Edward, 94

Hudson Institute, 98, 105, 108

human rights, 26, 28, 38, 40–44, 61, 219; abuses, 43, 58–59, 68, 118, 189–90,

selective engagement, 281
Sen, Hun, 240
Senate Foreign Relations Committee, 30, 96
Senate Intelligence Committee, 197, 198
Seoul, 228, 235
Serbia, 25, 33, 36, 75, 77–78, 155; ethnic cleansing, 78
Sestanovich, Stephen, 130
sexual harassment, 200, 209, 338n57
Shinseki, Eric, 171
Shultz, George, 125
Sinclair, Upton, 187
Singapore, 43, 65, 68
Singer, Paul, 102
Slaughter, Anne-Marie, 4, 105, 117–18, 123, 125, 299n41, 315n25
Slovakia, 32
Slovenia, 32
Smith, Adam, 290
Snowden, Edward, 214
social media, 6, 159–60, 205, 206, 227; Trump and, 6, 159, 239, 245, 254, 354n110, 355n118
Social Security, 258
Somalia, 24, 38, 49, 63, 66, 73, 76, 90, 170, 183, 232, 303n79; 1993 raid, 24
Sopko, John, 205
Soros, George, 102
South China Sea, 34, 131, 226, 271
South Korea, 5, 24, 38, 52, 228, 235, 248, 251, 252, 278, 329n77
South Sudan, 42, 67
Soviet Union, x, 47, 183, 257, 265; Cold War, 147–48, 150, 263; collapse of, 7, 21, 22, 23, 37, 62, 89, 131, 147, 150, 157, 168, 183; communism, 55, 147–48, 155; nuclear weapons, 147–48. See also Russia
Special Forces, 38, 49, 66, 76, 175, 232, 271
sphere of influence, 61, 64–66
State Department, ix, 40, 60, 96, 147, 239, 243, 276; QDDR, 59, 60
Stavridis, James, 122

Steinberg, James, 4, 111, 123, 130, 299n41
Stephanopoulos, George, 138
Stephens, Bret, 119, 120, 121, 153
Stewart, Jon, 122
Stewart, Mark G., 51
Stiglitz, Joseph, 172
Sudan, 48, 155
Sullivan, Jake, 4
Summers, Lawrence, 28, 215, 343n104
Syria, 5, 25, 50, 65, 66, 73, 75, 81, 131, 155, 165, 183, 225, 232, 266, 325n36; Assad regime, 5, 10, 33, 36, 42, 67, 78, 135, 149, 151, 229, 311n60; chemical attacks, 229; civil war, 5, 7, 36, 42, 83, 112, 129, 135, 143, 162, 170, 187, 217–18; Russia and, 33; U.S. relations with, 33, 78, 170–71, 187, 229, 239

taboos and dogmas, 142–43
Taguba, Antonio, 189, 190
Taiwan, 52, 226, 247
Talbott, Strobe, 62, 105
Taliban, 25, 36, 37, 65, 73, 75, 81, 83, 155, 185, 204, 241, 307n31, 327n59
Taming American Power (Walt), x
Tanzania, 30
taxes, 139, 170, 172, 282, 283, 288
technology, 24, 27, 44, 59–60, 84; advances in, 84, 85, 200–201, 300n60; digital, 27, 159
Tehran, 48, 52, 78, 249, 267, 270
terrorism, 8, 16, 22, 30–31, 45, 48–51, 59, 60, 65, 71, 72–74, 78, 84, 140, 151–56, 158–60, 165, 175–78, 208; blowback, 175–76; Bush policy, 48–50, 65, 140, 151, 154–56, 171, 177–78, 188–90, 195, 199–201, 303nn74–76, 335n23; Clinton policy, 48, 188; cyber threats, 5, 59, 60, 73, 84, 158–60, 171, 327n62; 9/11 attacks, 8, 48–49, 51, 62, 65, 145, 150, 151, 154, 156, 170, 175, 188–90, 195, 233, 267, 284; Obama policy, 190, 196–98, 234;

A NOTE ABOUT THE AUTHOR

Stephen M. Walt is the Robert and Renée Belfer Professor of International Affairs at Harvard University. He is the author of *The Origins of Alliances*; *Revolution and War*; *Taming American Power: The Global Response to U.S. Primacy*; and, with John J. Mearsheimer, *The Israel Lobby and U.S. Foreign Policy*. He writes frequently for *Foreign Policy*.